The
Supreme Court
Yearbook

1996–1997

The justices of the Supreme Court. Standing, from left, are Justices Ruth Bader Ginsburg, David H. Souter, Clarence Thomas, and Stephen G. Breyer; sitting, from left, are Justices Antonin Scalia and John Paul Stevens, Chief Justice William H. Rehnquist, and Justices Sandra Day O'Connor and Anthony M. Kennedy.

The
Supreme Court
Yearbook
1996–1997

Kenneth Jost

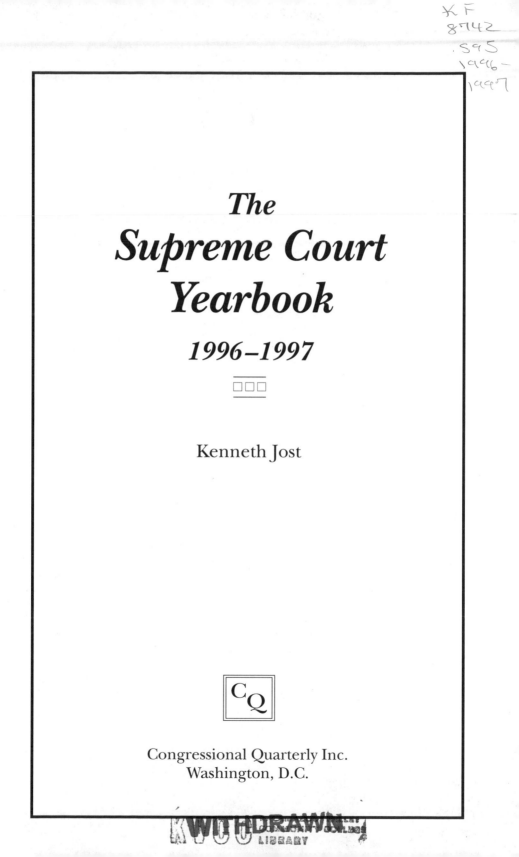

Congressional Quarterly Inc.
Washington, D.C.

Copyright © 1998 Congressional Quarterly Inc.
1414 22nd Street, N.W.
Washington, D.C. 20037

Photo credits: cover, 316, R. Michael Jenkins; frontispiece, Congressional Quarterly file photo; 296, 299, 311, 314, Collection, the Supreme Court Historical Society; 2, 37, 41, 51, Reuters; 30, Patrice Gilbert, *Legal Times;* 46, Scott J. Ferrell, Congressional Quarterly; 59, Kansas Department of Corrections; 67, *Star-Tribune/*Minneapolis-St. Paul; 134 (top), Bill Kostroun, *New Jersey Law Journal;* 134 (bottom), AP/Wide World Photos; 303, Joseph McCary; 307, Supreme Court; 312, White House.

Printed in the United States of America

ISBN   0-87187-919-0 (pbk)
ISBN   0-87187-920-4
ISSN   1054-2701

Contents

Preface   vii

1 *A Momentous Term*   1

2 *The 1996–1997 Term*   19

3 *Case Summaries*   74
    Business Law   79
    Courts and Procedure   83
    Criminal Law and Procedure   86
    Election Law   98
    Environmental Law   102
    Family Law   103
    Federal Government   103
    First Amendment   108
    Immigration Law   112
    Individual Rights   112
    Labor Law   120
    Property Law   126
    States   127
    Torts   131

4 *Preview of the 1997–1998 Term*   133

Appendix
    Opinion Excerpts   151
    How the Court Works   291
    Brief Biographies   303
    Glossary of Legal Terms   320
    United States Constitution   326

Index   345

Preface

When Chief Justice William H. Rehnquist spoke to a gathering of federal judges in Virginia the day after the Supreme Court issued the last of its opinions for the 1996–1997 term, many in the audience—and many of those watching on C-SPAN—expected him to talk about some of the blockbuster rulings of the past year.

The term ended with a climactic rush of headline-making rulings on such issues as physician-assisted suicide, indecent material on the Internet, and punishment for sexual offenders. Within a single week, the Court struck down three laws passed by Congress and overturned one of its own precedents. One month earlier, it had ruled that the president of the United States has no special protection from being sued in civil court, just like any other citizen.

The chief justice chose to disappoint, however. He mentioned the suit against President Bill Clinton only in passing—to say that it would not have much impact on most people's lives. He talked instead about cases that, as he told the audience, might be called "duds." One involved the rules for sentencing repeat offenders; another dealt with a defendant's right to withdraw a guilty plea before sentencing. A third case—a complicated bankruptcy dispute—dealt with how to determine the value of a pickup truck.

Rehnquist was making the point that even the Court's undramatic rulings have some impact on Americans' day-to-day lives. The Court's decisions help set the rules for disputes between creditors and debtors in bankruptcy cases, plaintiffs and defendants in civil suits, and prosecutors and defendants in criminal cases. They shape the power relationships not only between Congress and the president or between the national government and the states, but also between buyers and sellers, business and labor, and individuals and government.

Now in its eighth year, *The Supreme Court Yearbook* provides capsule summaries of each of the Court's decisions during the 1996–1997 term. The summaries, in Chapter 3, follow discussions of the justices' voting patterns in Chapter 1 and an overview of the Court's rulings along with detailed accounts of some of the most important cases in Chapter 2. A preview of the coming term is presented in Chapter 4. Excerpts from the term's major decisions appear in the Appendix.

My thanks again go to Toni House and the other members of the Supreme Court's public information office for their friendly and efficient assistance, and to the many lawyers, legal experts, and journalists whose comments and writings inform my own coverage. At Congressional Quarterly Books, thanks to Shana Wagger, Tracy Villano, and Talia Greenberg for overseeing the editing and production. Finally, thanks to my wife, Katie White, who helped in more ways than can be mentioned here.

1 | *A Momentous Term*

President Bill Clinton was at the top of his form. He had just negotiated an agreement with Republican congressional leaders that promised to balance the federal budget in five years. The economy was up, and so were Clinton's approval ratings. He left for Europe on the evening of May 26, 1997, expecting to win agreement on his plan to expand the North Atlantic Treaty Organization to include three of the former Communist countries in Eastern Europe.

Back in Washington, however, the Supreme Court had an unwelcome surprise. As the country settled in after a Memorial Day weekend, the Court on May 27 issued a unanimous ruling allowing a former Arkansas state employee to go ahead with a politically embarrassing civil lawsuit accusing Clinton of a crude sexual advance toward her while he was governor in his home state.

In Paris, White House aides acknowledged surprise that the Court had rejected so decisively Clinton's plea to delay the trial of Paula Jones's suit until after he left the White House. Clinton himself left it to his lawyers in Washington to comment about the case, but he told reporters the next day that he was concerned about the impact of the ruling on future presidents.

One month later, the Court turned its attention to the other branch of the national government: Congress. As the justices prepared for their summer recess, they issued three rulings within a week striking down laws that Congress had passed over the previous four years.

Two of the laws had won all but unanimous approval from the lawmakers. The Religious Freedom Restoration Act was enacted in the name of religious liberty. The Communications Decency Act sought to control sexual materials on the Internet. The third law— the so-called Brady Act—required local law enforcement agencies to conduct background checks on prospective gun buyers. Gun control supporters had pushed the bill through Congress after an eight-year struggle. Polls indicated the law had broad public support.

The lopsided votes in Congress and the public approval of the laws did not deter the Court, however, from flexing its constitutional muscles. The Brady Act, the Court declared, amounted an unconstitutional command from the federal government to sovereign state governments. The Internet law violated the First Amendment's protections for freedom of speech. And the religious freedom law infringed on states' rights as well as the Court's own prerogatives to define the extent—and the limits—of constitutional safeguards.

Retired Justice Harry A. Blackmun is helped down the steps of St. Matthew's Cathedral in Washington by the Court's marshal, Dale Bosley (left), and the Court's clerk, William Suter (right), after the funeral of the late justice William J. Brennan Jr. Brennan, a liberal who served on the Court from 1956 to 1990, died July 24, 1997, at the age of ninety-one. Other mourners included retired justice Byron R. White (right center) and five current justices (clockwise from bottom): Stevens, Souter, Breyer, Thomas, and Ginsburg.

Two hundred years earlier, Alexander Hamilton had reassured citizens of the new nation that the federal judiciary would be "the least dangerous branch" of the national government to be established under the Constitution. Whether dangerous or not, the Court was assuredly not the least powerful of the three branches. And now, a Court with a majority of justices ostensibly committed to judicial restraint appeared to observers across the ideological spectrum to be engaged in the kind of judicial activism associated with more liberal-oriented Courts of the past.

"Overall, this was a term of conservative judicial activism," said Erwin Chemerinsky, a liberal expert on constitutional law at the University of Southern California Law Center in Los Angeles. The rulings in major cases were striking, he added, not only for their conservative outcomes but also for the decisive margins and lack of a competing liberal viewpoint in at least some of the disputes.

Lawrence Lessig, a more conservative-oriented law professor at Harvard Law School, agreed that the term reflected an "activist" bent among the Court's conservatives, led by Chief Justice William H. Rehnquist. "It was Warren Court-ism on the right," Lessig said, referring to the era of liberal activism in the 1950s and '60s under Chief Justice Earl Warren. "I think it's great, but I think it's a little bit odd."

The description carried only so far, of course. In the term's most closely watched case, the Court voted unanimously to leave to state legislatures the wrenching question of physician-assisted suicide for terminally ill patients instead of recognizing a constitutional right for courts to define and enforce. In announcing the decision on June 26, Rehnquist made explicit the Court's unwillingness to take the dispute out of "the arena of public debate and legislative action."

"Throughout the Nation, Americans are engaged in an earnest and profound debate about the morality, legality, and practicality of physician-assisted suicide," Rehnquist wrote. "Our holding permits this debate to continue, as it should in a democratic society."

"This is a Court that does seem to be genuinely humbler" than previous Courts in the area of recognizing previously unrecognized rights, commented Eugene Volokh, a conservative constitutional law professor at UCLA Law School. All of the justices, Volokh said, believe that courts should defer to legislatures unless there is "a specific textual command" in the Constitution.

Many observers noted that the Court spent much of its term drawing lines between the states and the federal government and between the respective branches of the federal government. "The Supreme Court is redesigning the basic institutional architecture of our public lives," Paul Gewirtz, a professor at Yale Law School, commented to the *New York Times* at the end of the term.

On federalism issues, the rulings demonstrated the strong impulse among the Court's conservative bloc to confine the federal government's powers. "The rulings reflect the continuing Rehnquist Court perspective that the federal government is one of fairly strictly enumerated powers," said Douglas Kmiec, a conservative constitutional law expert at Notre Dame University Law School.

Chai Feldblum, director of a legislation clinic at Georgetown University Law Center in Washington and a liberal advocate on a range of civil liberties issues, said the Court also sent Congress a "signal that they are going to scrutinize very closely whether it has the power to enact the laws that it enacts."

"There is still a lot of power for Congress to pass a range of laws," Feldblum added. "But Congress will need to think more deliberately, work harder in terms of findings and background information, and perhaps be more careful of the breadth of the laws they pass."

The Court's rulings were not merely exercises in constitutional line-drawing, however. They dealt with issues of immediate impact in Americans' day-to-day lives. The ruling on physician-assisted suicide drew widespread approval from people who were appalled at the idea of doctors' deliberately administering lethal drugs to their patients. But it also evoked anguished criticism from people suffering with terminal illnesses who claimed for themselves the right to choose how to die.

The Internet decision—a ruling that united the Court's liberals and conservatives—prompted whoops of approval from the individuals and groups who travel the electronic frontier. But it also produced dismay and puzzlement among advocacy groups and parents who were looking for ways to shelter children from unwanted images imported into their homes by the new technology.

Regardless of views, however, Court-watchers were unanimous in pronouncing the term particularly important and particularly memorable. "An amazing term by any measure," Chemerinsky declared. "A monumental term," agreed Volokh. "It was a Supreme Court term that defied labels and made history," Linda Greenhouse, the *New York Times*'s veteran Supreme Court reporter, wrote in her wrap-up story. "It was a term that mattered."

The Conservative Majority

The Court's rulings were driven during the year by a conservative majority that was more cohesive than in some of the past few terms *(see Table 1-1)*. Rehnquist, in his eleventh term as chief justice, led a bloc of four other Republican-appointed justices who shared broadly similar views. The conservative majority generally favored the states in federalism disputes, took a skeptical view of most new claims of constitutional rights, and solidly backed law enforcement in criminal cases.

The other members of the Court's conservative bloc could be grouped into two pairs. Justices Antonin Scalia and Clarence Thomas were the staunchest conservatives and, as Chemerinsky put it, "ideological twins." For several terms, Scalia and Thomas had voted together more consistently than any other pair of justices. In the 1996–1997 term, however, their alignment reached a new height. They agreed in all but one of the eighty signed opinions issued during the year, for a remarkable agreement rate of 99 percent. (In the only case where they disagreed—a somewhat technical federal income tax issue—Scalia sided with the government, Thomas with the taxpayer.)

Scalia and Thomas also chafed at times under their conservative colleagues' reluctance to go farther or faster in dismantling liberal precedents. In one of the term's early rulings, Thomas wrote a dissenting opinion that hinted at overturning a 1956 precedent guaranteeing indigent criminal defendants a free trial transcript for purposes of an appeal. Scalia joined the opinion, but Rehnquist—who also dissented in the case—did not.

Justices Sandra Day O'Connor and Anthony M. Kennedy tempered their generally conservative views with occasional liberal votes as well as a measure of caution in their conservative stands. O'Connor wrote briefly in the Brady Act case to stress that the ruling left Congress other options to achieve the same goal. Kennedy wrote a concurring opinion in another important case—upholding state laws using civil commitment procedures to lock up

Table 1-1   Justices' Alignment, 1996–1997 Term

This table shows the percentage of decisions in which each justice agreed with each of the other members of the Court. Of the eighty signed opinions for the 1996–1997 term, thirty-six (or 45 percent) were unanimous.

The voting pattern showed two voting blocs somewhat more cohesive than in some of the past few terms. The conservative bloc includes Chief Justice Rehnquist and Justices O'Connor, Scalia, Kennedy, and Thomas. The moderate-to-liberal bloc consists of Justices Stevens, Souter, Ginsburg, and Breyer.

Each of the five conservative justices voted with each of the others at least 82 percent of the time. Scalia and Thomas were the most closely aligned: they voted together in all but one of the eighty signed opinions (99 percent). Each of the four liberal-leaning justices also voted with each of the other three at least 82 percent of the time. Souter and Ginsburg were the most closely aligned: they voted together in seventy-one out of eight cases (89 percent).

Justices O'Connor and Kennedy voted with the conservative bloc somewhat more often than in the 1995–1996 term. O'Connor and Kennedy agreed with each of the Court's most consistent conservatives, Scalia and Thomas, at least 82 percent of the time; in the previous term, O'Connor and Kennedy had lined up with Scalia and Kennedy less than 80 percent of the time.

Once again, the justices least often in agreement were Stevens with Scalia and Thomas. In the nonunanimous decisions, Stevens voted with Scalia in 9 percent of the cases, with Thomas in 11 percent.

	Rehnquist	Stevens	O'Connor	Scalia	Kennedy	Souter	Thomas	Ginsburg	Breyer
Rehnquist		22.7	67.4	72.7	72.7	50.0	75.0	47.7	43.2
		57.5	82.3	85.0	85.0	72.5	86.2	71.2	68.8
Stevens	22.7		30.2	9.1	40.9	68.2	11.4	70.5	70.5
	57.5		62.0	50.0	67.5	82.5	57.2	83.8	83.8
O'Connor	67.4	30.2		67.4	69.8	53.5	69.8	55.8	53.5
	82.3	62.0		82.3	83.5	74.7	83.5	76.0	74.7
Scalia	72.7	9.1	67.4		68.2	36.4	97.7	34.1	29.5
	85.0	50.0	82.3		82.5	65.0	98.8	63.8	61.2
Kennedy	72.7	40.9	69.8	68.2		59.1	70.5	52.3	52.3
	85.0	67.5	83.5	82.5		77.5	83.8	73.8	73.8
Souter	50.0	68.2	53.5	36.4	59.1		38.6	79.5	75.0
	72.5	82.5	74.7	65.0	77.5		66.2	88.8	86.2
Thomas	75.0	11.4	69.8	97.7	70.5	38.6		36.4	27.3
	86.2	57.2	83.5	98.8	83.8	66.2		65.0	60.0
Ginsburg	47.7	70.5	55.8	34.1	52.3	79.5	36.4		77.3
	71.2	83.8	76.0	63.8	73.8	88.8	65.0		87.5
Breyer	43.2	70.5	53.5	29.5	52.3	75.0	27.3	77.3	
	68.8	83.8	74.7	61.2	73.8	86.2	60.0	87.5	

Note: The first number in each cell represents the percentage of agreement in divided decisions. The second number represents the percentage of agreement in all signed opinions.

repeat sexual offenders—to warn against misusing the statutes as a supplement to criminal prosecutions.

O'Connor and Kennedy split off from their conservative colleagues less
often in the 1996–1997 term than in recent years, however. Overall, they
voted together with Rehnquist, Scalia, and Thomas somewhat more often
than in the 1995–1996 term. That year, they joined with the liberal-leaning
justices in two high-profile rulings that barred discrimination against women
at state-run military academies and overturned a Colorado initiative prohibiting enactment of laws to prohibit discrimination against homosexuals. This
term, O'Connor and Kennedy lined up with the conservative bloc in most of
the major rulings that divided neatly along ideological lines.

In addition, O'Connor and Kennedy wrote qualifying opinions less often than in other terms. "In the past, it was common for O'Connor and
Kennedy to write concurrences that took away much of the force of the
majority opinions," remarked Michael McConnell, presidential professor at
the University of Utah Law School and a longtime conservative advocate
before the Court. "That was much less so this time." There was one exception, however: O'Connor wrote a significant concurrence in the assisted-
suicide cases that left open the possibility of recognizing a constitutional
claim in individual cases in the future.

The strength of the conservative bloc could be seen in the term's most
closely divided decisions. The five conservative justices voted together in
nine out of seventeen cases decided by 5–4 votes, including such major rulings as the decisions on the Brady Act and on state sexual offender laws and
an important church-state ruling easing the rules on public aid to parochial
schools. In four other 5–4 decisions, four of the five conservatives voted
together in dissent; the Court's liberal bloc prevailed by winning over one of
the justices from the conservative wing.

More than any of the other conservatives, Rehnquist put his personal
stamp on the term. His end-of-term rulings in the assisted-suicide cases epito-
mized his aversion to judicial activism; his deference to legislative bodies,
especially state legislatures; and his reliance on history and tradition rather
than broader notions of fairness and justice to weigh claims of constitutional
rights under broadly written provisions like the Fourteenth Amendment's
Due Process Clause. The Court "must exercise the utmost care" in interpreting the Constitution, he wrote, "lest the liberty protected by the Due Process
Clause be subtly transformed into the policy preferences of the members of
this Court."

Rehnquist's philosophy of judicial restraint played out in some of his
other majority opinions. He led a 6–3 decision turning aside a minor political party's effort to overturn state "anti-fusion" laws that prohibited candidates from being listed on more than one party line on the ballot. The state's
interest in "ballot integrity" outweighed any First Amendment interests,
Rehnquist explained. Twice, he led solid majorities in turning back Fourth

Amendment challenges to police procedures in automobile traffic stops. And, in the final week of the term, he rebuffed a constitutional challenge to the newly adopted Line Item Veto Act and instead used the case to limit the ability of individual members of Congress to bring constitutional disputes into the courts. The Constitution, he declared, "contemplates a more restricted role" for federal courts.

For the first time in several terms, Rehnquist cast a lone dissenting vote in a case—and it too reflected his deference to state lawmakers. The ruling overturned a Georgia law requiring drug testing for candidates for state offices. The Court invalidated the law by an 8–1 vote as an unreasonable search under the Fourth Amendment. "Nothing in the Fourth Amendment," Rehnquist retorted, "prevents a State from enacting a statute whose principal vice is that it may seem misguided or even silly to the members of this Court."

Rehnquist wrote one other noteworthy majority opinion during the term—one that put him at odds with most of the other conservatives. He led a 6–3 majority in upholding most of a lower court's injunction limiting demonstrations by anti-abortion protesters at women's clinics in western New York. The ruling broke no new ground: it followed the Court's ruling in a 1994 case— also written by Rehnquist—in allowing limits on protests to protect access to clinics by patients and staff as long as the restrictions did not "burden more speech than is necessary. . . ." As in the earlier ruling, Scalia, Kennedy, and Thomas dissented.

Scalia also put a personal stamp on the term with his last-day ruling in the Brady Act case. He used the assignment to establish a precedent for looking to what he called "historical understanding and practice" as the major guide in determining disputes over the respective powers of the states and the federal government.

A longtime advocate of using "original intent" to interpret the Constitution, Scalia devoted slightly under half of his thirty-seven-page opinion to examining history from the writing of the Constitution to the present. The historical record showed, he argued, that the Framers of the Constitution never intended Congress to have the power to require state officials to carry out federal duties and that Congress, until recently, had never sought to impose such responsibilities on the states. The dissenting justices were forced to respond in kind, constructing equally detailed arguments to try to show that history was on their side rather than Scalia's.

"The forces of originalism have won the debate," commented Kmiec of Notre Dame law school. "Everybody on the Court is now relying on historical material to make their case. There's very little reliance merely on prior precedent as being sufficient to conclude a discussion."

Scalia's other majority opinions were less noteworthy—and all but one came in unanimous decisions. He authored a significant opinion holding that property owners have the same standing under the Endangered Species Act to bring court challenges to overenforcement of the law as environmentalists have to bring suits contesting underenforcement. He also wrote the opinion allowing state and local governments to suspend without pay a public employee who has been arrested for a crime.

In his votes and in his dissenting opinions, Scalia again staked out a position, along with Thomas, at the conservative end of the Court's ideological spectrum. They were the most frequent dissenters among the conservative bloc: Scalia was in the minority in seventeen cases, Thomas in sixteen *(see Table 1-2)*. And neither Scalia nor Thomas ever joined the four liberal justices in a 5–4 ruling.

In contrast to previous terms, however, Scalia's dissenting opinions lacked the harsh, sometimes personal rhetoric that even some conservative admirers had criticized. He did complain, in the abortion protest case, that the ruling made "a destructive inroad upon First Amendment law." But three years earlier, he had denounced the Court's original decision to uphold limits on anti-abortion demonstrators in much sharper terms—likening it at one point to the Court's decision upholding the internment of Japanese-Americans during World War II.

Scalia's ideological ally, Thomas, continued to take the lead in charting an ambitious conservative agenda for the future. In three cases, he wrote separate opinions suggesting that well-established precedents dating back several decades or more should be reconsidered or overturned. He argued against the Court's decision to extend the 1956 ruling on transcripts for indigent defendants to parental termination cases; if the case squarely presented the issue, Thomas added, "I would be inclined to vote to overrule" the prior ruling. In another case—a state tax dispute from Maine—he called for scrapping cases dating from the nineteenth century holding that the Constitution prohibits states from discriminating against interstate commerce. The so-called "negative Commerce Clause," Thomas said, "has no basis in the text of the Constitution, makes no sense, and has proved virtually unworkable in application."

Most provocatively, Thomas hinted in a concurring opinion in the Brady Act case that he would consider interpreting the Second Amendment's "right to bear arms" as limiting Congress's power to regulate firearms. "This Court has not had recent occasion to consider the nature of the substantive right safeguarded by the Second Amendment," Thomas wrote. "If, however, the Second Amendment is read to confer a personal right to 'keep and bear arms,' a colorable argument exists that the Federal Government's regulatory scheme, at least as it pertains to the purely intrastate sale or possession of firearms, runs afoul of that Amendment's protections."

Thomas noted that the Court's most recent decision on the Second Amendment—in 1939—upheld a federal law banning the possession of a sawed-off shotgun on grounds that the weapon could not contribute to "the common defense." But in a footnote, he cited an array of recent law review

Table 1-2   Justices in Dissent, 1996–1997 Term

Justice	8–1	7–2/6–2	6–3	5–4	Total	Percentage
		Division on Court				
Rehnquist	1	1	3	6	11	13.8
Stevens	5	6	3	9	23	28.8
O'Connor	—	1	4	5	10	12.6
Scalia	—	3	7	7	17	21.2
Kennedy	—	1	1	3	5	6.2
Souter	—	1	2	9	12	15.0
Thomas	—	2	7	7	16	20.0
Ginsburg	—	1	3	12	16	20.0
Breyer	—	4	3	10	17	21.2

Note: The totals reflect cases where justices dissented in whole or in part. There were eighty signed opinions during the 1996–1997 term. Because of a recusal, Justice O'Connor participated in seventy-nine cases.

articles arguing that the Second Amendment was not intended only to safeguard state militias, but also to establish an individual right to keep or bear arms. Thomas closed by invoking one of the great nineteenth-century justices. "Perhaps at some future date," Thomas wrote, "this Court will have the opportunity to determine whether Justice [Joseph] Story was correct when he wrote that the right to bear arms 'has justly been considered, as the palladium of the liberties of a republic.'"

Marking his sixth term on the Court, Thomas moved beyond the relatively minor tax and bankruptcy cases that are often assigned to junior justices. He authored one of the major opinions of the year: the 5–4 decision upholding state "sexual predator" laws. The opinion embodied the conservatives' core views: deference to state legislatures and skepticism of expansive interpretations of the Due Process Clause. The Kansas Supreme Court had struck down the law on the ground that it allowed a civil commitment on the basis of a "mental abnormality" rather than a "mental illness." Thomas rejected the argument. " . . . [W]e have never required State legislatures to adopt any particular nomenclature in drafting civil commitment statutes," he wrote. "Rather, we have traditionally left to legislators the task of defining terms of a medical nature that have legal significance."

In two other majority opinions, Thomas sided with the government in criminal cases. In one, he led a six-justice majority in requiring the federal Sentencing Commission to increase the possible maximum sentences for repeat drug or violent crime offenders. In another, he wrote the 5–4 decision rejecting a habeas corpus plea by a Virginia death row inmate who had drawn worldwide attention with his effort to reverse his murder conviction.

Thomas said that the inmate could not use a newly established rule on jury procedures in death penalty cases to overturn his nine-year-old conviction.

Thomas also wrote a significant patent law ruling upholding the so-called doctrine of equivalents—a judicially-created rule that protects patentholders against inventors who develop products or processes that are similar but not identical. He suggested, however, that lower courts had applied the doctrine too broadly, weakening the rule that patents generally should be strictly limited according to their terms.

The Court's centrist conservatives, O'Connor and Kennedy, authored majority opinions in two of the term's major decisions: a pair of closely divided, closely watched cases on separation of church and state. Both rulings added to the term's conservative impact, but they appeared to go in opposite directions. In one, O'Connor led a narrowly divided Court in making it easier for government to provide aid to students at parochial schools. In the other, Kennedy led the Court in striking down a law aimed at strengthening freedom for religious practices—over a strong dissent from O'Connor.

The parochial school assistance case amounted to a personal vindication for O'Connor. She had led four dissenters from a 1985 ruling that barred the New York City school system from using federal funds to provide remedial educational services for low-income students on the premises of parochial schools. Over the next decade, O'Connor complained about the ruling and joined decisions subtly undermining it. This term, she led a five-justice majority in agreeing to hear a renewed plea by the New York school system and then voting to overturn the twelve-year-old precedent. The prior ruling, O'Connor declared forcefully from the bench, "is no longer good law."

O'Connor had also disagreed with the legal holding in a 1990 church-state case that had made it harder for religious groups or individuals to gain exemptions from laws that interfered with their religious practices. Congress took up the issue and passed a law in 1993 that echoed O'Connor's position by establishing a stricter standard for states to meet in enforcing laws that had an incidental effect on religious practices. State and local governments challenged the law as an infringement of states' rights.

Kennedy led the Court in sustaining the attack on the law this term not only as a violation of states' rights but also as an intrusion on the Court's own prerogatives. The law, Kennedy declared in the 6–3 ruling, imposed "substantial costs" on the states, "both in practical terms of imposing a heavy litigation burden . . . and in terms of curtailing their traditional general regulatory power. . . ." Equally important, he said Congress had exceeded its lawmaking powers by attempting to define the substantive meaning of constitutional provisions in the face of a contrary ruling by the Court. "Our national experience teaches us," Kennedy wrote, "that the Constitution is preserved best when each part of the government respects both the Constitution and the proper actions and determinations of the other branches."

O'Connor said she agreed with Kennedy's views that Congress had exceeded its power in enacting the law. But she reiterated her disagreement with the precedent that the law was aimed at overturning. "I remain of the view that [the prior case] was wrongly decided," she declared in a dissenting opinion that she emphasized by reading from the bench.

Kennedy and O'Connor also split in two other major rulings in the term. Kennedy led a five-justice majority in upholding a federal law requiring cable operators to carry most local television stations on their systems; he said Congress had substantial grounds for believing the law would promote media diversity without imposing undue burdens on cable operators' editorial freedom. O'Connor sharply disagreed, faulting Kennedy for being too deferential toward Congress. "We are not . . . at liberty," she wrote, "to substitute speculation for evidence or to ignore factual disputes that call the reasonableness of Congress' findings into question."

In the other case—an important federalism dispute—Kennedy and O'Connor agreed on the result, but had a critical disagreement about the meaning of the decision for future cases. The issue was whether an Indian tribe could sue Idaho state officials in federal court to resolve a dispute about jurisdiction over a lake that lay along the tribe's reservation. Kennedy rejected the suit in what was ostensibly an opinion for the usual, five-justice conservative majority. But O'Connor led two other justices—Scalia and Thomas—in splitting off from a crucial passage where Kennedy proposed a new rule that would make it significantly harder for individuals to bring any suits against state officials in federal court.

In their other major opinions, O'Connor and Kennedy usually saw eye to eye with each other and with their fellow conservatives. O'Connor led a 5–4 decision that made it harder for plaintiffs in police brutality suits to recover damages from local governments. Kennedy authored the 5–4 decision in a case that upheld a plan reducing the number of black-majority congressional districts in Georgia to one.

But O'Connor and Kennedy were also the most likely of the conservatives to join with liberal justices in closely divided decisions. O'Connor provided the critical fifth vote in a decision that barred retroactive application of a new law restricting the ability of state prison inmates to use habeas corpus to challenge their convictions in federal court. She also split from the conservative bloc in a 5–4 decision that limited the protections from damage suits for private prison guards. For his part, Kennedy split from the other conservatives in a criminal procedure decision that blocked a prosecutor from introducing the details of a prior offense committed by the defendant. And both O'Connor and Kennedy joined in the 6–3 decision guaranteeing free trial transcripts for defendants in parental termination suits.

By positioning themselves in the middle of the Court's ideological spectrum, Kennedy and O'Connor again had the lowest and second-lowest percentage of dissenting votes. Kennedy had only five dissents among the eighty signed opinions, or 6 percent. It was at least the sixth consecutive year Kennedy had cast the fewest dissenting votes of any of the justices. O'Connor dissented in ten cases, or 12 percent of the total—just below Rehnquist's figure of eleven dissents.

More significantly, by hewing closer to the conservative position in major cases, O'Connor and Kennedy also helped give the year's decisions a strong conservative stamp. "The ones who can throw their weight around, who can make a difference, are O'Connor and Kennedy," UCLA professor Volokh remarked. "If O'Connor and Kennedy both vote conservative, they can really do a lot for the center-right program on the Court."

Conservative Court-watchers were generally pleased with the results. But there were disappointments. "The Court has shown admirable restraint, but at times they have gone overboard in restraint," commented Richard Samp, chief counsel of the conservative Washington Legal Foundation. As one example, Samp cited the Court's 5–4 decision rejecting a free speech challenge to the federal law requiring agricultural growers to pay for industrywide generic advertising. O'Connor and Kennedy helped form the majority to uphold the program.

In the main, though, conservatives had much to cheer— in particular, the rulings limiting the powers of Congress and the federal government. "This term will be remembered most of all, and more than any in recent memory, for the Court's contributions concerning the division, allocation, and separation of governmental power," noted Theodore Olson, a Washington attorney and a leader in the Federalist Society, which advocates a smaller role for the federal government. "I think the Court will continue that trend," Olson added, "because there's always going to be something nibbling around the margins."

The Left-of-Center Minority

The justices on the liberal end of the Court's ideological spectrum were a diverse and often less than cohesive group. Two of them—John Paul Stevens and David H. Souter—came to the Court as moderate Republicans appointed by moderate Republican presidents, Gerald R. Ford and George Bush respectively. The other two—Ruth Bader Ginsburg and Stephen G. Breyer—had been Democrats, but each served on the federal bench for more than a decade before being elevated to the Court by President Clinton during his first term.

None of the four could be described as a liberal in the Warren Court mold. "There is not a sitting Justice committed to a view of the Constitution as an engine of social change," Linda Greenhouse wrote in the *New York Times* at the start of the term. Stevens perhaps came closest to that description; he had shifted to the left on criminal law and constitutional issues in his two decades on the bench. But Souter, a former state attorney general, often voted with the conservatives on criminal law issues. Ginsburg was uncomfortable with expanding constitutional protections under the Due Process Clause. And Breyer had a mixed record on free speech issues and, along with Souter and Ginsburg, a relaxed view of the Fourth Amendment's limits on police searches.

Still, the liberal-leaning justices typically found common ground on some of the most important issues before the Court, putting them at odds with the conservative majority. They strongly resisted the Court's rulings to limit racial redistricting. They opposed the majority's moves to ease the rules on government aid to religion. And they dissented together from many of the decisions to turn back challenges in death penalty cases.

The two ideological blocs came closest to agreement in one important area: the First Amendment's free speech provisions. "That's one place where ideology seems to fall by the wayside for both the conservatives and liberals on the Court," Georgetown's Feldblum remarked. In most free speech cases, she said, "the First Amendment will prevail for this Court."

The decision to strike down the Communications Decency Act fit that pattern, as did several cases from the past few terms. But the Court this term also turned back free speech challenges to two federal regulatory schemes: the "must-carry" law for cable television and the industrywide generic advertising under agricultural marketing schemes. The ideological groupings were mixed in both cases, but the Court's liberal-leaning justices provided most of the votes for sustaining the two laws while conservatives accounted for three of the four dissenting votes in each.

Among the Court's left-of-center bloc, Stevens made the greatest impact on the term's decisions. He authored mostly unanimous opinions in two of the major cases: the ruling to strike the Internet indecency law and the decision to reject President Clinton's plea to postpone the Paula Jones sexual harassment suit. In both opinions, the scholarly, bow-tie-wearing justice wrote broadly, with an eye to history as well as to the present.

In the Clinton case, Stevens surveyed the history of presidential powers and court rulings affecting the president and found no bar under the Constitution to allowing a civil suit for unofficial conduct to proceed. "The fact that a federal court's exercise of its traditional Article III jurisdiction may significantly burden the time and attention of the Chief Executive is not sufficient to establish a violation of the Constitution," he wrote.

In the Internet case, Stevens opened with a primer that praised the "vast democratic fora" provided by the Internet and closed with a warning against restricting its growth through governmental regulation. "As a matter of constitutional tradition," Stevens wrote, "governmental regulation of the content of speech is more likely to interfere with the free exchange of ideas than to encourage it."

Stevens wrote with similar breadth in leading the liberal dissenters in the term's last-day ruling in the Brady Act case. "If Congress believes that such a statute will benefit the people of the Nation, and serve the interests of cooperative federalism better than an enlarged federal bureaucracy," Stevens concluded, "we should respect both its policy judgment and its appraisal of its constitutional power."

In addition, he wrote an important concurring opinion in the assisted-suicide cases that, as University of Utah professor McConnell noted, "reads more like a dissent." The rulings, Stevens argued, "[do] not foreclose the possibility that some applications of the [state laws] may impose an intolerable intrusion on the patient's freedom."

As in past terms, Stevens ranked highest among the justices in dissents. He cast dissenting votes in twenty-three of the eighty signed opinions—or 29 percent. He also led the justices in lone dissents, with five; Rehnquist's solo dissent was the only other during the term. Many of Stevens's dissents came in criminal law cases, where he supported broader rights for suspects and defendants than the majority was willing to recognize. But Stevens also led a unanimous Court in an important decision that reinforced a two-year-old ruling generally prohibiting no-knock searches by police.

Souter, marking his seventh term, had, like Stevens, moved away from the moderate stance of his early years to a more liberal position in recent terms. His position as a former state attorney general notwithstanding, Souter, as a Supreme Court justice, sided with the national government in most federalism disputes. His was also the strongest voice on the Court for strict separation of church and state. And, although he usually backed the government in criminal law cases, he joined the liberal justices in dissenting from rulings on capital punishment.

His dissents drew notice and favorable comment from liberal Court-watchers. "Souter has really taken on the role of the eloquent dissenter," USC professor Chemerinsky remarked. "He came to be the liberal conscience in dissent."

As one example, Souter used his dissent in the parochial school aid case to lecture the conservative majority on the reasons for prohibiting government subsidies for religious organizations. "The rule expresses the hard lesson learned over and over again in the American past," Souter wrote, "that religions supported by governments are compromised just as surely as the religious freedom of dissenters is burdened when the government supports religion."

Souter also wrote dissenting opinions in two federalism cases. In the Brady Act case, he conceded that he found the issue "closer than I had anticipated," but ultimately concluded that the Framers had expected Congress to have the power to order state officials to enforce federal laws. In the second case—the dispute over federal court suits against state officials— Souter said the ruling would "redefine and reduce" the ability of private citizens "to vindicate federal rights."

Like Stevens, Souter also wrote a concurrence in the assisted-suicide case that expressly challenged the legal reasoning in the majority opinion. In contrast to Rehnquist's reliance on history and tradition to uphold the ban on physician-assisted suicide, Souter said the issue was whether the laws amounted to "arbitrary impositions" or "purposeless restraints." Souter's approach clearly gave more discretion to courts in examining the laws, and he expressed his ultimate decision to uphold the statutes in tentative terms. The Court should "stay its hand" for now, he wrote, to allow "reasonable legislative consideration" on the issue.

Souter's majority opinions were less noteworthy than his dissents. He led a 5–4 majority in a densely statutory decision that limited the scope of the recently enacted federal habeas corpus restrictions; he explained from the bench that he would read only a short summary to avoid putting spectators to sleep.

Several other of his decisions were extremely limited. For example, he led a narrow majority in a racial redistricting decision that upheld a federal judge's power, in effect, to prod opposing parties into a settlement rather than return the challenged district to the legislature to redraw. Rehnquist split off from the conservative bloc to provide the needed fifth vote for the decision.

Ginsburg, in a productive fourth term on the Court, appeared to be developing a niche as the Court's expert on civil procedure. The specialty produced her most important majority opinion. The decision upset a massive asbestos-injury class action settlement and limited the ability of plaintiffs' attorneys and industry representatives to reach similar global agreements in future mass tort cases. The asbestos settlement, Ginsburg said, went beyond the federal rules on class action suits. And courts, she stressed, "are not free to amend a rule" on their own.

In a similar vein, Ginsburg chided a federal appeals court for its handling of a constitutional challenge to an Arizona "official English" ballot initiative. The Ninth U.S. Circuit Court of Appeals had ruled the measure unconstitutional despite significant procedural reasons indicating the suit should have been dismissed—and without waiting for an official interpretation of the initiative from the state supreme court. "A more cautious approach was in order," Ginsburg wrote in a unanimous opinion that set the appeals court's ruling aside.

Even more dramatically, Ginsburg upbraided the Court's conservative majority on procedural grounds in the parochial school aid case. The decision to let the New York City schools gain a rehearing in the case twelve years after the original decision was unprecedented and unwise, Ginsburg said. And the result, she warned, would be to invite losing parties in other cases to ask the Court to reconsider prior rulings based not on the law but on "speculations" about the effect of changes in the Court's membership.

Ginsburg produced three other important majority opinions. In one, she led the Court in upholding an expansive prosecution theory for insider trading cases under federal securities law. The opinion was closely reasoned and free of rhetoric, but no less critical for the government in supporting efforts to police the nation's securities markets. In another, Ginsburg wrote a nearly unanimous opinion striking down the Georgia law requiring drug testing for state candidates. The law, Ginsburg wrote, "diminishes personal privacy" for no purpose other than to display the state's opposition to drug abuse.

Earlier in the term, Ginsburg authored the ruling in the decision guaranteeing trial transcripts for indigents in parental termination cases. The case involved the state's "awesome authority" to sever a parent's relation with her child, Ginsburg explained. Given the stakes for the parent, she continued, the state should not be allowed to "bolt the door to equal justice."

Ginsburg had the unwanted distinction during the term of being the most frequent dissenter in the Court's 5–4 decisions, casting minority votes in twelve of the seventeen one-vote rulings. In most of the cases—nine—she sided with the other liberal-leaning justices. But in two of the cases, she positioned herself with three of the Court's conservatives—voting to strike down the cable television must-carry law and to uphold a state tax provision challenged on federalism grounds.

As the junior justice, Breyer was not receiving choice assignments for majority opinions. But he also appeared to be developing a niche as the Court's specialist in liability law. He held generally conservative views—skeptical of expansive liability theories and interested in streamlining tort litigation. Those views put him sometimes in the majority and sometimes in dissent.

Most notably, Breyer dissented, along with Stevens, from the decision to block the asbestos class action settlement. His opinion catalogued the problems courts face in mass tort litigation: crowded dockets, long delays, large legal fees, and the risk of overcompensating plaintiffs with minor injuries and undercompensating people with more serious injuries. The majority, he said, "understates the importance of settlement in this case."

Breyer wrote the majority opinion in another asbestos-related case, this one limiting recovery to railway workers exposed to asbestos in their jobs but free of any medical symptoms. The workers, who sued under a federal law establishing tort remedies for railway employees, sought to recover for emotional distress resulting from the fear of developing asbestos-related diseases in the future. But Breyer said that theory would open the door to "unlimited and unpredictable liability."

His concerns about civil litigation also surfaced in the separate opinion Breyer wrote in the ruling on the sexual harassment suit against President Clinton. Instead of joining the Court's opinion, Breyer wrote a concurrence that called for more safeguards against the burdens of litigation on the office of the president. Breyer said the majority's anticipation of few civil suits against the president could "turn out to be misplaced." And he said he was uncertain that lower courts would be able to manage such suits without "significantly interfering with the discharge of Presidential duties."

In two other opinions, Breyer was more favorable toward tort plaintiffs. He led a 5–4 decision in refusing to give private prison guards the same legal protection from damage suits enjoyed by guards employed by the government. The opinion relied almost completely on economic analysis, ending with the conclusion that private prison companies would "adjust their behavior" in response to the risk of civil damage awards. In the other ruling, Breyer wrote an opinion expanding liability for some boat manufacturers. In that decision too, Breyer relied on economic reasoning. The ruling, he said, would encourage safer product design by boat manufacturers.

In other areas, Breyer aligned himself with the center-left bloc of justices. He led the four dissenters in the racial redistricting ruling in the Georgia case, echoing prior dissenting opinions in warning against "judicial entanglement" in the districting process. He also wrote the limited dissent in the ruling upholding the Kansas sexual predator law. Breyer said the defendant had been subjected to retroactive punishment, but agreed with the majority that states could enact such laws as long as they were applied to future cases. And, in the police brutality suit, Breyer wrote a dissent calling for a re-examination of a 1978 precedent that imposed liability on local governments for constitutional violations by employees only under limited circumstances.

Relegated to dissents in so many cases, the liberal justices appeared to be trying to lay the groundwork for a change in the Court's direction in some areas in the event of a change in the Court's membership. "They undoubtedly have to perceive themselves as the minority in many areas of the law," Chemerinsky commented. But O'Connor's success in reversing the ruling on aid to parochial schools a decade later provided an example of how today's minority can become tomorrow's majority on an issue.

Court-watchers differed on how well the liberal justices were doing in marshaling arguments for a later day. Liberal experts, such as Chemerinsky and Feldblum, gave them good marks for laying out alternative views. But conservative constitutional law experts were less impressed. Notre Dame professor Kmiec noted that the liberal justices failed to agree on a unified position in some of the conservatives' major victories. "They would be more effective if they could agree on a writer," Kmiec said. "That suggests they're not speaking with one voice."

No Changes in Sight?

For the moment, the prospects for a fifth vote on the Court's left side did not appear promising. Despite recurrent rumors over several years, Rehnquist showed no visible signs of preparing to step down. The Court's next two justices in order of seniority—the liberal Stevens and the centrist-conservative O'Connor—both appeared to be in good health after having survived bouts in recent years with prostate cancer and breast cancer respectively. Stevens was hospitalized in February because of an obstructed coronary artery; but he was released after a couple of days and pronounced "symptom-free."

A rumor percolated in late June that Justice Scalia might be considering retirement, frustrated that the conservative bloc has been too timid in overturning liberal precedents of bygone days. Nothing materialized, however. And Kennedy, who turned sixty-one in July, and Thomas, not yet fifty, both appeared ready to serve well into the next century.

Still, President Clinton had three more years in office, and history favored his having the chance to make at least one more appointment to the Court. Only twice since the Civil War had a president gone for a complete four-year term without making an appointment to the Court. Jimmy Carter made no appointments during his presidency (1977–1981), and Franklin D. Roosevelt had no vacancies to fill in his first term (1933–1937).

If Clinton were to have a vacancy to fill, Court-watchers expected him to follow his pattern in choosing Ginsburg and Breyer by selecting another moderately liberal, sitting federal court judge. (There was speculation he might want to appoint the Court's first Hispanic justice.) Clinton had to reckon with the likelihood of a close examination of any nominee by the Republican-controlled Senate. Conservative GOP senators signaled their concerns about "activist" judges during the year by calling for the impeachment of some lower court federal jurists. Nothing came of the effort, but the episode served as a cautionary reminder to a White House already reluctant to enter into tough confirmation fights for federal judicial appointments.

If Stevens were to retire, Clinton's appointment might actually shift the balance of power on the Court toward the center— just as Breyer's selection to replace the liberal Justice Harry A. Blackmun did. But if one of the conservatives were to retire, Clinton might have the power to create a fragile majority of moderate-to-liberal justices.

Would a new "Clinton court" reverse the direction that the Rehnquist Court had taken? Notre Dame's Kmiec said the liberal justices were hurting their chances with their sometimes fragmented dissents. "That's where the next majority opinions come from after a change of personnel," Kmiec said. "If they individually write, they don't create a body of jurisprudence that will be readily turned into opinions at a later time."

Volokh at UCLA acknowledged that a left-of-center majority might "undo" some Rehnquist Court decisions. But he also noted that under Chief Justice Warren E. Burger, the Court in the 1970s and early '80s disappointed conservatives by failing to overturn many of the liberal precedents from the Warren Court era.

USC's Chemerinsky, however, gave better odds on the chances of a new course at the Court. "The pendulum has gone back and forth through American history," Chemerinsky said. "And there's no reason to think that it won't swing back again."

2 | *The 1996–1997 Term*

With one week left to go before the expected start of its summer recess, the Supreme Court had sixteen cases remaining to be decided, one-fifth of the total for the year. The backlog distressed even the members of the Court. "It's the worst I've seen in years," one unidentified justice told National Public Radio's Supreme Court reporter Nina Totenberg.

If Chief Justice Rehnquist had his way, however, the Court was sure to finish by the end of the week. Rehnquist was a stickler for staying on schedule. "Everything is on time with the Chief Justice," Justice Thomas once remarked. Rehnquist had an additional reason for wanting to wrap up: he had airplane tickets to fly to Rome on Sunday.

By week's end, Rehnquist was free to travel. In the span of five days—June 23 through June 27—the Court issued sixteen signed opinions, two more per curiam decisions, and a final orders list denying review in more than 150 cases. Rehnquist missed the final session; he was speaking in Virginia to the annual meeting of federal judges for the Fourth Circuit. So it fell to Justice Stevens, next in seniority, to announce that the Court had disposed of all cases ready for decision and would recess until the first Monday in October, when the October 1996 term would formally end and the new term begin.

For the justices and the Court staff, the week's pace was dizzying. Opinions were reworked, reprinted, and recirculated to all nine chambers up to the last minute. One justice went for two days without sleep, according to Joan Biskupic's after-the-fact account in the *Washington Post.* On Thursday, Court officials were still uncertain whether the justices would finish the next day.

The week was also hectic for the lawyers, experts, and advocacy groups that followed the Court's decisions. The head of one interest group came to the Court one morning with a press release ready to applaud an anticipated decision. The release had to be trashed; the justices went against the group's position in the case.

When the opinions had all been digested, conservative advocacy groups could count a number of major victories—capped by the term's final decision striking down a provision of the Brady gun-control act on states' rights grounds. But liberal interest groups also had some cause for cheer, most notably, the ruling in a suit by the American Civil Liberties Union (ACLU) to strike down the law seeking to regulate sexual indecency on the Internet.

Above all, the Court struck observers as assertive and ambitious in taking on disputed legal issues. "Overall, it was quite an aggressive term, both in seeking out issues and resolving them," said Alan Morrison, a longtime

Table 2-1   Laws Held Unconstitutional

The Supreme Court issued seven decisions during the 1996–1997 term that held unconstitutional federal laws or state laws or constitutional provisions.

Decisions (in chronological order)	Law Held Invalid
Federal Laws	
Babbitt v. Youpee [p. 106]	Indian Land Consolidation Act
City of Boerne v. Flores [p. 109]	Religious Freedom Restoration Act
Reno v. American Civil Liberties Union [p. 110]	Communications Decency Act
Printz v. United States [p. 104]	Brady Handgun Violence Prevention Act
State Laws	
Lynce v. Mathis [p. 92]	Florida law retroactively canceling early prison release credits
Chandler v. Miller [p. 118]	Georgia law requiring drug testing for candidates for state offices
Camps Newfound/Owatonna, Inc. v. Town of Harrison [p. 129]	Maine tax exemption for charities only if they mostly serve state residents

public interest lawyer with the liberal Public Citizen Litigation Group in Washington.

"It was a fairly good term," said Scott Bullock, a staff attorney with the Institute for Justice, a conservative public interest legal center, "especially in terms of the Court reasserting itself by striking down congressional legislation that exceeds constitutionally limited powers."

The Court's assertiveness was reflected in the number of federal and state laws it struck down during the term. Four federal laws were invalidated. And, despite the conservative majority's interest in strengthening state prerogatives, the Court also struck down three state laws on federal constitutional grounds *(see Table 2-1)*.

On another measure of judicial activism—overturning its own precedents—the Court appeared less aggressive. It explicitly scrapped one of its prior decisions only once during the term; in past terms, the justices had often discarded two or three precedents *(see Table 2-2)*. But the decision was a notable example of the Court's willingness to depart from the doctrine of stare decisis ("let the decision stand"). The rejected ruling, which set limits on government aid to students at parochial schools, was only twelve years old. And the Court overturned the prior decision, by a 5–4 vote, through an unprecedented use of a procedural rule. The Court reconsidered the 1985

Table 2-2   Reversals of Earlier Rulings

The Supreme Court issued one decision during the 1996–1997 term that explicitly reversed a previous ruling by the Court. The ruling brought the number of such reversals in the Court's history to at least 212.

New Decision	Old Decision	New Holding
Agostini v. Felton	*Aguilar v. Felton* (1985); *School Dist. of Grand Rapids v. Ball* (1985)	Allows government aid to church-related school

ruling in a plea brought by the New York City school system, which had been the losing party in the original case. Dissenting justices said the move amounted to granting an "anytime rehearing" that could invite similar moves by losing litigants aimed at taking advantage of changes in the Court's membership.

The Court also admonished the federal judiciary. The justices made clear in a number of rulings that federal judges should take a lower profile and defer more often to elected officials or to state courts. In the most closely watched case of the term, the Court unanimously overturned rulings by two federal appeals courts striking down state laws banning physician-assisted suicide for people with terminal illnesses. The issue, Rehnquist wrote, was for popularly elected state legislatures to decide, not the courts.

A similar effort to rein in federal judges showed up in other cases. The Court said a federal judge in Philadelphia went beyond federal procedural rules governing class-action suits in approving a massive settlement of future asbestos-injury claims. It rebuked a federal appeals court for reaching out to decide the constitutionality of Arizona's "official English" initiative. It also gutted a broad class-action suit contesting Arizona's compliance with a federal child-support enforcement scheme, saying the issue was for federal officials rather than courts to assess. And it repudiated a line of cases from the federal appeals court in Washington that had allowed individual members of Congress to bring legal challenges to the constitutionality of laws or executive branch actions. The courts, Rehnquist wrote, should normally stay out of political disputes between the executive and legislative branches.

State courts also felt the Court's rebuke in a handful of cases—notably, in reversals of three decisions where state justices had strengthened protections in criminal law settings. Most significantly, the Court reversed a decision by the Kansas Supreme Court that had overturned the state's recently enacted law providing for indefinite civil commitment for "violent sexual predators." The Kansas court said the ruling violated sexual offenders' due process rights by allowing confinement without a finding of "mental illness," but the Court disagreed. The Court also overturned rulings by supreme courts in two states, Ohio and Maryland, that had limited police powers to question or search automobile drivers or passengers after a traffic stop.

State supreme courts were also reversed in two cases for refusing to extend individual rights. The Court said the Wisconsin Supreme Court was wrong to carve out a broad exception for drug cases to its 1994 decision restricting no-knock searches by police. The Mississippi Supreme Court was overturned for refusing to provide free trial transcripts for an indigent mother seeking to appeal a decision terminating her parental rights to her young children.

Throughout the term, the Court seemed to be re-emphasizing its own supremacy in the constitutional scheme. That theme emerged most forcefully in the final-week decision to strike down the Religious Freedom Restoration Act (RFRA). The 1993 law, which required states to give greater leeway to groups claiming a First Amendment exemption from state or local laws, contradicted the Court's own decision on the issue only a few years earlier. In striking down the statute, the Court held that it infringed not only on states' rights but also on the Court's own powers to define constitutional rights.

The decision to strike down such a widely popular law caught many experts by surprise. But, as Professor William van Alstyne of Duke University Law School remarked, the Court saw the issue as "who ultimately decides the interpretation and meaning of the Constitution." Justice Kennedy, writing for the Court, answered that question by harking back to Chief Justice John Marshall's famous assertion of judicial power in *Marbury v. Madison,* the 1803 ruling that first established the Court's power to strike down a law passed by Congress. Whatever powers Congress may have, Kennedy wrote, the judiciary retains "the duty to say what the law is."

States appeared to be the biggest beneficiaries of the Court's assertiveness during the term. The Brady Act decision wiped out a federal mandate that local law enforcement agencies conduct background checks on prospective gun purchasers. The ruling to strike down the RFRA appeared likely to dampen the flurry of suits by inmates attacking prison restrictions as infringing on their religious practices. In addition, the Court somewhat strengthened the Eleventh Amendment's restrictions on suits against states or state officials in federal court. States also benefited from the Court's general policy of backing law enforcement in criminal cases.

The federalism rulings cheered the conservative advocates of a reduced role for the national government. "Instead of purporting to resolve contentious moral questions for itself or even allowing Congress to step in in the absence of real constitutional authority to do so, it has left the decisions to state and local governments," said Michael McConnell of the University of Utah Law School.

Some critics echoed the warnings of the dissenting justices that the Court's rulings could hamper the federal government's ability to deal with national problems. "Now we have a set of rulings showing the Court wants to limit Congress to its enumerated powers," Cass Sunstein, a professor at the University of Chicago Law School, remarked. "The Court hasn't been in that business since the early New Deal."

Many advocates and experts, however, said the impact of the decisions was likely to be less than the supporters hoped or the critics feared. "The idea that the Brady bill's downfall suggests a return to the pre–New Deal Court is nonsense," Gerald Gunther, a longtime constitutional law expert at Stanford Law School, told the *National Law Journal.*

Several advocates of limiting federal power noted that Congress had other ways to get the states to help carry out federal regulatory schemes. In particular, they pointed to Congress's frequent use of its spending powers to provide funds for states to enforce federal laws or to reduce financial aid for failing to comply with federal directives. "That's clearly an approach that can be done in most situations where Congress feels a need for state officials to be carrying out a task," Ohio State Solicitor Jeffrey Sutton said.

Still, experts and advocates pointed to a number of federal laws susceptible to challenge under the Brady Act ruling. As one example, they pointed to the Motor Voter Act, which required states to adopt procedures aimed at simplifying voter registration. In addition, lower courts were already considering challenges to federal laws that cited the Court's 1995 decision limiting Congress's power under the Constitution's Commerce Clause. In that case, the Court struck down a law prohibiting possession of a firearm near a school, saying the act exceeded Congress's power to regulate interstate commerce. The ruling spurred challenges to laws making carjacking a federal crime, allowing victims of domestic violence to sue in federal court, and making it a crime to cross state lines to avoid child support.

Those challenges had yet to reach the Court, and experts disagreed about their likely outcome. But even some critics of broad federal powers were playing down the likely impact of the Court's recent decisions. "I don't know of anybody who's pushing for a return to the pre–New Deal era when the federal government didn't get that involved in the day-to-day lives of American citizens," said Richard Samp of the conservative Washington Legal Foundation.

The Court's criminal law rulings were generally good news for state and federal law enforcement alike. Federal and state prosecutors won fourteen of the sixteen signed opinions in cases involving criminal prosecutions or federal habeas corpus petitions. In addition, prosecutors had a much higher chance of persuading the Court to review their appeals. Defendants and inmates filed the vast majority of petitions with the Court, but prosecutors persuaded the Court to grant review in ten cases while defendants and inmates gained review in only eight. And prosecutors won all of the cases where the Court granted review at their request.

"It was generally a bad term for rights of criminal defendants," said Lisa

Kemler, a Washington-area attorney who followed the Court for the National Association of Criminal Defense Lawyers.

The most important of the law enforcement victories during the term was technically a civil case: the decision upholding the Kansas law providing for indefinite civil commitment in a mental institution for repeat violent sexual offenders. The ruling "means that some people are going to spend the rest of their lives incarcerated," said USC law professor Erwin Chemerinsky, a critic of the decision.

In more traditional criminal law areas, the justices voted by substantial majorities in two cases to give police broader discretion in automobile searches. In an Ohio case, the Court held that police can continue interrogating a motorist after completing a traffic stop even if they do not tell the driver he is free to leave. In a Maryland case, the Court ruled that in the interest of officers' safety, police can order a passenger as well as the driver out of a car after a traffic stop. All of the justices agreed on the legal holding in the Ohio case, and only Stevens and Kennedy dissented from the rule in the Maryland dispute.

By a narrower majority, the Court also continued to raise barriers for state prison inmates challenging their convictions in federal habeas corpus cases. In two 5–4 decisions, the Court denied habeas corpus petitions by death row inmates in Florida and Virginia by invoking its 1989 decision that bars the use of newly established constitutional requirements to overturn state court convictions or sentences. In both cases, the dissenters argued that the constitutional rights claimed by the inmates had been well established at the time of their trials.

Federal prosecutors won a number of significant victories, including an important ruling in a closely watched insider trading case. The 6–3 decision upheld a legal theory crafted by the Securities and Exchange Commission called the "misappropriation doctrine." The doctrine was used in civil or criminal proceedings against people who engaged in securities trading on the basis of confidential information they gained not from a traditional corporate insider position, but from some other position of trust. The ruling came in the case of a Minneapolis attorney who made a multimillion-dollar profit in securities trading by using information about an impending tender offer he learned from a partner in his law firm.

In another high-profile criminal case, the government gained a new appellate court hearing on its use of a Reconstruction-era civil rights statute to prosecute a former Tennessee judge charged with sexually assaulting several women in his chambers. The statute made it a federal crime for a state official to violate a person's civil rights "under color of law." The Court said the appeals court had used an overly narrow test to determine whether the law protected a woman's right to be free from sexual assault.

Federal prosecutors also won favorable interpretations of the federal sentencing guidelines in two cases, allowing longer prison terms for repeat drug or violent crime offenders and for people who use weapons in committing drug offenses. In a third case the Court, in an unsigned opinion, ruled that federal judges can take into account charges that the defendant has previously been acquitted of when sentencing that defendant. Dissenting judges said the decision was "repugnant" to the presumption of innocence.

Against the generally pro-prosecution rulings, civil liberties advocates and criminal defense lawyers could count only a few, limited victories—such as the Court's refusal in the Wisconsin case to allow police to conduct no-knock searches in all serious drug cases. "There's no drug exception to the Fourth Amendment," said Steven R. Shapiro, national legal director of the American Civil Liberties Union. "From this Court, that was a very important statement." Even so, the Court upheld the defendant's conviction, saying police had sufficient reason in the case to justify entering his motel room without knocking.

The Court also limited the effect of a newly enacted law that Congress passed to restrict federal habeas corpus remedies for state prisoners. By a 5–4 vote, the Court held that Congress did not intend for most of the provisions of the 1996 law—the Antiterrorism and Effective Death Penalty Act—to apply to habeas corpus petitions pending when it took effect. "That would surprise most of the members of Congress who passed the law," said Kent Scheidegger, an attorney with the pro–law enforcement Criminal Justice Foundation in Sacramento.

The term's rulings on civil rights and civil liberties reflected established Rehnquist Court themes: a generally broad construction of free speech, but a narrow approach to substantive due process rights; a broad reading of federal civil rights statutes, but opposition to race-specific remedies; and a restrictive view to civil rights damage suits.

Free speech advocates celebrated the ruling striking down the Internet anti-indecency law not only for the specific result, but also for the Court's message in doing so. "The Court said in the strongest possible terms that this was a revolutionary new medium of communication and that it could only reach its full potential if it was granted maximum First Amendment protection," said the ACLU's Steven Shapiro.

In two other cases, however, the Court upheld federal laws challenged on free speech grounds, both times by 5–4 votes. The Court rejected a challenge to the so-called cable television must-carry law that required local cable systems to carry the signals of most local broadcast stations. It also turned back a challenge by some California fruit growers to a federal agricultural marketing scheme that required them to pay part of the cost of an industrywide generic advertising program.

The Court also rejected a First Amendment challenge to state laws that prohibit candidates from being listed on the ballot by more than one political party. The so-called anti-fusion laws were on the books in about forty states. By a 6–3 vote, the Court held that the statutes imposed only minor burdens on political association but served important interests of preventing voter confusion or ballot manipulation.

The Court also confronted a free speech challenge to a federal judge's injunction limiting anti-abortion demonstrations at women's clinics in western New York. The ruling upheld most of the injunction, but struck down a provision requiring demonstrators to stay at least fifteen feet away from clinic patients and staff. The Court said that provision burdened more speech than necessary to protect access to the clinics.

The rulings upholding state laws banning assisted suicide reflected the Court's reluctance to find new substantive rights embedded in the Due Process Clause. On the other hand, the Court did rely on due process as well as equal protection in creating a new procedural right this term: the right to a free transcript for indigents in parental termination cases. The ruling, in a Mississippi case, said the state should not "bolt the door to equal justice" by effectively denying an indigent the opportunity to appeal a parental termination order.

Traditional civil rights groups suffered another in a series of setbacks on the issue of racial redistricting. The Court upheld a lower court's decision to reduce the number of majority-black congressional districts in Georgia to one. The decision came by the same 5–4 majority that had prevailed since the Court first allowed white voters to challenge racially motivated redistricting plans in 1993.

"These cases have been an unbroken line of defeats for African-American voters who have sought a voice in elections," said Theodore Shaw, associate counsel for the NAACP Legal Defense and Educational Fund. But groups opposed to racial preferences applauded the decision. "The Court again showed its willingness to strike down government programs based on race," said Scott Bullock of the Institute for Justice. The impact of the decision was softened, however, by the fact that two African-Americans originally elected from majority-black districts were re-elected in November in the newly reconfigured, majority-white districts.

In another voting rights case, the Court made it somewhat harder for minorities to block redistricting in jurisdictions that are required under the Voting Rights Act to obtain prior approval from the Justice Department for changes in election practices or procedures. The ruling, in a case affecting an all-white rural school board in Louisiana, held that preclearance can be denied only if the changes leave minority voters worse off in voting rights. Civil rights groups wanted to block the school board's redistricting plan because it included no majority-black districts.

Civil rights groups fared better with a Voting Rights Act challenge to Mississippi's decision not to use the simplified voting registration procedures mandated for federal elections for state and local balloting as well. The Court said the dual-registration plan needed to be submitted for prior approval.

And the Court in two cases somewhat broadened the scope of the federal anti–job discrimination law, Title VII of the Civil Rights Act of 1964. All three decisions were unanimous.

The Court's rulings in civil rights damage suits were mixed. In one important ruling, the Court made it harder for police brutality victims to recover damages from local governments for inadequately training or screening officers. The ruling threw out a jury verdict that an Oklahoma county was guilty of "deliberate indifference" when the local sheriff hired as a deputy a twenty-one-year-old relative with a lengthy criminal record. In another excessive force case, however, the Court refused to give private prison guards the same legal protection in damage suits enjoyed by government-employed guards.

The most closely watched civil rights damage suit was also the least likely to have wide impact: the sexual harassment suit by Paula Corbin Jones against President Clinton. In rejecting Clinton's plea to postpone the suit until after he left office, the Court emphasized Jones's interest in bringing the case to trial without undue delay. But the Court also rejected Clinton's warning that a ruling for Jones would encourage "a large volume of politically motivated" litigation against future presidents. "History indicates that the likelihood that a significant number of such cases will be filed is remote," Justice Stevens wrote.

In a term with relatively few major business law cases, business groups generally did not have a lot to cheer. "There were some significant victories, but some losses that give us concern," said Stephen Bokat, general counsel and vice president of the U.S. Chamber of Commerce. "A lot of what this Court has done is reinforce states' rights, and business interests are not always consistent with that kind of view of things."

Surprisingly perhaps, Bokat listed business's biggest victory as the Court's ruling in the Internet case. The Chamber of Commerce was one of several business groups that filed briefs supporting the civil liberties organizations that first challenged the law. "More and more businesses are using the Internet to sell their products," Bokat explained. "We felt that having unconstitutional restrictions on speech on the Internet had a lot of potential problems down the line for business."

But business groups lost the two free speech challenges that they started: the cable industry effort to throw out the "must-carry" law and the growers' effort to get out of paying for generic advertising under federal agricultural marketing schemes. Both cases were decided by 5–4 votes, and in both cases the Court took a relaxed view of the First Amendment rights of the businesses challenging the laws. Indeed, in the agricultural marketing case, the Court treated the law as an economic regulation with no free speech aspects requiring special scrutiny.

The Court gave business groups similarly mixed results in another important area: tort litigation. In one closely watched case, the Court barred railway workers suing under a federal law from recovering damages for exposure to toxic substances if they show no symptoms of disease. Bokat said he hoped other courts confronted with "exposure-only" suits under state law would follow the Court's logic and also deny recovery.

Business groups suffered a major setback, however, with the decision to throw out the asbestos litigation settlement. Twenty former asbestos manufacturers had agreed to the multibillion-dollar settlement in order to resolve all future asbestos-related claims that might be brought against them. But the Court, by a 6–2 vote, said the accord did not meet the requirements for a class action under the Federal Rules of Civil Procedure. "A lot of people expected the Court to be more flexible and pragmatic," said Maureen Mahoney, a Washington attorney and former Supreme Court law clerk.

The Court ruled for labor over business in a number of workplace-related cases. Most significantly, the Court rejected an effort to use the federal pension and benefit protection law known as ERISA—the Employee Retirement Income Security Act—to override state laws requiring employers to pay "prevailing wages" on public works projects. Business groups have generally favored broad preemption for ERISA and other federal laws. In another ERISA case, the Court ruled that workers can recover damages under the law if an employer fires them for the purpose of taking away their health or welfare benefits. Employers also lost the two cases that expanded the scope of the federal anti–job discrimination law.

In other business cases, the Court gave government contractors a partial victory by refusing to give retroactive effect to a 1986 law making it easier for private individuals to bring false claim suits against them. But the ruling left open other important issues about the scope of the law for future cases. Property owners and industry groups that have tangled with land-use restrictions under the Endangered Species Act won a unanimous decision that they have legal standing to sue federal agencies for overenforcement of the law. But business groups lost a challenge to an Ohio tax scheme that imposed a sales tax on out-of-state natural gas producers and marketers while exempting regulated natural gas utilities within the state.

Assisted Suicide

No Right to Physician's Help in Ending Life

Washington v. Glucksberg, decided by a 9–0 vote, June 26, 1997; Rehnquist wrote the opinion. *(See excerpts, pp. 258–264.)*

Vacco, Attorney General of New York v. Quill, decided by a 9–0 vote, June 26, 1997; Rehnquist wrote the opinion. *(See excerpts, pp. 264–268.)*

Dr. Timothy Quill startled the medical profession in 1992 by admitting in an article in a medical journal that he had helped a cancer-stricken patient die by prescribing heavy doses of painkilling medication. New York prosecutors tried but failed to indict the Rochester internist for medical misconduct.

Two years later, Quill joined with two other New York doctors and three people with terminal illnesses in a lawsuit aimed at protecting doctors from the state law that made it a crime to assist a person to commit suicide. Meanwhile, doctors and patients in the state of Washington were waging a similar court fight to try to establish a constitutional right for terminally ill patients to have a physician help them end their pain and hasten their death.

Federal appeals courts upheld the claims in both cases, sharpening a growing national debate over the legality and morality of physician-assisted suicide. This term, the Court overturned both decisions, rejecting the doctors' and patients' constitutional claims for now and leaving the emotional issue for legislators to decide.

Modern medicine had helped lay the groundwork for the cases by introducing technological advances that helped many people with terminal illnesses live longer but for others merely prolonged the process of death. From news accounts or personal experiences, Americans became familiar with the stories and images of people suffering under constant, irreversible pain who said they would rather die with dignity than live in agony.

Many medical experts said that doctors confronted with such requests often complied, as Quill had done, by prescribing large amounts of medication that they knew would result in the patient's death. But the practice collided with medical ethics and criminal law. The Hippocratic Oath itself said a physician should not "give a deadly drug to anybody if asked for it." And the American Medical Association reaffirmed as late as 1996 that physician-assisted suicide was "fundamentally incompatible with the physician's role as healer."

Legally, all but a few states made it a crime to assist someone to commit suicide, either by specific statute or by implication as a matter of common law. But advocates of physician-assisted suicide maintained that there were no court decisions upholding the prosecution of a doctor for helping a terminally ill patient to die. Indeed, Michigan authorities tried but failed to convict the most prominent doctor who advocated physician-assisted suicide: Dr. Jack Kevorkian. Beginning in 1990, the retired pathologist assisted more than fifty people to die, but juries in three trials refused to convict him.

The issue of treating terminal patients had first gained national attention as a legal question in 1976 with the case of a young New Jersey woman, Karen Ann Quinlan, who was left in a coma after an automobile accident. The New Jersey Supreme Court allowed Quinlan to be removed from a respirator, and the Supreme Court let the ruling stand. More than a decade later, the Court agreed to take up the issue itself in a similar case involving a

A member of the group "Not Dead Yet" demonstrates against physician-assisted suicide after Supreme Court arguments on the issue January 8. The Court ruled June 26 that states can prohibit doctors from helping terminally ill patients to end their lives.

Missouri woman, Nancy Beth Cruzan, who was in a "permanent vegetative state" after an auto accident.

The justices unanimously agreed that an individual has a constitutional right to refuse unwanted, life-sustaining medical treatment. But by a 5–4 vote, the Court held in *Cruzan v. Director, Missouri Department of Health* that states could require "clear and convincing evidence" of a patient's previously expressed wish to die before allowing family members to terminate life-support systems. Some commentators depicted the Court's ruling as approving a "right to die." But in his opinion for the Court, Chief Justice Rehnquist linked the holding to what he depicted as a well-established right to refuse medical treatment. *(See* Supreme Court Yearbook, 1989–1990, *pp. 10–12.)*

Still, advocates of physician-assisted suicide viewed the ruling as a precedent on their side. And through the 1990s they pressed the case for what they preferred to call physician-assisted dying through ballot initiatives, court cases, and policy debates in medical and legal circles and in the court of public opinion.

Polls found that Americans were divided and ambivalent on the issue. By the time the Court took it up, surveys showed a majority of people in favor of making it legal for a doctor to help a patient commit suicide. But three states had mixed results on ballot measures to legalize the practice. Voters in Washington and California rejected assisted-suicide initiatives in 1991 and 1992 respectively. But Oregon voters in 1994 narrowly approved a measure to permit physician-assisted suicide for terminally ill patients under regulatory safeguards; the measure was blocked by a federal court ruling, however, and opponents placed a proposal to repeal the law on the November 1997 ballot.

Meanwhile, most states responded to the Court's *Cruzan* decision by enacting laws that allowed individuals to write a so-called "living will" with legally binding instructions to permit a doctor to terminate life-support systems in the event they were unconscious or unable to communicate their wishes. None of the laws included provisions to legalize physician-assisted suicide. Most legislators and medical and legal experts saw a distinction between the passive action of withdrawing life-sustaining treatment and the active step of providing medication deliberately to cause the patient's death.

The lawsuits in Washington and New York, however, attacked that distinction as part of a two-pronged legal strategy to legalize physician-assisted suicide. The two suits—both filed in 1994—argued that the states were violating the constitutional requirement for equal protection of the laws by allowing some terminal patients to end their lives by withdrawing life-support systems but denying an equivalent choice to people with other terminal diseases. The suits also claimed the laws violated substantive due process by interfering with an individual's fundamental right to control the manner of one's death.

The patients in the two cases presented compelling stories. In New York, an elderly woman with thyroid cancer and two men with AIDS all said they were suffering unbearably under late stages of terminal diseases. Each said he or she wanted to have drugs available if they reached the point where they felt they could endure the suffering no longer.

In Washington, three patients presented similar claims: an elderly woman bedridden with cancer, an elderly man with pulmonary disease connected to an oxygen tank at all times, and a middle-aged man with AIDS. Four doctors joined in bringing the claim, along with an advocacy group, Compassion in Dying, that had helped push the unsuccessful 1991 initiative in the states. The physicians included Harold Glucksberg, a Seattle internist who specialized in the care of cancer patients.

Lower courts divided in the two cases. A federal judge in Seattle agreed with the plaintiffs in May 1994 that the law banning assisted suicide was unconstitutional. The federal judge in the New York case, however, rejected the constitutional claims in December. The two cases then went before federal appeals courts, which issued separate rulings only a month apart in spring 1996 agreeing with the doctors' claims. By that time, the patients who had been plaintiffs had all died, but the doctors were allowed to represent the interests of other terminally ill patients.

In the Washington case, the Ninth U.S. Circuit Court of Appeals ruled on due process grounds that the state's ban on assisted suicide was unconstitutional as applied to terminally ill patients. "Not only is the state's interest in preventing such individuals from hastening their deaths of comparatively little weight," Judge Stephen Reinhardt, a prominent liberal jurist, wrote in the March 6 decision, "but its insistence on frustrating their wishes seems cruel indeed." The vote by the eleven-judge panel was 8–3; the court did not rule on the equal protection issue.

In its ruling in the New York case, the Second U.S. Circuit Court of Appeals rejected the due process argument, citing Supreme Court precedents that discouraged the recognition of new "fundamental" rights. But the appeals court agreed with the equal protection attack on the law. "It simply cannot be said," Judge Roger Miner, a conservative Republican-appointed judge, wrote in the April 2 decision, "that those mentally competent, terminally ill patients who seek to hasten death but whose treatment does not include life support are treated equally."

Both states asked the Court to review the decisions, and the justices granted the petitions as the new term was about to begin. The cases brought forth a flood of more than sixty briefs from advocates on both sides of the issue. Those urging the Court to uphold the ban on physician-assisted suicide included the American Medical Association, Catholic and other religious groups, anti-abortion organizations, and disability rights groups. The American Civil Liberties Union was the major group on the other side; other briefs came from a group calling itself Americans for Death With Dignity and from various law professors, religious leaders, and bioethicists.

The Clinton administration sided with the states in carefully structured briefs. Terminally ill patients had a "liberty interest" in limiting their suffering, the administration argued, but the interest was outweighed by the government's interests in preserving life and in preventing abuses that could come from legalized physician-assisted suicide.

The Court scheduled arguments in the two cases for January 8. The courtroom was packed for the successive hour-long arguments. Outside, a hundred or more demonstrators lined the sidewalks. Opponents of physician-assisted suicide, many of them in wheelchairs, chanted, "Not dead yet." A smaller group from the pro-suicide Hemlock Society carried signs reading, "We support physician-assisted suicide."

The states' lawyers went first in each case, but it was the attorneys seeking to uphold the rulings in favor of physician-assisted suicide who found themselves on the defensive. Justices across the ideological spectrum indicated skepticism about the constitutional claims and a strong inclination to leave the issue to legislators.

"Surely legislatures have much more flexibility and much greater capacity to make those decisions than we do," Justice Kennedy asked the lawyer in the Washington case, Kathryn L. Tucker. "You're asking us to declare unconstitutional the laws of 50 states."

"Everything you've said could go on in a legislative chamber," Justice Ginsburg told Tucker. "Where do we draw the line?"

The attorneys for the states pitched their cases to that sentiment. William L. Williams, a senior assistant attorney general, opened his argument defending the state's "legislative judgment to prohibit assisted suicide." In his turn, New York Attorney General Dennis Vacco said the issue was "whether the state must remain neutral in the face of a decision of one of its citizens to help another kill herself." In the state's view, Vacco continued, "the Constitution does not require this to be the case."

For their part, Tucker and Harvard law professor Laurence Tribe, representing the doctors and patients in the New York case, labored to fit their arguments within Court precedents. When Tucker argued that the *Cruzan* decision had established a broad right to choose medical treatment, Rehnquist shot back: "I don't think there was language like that in *Cruzan*." And Tribe fared badly with his equal protection argument that the state had no reason to prohibit assisted suicide while legalizing the practice of withdrawing life support. The difference, Kennedy said, "is based on the distinction between allowing events to take their own course and third-person intervention."

The justices' one-sided questioning foreshadowed the Court's decisions unanimously rejecting the challenges to the two state laws on June 26. The due process claim failed, Rehnquist said, because the country's "consistent and almost universal tradition" barred any right to suicide or assistance in doing so. The equal protection argument failed, he said, because of the "important and logical" reasons for the distinction between permitting the withdrawal of life-sustaining treatment and prohibiting physician-assisted suicide.

Rehnquist wrote separate opinions in the two cases, both of them sparely written and relatively short: thirty-two pages in the Washington case, fourteen in the New York ruling. He opened his opinion in the Washington case by stressing that laws banning assisted suicide were "longstanding expressions of the States' commitment to the protection and preservation of human life." After tracing the history of laws against suicide from colonial times, Rehnquist also emphasized that the issue had been debated in recent years and the laws "generally" reaffirmed by voters and legislators.

On that basis, Rehnquist concluded that there was no tradition of recognizing a right to assisted suicide. In addition, he rejected the doctors' argument that the Court's decisions in *Cruzan* or the abortion-rights cases established a broad right of personal autonomy that included the right to assisted suicide.

The assisted-suicide ban still had to be "rationally related to legitimate government interests," Rehnquist said, but that requirement was "unquestionably met." The ban, he said, promoted the state's "unqualified interest in preservation of human life." Legalizing physician-assisted suicide, he said, "could make it more difficult for the State to protect depressed or mentally ill persons, or those who are suffering from untreated pain, from suicidal impulses."

Rehnquist listed other purposes served by the ban. Allowing assisted suicide, he said, could "undermine" the doctor-patient relationship by "blurring the time-honored distinction between healing and harming." The ban also protected "vulnerable groups—including the poor, the elderly, and disabled person—from abuse, neglect, and mistakes." Finally, he said, "the State may fear that permitting assisted suicide will start it down the path to voluntary and perhaps even involuntary euthanasia." As evidence, Rehnquist cited "the Dutch government's own study" that found instances of abuse after voluntary euthanasia was legalized there.

The state's interests "are unquestionably important and legitimate," Rehnquist concluded, and the assisted-suicide ban "at least reasonably related to their promotion and protection." The ban therefore did not violate the Fourteenth Amendment, he said. In a footnote, Rehnquist acknowledged Justice Stevens's argument in his concurring opinion that the decision did not preclude a successful claim by a plaintiff "in a more particularized challenge." "Our opinion does not absolutely foreclose such a claim," Rehnquist wrote. But, he continued, "such a claim would have to be quite different from the ones advanced" in this case.

Rehnquist, whose wife Nina died in 1991 after a long battle with ovarian cancer, ended his opinion by noting the "earnest and profound" debate about physician-assisted suicide around the country. "Our holding permits this debate to continue, as it should in a democratic society," he said.

In the New York case, Rehnquist easily rejected the argument that the state was violating equal protection by allowing some terminally ill patients to end their lives by withdrawing life support but denying other people with terminal conditions a way to hasten their deaths.

"By permitting everyone to refuse unwanted medical treatment while prohibiting anyone from assisting a suicide, New York law follows a longstanding and rational distinction," Rehnquist wrote. After listing the reasons discussed in the Washington case for prohibiting assisted suicide, Rehnquist concluded that they "easily satisfy the constitutional requirement that a legislative classification bear a rational relation to some legitimate end."

Four justices joined Rehnquist's opinions in the companion cases: O'Connor, Scalia, Kennedy, and Thomas. In a concurring opinion, however, O'Connor appeared to qualify her support.

O'Connor stressed that there were "no legal barriers" in either state to a terminally ill patient's obtaining pain-killing medication from a physician "even to the point of causing unconsciousness and hastening death." On that basis, she said the state's interest in "protecting those who might seek to end life mistakenly or under pressure" was sufficient to justify the ban on physician-assisted suicide.

The other four justices concurred in the results in both cases, but not in Rehnquist's opinion. Stevens and Souter both wrote lengthy, lone opinions suggesting that individual cases involving terminally ill patients might be decided differently. ". . . [T]he so-called 'unqualified interest in the preservation of human life' is not itself sufficient to outweigh the interest in liberty that may justify the only possible means of preserving a dying patient's dignity and alleviating her intolerable suffering," Stevens wrote at the end of his joint opinion in the two cases.

Souter, who wrote separately in the two cases, used his opinion in *Glucksberg* to challenge Rehnquist's approach in deciding due process claims. Citing a dissent by Justice John Marshall Harlan in a 1961 case, Souter proposed a more open-ended test. Courts should strike down laws, Souter said, that result in "arbitrary impositions" or "purposeless restraints" that are "at odds with the Due Process Clause of the Fourteenth Amendment." But he said that "at this time" he was satisfied that legislatures "were relatively more competent" to deal with the issue of physician-assisted suicide than courts. Souter also wrote a one-paragraph opinion in *Vacco* rejecting the equal protection challenge to the New York law.

Ginsburg and Breyer both said they joined in O'Connor's opinion, but not in Rehnquist's. Ginsburg did not write separately. But Breyer underlined O'Connor's emphasis on the legality of providing terminally ill patients with pain-relieving medications "despite the risk that those drugs themselves will kill." If the law prevented "palliative care," Breyer said, "the Court might have to revisit its conclusions in these cases."

The opponents of physician-assisted suicide cheered the ruling. "This ruling will protect Americans from a regime that says it's cheaper to kill patients than to treat them," New York Attorney General Vacco told a news conference.

Both Tribe and Tucker emphasized, however, that five of the justices had left open the possibility of future constitutional challenges in individual cases. "They are saying that a person with no dignified way to die could still bring a challenge to those laws," Tribe said.

Vacco maintained that legislators were more likely than courts to help find ways to relieve the suffering of people with terminal diseases. "If it's kept in the legislatures," he said, "it will be more focused on this issue of treating pain and less on this question of rights."

But Quill voiced regret that the ruling left unchanged what he called the "underground practice" of doctor-assisted deaths. "We are back to the status quo, which is an arbitrary, secretive process for those doctors who are willing to help patients hasten their death," he said.

Freedom of Speech

Court Rejects Law to Limit "Indecency" on Internet

Reno, Attorney General v. American Civil Liberties Union, decided by 9–0 and 7–2 votes, June 26, 1997; Stevens wrote the opinion; O'Connor and Rehnquist dissented in part. *(See excerpts, pp. 243–258.)*

To the millions of people around the world who used it, the Internet presented a cornucopia of information and a powerful communications medium unprecedented in human history. Seated at a computer terminal, any man, woman, or child was only a mouse-click away from vast storehouses of knowledge or instantaneous conversations with people of like-minded interests anywhere in the wired world.

Critics, however, saw a dark side to the easy availability of online communications: the very real risk that youngsters would come into contact, inadvertently or otherwise, with sexually explicit material inappropriate for their years. To try to control indecency in cyberspace, Congress in 1996 made it a federal crime to display sexually offensive text or images on interactive computer networks in a manner that was accessible to minors. But this term, the Court ruled the law unconstitutional in a mostly unanimous decision that took the First Amendment for the first time into the new world of cyberspace.

The law—the Communications Decency Act—was a small part of an omnibus telecommunications bill aimed mostly at reducing government regulation. The major supporters included culturally conservative senators from both parties, such as Nebraska Democrat James Exon and Indiana Republican Dan Coats. They warned—as Exon put it during floor debate—that online networks were putting "the worst, most vile, most perverse pornography . . . only a few click-click-clicks away from any child."

Opponents minimized the problem. They argued that sexually explicit material was relatively rare on online networks and typically carried an onscreen warning. But Coats countered that warnings were "like taking a porn shop and putting it in the bedroom of your children and then saying, 'Do not look.'"

In its final form, the law included three criminal provisions. The act prohibited anyone from knowingly transmitting indecent material on an interactive computer network to persons under the age of eighteen. It also prohibited sending material that depicted "sexual or excretory activities or organs" in a "patently offensive way" to a "specific child" under the age of eighteen or displaying such material "in a manner available to" anyone under the age of eighteen.

The act provided criminal penalties of up to two years in prison and fines of up to $25,000. It also established defenses from prosecution for anyone who restricted access to indecent communications by means of a credit card, adult access code, or the like, or who took "in good faith" other, unspecified "reasonable, effective, and appropriate actions" to limit access to minors.

President Clinton backed the provision, but gave it only limited attention when he signed the telecommunications act on February 8, 1996. Computer-users marked the day with protests. Some managers of sites on the World Wide Web turned the background color of their web pages black in mourning.

Christopher Hansen, lead attorney for the American Civil Liberties Union in the Internet indecency case, takes questions at a news conference June 26 after the Supreme Court decision striking down the Communications Decency Act.

More concretely, electronic speech and other First Amendment advocacy groups immediately went to court to try to overturn the indecency provisions. Parallel suits were filed by a coalition of online user groups led by the American Civil Liberties Union and by a second, more establishment-oriented coalition led by the American Library Association. The suits contended that the law violated the free speech rights of minors and adults alike. The only way to make sexually explicit material completely inaccessible to youngsters, the suits contended, was to suppress it altogether. And, the suits pointed out, indecent—as opposed to obscene—material was constitutionally protected, at least as to adults.

The argument turned on distinctions the Court had drawn in previous rulings on laws regulating minors' access to sexual materials. The Court had recognized a strong governmental interest in limiting the availability of sexually explicit materials to youngsters. But it had also ruled that the government could not carry regulations so far as to limit adults' access to such material as long as it was not obscene. On that basis, for example, the Court in 1989 struck down a federal law prohibiting so-called "dial-a-porn" services (*Sable Communications of Cal., Inc. v. FCC*).

Legislative supporters expected the Internet indecency law to be challenged and provided in the act that any suit would be heard by a three-judge federal court, with a direct appeal to the Supreme Court. The trial of the two cases before a three-judge panel in Philadelphia turned into a technological demonstration as well as a legal argument. Plaintiffs brought in computer terminals to demonstrate the wonders of the Internet. Software experts testified that using so-called nanny filters to screen out objectionable material at the computer was technologically superior to tagging material at the source.

The judges were convinced. The court issued a unanimous ruling on June 13, 1996, that the indecency provisions were unconstitutional. Each of the judges wrote a separate opinion; combined, they ran 175 pages. All three judges found that the law restrained constitutionally protected speech and that the legal defenses were technologically or commercially infeasible for many users. Two of the judges also found the challenged provisions unconstitutionally vague. The Clinton administration appealed.

When he opened his argument defending the law on March 19, Deputy Solicitor General Seth Waxman told the justices that the Internet was both a "revolutionary advance in technology" and "a revolutionary means for displaying patently offensive sexually explicit material to children in the privacy of their homes." With 8,000 sexually explicit sites on the World Wide Web, Waxman said, the Internet "threatens to render irrelevant all previous efforts to protect children from sexually indecent material."

But Waxman encountered tough questions from justices across the ideological spectrum. O'Connor asked what a library was supposed to do if it wanted to put material on a web site that might be deemed indecent. Breyer said the law could make "every high school student guilty of a federal crime and subject to two years in prison" for talking over the Internet with other students about their sexual experiences. Souter asked whether parents could be sent to prison for allowing their children to view indecent material on a home computer.

In his turn, Washington attorney Bruce J. Ennis opened with a four-point attack on the law. The act, he said, "bans speech. It will not be effective. There are less restrictive alternatives that would be much more effective. And the combination of an imprecise standard, coupled with the threat of severe criminal sanctions, will chill much speech that would not be indecent."

Ennis pointed to the Internet's pervasiveness: forty million speakers, he said, used news groups, chat rooms, or "list servs"—computer jargon for automatic mail lists. It was "not technologically possible," he said, to screen out underage users from these cyberspace forums. But, he added later, software programs were on the market—and more were being developed—to allow parents to block out sexual material.

The justices probed Ennis's points with more curiosity than skepticism. Rehnquist asked Ennis to elaborate on the difficulty of screening users by age. O'Connor noted newspaper articles that questioned the effectiveness of blocking software. Only Scalia seemed overtly skeptical, questioning parents' ability to monitor their children's computer use on their own. If he spent time monitoring his teenager's use of the Internet, Scalia said, "I'd know even less about this case than I know today."

The Court's ruling came on the next-to-last day of the term, and it was almost all that computer advocacy groups had hoped for. Stevens began with a compact and literate primer on the Internet, quoting the lower court's description of it as a "unique and wholly new medium of worldwide human communication." He acknowledged that sexually explicit material was "widely available," but emphasized that users "seldom encounter such material accidentally." And he emphasized that age verification was impossible for some cyberspace forums—such as chat rooms—while credit card verification would burden some noncommercial web sites and completely shut out adults who did not have credit cards.

On a threshold issue, Stevens said that none of the justifications that the Court had recognized for upholding government regulation of broadcasting or cable television applied to computer networks. There was no history of government regulation or resource scarcity, as in broadcasting or cable, and the Internet was not as "invasive" as radio or television. ". . . [O]ur cases provide no basis," he concluded, "for qualifying the level of First Amendment scrutiny that should be applied to this medium."

From there on, Stevens found little merit in the law or the government's arguments defending it. The law, he said, contained "many ambiguities" that were "problematic" given the "severity of criminal sanctions" it established. The law "unquestionably silences some speakers whose messages would be entitled to constitutional protections," Stevens continued. And the use of community standards to define "indecent" or "patently offensive" could easily result in banning "discussions about prison rape or safe sex practices, artistic images that include nude subjects, and arguably the card catalogue of the Carnegie Library."

Stevens dismissed the government's arguments in response almost out of hand. Most significantly, he said that Internet speakers could not rely on the defenses provided in the law. "Tagging" sexual material would not be "effective," as the law required, unless blocking software was universal. And credit card or access code verification was "not economically feasible for most noncommercial speakers."

Finally, Stevens strongly rejected the government's argument that the growth of the Internet required some controls on indecency, lest people turn off their computers for fear of exposing their children to sexually offensive materials. "We find this argument singularly unpersuasive," Stevens said in a passage he emphasized from the bench. ". . . [G]overnmental regulation of the content of speech is more likely to interfere with the free exchange of ideas than to encourage it."

The ruling was all but unanimous. Six justices joined in Stevens's opinion: Scalia, Kennedy, Souter, Thomas, Ginsburg, and Breyer. In a partial dissent, Justice O'Connor, joined by Chief Justice Rehnquist, agreed that the "display" provision and some applications of the "indecency transmission" and "specific person" provisions were unconstitutional because they would have the effect of "restricting adults' access to protected materials." But O'Connor said she would uphold the ban on sending indecent materials if the speaker knew that "all of the recipients are minors"—a definition that computer users said would exclude most cyberspace forums.

Internet advocates cheered the ruling. "The Supreme Court has written the Bill of Rights for the 21st century," declared Jerry Berman, executive director of the Center for Democracy and Technology. Reporters and headline-writers similarly depicted the decision as momentous. "The First Amendment went digital yesterday," Joan Biskupic wrote in the *Washington Post.*

Some supporters of the law were bitter. The Court was "telling families to fend for themselves in an Internet of raw indecency," Senator Coats declared. He vowed to introduce new legislation. President Clinton voiced milder regret about the decision and promised to work on other ways to help parents limit youngsters' access to indecency. But even before the Court ruling, an administration task force had drafted a report that envisioned only minimal governmental regulation of the Internet.

Separation of Powers

No Immunity for President in Civil Suits

Clinton v. Jones, decided by a 9–0 vote, May 27, 1997; Stevens wrote the opinion. *(See excerpts, pp. 168–176.)*

Two legal clouds hung over Bill Clinton as he prepared for his second term in the White House. The first—the independent counsel investigation of the "Whitewater" affair—involved financial dealings and legal maneuverings too complex and too murky for much of the public to fathom. But the second was straightforward and easily understood: a civil suit by a former Arkansas state employee, Paula Corbin Jones, accusing Clinton of making a crude sexual advance toward her while he was governor of Arkansas.

Clinton denied that the alleged incident had occurred. But six years after Clinton might or might not have met Jones in a Little Rock hotel room, her sexual harassment suit led to a Supreme Court ruling with ominous implications for Clinton and perhaps for future presidents. The Court ruled, unanimously, that the president enjoys no automatic immunity from civil lawsuits while serving in the White House.

The ruling cleared the way for Jones's lawyers to question Clinton under oath about the accusation. Barring a settlement or a dismissal on other legal grounds, Clinton faced the prospect of a trial that could prove to be personally embarrassing and politically damaging. But the ruling appeared

Paula Jones, with her attorneys Joseph Cammarata (left) and Gilbert Davis, makes a statement outside the federal courthouse in Little Rock on August 22, almost three months after the Supreme Court cleared the way for her to pursue her sexual harassment suit against President Clinton.

to win broad approval as a vindication for the rule of law. "No American, not even an incumbent president, is beyond the law's reach," the *New York Times* approvingly editorialized the day after the decision.

Paula Jones's path to the nation's highest court began in 1991 when the unmarried, twenty-four-year-old high school graduate was working as a $12,000-a-year clerk in the Arkansas Industrial Development Commission. The commission sponsored a conference at Little Rock's Excelsior Hotel on May 8; Jones was staffing a registration desk in the lobby. According to her account three years later, Clinton, then forty-four, apparently noticed her as he arrived at the hotel and, after reaching his suite, asked state trooper Danny Ferguson to summon Jones to join him.

Once she was inside, Jones claimed, Clinton began making suggestive remarks and physical advances, which she rebuffed. But—as she told the story —Clinton continued by pulling down his trousers, exposing himself, and asking for oral sex. Again, she refused: "Look, I'm not that kind of girl," she claimed to have told Clinton. With that, Clinton was said to have backed off, dismissing Jones with a cautionary suggestion to keep quiet about the incident.

Jones later claimed to have told several friends about the incident over the next few days. But she made the accusation public only after stories appeared in December 1993 and January 1994 that charged Clinton with having often used Arkansas state troopers while governor to arrange sexual liaisons. In one of the stories, published in the *American Spectator,* a conservative magazine, an unidentified trooper was quoted as naming "Paula" as one of the women he had arranged for Clinton to meet.

Even without a last name, Jones said she was recognizable in the story, and she felt she had been defamed. She responded by going public with her version of the events at a news conference arranged by a conservative, anti-Clinton organization. Through his press secretary, Clinton denied ever having met Jones. The story simmered inconclusively for nearly four months as Jones conferred with lawyers. Then, just as a three-year deadline for filing a lawsuit was about to expire, Jones's lawyers filed a suit in federal court in Little Rock. The suit, filed May 6, 1994, charged Clinton with violating her civil rights, conspiracy, infliction of emotional distress, and defamation. She asked for actual damages of $75,000 and punitive damages of $100,000 on each of the four counts.

Instead of meeting the accusation squarely in court, Clinton's lawyers filed a legal motion asking, on grounds of presidential immunity, to delay all proceedings in the suit until Clinton was out of office. U.S. District Court Judge Susan Webber Wright refused in December 1994 to dismiss the suit outright or to block the pretrial evidence-gathering process called discovery. But Wright, appointed to the bench in 1990 by President George Bush, did order that any trial in the case be "stayed"—held in abeyance—until after Clinton's presidency.

Both sides appealed to the Eighth U.S. Circuit Court of Appeals. In January 1996, the appeals court handed Clinton a setback. By a 2–1 vote, the court held that the president was not entitled to any official immunity for events unrelated to his conduct in office. It also rejected Clinton's arguments that judicial management of the litigation while he was president would pose separation-of-powers problems. On that basis, the court ruled Judge Wright was wrong to stay the trial until after Clinton left office.

Clinton's lawyers took the case to the Supreme Court, which agreed in late June to hear the case. In addition to giving Clinton another chance to present his legal plea, the justices' action put legal proceedings on hold until after the November election—blunting any possible discussion of character issues during Clinton's bid for re-election.

For the Court, the case presented an immunity claim never before raised in any court. Extensive research found only three instances in which sitting presidents had been involved in civil suits for unofficial conduct before entering the White House. Two complaints against Theodore Roosevelt and Harry S Truman were dismissed before they took office and the dismissals upheld after their respective inaugurations. More recently, an automobile accident case was filed against John F. Kennedy during the 1960 campaign. After taking office, Kennedy sought to stay the case under a 1940 law that gave members of the armed forces grounds to delay proceedings in civil suits. A federal judge denied the motion, and the case was then settled.

The Court, however, had recognized a broad claim of presidential immunity for official conduct in a decision in 1982 involving former president Richard M. Nixon. The ruling in *Nixon v. Fitzgerald* stemmed from a civil suit by a former Air Force whistleblower who blamed Nixon for his firing. By a 5–4 majority, the Court held that the president was "entitled to absolute immunity from damages liability predicated on his official acts."

Clinton's case came before the Court on January 13, only one week before the president's second inauguration. The president's attorney was Robert S. Bennett, a media-savvy, $400-an-hour Washington lawyer with a record of having successfully defended a number of public officials against misconduct charges. Acting Solicitor General Walter Dellinger also was to appear as a "friend of the court," supporting Clinton's immunity plea.

Bennett sought to minimize the president's plea. "All we're saying," Bennett told the justices, "is we'll give Ms. Jones her day in court, but let's not do it now." But both he and Dellinger faced a barrage of sharply skeptical questions from the justices.

Scalia mocked the president's argument that the lawsuit would interfere with his duties. "The notion that he doesn't have a minute to spare is not credible," Scalia said. Kennedy voiced concern that Clinton could use the delay in the trial to Jones's disadvantage. "He's in a very dominant position," Kennedy said. O'Connor questioned whether a president would be entitled to delay other kinds of civil suits. What about a child custody dispute, she asked, "where we have to know where the child is going to live?"

Jones's lawyer, Gilbert K. Davis, encountered some rough moments, too. Chief Justice Rehnquist, among others, chided him for failing to give a clear answer on how a trial judge should handle a presidential request for a delay in the proceedings because of conflicts with official duties. But afterward, Davis and his co-counsel, Joseph Cammarata, professed optimism about the outcome.

The Court's ruling came four months later, on May 27, as Clinton was in Europe to promote an important diplomatic initiative: NATO expansion. The courtroom fell silent as Chief Justice Rehnquist recognized Justice Stevens to announce the decision. In a firm voice, Stevens summarized the ruling: no immunity for Clinton; no reason to stay the trial or discovery until after he left office. Reporters hurriedly filed out of the press gallery the moment Stevens finished.

Stevens's twenty-eight page written opinion opened by stating that the president's plea deserved "respectful and deliberate consideration." But, he continued, the claim for "temporary immunity" from civil suits for unofficial conduct "cannot be sustained on the basis of precedent." The Court had always limited official immunity to conduct relating to official duties, Stevens said. Nor did separation of powers principles require immunity, since the judiciary was not attempting to increase its power at the president's expense. In addition, Stevens said, the Court had recognized that the president can be required to respond to subpoenas or other judicial orders—most notably, in *United States v. Nixon*, the 1974 Watergate tapes case that helped end Nixon's presidency.

Still, Stevens said that the question whether Clinton was entitled to a delay as a matter of discretion was "closer" than the appeals court thought. "The high respect that is owed to the office of the Chief Executive," he said, "is a matter that should inform the conduct of the entire proceeding, including the timing and scope of discovery." Nevertheless, he concluded that the "lengthy and categorical stay" that Judge Wright granted took "no account whatever of [Jones's] interest in bringing the case to trial."

Stevens ended by casting doubt on Clinton's warnings that a ruling against his position could pave the way for "frivolous and vexatious" litigation against future presidents. "History indicates that the likelihood that a significant number of such cases will be filed is remote," Stevens said.

All of the justices joined Stevens's opinion except Breyer, who wrote a sixteen-page opinion concurring in the judgment. Breyer said he agreed with the majority that the Constitution does not "automatically grant" the president immunity from civil suits for unofficial conduct. But he also said he was concerned about the possibility that civil suits could result in a "distraction" for an incumbent president and interfere with his official duties. To guard against that possibility, Breyer said the Court should have recognized a constitutional principle that courts must avoid any "interference with a President's ability to carry out his public responsibilities."

The ruling elated Jones's lawyers. "The Supreme Court of the United States has made it possible for Paula Jones, a courageous American, to finally get her day of justice," Cammarata told a news conference a few hours after the ruling. But Bennett insisted the president had nothing to fear from the suit going forward. "When all is said and done, it will be clear that President Clinton did nothing wrong," he said on CNN's "Larry King Live" that night.

For his part, Clinton, in Europe, declined to comment directly on the ruling, but told reporters: "As to what might happen to future presidents, I am concerned about that."

Political and legal observers alike speculated, however, that the case could be settled without going to trial. Bennett himself hinted at the possibility on the Sunday morning talk shows June 1, suggesting that Clinton might be willing to make a donation to a charity of Jones's choosing to try to resolve the case. But Bennett ruled out any direct apology. Jones's attorneys countered by insisting on vindication for their client. "What Paula Jones wants is her good name and reputation restored," Cammarata said. He added that Jones was "entitled to some compensation" for "the three years of hell that she's been put through."

The legal maneuverings continued over the summer. Clinton's lawyers filed an answer to the complaint in federal court in Little Rock just before the Fourth of July holiday weekend. Clinton "adamantly" denied Jones's accusations, the legal pleading stated. "At no time did the president make sexual advances toward the plaintiff," the Clinton document said. In addition, though, the lawyers asked the judge to dismiss Jones's complaint on the ground that the allegation—even if true—was only "a single overture" that would not amount to a violation of law. In August, Judge Wright dismissed the defamation count of the complaint but refused to drop any of the others. She also scheduled the trial to begin on May 27, 1998, in Little Rock.

Then, in September, the case took a bizarre turn when Davis and Cammarata asked for and were granted permission to withdraw as Jones's attorneys because of what they described in a formal motion as "fundamental differences" with her. It was widely reported that Jones had rejected a recommendation from the two lawyers that she accept a $700,000 settlement of the suit. Jones had balked, the reports stated, because the proposed settlement did not include a full apology from the president.

Gun Control

Brady Act's "Background Checks" Struck Down

Printz, Sheriff/Coroner, Ravalli County, Montana v. United States, decided by a 5–4 vote, June 27, 1997; Scalia wrote the opinion; Stevens, Souter, Ginsburg, and Breyer dissented. *(See excerpts, pp. 273–290.)*

In the years after her husband was wounded in the attempted assassination of President Ronald Reagan in 1981, Sarah Brady became an unrelenting advocate of tighter gun control laws. In 1993, she finally achieved her goal of a federal law imposing a five-day waiting period before anyone could purchase a handgun. During that time, the act required local law enforcement officials to conduct a background check to identify people who were ineligible to buy a gun under federal law.

Most major law enforcement organizations supported the law. But a few local sheriffs, strongly opposed to gun control, mounted constitutional challenges to the measure, contending that Congress exceeded its power in forcing local officials essentially to administer a federal regulatory system. This term, the Court agreed, in a 5–4 decision that once again showed the conservative justices' determination to rein in the powers of the federal government vis-à-vis the states.

James S. Brady, Reagan's former press secretary, was seated in his wheelchair next to President Clinton when the Brady Handgun Violence Prevention Act was signed into law on November 30, 1993. Brady had been permanently disabled since March 30, 1981, when he was wounded in John

Former presidential press secretary James K. Brady joins Maryland Attorney General Joseph Curran on the Supreme Court plaza in a news conference early in the term about the challenge to the Brady gun control law. The Court on June 26 struck the law down on states' rights grounds.

Hinckley Jr.'s attempted assassination of President Reagan. Sarah Brady became the head of the national advocacy group Handgun Control four years later. Over the next nine years, she tirelessly urged Congress to pass a law to take action to restrict the easy availability of handguns.

Congress in 1968 had prohibited firearms dealers from selling handguns to convicted felons, drug users, persons with an adjudicated mental illness, and anyone under the age of twenty-one. Enforcement of the provision, however, was spotty. To remedy the problem, gun control groups wanted time for law enforcement agencies to conduct a background check on the purchaser before the sale went through.

Anti–gun control organizations, led by the powerful National Rifle Association (NRA), strongly opposed the waiting period. They argued for an alternative: a computerized "instant-check" system operated by the federal government that could immediately determine the prospective handgun purchaser's eligibility under federal law. Gun control groups countered that the federal government did not have the information needed to create the massive database required for an effective instant-check system. The only viable procedure for now, they said, was for local law enforcement officials to conduct the background checks.

The dispute became the key issue in the congressional debate over the bill. In 1991, both the House and the Senate approved a five-day waiting period, but Senate Republicans blocked final action on the bill in 1992. But the gun control groups' prospects were lifted by Bill Clinton's election as president. Clinton backed the Brady bill during his campaign and, once in office, urged the Democratic-controlled Congress to pass the measure promptly.

In its final form, the law required law enforcement officials to conduct the background check only for an interim period. The law mandated that the federal government have the instant-check system that gun control opponents called for up and running by 1998. Still, the NRA and other gun control opponents criticized the law. And, with assistance from the NRA, like-minded sheriffs mounted constitutional challenges.

Out in western Montana, Ravalli County Sheriff Jay Printz simply refused to carry out the federal mandate. "I've got too much to do, and here they are telling me I have to do federal background checks," Printz declared. In southeastern Arizona, Graham County Sheriff Richard Mack felt the same way. "The federal government has no right to divert my attention from Graham County matters to serve their agenda," he said.

Mack and Printz filed separate federal court suits in 1994 claiming that the Brady Act violated the constitutional protections for states' rights, including the Tenth Amendment. The linchpin of their argument was a 1992 Supreme Court precedent, *New York v. United States*. In that case, the Court voted 6–3 to strike down a federal law that, in effect, required states either to establish a federally prescribed system for disposing of wastes from nuclear power plants or to take responsibility for the radioactive wastes themselves. "The federal government may not compel the states to enact or administer a federal regulatory program," Justice O'Connor wrote for the majority.

Federal judges in both of the cases agreed that the law—as the judge in Printz's case put it—"substantially commandeers state executive officials . . . to administer a federal program." But the Ninth U.S. Circuit Court of Appeals, after consolidating the two cases, issued a 2–1 ruling in September 1995 upholding the law. The act, the majority said, required states to undertake only a minor, administrative function.

The sheriffs and the Clinton administration joined in urging the Court to review the decision to settle the issue. Gun control advocates professed confidence the law would be upheld. But they were confronting a Court that had twice within the previous two years struck down other federal laws on states' rights grounds.

Representing the sheriffs in the arguments before the Court on December 3, attorney Stephen Halbrook began by detailing the burdens on the two sheriffs' offices of complying with the law. Under questioning, though, he went further. "These departments could have plenty of officers and not much to do, and these requirements would still be unconstitutional," Halbrook said.

Later, Halbrook took his position even further, contending that Congress even had no power to order the sheriffs to give the federal government the criminal record information it would need to set up the instant-check system. "That's an extreme position," O'Connor remarked.

But Acting Solicitor General Walter Dellinger took the brunt of the justices' questions as he attempted to defend the law. Could the states require the federal government to provide similar assistance in carrying out a regulatory program, Justice Kennedy asked. When Dellinger said the Supremacy Clause prevented the states from issuing an order to the federal government, Kennedy had a quick retort. "But there's a federal design here," Kennedy said. "Isn't it the idea that we can't have one government interfere with another?"

The Court's decision, announced on the final day of the term, June 27, gave the critics of expansive federal powers a significant legal victory. "The Federal Government may neither issue directives requiring the States to address particular problems, nor command the States' officers, or those of their political subdivisions, to administer or enforce a federal regulatory program," Scalia wrote for the five-justice majority. "Such commands are fundamentally incompatible with our constitutional system of dual sovereignty."

Scalia acknowledged that the issue could not be decided by looking simply to the text of the Constitution. But he found that "historical practice," "the Constitution's structure," and "this Court's jurisprudence" all pointed toward limiting federal power over state officials.

As to history, Scalia went back to the ratification of the Constitution and the early Congresses to show that federal lawmakers had not, until recently, attempted to "command the States' executive power" except under a specific constitutional provision. And the recent laws, he said, were either distinguishable or unpersuasive in showing an established practice to support the Brady Act provisions.

Scalia also said constitutional principles of state sovereignty argued against allowing Congress to require state officials to administer federal mandates. "The power of the Federal Government would be augmented immeasurably if it were able to impress into its service—and at no cost to itself—the police officers of the 50 States," he wrote. In addition, Congress could improperly reduce presidential powers by "simply requiring state officers to execute its laws."

Finally, Scalia turned to the Court's precedents. He pointed first to a pair of decisions in the 1980s that upheld federal statutes only after interpreting them to stop short of commanding states to adopt specific regulatory policies. Then he turned to the ruling in New York, which he said conclusively established that Congress had no power to direct the states' policymaking prerogatives. He ended by rejecting the government's arguments that the Brady Act's objectives justified the minimal intrusion on state officials. "It is the very principle of separate state sovereignty that such a law offends," Scalia wrote, "and no comparative assessment of the various interests can overcome that fundamental defect."

Chief Justice Rehnquist and Justices O'Connor, Kennedy, and Thomas concurred in Scalia's opinion. In a brief concurrence, O'Connor said the ruling would not prevent Congress from contracting with states to carry out federal programs or from imposing "ministerial reporting requirements" on the states. Thomas also wrote a concurring opinion, significantly suggesting that the Second Amendment's "right to bear arms" provision might limit Congress's ability to regulate intrastate sale of firearms.

Stevens opened the major dissent by arguing that Congress's power to "impose affirmative obligations on executive and judicial officers of state and local governments" was "firmly supported by the text of the Constitution, the early history of the Nation, decisions of this Court, and a correct understanding of the basic structure of the Federal Government." Emphasizing his points by reading a summary from the bench, he warned that the ruling would even limit Congress's powers in a national emergency. A military draft, a mass inoculation program, or the threat of an international terrorist "may require a national response before federal personnel can be made available to respond," he said.

Souter, Ginsburg, and Breyer joined Stevens's opinion. In a separate dissent, Souter said he found the case "closer than I anticipated." But Souter said passages in the *Federalist Papers* showed that both Alexander Hamilton and James Madison thought Congress would have the power to command state officials to carry out federal directives. Breyer, in a briefer opinion, pointed to the example of some European countries with federal systems as showing that local control was enhanced rather than diminished by using local officials rather than creating "federal bureaucracies" to carry out federal directives.

The ruling elated the sheriffs who brought the challenge. "It's a great day for America," said Mack, who had been defeated for re-election in a campaign centered around his opposition to the law but was then appointed a deputy sheriff. In Montana, Printz said the ruling would allow him to "get back to our essential job, instead of shuffling Brady paperwork."

Gun control proponents, however, insisted the ruling would have only minimal effect. About half the states had their own laws requiring background checks on gun buyers, they said, and law enforcement officials in other states were likely to continue the checks on a voluntary basis. "Nationwide, law enforcement fought for this provision," Sarah Brady said on ABC's "This Week" two days after the ruling. "They're going to continue for the most part to do the background checks."

Church and State

Congress Exceeded Power with Religious Freedom Law

City of Boerne v. Flores, Archbishop of San Antonio, decided by a 6–3 vote, June 25, 1997; Kennedy wrote the opinion; O'Connor, Souter, and Breyer dissented. *(See excerpts, pp. 231–242.)*

A seventy-year-old Catholic church in a small West Texas city was the unlikely setting this term for a multifaceted constitutional conflict that pitted church against state, federal powers against states' rights, and Congress against the Supreme Court. The dispute ended with a paradoxical result: a Court generally favorable to religion struck down a law aimed at protecting religious liberty that had been endorsed by virtually every major religious organization and adopted four years earlier with nearly unanimous support in Congress.

The Rev. Anthony Cummins had no intention of starting a constitutional confrontation when he asked his Archbishop to approve plans to expand the St. Peter's Church in Boerne, a small city outside San Antonio. Cummins's congregation had outgrown the picturesque church, built in the mission architectural style in 1923. The sanctuary seated about 230 worshipers; on some days, forty to sixty parishioners had to be turned away.

When Cummins sought a building permit to enlarge the church, however, he was turned down. City officials told him the church lay within a historic district and any construction affecting landmark buildings within the district had to be approved by the Historic Landmark Commission.

Through the Archbishop of San Antonio, Cummins took the issue to federal court. The suit claimed, among other things, that the city's action violated a new federal law aimed at protecting religious freedom.

The law was the Religious Freedom Restoration Act—sometimes called by the acronym RFRA. Congress passed the law in 1993 to make it easier for religious organizations or individuals to win exemptions from laws that had an incidental impact on their actions or practices.

In passing the law, Congress wanted in effect to overturn a ruling by the Court a few years earlier that made it virtually impossible for religious groups to claim exemptions from generally applicable state or local laws. In that case—*Employment Division v. Smith*—the Court in 1990 rejected a claim by two Native Americans to a right to smoke the hallucinogen peyote as part of their traditional religious practices. *(See* Supreme Court Yearbook, 1989–1990, *pp. 15–17.)*

The Court's 6–3 ruling in *Smith* represented a shift in its handling of cases brought under the provision of the First Amendment that bars laws prohibiting the "free exercise" of religion. The Court had handed down a few cases in the 1960s and '70s that had essentially allowed the Free Exercise Clause to trump otherwise valid laws unless the government could show a "compelling state interest" in enforcing the law. In one ruling, the Court in 1963 overturned a state's refusal to allow unemployment compensation for a Seventh-Day Adventist who declined to work on Saturday (*Sherbert v. Verner*). In another, the Court in 1972 excused Amish children from mandatory public school attendance laws after eighth grade (*Wisconsin v. Yoder*).

In *Smith*, however, Justice Scalia led a five-justice majority in holding that the Free Exercise Clause did not bar the enforcement of "a valid and

St. Peter's Church in Boerne, Texas, was the focus of a church-state dispute before the Supreme Court. The case led to the Court's ruling on June 25 striking down the Religious Freedom Restoration Act.

neutral law of general applicability" that was not "specifically directed" at a religious practice. Four of the justices sharply challenged Scalia's new rule—among them, O'Connor. She agreed that Oregon had a compelling interest in enforcing its drug laws and, thus, concurred in the result in the case. But she called Scalia's new standard for judging free-exercise claims "incompatible with our nation's fundamental commitment to individual religious liberty."

The ruling drew a sharply negative reaction outside the Court. A coalition of religious and civil liberties groups from across the ideological spectrum drafted a bill to restore the previous, friendlier test for religious liberty claims. The bill provided that a state or local law could not "substantially burden a person's exercise of religion" unless the government could demonstrate that the burden was "in furtherance of a compelling government interest" and was "the least restrictive means of furthering" that interest.

Congress approved the law without dissent in the House and with only three no votes in the Senate. President Clinton hailed the new protection for religious freedom as he signed the bill into law on November 16, 1993. But the law stirred controversy among state and local officials as they began confronting religious liberty claims brought under its provisions.

Successful claims under the law appeared to be relatively modest. An Amish group in Wisconsin escaped fines for refusing to post orange safety triangles on their horse-drawn buggies. A group of Jehovah's Witnesses in California avoided a requirement to take a loyalty oath as a condition of employment with the state. But state corrections authorities faced a host of religious liberty claims from prisoners that, fanciful or not, took time and energy to defeat in court. One inmate, for example, contended that the biblical injunction to "be fruitful and multiply" gave him a right to conjugal visits in prison.

In Boerne, city officials responded to the church suit by claiming that RFRA was an unconstitutional limitation on the prerogatives of state and local governments. U.S. District Court Judge Lucius Desha Bunton III in San Antonio agreed, but the federal appeals court in New Orleans reversed the ruling and reinstated the law. The city, backed by state and local governments around the country, decided to take the issue to the Supreme Court.

The Court had dealt with Congress's power to protect constitutional rights against the states most extensively in rulings upholding the federal Voting Rights Act of 1965. Congress had claimed the power to override state voting procedures under section 5 of the Fourteenth Amendment. The amendment barred states from denying citizens due process or equal protection of the laws and, in section 5, gave Congress "power to enforce" the amendment's provisions "by appropriate legislation."

In a series of rulings dating from 1966, the Court rejected challenges to civil rights laws enacted under the authority of section 5. The Rehnquist Court, however, was skeptical of broad claims of congressional power. In addition, unlike the Voting Rights Act, the religious freedom law was aimed not at protecting the rights specifically granted by the Fourteenth Amendment, but at provisions of the Bill of Rights that came to be enforced against the states many years later.

Representing the city, Marci Hamilton, a professor at Cardozo Law School in New York, opened her plea to the Court on February 19 to invalidate the law by insisting that the case was "not about religious liberty" but "about federal power." She called RFRA "the worst form of legislative overreaching."

Justice Scalia eagerly embraced Hamilton's argument. Isn't it a "massive alteration" of the Fourteenth Amendment, he asked, to say that Congress can enforce every provision of the Bill of Rights? "It's staggering," Hamilton responded.

But Justice Breyer disagreed. "Why is it staggering," he challenged Hamilton, "for Congress to be able to say when there are laws that affect [religious] freedom, they should be looked at closely?"

In his turn, H. Douglas Laycock, a law professor at the University of Texas and a major draftsman of the statute, said Congress had followed established practices in enacting the law. "Congress has always understood that it has power to make constitutional rights effective and to go beyond the floor set by this Court," he said.

But he was quickly challenged by Justice O'Connor. Did he admit, O'Connor asked, that Congress "cannot come in and overrule a decision of this Court . . . by legislation." Laycock said the Court still had responsibility to interpret the law, but other justices were unsatisfied. The law did not give the Court much "running room," Justice Kennedy said.

Four months later, Kennedy led the Court in a ruling that rebuked Congress for intruding on the power of the judicial branch. "The power to interpret the Constitution in a case or controversy remains in the judiciary," Kennedy declared. Congress has no power, he continued, "to decree the substance of the Fourteenth Amendment's restrictions on the states." And with its sweeping terms, Kennedy said, RFRA amounted to "a considerable congressional intrusion into the States' traditional prerogatives and general authority to regulate for the health and welfare of their citizens."

Four justices—Chief Justice Rehnquist and Justices Stevens, Souter, and Thomas—joined all of Kennedy's opinion; Scalia joined all but a part that relied on the legislative history of the Fourteenth Amendment. In addition, Stevens wrote a short concurrence, saying that RFRA also amounted to an improper "governmental preference of religion" in violation of the Establishment Clause.

In her dissent, O'Connor agreed with the majority on its ruling on congressional power. "Congress lacks the ability," she wrote, "independently to define or expand the scope of constitutional rights by statute." But she argued again that the Court had made a mistake with its 1990 ruling and called for a reargument to consider overturning the decision.

". . . [I]n light of both our precedent and our Nation's tradition of religious liberty, *Smith* is demonstrably wrong," O'Connor declared, emphasizing the dissent by reading portions from the bench. At length, O'Connor cited the history of the First Amendment to try to show that the Framers intended to require government to make accommodations for religious practices that might conflict with general laws.

Breyer, who joined most of O'Connor's dissent, and Souter, who wrote separately, echoed her call for reconsidering the *Smith* decision. But neither one took a position on the question of Congress's power to enact RFRA under the Fourteenth Amendment.

The Court's ruling drew intense reaction from across the ideological spectrum. Senate Judiciary Committee Chairman Orrin Hatch, a conservative Utah Republican, said the Court had "once again acted to push religion to the fringes of society." Rep. Charles Schumer, a liberal New York Democrat who had sponsored the law in the House, said the Court had "turned its back on America's proud history of religious freedom."

Religious leaders also decried the ruling. "Every church and synagogue, every religious person in America is going to be hurt by this decision," said Oliver Thomas, counsel on religious liberty for the National Council of Churches. And they joined with supportive lawmakers in promising to devise new ways to accomplish their goals. Options being discussed included state laws to protect free-exercise claims, a more narrowly framed federal law, or—an admitted longshot—a constitutional amendment.

But Hamilton, the winning lawyer in the case, defended the ruling. "Congress does not have the power to amend the Constitution unilaterally," she said on PBS's "NewsHour." Religious groups still had strong legal protections, she added. The only problem with RFRA, she said, "was that it told churches, synagogues, et cetera, that they had a right not to get along with their community."

In August, Boerne officials reached a compromise agreement with the church over the planned rebuilding. Under the accord, about 80 percent of the building was to be left intact, but the church was to be allowed to enlarge the sanctuary by 850 seats—a nearly four-fold increase in capacity.

Church and State

Court Erases Precedent to Back Aid for Parochial Schools

Agostini v. Felton, decided by a 5–4 vote, June 23, 1997; O'Connor wrote the opinion; Souter, Stevens, Ginsburg, and Breyer dissented. *(See excerpts, pp. 215–230.)*

For more than a decade, the New York City school system used a cumbersome and expensive procedure to provide federally funded, remedial education for low-income students at parochial schools. Acting under a court order designed to maintain separation of church and state, the school system leased mobile vans, parked them on the street adjacent to parochial school grounds, and brought the parochial students in to be taught by public school teachers in what was technically a public school classroom.

The system grated on school administrators and parochial school parents. But the procedure was required by a Supreme Court ruling in 1985 that barred the city's earlier practice of sending teachers directly into parochial school buildings. This term, however, the Court overturned that ruling in a decision that cheered the critics of strict limits on government involvement with religious institutions.

The Court had struggled with the issue of church-school aid for decades. In a succession of rulings beginning in the late 1940s, the Court approved reimbursing parochial school students for transportation costs or lending textbooks for use at church-affiliated schools. But it barred more direct assistance to parochial schools, such as teacher salary supplements or grants for building maintenance and repairs.

The rulings generated both confusion and criticism. But the Court in 1985 reaffirmed its basic approach in a pair of rulings involving efforts by local school systems to provide aid to low-income students at parochial schools.

Congress in 1965 established an aid program—known as Title I—to provide remedial instruction to low-income students. New York City and Grand Rapids, Michigan, were two of many cities that tried to use the funds to teach the many low-income students attending Catholic schools.

In Grand Rapids, the school system created what it called a "shared time" program of providing remedial and enrichment classes to students at nonpublic schools during regular school hours or after the school day. New York City similarly provided services by sending public school teachers and counselors into parochial school buildings. New York administrators devised elaborate procedures to try to ensure that the program operated in accord with religious neutrality—even to the point of removing all religious symbols from classrooms used for Title I services.

The safeguards did not satisfy critics of parochial school aid. A group of taxpayers filed suit in 1978 challenging the New York City procedures as a violation of the First Amendment's provision that bars government "establishment of religion." Although a federal district court judge rejected the suit, the federal appeals court in New York strictly applied Supreme Court precedents to rule it unconstitutional.

The New York City case and a similar challenge to the Grand Rapids program reached the Court in its 1984–1985 term. By a 5–4 vote, the Court in *Aguilar v. Felton* held New York's program unconstitutional because it resulted in an "excessive entanglement of church and state in the administration of [Title I] benefits." The Court similarly voted to bar the Grand Rapids program either during school hours (7–2) or after hours (5–4) (*Grand Rapids School District v. Ball*).

Over the next decade, the Court eased its rules on financial aid for students attending church-affiliated schools. Just one year after *Aguilar*, it unanimously approved the use of funds from a federal aid program for the handicapped to help a blind ministerial student (*Witters v. Washington Department of Services for the Blind*). In 1993, the Court extended the logic of the ruling from higher education into secondary schools with a 5–4 decision that allowed the use of public funds to pay for a sign-language interpreter for a deaf parochial school student (*Zobrest v. Catalina Foothills School District*). *(See* Supreme Court Yearbook, 1992–1993, *pp. 29–31.)*

The change in direction stemmed in large part from changes in the Court's membership. By 1993, three of the justices in the majority in the *Aguilar* and *Grand Rapids* rulings had retired: William J. Brennan Jr., Thurgood Marshall, and Lewis F. Powell Jr. Two of the new justices—Kennedy, who followed Powell, and Thomas, who succeeded Marshall—took a more relaxed view of government aid to religion.

In 1994, the Court's conservatives used another church-state case to publicly signal their interest in reconsidering and possibly overturning the *Aguilar* decision. The 6–3 ruling in *Board of Education of Kiryas Joel School District v. Grumet* nullified a New York law that effectively created a special school district for an Orthodox Jewish community. But Justices O'Connor and Kennedy, who joined the majority, wrote separate opinions calling for a new look at *Aguilar*—as did Scalia, in a dissent joined by Rehnquist and Thomas. *(See* Supreme Court Yearbook, 1993–1994, *pp. 49–52.)*

New York school administrators took the comments as an invitation to try to wipe out a decision that they said had forced them to spend $100 million of Title I funds on mobile vans and the like instead of educational services. But they faced an obstacle: the Court had only a very limited procedure for rehearing a case.

The school system's lawyers, however, seized on a provision in the Federal Rules of Civil Procedure—Rule 60(b)—that allows trial judges to "relieve a party . . . from a final judgment" if "it is no longer equitable that the judgment should have prospective application." Relying on the rule, the school system asked U.S. District Court Judge John Gleeson to lift the *Aguilar* injunction. It pointed to the costs of compliance, the change in Supreme Court decisions, and the comments by a majority of justices in *Kiryas Joel* indicating that *Aguilar* was no longer good law.

Gleeson acknowledged the shift on the Court, but rejected the plea. "*Aguilar*'s demise," he said, "has not yet occurred." In a brief opinion, the federal appeals court in New York agreed. The school system then asked the Court to review the ruling. The Clinton administration joined in the plea, urging the Court to use an unprecedented procedure to overturn one of its legal rulings issued only twelve years earlier.

When the case was argued April 15, the school system's lawyer and Acting Solicitor General Walter Dellinger both faced sharp questioning on the procedural and substantive issues. "I do not know of any use of [Rule] 60(b) essentially to gain a rehearing in this Court," Justice Ginsburg told Dellinger—who candidly agreed. O'Connor also appeared troubled. "Under 60(b), we have to find that that judge abused his discretion in refusing to reopen the case," she remarked. "How do we deal with that?"

Other justices strongly defended the line drawn in *Aguilar* to limit government aid to parochial schools. Justice Souter called the ruling "an attempt to draw a visual line between what the [parochial] school is attempting to accomplish and what secular funds are providing."

But there was also criticism of the ruling. Scalia complained that the decision hurt low-income parents who sent their children to parochial schools. "Those parents must forgo that subsidy even for remedial services," he remarked. The decision, Scalia added, represented "an absolutist view of the Establishment Clause." O'Connor agreed. The Title I program "worked just fine" in New York, she said, "until this Court got the notion that it somehow violated the Establishment Clause."

Two months later, O'Connor led a five-vote majority in setting aside the procedural difficulties to overturn the *Aguilar* ruling. O'Connor said that neither the costs of complying with the ruling or the comments by the justices in the 1994 decision would justify reconsidering *Aguilar*. But she said that the use of Rule 60(b) would be proper if the Court's subsequent decisions had "undermined" the *Aguilar* decision.

Proceeding to examine those rulings, O'Connor said that the *Witters* decision in 1986 and the *Zobrest* decision in 1993 had "modified" the Court's approach to "religious indoctrination." First, she said, the rulings rejected "the presumption" that placing public employees on parochial school grounds was always impermissible. Second, she continued, the Court had also "departed" from the rule that all government assistance that "directly aids the educational function of religious schools" is invalid.

With those considerations discarded, O'Connor proceeded to re-examine whether New York's Title I program improperly advanced religion—and concluded that it did not. The program, she said, "does not result in governmental indoctrination; define its recipients by reference to religion; or create an excessive entanglement" between church and state. *Aguilar*, she concluded, was "no longer good law."

O'Connor added that there was no reason not to overturn the precedent in the New York case itself. " . . . [I]t would be particularly inequitable," she wrote, to wait for another case while the city was forced to spend "millions of dollars" on mobile vans and leased sites "when it could be spending that money to give economically disadvantaged children a better chance at success in life. . . ." Rehnquist, Scalia, Kennedy, and Thomas joined her opinion.

The dissenting justices forcefully criticized the ruling on procedural and substantive grounds. Souter said *Aguilar* established a "sensible" line limiting government aid to religious schools. Under the new ruling, he warned, state and local governments would be free to pay for "the entire cost of instruction provided in any ostensibly secular subject in any religious school." Stevens, Ginsburg, and Breyer joined his opinion.

Separately, Ginsburg—joined by the other three dissenters—said the decision allowed the use of a procedural rule for trial courts to obtain an " 'anytime' rehearing" by the Court. The result, she said, was to undermine what she called the Court's "responsive, non-agenda-setting character."

Groups favoring stricter separation of church and state criticized the ruling, even though it had been anticipated. "Thanks to this misguided decision, taxpayers will be called on to pay for state-funded teachers inside religious schools," said Barry Lynn, executive director of Americans United for Separation of Church and State.

In New York, however, the ruling was hailed by school officials and by the principals at Catholic schools who had been forced to work under the makeshift arrangements required by the old ruling. Ted Staniecki, principal of the School of the Incarnation, recalled that 200 of the school's 520 students had to traipse out to vans parked alongside the school to receive remedial instruction. "We finally got some common sense," Staniecki told the *New York Times* after the decision.

Criminal Law

States Allowed to Confine Sexual "Predators"

Kansas v. Hendricks, decided by a 5–4 vote, June 23, 1997; Thomas wrote the opinion; Breyer, Stevens, Souter, and Ginsburg dissented. *(See excerpts, pp. 204–215.)*

Leroy Hendricks had a thirty-year record of sex crimes against children covering almost all of his adult life outside prison walls. Once, when asked in court whether he could promise not to molest children if released, he answered, "The only way to guarantee that is to die."

The state of Kansas instead turned in 1994 to a newly enacted "sexual predator" law to commit Hendricks to a secure, mental hospital on an indefinite basis. This term, the Court upheld the law in a ruling that promptly encouraged other states to consider following Kansas's example in dealing with recidivist sex offenders.

Hendricks—the first person to be committed under the 1994 Kansas law—began abusing children in 1955 at the age of twenty when he exposed his penis to two young girls and asked them to touch it. Over the next thirty years, he accumulated five convictions for molesting a total of ten children—boys and girls, as young as seven or eight years old. Shortly after being paroled in 1972, he began to abuse his own stepdaughter and stepson, forcing them to engage in sexual activity over a four-year period.

In 1984, Hendricks was convicted of attempting to fondle two thirteen-year-old boys in the electronics shop where he worked. Although he faced a maximum prison sentence of forty-five to 180 years, the prosecutor agreed to a plea bargain of five to twenty years. Because of good time credits earned while in prison, Hendricks was scheduled to be released in August 1994.

Kansas, however, had just passed a law aimed at isolating repeat sexual offenders beyond their prison terms. The Sexually Violent Predator Act authorized what it described as civil confinement for persons who had been found guilty of a sexually violent crime and diagnosed as suffering from a mental abnormality or personality disorder which "makes the person likely to engage" in predatory acts of sexual violence in the future.

The law provided a number of safeguards—most notably, the requirement that the state prove the elements of the act beyond a reasonable doubt. Individuals were entitled to an attorney and mental health examinations, at public expense for indigents. The act also required the committing court to review a person's record at least once a year to determine whether continued detention was warranted. In addition, someone committed under the law could petititon for release at any time.

The Kansas law raised questions, however, under some Supreme Court precedents. In 1992, the Court ruled that a person could not be confined to a mental institution only because he was dangerous; the government also had to show the person was mentally ill (*Foucha v. Louisiana*). In an earlier case—*Addington v. Texas* (1979)—the Court required "clear and convincing evidence" to justify an involuntary civil commitment—a higher standard than the preponderance of the evidence test that the Kansas law used to determine the likelihood of future sexual offenses. In addition, the use of the law against anyone for crimes committed before its enactment raised questions under the Constitution's Ex Post Facto Clause, which generally prohibits retroactive punishment.

Leroy Hendricks

Shortly before Hendricks's scheduled release, the same prosecutor who had negotiated the plea bargain ten years earlier filed a petition to commit Hendricks under the new Kansas law. Testifying in the proceeding, Hendricks admitted that he could not control "the urge" to molest children when he got "stressed out." He agreed with the state's psychologist that he suffered from pedophilia and described treatment programs for the condition as "bull——." The psychologist testified that Hendricks met the critieria under the law and, specifically, that he was likely to commit sexual offenses against children in the future if not confined. Hendricks countered with testimony from a psychiatrist who said it was not possible to predict with any accuracy the future dangerousness of a sex offender.

After hearing the testimony, a jury unanimously agreed that Hendricks was a violent sexual predator, and the judge ordered him committed. Through his attorney, Hendricks then challenged the law on constitutional grounds. He claimed, first, that the law violated due process by authorizing his confinement on the basis of a "mental abnormality," instead of a diagnosed mental illness. In addition, he said the commitment amounted to successive and retroactive punishment for his previous crimes, in violation of the Double Jeopardy Clause and the Ex Post Facto Clause.

The trial judge rejected the plea. But the Kansas Supreme Court, in a 6–1 ruling, agreed with Hendricks's argument that confining him without a finding of mental illness violated his "substantive due process rights." The court did not rule on the double jeopardy and retroactive punishment claims. The state asked the Court to review the ruling, and the justices granted the petition.

Kansas Attorney General Carla J. Stovall began her defense of the law on December 10 by describing it as a "hybrid" combining punishment with treatment. But she quickly encountered skeptical questions. "It seems to be a new kind of category of commitment," Justice O'Connor interjected. Could the state lock up anyone diagnosed with a mental abnormality, O'Connor asked, and then prove he was dangerous too?

Other justices joined in probing how far the state's argument could extend. Would someone be entitled to release if the state failed to provide treatment, Souter asked. Hesitantly, Stovall appeared to agree. Could an armed robber be committed as a "sociopathic personality," Breyer asked. Stovall demurred. The medical diagnosis in Hendricks's case was "much greater than in your example," she told Breyer.

But the justices voiced equal discomfort with the argument from Hendricks's attorney. The lawyer, Thomas J. Weilert, contended that the state could not commit Hendricks except for his own good. The Kansas Supreme Court, Weilert stressed, found that Hendricks was not receiving treatment at the time of its decision. Since then, he acknowledged, the state had put Hendricks in group therapy sessions, but there was "no evidence" that the treatment was effective.

Under questioning, however, Weilert conceded that Hendricks presented a danger to society. "There's no doubt," he said, "that Mr. Hendricks presents a risk of committing a criminal act" if released. "What's the state supposed to do?" Chief Justice Rehnquist interrupted. "Just wait until he gets out and does it again?"

The Court's decision, announced by Justice Thomas on June 23, accepted the state's arguments. Civil commitment had historically been used, Thomas said, to confine someone who was mentally ill and presented a danger to himself or society. The Kansas law satisfied that test by requiring "a finding of future dangerousness" linked to the existence of a mental abnormality or personality disorder that "makes it difficult, if not impossible, for the person to control his dangerous behavior."

The state was not required to make a finding of "mental illness," Thomas continued. The Court, he said, had "never required State legislatures to adopt any particular nomenclature in drafting civil commitment statutes." Pedophilia was recognized by mental health professionals as "a serious mental disorder," he said. And Hendricks himself acknowledged that he "cannot control the urge" to molest children. On that basis, Thomas concluded, the Kansas law "plainly suffices for due process purposes."

Thomas rejected the double jeopardy and retroactive punishment issues by stressing that the Kansas law provided for civil commitment rather than criminal punishment. Kansas described its law as civil in nature. The law was not aimed at the criminal law goals of retribution or deterrence, Thomas said, and the possibility of indefinite commitment did not necessarily reflect a criminal law purpose either.

Finally, Thomas rejected Hendricks's argument that the Court's prior rulings had established a requirement for treatment under civil commitment statutes. ". . . [N]othing in the Constitution," Thomas wrote, "prevents a State from civilly detaining those for whom no treatment is available, but who nevertheless pose a danger to others."

The vote in the case was 5–4, with Chief Justice Rehnquist and Justices O'Connor, Scalia, and Kennedy joining Thomas's opinion. Kennedy added a brief concurrence to warn against the use of the law to supplement criminal prosecution. "If the civil system is used to simply impose punishment after the State makes an improvident plea bargain on the criminal side," he wrote, "then it is not performing the proper function."

The limited dissent did not challenge the basic premise of the sexual predatory laws, only its retroactive application. Breyer began his dissenting opinion by saying he agreed that the Kansas law's definition of "mental abnormality" satisfied the substantive requirements of the Due Process Clause. But, he continued, the law "did not provide Hendricks . . . with any treatment until after his release date from prison and only inadequate treatment thereafter."

On that basis, Breyer concluded the law was "not simply an effort to commit Hendricks civilly, but rather an effort to inflict further punishment on him." For that reason, use of the law against Hendricks violated the Ex Post Facto Clause, Breyer said. But he closed by stressing that states were free to enact what he termed "dangerous sexual offender statutes" if they operated prospectively. And a law could even be applied retroactively, he ended, "if the confinement it imposes is not punishment. . . ." Stevens and Souter joined all of Breyer's opinion; Ginsburg joined only the part on the Ex Post Facto Clause, but did not write separately to explain her views on the due process issue.

In Kansas, Attorney General Stovall praised the ruling. "It means we can continue to protect the public from the worst kind of criminals," she said. But Wendy McFarland of the Kansas chapter of the American Civil Liberties Union, which supported Hendricks's plea, criticized the decision. "Anticipating crimes before they've been committed and penalizing them before they happen is a precedent that should frighten every American," she told the Associated Press.

The ruling appeared to ease legal doubts about similar laws already on the books in five other states: Arizona, California, New Jersey, Washington, and Wisconsin. In addition, it seemed likely to encourage other states to follow suit. The New York Senate approved a similar bill within two days of the decision, although the measure died in the state Assembly.

Hendricks himself declined to comment on the ruling, but several of the other men housed with him at the Larned State Security Hospital in Kansas voiced disappointment. "My behavior and I are two different things," Donald Hunt, committed for pedophilia, told the Associated Press, "but I know the public sees me as my behavior."

Class Actions

"Sprawling" Asbestos Settlement Barred by Court

Amchem Products, Inc. v. Windsor, decided by a 6–2 vote, June 25, 1997; Ginsburg wrote the opinion; Breyer and Stevens dissented in part; O'Connor did not participate. *(See excerpts, pp. 176–190.)*

Millions of American workers were exposed to asbestos at their jobs over a period of decades with no warning that dust and fibers from the insulating material could cause serious and sometimes fatal respiratory problems. Tens of thousands of the asbestos-exposed workers or their survivors brought damage claims in state and federal courts, seeking millions of dollars in compensation from manufacturers of asbestos products.

As the damage claims mounted—spurred by favorable court rulings—the litigation created administrative headaches for the courts and financial nightmares for some of the companies. To try to end the litigation, a coalition of twenty former asbestos manufacturers in 1993 struck an unprecedented deal with plaintiffs' lawyers calling for a $1.3 billion fund to settle all future asbestos-injury claims out of court. But this term, the Court rejected the scheme in an important ruling that limited the defensive use of class-action settlements to resolve mass torts.

The dispute arose against a complex factual and legal background. The dangers of asbestos exposure were known as early as the 1930s, but millions of workers—many of them in oil refineries or naval shipyards—continued to be exposed into the 1950s and later. After a long latency period, asbestos-related injuries began to appear in large numbers in the 1960s. By the end of the decade, asbestos victims started filing what was first a wave of lawsuits and then a veritable flood.

State and federal court systems struggled to cope with the cases, which numbered 150,000 in federal courts alone as of 1997. A report by a special committee of federal judges in 1991 cited some of the problems the courts faced: crowded dockets, lengthy trials, long delays, repetitive litigation, and high "transaction costs" that threatened to eat up any money that could be paid to current and future victims.

Asbestos manufacturers were also suffering under the litigation. One of the leading companies, Johns Manville Corp., sought bankruptcy protection in 1983 to stem the financial payouts. Other companies looked for less drastic ways to try to cap their costs and put the litigation behind them.

The judicial committee recommended federal legislation to create a national asbestos-dispute resolution system. When Congress failed to act on the proposal, federal judges responded in 1991 by consolidating all pending federal cases in a single district court in Philadelphia. A committee of plaintiffs' lawyers was appointed to manage the litigation on one side; twenty of

Requirements for Class Action Suit

Numerosity	"class [so large] that joinder of all members is impracticable"
Commonality	"questions of law or fact common to the class"
Typicality	named parties' claims or defenses "are typical of the class"
Adequacy of Representation	representatives "will fairly and adequately protect the interests of the class"

Federal Rule of Civil Procedure 23(a)

common questions must "predominate over any questions affecting only individual members"

class resolution must be "superior to other available methods for the fair and efficient adjudication of the controversy"

Federal Rule of Civil Procedure 23(b)(3)

the companies named as defendants had already formed the Center for Claims Resolution (CCR) to handle cases from their side.

Through the end of 1996, the center processed some 180,000 cases. But lawyers for the companies worried about future cases from people who had developed asbestos-related diseases but not yet filed claims and from people who had not yet developed symptoms but might become ill in the future. The solution they negotiated with plaintiffs' lawyers was a 106-page agreement to establish a $1.3 billion fund to handle all future asbestos-related claims against the companies outside the court system.

Procedurally, the plaintiffs' attorneys drew up a class-action lawsuit brought in the name of nine individuals on behalf of all people in the United States who had been exposed to asbestos or asbestos products manufactured by the companies through their work or whose spouse or family member had been so exposed. The complaint was filed in federal court in Philadelphia on January 15, 1993, simultaneously with an answer by the defendants, a proposed settlement agreement, and a joint motion to certify the suit as a class action under the Federal Rules of Civil Procedure.

The federal class action rules were designed to allow people with common legal claims, often too small to be tried on an individual basis, to consolidate their suits for a single proceeding. The multiple provisions of Rule 23 required that the class of plaintiffs be "numerous" and their claims be "common" and that the individually named plaintiffs' have "typical" claims and be able to "adequately represent" the interests of the class. In a significant amendment in the 1960s, the rules allowed a judge to make a class action binding on anyone who shared the legal claim unless an individual—after getting notice of the suit—chose to "opt out" of the proceeding. Two additional requirements applied: common issues must "predominate" over other questions and class resolution must be "superior to" other methods of adjudicating the dispute.

The new provision led to a widening use of class actions first in consumer suits and then in other kinds of mass tort cases, including environmental and occupational injury suits. Beginning in the late 1980s and early '90s, lawyers on both sides of such cases began using the provision to negotiate so-called global settlements: complex administrative schemes, subject to court approval, to compensate individual claimants for their injuries. The settlements, which usually called for substantial fees for the plaintiffs' attorneys, often provoked controversy—either because they cost too much or paid victims too little or both.

The asbestos settlement represented a further, and even more controversial, development: the creation of a so-called settlement class before a suit was filed. The lawyers who negotiated such agreements saw the device as a cost-effective way to provide compensation for victims and cap costs for corporate defendants. But critics viewed the procedure as an invitation to collusive deals that benefited the class-action lawyers and companies involved but gave inadequate compensation to people who had been injured.

For courts, a pivotal legal question was how to consider the proposed settlement in making the preliminary decision whether to "certify the class" under Rule 23. Until 1995, the judges who handled the small number of such cases raised no special concerns about the procedure. In the asbestos case, U.S. District Court Judge Lowell A. Reed Jr. approved the settlement in 1994 after finding that adequate notice had been given, class certification was appropriate, and the agreement was fair and noncollusive.

In 1995, however, the federal appeals court in Philadelphia—the Third Circuit—held in a separate case that a judge could not certify a settlement class without finding that all provisions of Rule 23 were scrupulously met and could not consider the benefits of a settlement in making that decision. The opinion was authored by Judge Edward R. Becker. Coincidentally, Becker was picked for the three-judge panel to hear an appeal of the asbestos-class settlement ruling brought by potential plaintiffs who objected to the terms of the deal and the procedure for approving it.

Unsurprisingly perhaps, Becker led the appellate panel in decisively rejecting the asbestos accord. He reiterated that Rule 23's requirements must be met without taking the settlement into account. But he also said the panel had considered the terms of the settlement before reaching its conclusions that the criteria had not been satisfied. Becker said the potential members of what he called a "humongous" class had divergent interests; on that basis, he said that common issues did not "predominate" and that the named plaintiffs could not "adequately represent" the interests of the whole class.

The asbestos companies, backed by business groups, urged the Court to review the ruling. They said the decision upset a carefully worked out settlement, conflicted with other appellate rulings on the issue, and threatened the use of a valuable judicial management tool for resolving mass tort cases.

When the case was argued before the Court on February 18, however, several of the justices sharply questioned both the procedure and the terms of the settlement. Ginsburg began by attacking the breadth of the agreement. The accord, Ginsburg said, "stops every court in this country . . . from dealing with any of these claims." Scalia followed by questioning the notice to class members. "How would any notice be adequate," he asked, "to protect people who do not know they have been exposed?" Stephen Shapiro, the Chicago attorney defending the settlement, appeared to make little headway in answering the justices' concern.

In his turn, Harvard law professor Laurence Tribe, representing asbestos victims opposed to the settlement, faced less critical questioning. Justices Breyer and Stevens both evinced some sympathy for a judge's desire to resolve mass tort cases quickly. But Tribe shot back that it was for Congress, not the courts, to impose a settlement that protected industry from suits into the indefinite future.

It was Ginsburg who wrote for the Court four months later in a broadly framed opinion June 25 rejecting the settlement. Initially, Ginsburg agreed that a settlement ought to be considered in weighing whether Rule 23's requirements were met for class certification. But the "global compromise" negotiated by the plaintiffs' lawyers and asbestos company attorneys, she said, had "no structural assurance of fair and adequate representation for the diverse groups and individuals affected." The "sprawling" class did not meet the federal rules' requirements, she said, and judges were "not free to amend a rule" just to simplify the management of a complex case.

Ginsburg acknowledged the argument that a nationwide administrative claims system would be "the most secure, fair, and efficient means of compensating victims of asbestos exposure." But, she continued, "Congress has not adopted such a solution." Without legislative authorization, she concluded, the class action rules "cannot carry the large load that CCR, class counsel, and the District Court heaped upon it."

Chief Justice Rehnquist and Justices Scalia, Kennedy, Souter, and Thomas joined Ginsburg's opinion; Justice O'Connor did not participate in the case because she owned stock in one of the companies involved.

In a largely dissenting opinion, Justice Breyer faulted Ginsburg for second-guessing the trial court and for underestimating "the need for settlement in this mass tort case." Although he joined the majority's legal holding on the relevance of a settlement to approving a class action, he insisted— contrary to Ginsburg—that the appeals court gave the accord no weight.

The case, Breyer said, should be returned to the appeals court for a new decision under a proper standard. Stevens joined the dissent.

Experts and advocates on both sides of the issue agreed the decision not only undid the asbestos accord but also appeared to doom similar agreements in other mass tort cases. Some observers predicted, however, that the ruling could help spur the federal judiciary's policymaking body to approve a pending amendment to Rule 23 aimed at easing the requirements for certifying a "settlement class."

The nation's largest plaintiffs' attorneys group, the Association of Trial Lawyers of America, praised the decision for rejecting what it called a "one-size-fits-all" settlement. But Larry Fitzpatrick, president of the asbestos companies' center, insisted that it would try to preserve "elements" of the agreement in some form. "We're not going back to the old system of wasteful litigation," he said.

Securities Law

Government Backed in "Insider Trading" Prosecution

United States v. O'Hagan, decided by 6–3, 7–2, and 9–0 votes, June 25, 1997; Ginsburg wrote the opinion; Thomas, Rehnquist, and Scalia dissented in part. *(See excerpts, pp. 190–204.)*

James O'Hagan made a $4.3 million killing in securities trading in 1988, but he owed his good fortune to something other than hard work, skill, or luck. The Minneapolis attorney picked up confidential information about a big corporate takeover, bought up stock and call options in the target company, and then sold the securities for a hefty profit after the takeover attempt became public.

The Securities and Exchange Commission said O'Hagan violated federal securities law and instigated a criminal prosecution that ended in the attorney's convictions on a variety of securities fraud and mail fraud counts. O'Hagan won a reversal from a federal appeals court, but this term the Supreme Court reinstated the convictions in an important ruling that erased legal doubts about one of the SEC's main weapons to combat insider trading.

The SEC had long used the broadly written antifraud provision of the Securities Exchange Act of 1934—section 10(b)— and the agency's implementing regulation—Rule 10b-5—to go after corporate insiders for using material, nonpublic information to trade in a company's securities. The theory applied not just to company employees but also to anyone who had a "fiduciary relationship" with the company—like a lawyer, banker, or someone else in a position of trust or confidence. The SEC also expanded the theory to go after "tippees"—someone an insider "tipped off" about the information. But the commission needed a different theory to reach other people who had access to confidential information but did not work for or have a fiduciary relationship with the company whose stock they were trading. The gap was especially significant in tender offers, where attorneys and bankers representing a takeover target often learned of the buyer's intentions before they became public.

One of the commission's answers was its so-called "misappropriation theory." The SEC argued that someone who learned of confidential information through a fiduciary relationship and then used it to trade in securities had committed a "deception" for purposes of triggering the securities antifraud laws. In addition, the commission adopted a new rule in 1980—Rule 14e-3(a)—specifically dealing with

James O'Hagan

tender offers. The rule prohibited anyone from using nonpublic information to trade in the stock of a company that was the subject of a planned tender offer if the individual knew that the information came, directly or indirectly, from either the offering company, the target company, or any of their officers, directors, or employees.

The SEC and federal prosecutors used the misappropriation theory aggressively in the 1980s and won acceptance of its approach from the federal appeals court in New York, which heard many of the most important securities fraud cases. But the Supreme Court twice skirted a direct ruling on the theory. In 1980, it reversed on limited grounds the securities fraud conviction of a financial printing house employee who gleaned information from documents he was handling to trade in stocks (*Chiarella v. United States*). Then in 1987, the Court divided 4–4 in a case against a *Wall Street Journal* columnist, R. Foster Winans, who used information gained in his job for stock-trading. The tie vote in *Carpenter v. United States* left Winans's conviction standing, but established no legal precedent.

O'Hagan's case gave the Court a chance to rule on both the misappropriation theory and the SEC's tender-offer Rule 14e-3(a). O'Hagan had been a partner in a prestigious Minneapolis law firm, Dorsey & Whitney. In summer 1988, the firm was hired as local counsel for the British-based conglomerate Grand Metropolitan PLC in connection with its planned takeover of the Minneapolis-based Pillsbury Company. O'Hagan was not working on the deal himself, but confirmed his suspicions about the impending tender offer in a brief conversation with the head of the firm's corporate department.

The information was especially valuable for O'Hagan, who was a heavy stock market player and who needed cash at the time to try to cover up a separate crime: theft of about $3 million from client trust accounts. Armed with the nonpublic information, O'Hagan invested heavily in Pillsbury stock options and stock in August and September. Then, when Grand Met announced its tender offer in October, O'Hagan sold the securities for a profit of $4.3 million.

The American Stock Exchange's options surveillance department detected O'Hagan's trading and reported it to the SEC, which did more investigating and then turned the case over to federal prosecutors in Minneapolis. A federal grand jury indicted him on fifty-seven counts of securities fraud, fraudulent trading in connection with a tender offer, and mail fraud. At trial, O'Hagan argued that Grand Met's plan to acquire Pillsbury was already public knowledge when he bought the securities, but the jury disagreed and convicted him on all counts. O'Hagan, who had already been convicted and sentenced in state court in the theft case, was given an additional eighteen-month prison term and ordered to forfeit the profits from the trades plus interest.

But the federal appeals court in St. Louis reversed all of the federal convictions. In a 2–1 decision, the appeals court rejected the government's misappropriation theory on the grounds that O'Hagan's violation of his fiduciary duty of confidentiality to his law firm did not amount to a deception under federal securities law and, in any event, was not "in connection with the purchase or sale of a security," as required by the statute. As for the tender-offer counts, the court held that the SEC's broadly written ban on trading by people with inside information went beyond its statutory authority to prevent "fraudulent, deceptive, or manipulative" conduct. The court also threw out the mail fraud counts, saying they rested on the securities fraud charges.

The government's lawyer opened his argument to the Court on April 16 by stressing the importance of the case to the public belief in the integrity of the stock market. "Investors in the securities market rely on the fact that the markets are essentially honest," Deputy Solicitor General Michael Dreeben told the justices.

But defense attorney John French insisted the government had overstepped in prosecuting O'Hagan. "I don't believe Congress was attempting to regulate conduct between lawyers and firms," French argued.

Some of the justices appeared troubled by the government's theory for prosecuting O'Hagan. "Where is the connection between 'the deceptive device' and 'the purchase or sale' of the security?" Chief Justice Rehnquist asked Dreeben, quoting the statutory language. O'Hagan "didn't deceive anyone who sold him the securities," Rehnquist said.

Justice O'Connor pressed Dreeben on how far the government's theory could extend. Could the government prosecute a lawyer who "inadvertently" let his daughter know secret information that she later used in stock trading, O'Connor asked. "Probably not," Dreeben conceded.

But other justices sounded more sympathetic to the government's side. O'Hagan's conduct was clearly deceptive, Breyer said. "It deceives everybody in the firm for which he works," he said.

The Court's ruling, announced on June 25 in its final week, represented a major victory for the SEC. The Court approved the misappropriation theory by a 6–3 vote and the tender-offer rule by a 7–2 margin. In a detailed, 35-page opinion, Justice Ginsburg agreed with the government that O'Hagan's misappropriation of confidential information deceived the other members of his law firm, satisfying the securities law's definition of deceptive conduct. "A fiduciary who pretends loyalty to the principal while secretly converting the principal's information for personal gain dupes or defrauds the principal," she wrote. O'Hagan's deception was also "in connection with" securities trading, Ginsburg continued, because the fraud was "consummated" only when he used the information to buy and sell the stock.

As for Rule 14e-3(a), Ginsburg said the regulation fell within the SEC's authority under the statute to enact rules "reasonably designed to prevent" fraudulent trading. "It is a fair assumption," she wrote, "that trading on the basis of material, nonpublic information will often involve a breach of a duty of confidentiality to the bidder or target company or their representatives."

Finally, Ginsburg said the appeals court's decision to overturn the mail fraud counts rested on procedural grounds linked to its rulings on the other charges. On that basis, she set aside the appeals court's ruling on those counts, but also remanded the case for consideration of other objections O'Hagan had raised. Five justices joined Ginsburg's opinion in full: Stevens, O'Connor Kennedy, Souter, and Breyer. Scalia joined some of the opinion, but dissented on the securities fraud counts.

In the main dissent, Thomas argued for overturning the securities fraud and tender-offer convictions. At length, Thomas contended that the government had failed to provide a "coherent" explanation for its misappropriation theory. O'Hagan's deception of his law firm, Thomas suggested, had "no impact on the integrity" of his stock trades or on "the confidence or integrity of the market." As for the tender-offer rule, Thomas said it went beyond the SEC's authority by using a definition of fraud broader than the Court had approved in prior securities law rulings. Thomas agreed, however, that the mail fraud counts could stand. Rehnquist joined Thomas's opinion.

Scalia voted with the majority to uphold the tender-offer and mail fraud convictions, but dissented on the securities fraud charges. He took a different approach than Thomas, however. He argued simply that a standard method of narrowly interpreting criminal law provisions—the so-called rule of lenity—limited the antifraud section to deceptions of a party to a securities transaction.

The ruling cheered the SEC and other advocates of strict insider trading enforcement. SEC Chairman Arthur Levitt Jr. said the ruling "reaffirms the SEC's efforts to make the stock market fair to all people, whether you're a Wall Street veteran or a Main Street newcomer." But some securities lawyers complained that the ruling still left the definition of illegal insider trading unclear. "Now Congress will not be motivated to create a statutory definition of insider trading," Edward Brodsky, a partner at the New York firm of Proskauer Rose, told the *New York Law Journal.* "People should be clearly forewarned what constitutes a crime," he added.

Cable Television

"Must-Carry" Law Upheld in Victory for Broadcasters

Turner Broadcasting System, Inc. v. Federal Communications Commission, decided by a 5–4 vote, March 31, 1997; Kennedy wrote the opinion; O'Connor, Scalia, Thomas, and Ginsburg dissented. *(See excerpts, pp. 151–168.)*

The broadcasting and cable television industries returned to the Court for a second time this term with a dispute over a federal law requiring cable systems to carry the signals of local TV stations. Three years earlier, the Court appeared to give cable companies a boost in their effort to invalidate the 1992 provision on First Amendment grounds. But this term, the Court voted 5–4 to uphold the "must-carry" provision, accepting Congress's belief that the law would help preserve local broadcasters, promote media diversity, and promote fair competition in television programming.

The passage of the 1992 law capped a long history of rivalry between the two industries. Broadcasters had helped stifle the growth of cable through the 1950s and 1960s by persuading the Federal Communications Commission (FCC) to impose restrictive regulations on cable systems. But cable operators began chipping away at those regulations through court challenges in the 1970s and, by the 1980s, had begun to take away audience and advertising from established broadcasters.

The broadcasting industry responded by urging first the FCC and then Congress to require cable operators to carry local television stations on their systems. With the growth in the number of cable subscribers, the broadcasters argued, cable systems had the power to limit local stations' audience by dropping them from their lineups. And, the broadcasters contended, cable had an incentive to do just that—in order to limit a competitive communications medium.

Twice, the FCC adopted a form of must-carry rule only to be overturned each time by the federal appeals court in Washington, which ruled the agency did not have sufficient evidence to justify the provision. Rebuffed, broadcasters turned to Congress, which in 1992 included a must-carry provision in an omnibus cable regulation bill enacted over President George Bush's veto.

The cable industry challenged the law in court. Cable operators argued it violated their constitutional right to determine their programming; cable programmers said it violated their First Amendment rights by giving broadcasters preferential access to cable systems. The FCC, backed by broadcasters, argued that the law was structural regulation that did not affect First Amendment interests at all or, at most, imposed minimal burdens that were justifiable given Congress's objectives.

A special three-judge court upheld the law in a 2–1 ruling in 1993, and cable operators appealed to the Supreme Court. The justices failed to resolve the issue, however. By a 5–4 vote, the Court sent the case back to the lower court for a new hearing. Eight of the justices ruled that the cable industry was entitled to a greater measure of First Amendment protection than the lower court had recognized. But they were divided equally on how to resolve the case.

One group, led by Justice O'Connor, wanted to strike the law down; the other, led by Justice Kennedy, said the lower court should re-examine the law under the "intermediate scrutiny" test used in some First Amendment cases—whether the law furthered an important governmental interest and was narrowly tailored to serve that interest. The tie was broken by Justice Stevens, who favored upholding the law but voted to send the case back to avoid a deadlock. (*See* Supreme Court Yearbook, 1993–1994, *pp. 52–55.*)

On remand, the three-judge court again upheld the must-carry law, by the identical 2–1 vote. So the case returned to the Court. When the case was argued on October 7—the first day of the new term—the most closely watched justice was the Court's only new member since the first ruling: Breyer.

Appointed at the end of the 1993–1994 term, Breyer replaced Justice Harry A. Blackmun, who had voted with the plurality in sending the must-carry case back for a second look. Thus, if Breyer joined the previous dissenters, must-carry would go down. Cable industry leaders hoped Breyer's expertise in economics and regulation would make him skeptical of the justifications for must-carry. Regardless, they thought the Court's unwillingness to uphold the law on the first go-around boded well for their chances this time.

The arguments seemed to go badly for the broadcasters. The dissenters in the first ruling indicated no change of heart. Why would the loss of a few stations be "so horrible," Justice Scalia asked Acting Solicitor General Walter Dellinger, who was defending the law. "Most communities have only one newspaper." In addition, some of the justices who had joined the plurality ruling the first time seemed skeptical of the need for the law. Souter noted that even though broadcast stations were dropped a total of 8,000 times during the seven years before must-carry's enactment, only thirty-one stations went under.

Most significantly, Breyer seemed to have strong doubts about the law, repeatedly challenging the government's position. "I can't find empirical evidence" to justify the law, he declared at one point.

The ruling to uphold the law on March 31 thus came as a big surprise to the lawyers and observers who had followed the case. The justices' lineup was all but unchanged from the first decision. This time, Kennedy led a fragile majority of five in upholding the statute, while O'Connor again led four dissenters in calling for striking the law down. Breyer cast the pivotal vote: he joined most of Kennedy's opinion, but split off from what Breyer called the majority's "anticompetitive rationale" to justify the must-carry provision.

In a detailed recitation of the evidence before Congress, Kennedy said lawmakers had a "substantial basis" for concluding that "a real threat justified enactment of the must-carry provisions." He said cable operators had "systemic reasons" for wanting to "disadvantage" local broadcasters, which competed with cable systems for audience and advertisers. Congress had evidence that cable operators were dropping broadcasters from their line-ups, that some broadcasters were experiencing financial problems, and that local stations' financial strength could "deteriorate" if they were not carried on cable systems.

Kennedy also concluded that the must-carry provisions were narrowly tailored to further Congress's goals of preserving local broadcasters, promoting media diversity, and promoting fair competition. He said the burdens on cable operators were "modest." Cable systems had been able to meet their must-carry obligations 87 percent of the time by using "previously unused channel capacity," Kennedy said.

Kennedy ended with an explicit deference to Congress on the issue. "Judgments about how competing economic interests are to be reconciled in the complex and fast-changing field of television," he wrote, "are for Congress to make." Chief Justice Rehnquist and Justices Stevens and Souter joined his opinion in full.

Breyer joined all of Kennedy's opinion except for the discussion of the competition issues. The act, Breyer wrote, "undoubtedly seeks to provide over-the-air viewers who lack cable with a rich mix of over-the-air programming by guaranteeing the over-the-air stations that provide such programming with the extra dollars that an additional cable audience will generate." On that basis, Breyer said he was convinced that the law "survives 'intermediate scrutiny,' whether or not the statute is properly tailored to Congress' purely economic objectives."

In her dissenting opinion, O'Connor faulted the majority for deferring too much to Congress. She said the law was not "a measured response" to concerns about cable's monopoly powers, while the interest in promoting media diversity was "poorly defined."

"Congress has commandeered up to one third of each cable system's channel capacity for the benefit of local broadcasters," O'Connor wrote, "without any regard for whether doing so advances the statute's alleged goals." Justices Scalia, Thomas, and Ginsburg joined her opinion.

Cable operators, who had generally expected the law to be struck down, voiced disappointment but resignation. "We've been living under these rules since 1992," Michael Luftman, a spokesman for Time Warner Cable, said, "so basically this means that nothing is going to change."

Broadcasters who expected to benefit from the ruling were pleased. "We're speaking softly, but carrying a big stick," Barry Diller, chairman of the Home Shopping Network, told *Broadcasting and Cable* magazine. Diller's string of UHF stations could claim protected carriage on cable systems under the law. A spokeswoman for public television stations said the ruling "provides an important legal and policy precedent in support of access for noncommercial educational services."

Ironically, though, the major commercial television networks had mixed views about the decision. ABC, CBS, Fox, and NBC each had launched new cable programming channels or bought interest in cable networks. For them, the ruling made it harder to win carriage for their cable ventures on local systems that had less and less unused channel capacity with the increased diversity in video programming.

Women's athletics was coming into its own in the 1990s, drawing increased attention in high schools and colleges around the country and competing for spectators and prize money in several professional sports. Much of the credit for the advance went to a federal law, Title IX of the Education Amendments of 1972, which prohibited discrimination on the basis of sex at any school receiving federal funds.

The act was widely hailed for correcting the historic neglect of women athletes in high schools and colleges. But some people thought a federal appeals court carried the law too far with a ruling in November 1996 that required Brown University in Rhode Island to match the total number of varsity positions for men and women with their overall percentages in the student body.

The ruling by the First U.S. Circuit Court of Appeals in Boston shook the world of intercollegiate athletics. More than sixty colleges and universities joined the Ivy League school in urging the Supreme Court to review the decision, which they said amounted to gender-based quotas for women athletes. Many feared that the ruling, if upheld, would force them to put more money into women's sports at the expense of men's athletics.

The Court, however, spurned the colleges' plea. It issued a one-sentence order on April 21 declining to grant Brown's petition for certiorari— the legal term for the Court's review of a ruling from a state tribunal or a lower federal court. Officially, the action did not indicate approval of the ruling; the justices often stress that there are any number of reasons for declining to take up a case besides the merits of the lower court ruling.

Still, lawyers on both sides of the case said the justices' action would reverberate beyond the four New England states covered by the First Circuit. Lynette Labinger, lawyer for the Brown female athletes who filed the original suit in 1992, told the *Washington Post* that the Court's decision to let the ruling stand would send "a very clear and unequivocal message" to universities that they should "see if there is anything to do [under Title IX] and do it." The opposing lawyer, Maureen Mahoney, a Washington attorney who represented Brown in its high court appeal, told the *Post* that the ruling amounted to "compelled affirmative action" that could provoke "a backlash" against women's athletics.

As the Brown case illustrated, the Court can have an impact on Americans' lives just by doing nothing. The Court declines to hear the vast majority of cases that losing litigants bring to it in hopes of gaining the justices' attention. Sometimes, the Court's decision postpones a legal showdown, perhaps until other courts have had a chance to weigh in on the issue. In other cases, however, the move may signal that an issue is effectively settled. In any event, the justices' decision not to review a case amounts to the last word for the opposing parties.

That point was driven home this term at the highest level of the federal government. First Lady Hillary Rodham Clinton unsuccessfully asked the Court to review her effort to block a grand jury subpoena obtained by independent counsel Kenneth Starr for notes of her conversations with lawyers about matters related to the Whitewater investigation. Mrs. Clinton claimed the notes were protected by attorney-client privilege, but the Eighth U.S. Circuit Court of Appeals in April rejected the plea. The appeals court said there was no lawyer-client privilege between government lawyers and public officials, at least in the context of a federal grand jury investigation.

In urging the Court to take up the case, lawyers for the White House and the Justice Department contended that the ruling infringed on attorney-client privilege and threatened the ability of government officials to confer candidly with government attorneys. Starr countered that the decision recognized both the historic power of grand juries and the obligation of government attorneys to report evidence of wrongdoing. The issue stirred debate among legal ethics experts; it also provoked much speculation about the impact the notes could have on Starr's Whitewater investigation.

The Court's decision not to hear the case—called *Office of the President v. Office of the Independent Counsel*—came as a surprise to many legal observers and a shock to the White House. Some observers speculated the justices might have feared that hearing the case would have the effect of further prolonging the Whitewater investigation, then in its fourth year. Whatever the justices' reasons, their refusal left Mrs. Clinton with no alternative to producing the notes; lawyers turned the notes over to Starr's office that evening.

All told, the Court put a total of 140 cases on its calendar for the 1996–1997 term—midway between the figures of 145 for the previous term and 136 for the 1994–1995 term. Those cases were drawn from a total docket of 7,602 cases—a negligible increase over the previous term's total of 7,565 but below the record level of 8,100 cases in the 1994–1995 term. *(See Figure 3-1.)*

The justices issued eighty signed opinions during the term. That was a slight increase over the previous term's figure of seventy-five signed opinions. However slight, the increase was notable: the number had been falling steadily since Rehnquist became chief justice at the beginning of the 1986–1987 term. *(See Figure 3-1.)*

The drop in the number of opinions had produced much speculation among Court-watchers, who offered various possible explanations. Some said the Court was deliberately lowering its profile or that lower courts were producing opinions more in line with the Court's conservative majority. Some observers also posited that the liberal justices might be reluctant to take up

Figure 3-1   Supreme Court Caseload, 1960 Term–1996 Term

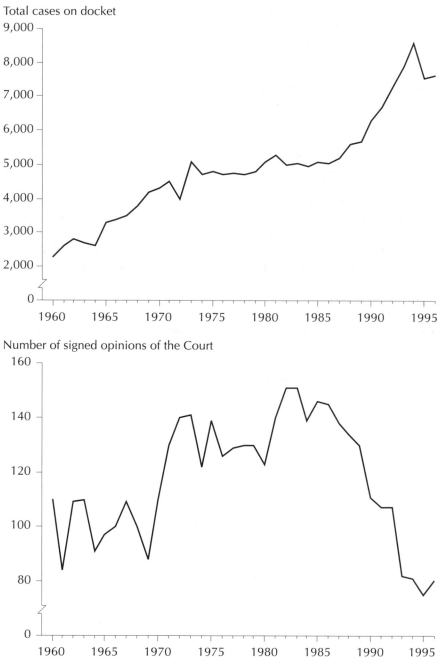

Total cases on docket

Number of signed opinions of the Court

some cases for fear of losing and cementing a precedent unfavorable to their views.

A new theory was offered during the year by a longtime student of the Court. David M. O'Brien, a political scientist at the University of Virginia, said he had found in historical research that the decrease may have been due in part to a fading away of an informal, internal procedure at the Court known as "join 3."

Briefly, the procedure is a modification of the Court's rule requiring the votes of four justices to agree to hear a case. Justices who do not feel strongly about a case may nonetheless accommodate their colleagues by agreeing to cast the fourth vote needed to accept a case.

Although Court scholars have known of the practice, O'Brien shed new light on its relative importance in the Court's overall docket based on the papers of the late Justice Thurgood Marshall. After reviewing Marshall's bench memos for the period 1979–1990, O'Brien said he found that join-3 votes had been cast by justices in 408 out of the 1,556 cases argued—or about 26 percent of the time. In some of those cases, he said, the join-3 votes were not essential. But join-3 votes were needed for 192 cases—or about 12 percent of the total.

The practice "clearly lowered the threshold for granting a case," O'Brien told Tony Mauro, who reported on the research in his "Courtside" column in *Legal Times*. And O'Brien said that the practice appeared to have receded after Marshall's retirement from the Court in 1990. He said that he had been told that Chief Justice Rehnquist and Justice O'Connor might still cast join-3 votes, but that the newer justices did so only very rarely.

For whatever reasons, the justices decided to pass up a host of interesting and important issues during the term. Twice, the justices declined to hear challenges to the military's "don't ask, don't tell" policy on homosexuals. They refused to hear a challenge to a Baltimore ordinance banning billboards for tobacco and alcoholic beverages. They also declined to hear a challenge by anti-abortion protesters to a federal law protecting access to abortion clinics.

Some of the issues were all but certain to return to the Court. For example, another challenge to the military's policy on gays was working its way through federal courts in New York. On other issues, however, the Court's inaction may have been a signal that the justices were content to let lower federal courts handle the issue, at least for the time being.

The Court also issued the unusually high number of nine *per curiam* or unsigned opinions on a summary basis—without hearing oral arguments. The procedure is usually reserved for cases where lower courts made clear errors, and the vote is typically unanimous. This term, six of the nine *per curiam* opinions were unanimous; the justices divided 7–2 in two of the *per curiam* opinions and 6–3 in the other.

Overall, the Court had somewhat more unanimous decisions and somewhat more one-vote decisions than in the previous term. Out of eighty signed opinions, the Court was unanimous in thirty-six—or 45 percent—of the cases; in the 1995–1996 term, 41 percent of the decisions were unanimous. There were seventeen 5–4 decisions—or 21 percent of the total, compared to 17 percent in the previous term. The Court divided 8–1 in six cases (8 percent), 7–2 or 6–2 in ten cases (12 percent), and 6–3 in eleven cases (14 percent). *(See Figure 3-2.)*

Following are case summaries of the eighty signed opinions and nine *per curiam* opinions the Court issued during the 1996–1997 term. They are organized by subject matter: business law, courts and procedure, criminal law and procedure, election law, environmental law, family law, federal government, First Amendment, immigration, individual rights, labor law, property law, states, and torts.

Figure 3-2   Vote Divisions on Cases Decided in 1996–1997 Supreme Court Term

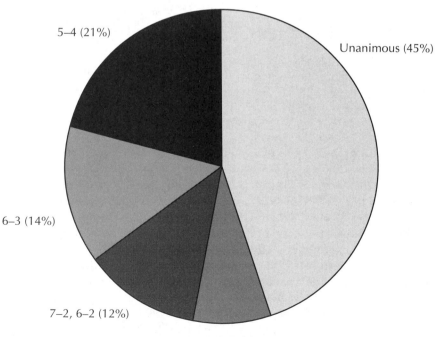

5–4 (21%)

Unanimous (45%)

6–3 (14%)

7–2, 6–2 (12%)

8–1 (8%)

Business Law

Banking

Atherton v. Federal Deposit Insurance Corporation, decided by a 9–0 vote, January 14, 1997; Breyer wrote the opinion.

Federal law sets an intermediate standard of gross negligence for imposing liability in suits against directors or officers of federally chartered banks, but states can adopt a lower standard of simple negligence.

The unanimous ruling—a partial setback for government regulators— came in a suit by the Federal Deposit Insurance Corporation blaming officials of a defunct savings and loan institution in New Jersey for causing its collapse by approval of bad real-estate loans. The government claimed that "federal common law" allowed the officers and directors to be held liable for the thrift's financial losses on proof of ordinary negligence. The defendants maintained that a law passed in 1989 to deal with the savings-and-loan crisis required proof of gross negligence. The Third U.S. Circuit Court of Appeals agreed with the government.

The Court first held that federally chartered banks were not subject to a federal common law standard. Breyer said there was no need for a uniform federal standard to supersede state liability rules. But Breyer said that the federal statute established "a floor" requiring that bank officers and directors "must meet at least a gross negligence standard." States were free, he added, to establish a "stricter standard," such as ordinary negligence. But they could not require proof of intentional or reckless conduct before liability could be imposed.

Research by the attorneys for the bank officials indicated that most states to rule on the issue, including New Jersey, used a gross negligence standard.

Bankruptcy

Associates Commercial Corp. v. Rash, decided by an 8–1 vote, June 16, 1997; Ginsburg wrote the opinion; Stevens dissented.

A debtor in a bankruptcy reorganization who chooses, over a creditor's objections, to keep rather than surrender property that serves as collateral on a loan must pay the creditor the replacement value of the property.

The ruling—a victory for creditors—settled a conflict between federal courts of appeals over what valuation method should be used in a so-called "cramdown" procedure in a bankruptcy reorganization. The procedure allows a debtor, as part of a court-approved reorganization, to retain property over the objections of a secured creditor who has a lien on the property. But the debtor—who "crams the plan down the creditor's throat"—must agree to pay the creditor the value of the property. Some courts ruled that the value of the property was the debtor's cost to replace it; others ruled the value was the lower amount that the creditor could recoup in a foreclosure sale.

In a densely statutory ruling, the Court held that the Bankruptcy Code called for the replacement-value standard. The value of the property, Ginsburg wrote, "is the price a willing buyer in the debtor's trade, business, or situation would pay to obtain like property from a willing seller."

In a lone dissent, Stevens said the statute, while "not entirely clear," appeared to favor a foreclosure-value standard, which he said also "best comports with economic reality."

Maritime Law

Saratoga Fishing Co. v. J.M. Martinac & Co., decided by a 6–3 vote, June 2, 1997; Breyer wrote the opinion; Scalia, O'Connor, and Thomas dissented.

Boat manufacturers may be held liable in product-defect suits for damage to property or equipment added by someone who bought the vessel and then resold it to a second purchaser.

The liability-expanding rule came in a suit brought by a California based tuna-fishing company, Saratoga Fishing Co., against the manufacturer of a boat that sank after an engine room fire in 1986. Saratoga bought the vessel from a second company, which had outfitted the boat with nets and other equipment for tuna-fishing. The original manufacturer, J.M. Martinac & Co., a Washington State concern, sought to limit its liability under the Court's 1986 ruling, *East River S.S. Corp. v. Transamerica Delaval, Inc.* In that decision, the Court held that an admiralty plaintiff cannot recover for the physical damage that a defective product causes to "the product itself" unless covered by a contract warranty. Applying that rule, the Ninth U.S. Circuit Court of Appeals barred Saratoga's recovery from the Martinac company on the ground that the added equipment was part of the ship when the vessel was resold to Saratoga.

By a 6–3 vote, the Court disagreed. "Equipment added to a product after the manufacturer . . . has sold the product to an initial user," Breyer wrote, "is not part of the product itself that has caused the physical harm." Breyer said that barring recovery from the manufacturer for damage to added equipment would reduce the incentive to produce safe products.

In a dissenting opinion, Scalia, joined by Thomas, said the Court should have awaited other lower court rulings on the issue before deciding it. On the merits, Scalia said he favored a different rule that would limit damages to whatever warranty the intermediary outfitter provided to Saratoga. Separately, O'Connor agreed that the Court should have taken up the case but sided with Scalia on the substantive issue.

Patents

Warner-Jenkinson Co., Inc. v. Hilton Davis Chemical Co., decided by a 9–0 vote, March 3, 1997; Thomas wrote the opinion.

The Court reaffirmed but narrowed somewhat a judicially-created doctrine that protects patentholders against inventors who develop products or processes that are similar but not identical.

The unanimous decision rejected arguments that Congress implicitly repealed the so-called doctrine of equivalents when it revised the federal Patent Act in 1952. The doctrine allows a patentholder to win an infringement claim even if a rival product or process is not identical as long as there is "equivalence" between its elements and the elements of the patented invention.

Writing for the Court, Thomas said that Congress could repeal the doctrine, but had not done so in the 1952 law. Thomas said, however, that the doctrine had "taken on a life of its own" in the courts and should not be applied so broadly as to weaken the rule that patents generally are confined to their explicit terms.

The decision sent back for further consideration a dispute between two chemical companies with rival processes for purifying food dyes. The patentholder, Hilton-Davis Chemical Co., had won a jury verdict in its infringement suit by relying on the doctrine of equivalents. The Court instructed the appeals court to re-examine the case in light of its opinion. But the justices declined to rule on one of the issues the two companies had argued: whether the doctrine can be applied only by a judge, not by a jury.

Taxation

Commissioner of Internal Revenue v. Estate of Hubert, decided by a 7–2 vote, March 18, 1997; Kennedy wrote the plurality opinion; Scalia and Breyer dissented.

The Court allowed the administrator of a nearly $30 million estate to avoid taxes on income generated by the legacy that was used to pay expenses of administering the estate.

The ruling rejected the Internal Revenue Service's position on a recurrent issue in wrapping up estates. The federal estate tax allows a deduction for amounts passed to a spouse or charity. Generally, the deduction must be reduced—and the taxable amounts increased—by the value of assets used to pay for wrapping up the estate. The IRS contended that no deduction could be claimed for income generated during administration by assets being passed to a spouse or a charity. Federal appeals courts were divided on the issue.

The Court rejected the IRS's position by a 7–2 vote, but the majority justices reached their decision by slightly different reasoning. In the plurality opinion, Kennedy, joined by Rehnquist, Stevens, and Ginsburg, concluded that the marital or charitable deduction, based on the value of the bequest at the time of the death, already reflected the income-earning potential of the assets.

In an opinion concurring in the judgment, O'Connor, joined by Souter and Thomas, said the regulations appeared to establish a test of "quantitative materiality" for determining the deduction and said the criterion was not met by "the unusual facts in this case." O'Connor added that the "maze of regulations and rulings" on the question was confusing and urged the IRS to "promulgate new regulations and make the issue clear."

In a dissent, Scalia, joined by Breyer, said the ruling "creates a tax boondoggle never contemplated by Congress and announces a test of deductibility virtually impossible for taxpayers and the IRS to apply."

O'Gilvie v. United States, decided by a 6–3 vote, December 10, 1996; Breyer wrote the opinion; Scalia, O'Connor, and Thomas dissented.

People who receive punitive damages in lawsuits must pay federal income taxes on them.

The 6–3 ruling backed the government's interpretation of a federal tax code provision that allows taxpayers to avoid taxation on "any damages received . . . on account of personal injuries or sickness." Federal appeals courts had divided on whether the exclusionary provision applied to punitive damages. The Court agreed to settle the issue in a case involving a $10 million punitive damage award won by the husband and children of a woman who died of toxic shock syndrome.

In the majority opinion, Breyer said punitive damages do not qualify for the exclusion because they are not received "on account of" personal injuries, but "on account of a defendant's reprehensible conduct and the jury's need to punish and deter it." Breyer acknowledged the statute was ambiguous and buttressed his conclusion by citing a variety of sources, including the Court's 1995 ruling in *Commissioner v. Schleier* that damages in age discrimination cases are subject to taxation.

Writing for the dissenters, Scalia said the statutory exemption "unambiguously covers punitive damages that are awarded on account of personal injuries."

United States v. Brockamp, decided by a 9–0 vote, February 18, 1997; Breyer wrote the opinion.

A taxpayer's mental disability cannot, under existing law, excuse a late filing for a refund of overpaid taxes.

The ruling backed the government in seeking to overturn a pair of decisions by the Ninth U.S. Circuit Court of Appeals. In one case, a California woman said her late father overpaid his taxes by $7,000 because of senility; in the other, a taxpayer blamed alcoholism for a late filing. The appeals court allowed both filings under the so-called equitable tolling doctrine, which allows a court to extend statutory time limits for equitable reasons.

Unanimously, the Court held that the equitable tolling doctrine cannot be used to extend the time limit for seeking a tax refund. Breyer said the "highly detailed" deadlines set out in the tax code "indicate to us that Congress did not intend courts to read other unmentioned, open-ended, 'equitable' exceptions into the statute. . . ."

All other federal appeals courts to rule on the issue had rejected similar claims for late-filed refunds. The Clinton administration, aware of the case, asked Congress to allow extensions of time for disabled taxpayers; the proposal was still pending at the end of the summer.

United States v. Jose, decided by a 9–0 vote, December 2, 1996; *per curiam* (unsigned) opinion.

The government can immediately appeal a federal court order limiting the enforcement of an Internal Revenue Service summons issued in a tax investigation.

The unanimous decision allowed the IRS to contest a federal judge's order that the agency's civil investigation branch give a taxpayer five days' notice before transferring any records to the agency's branch for criminal investigations. The Ninth U.S. Circuit Court of Appeals had dismissed the IRS's appeal, saying it was "not ripe for review."

In an unsigned opinion issued without hearing arguments, the Court said the lower court ruling was a final order that could be appealed. "Finality, not ripeness, is the doctrine governing appeals," the Court wrote.

The Court said it was expressing no opinion about the validity of the lower court's restriction on the IRS summons. It noted that two federal appeals courts had upheld such restrictions, while one had ruled that lower courts have no authority to limit IRS summonses.

Courts and Procedure

Appeals

M.L.B. v. S.L.J., decided by a 6–3 vote, December 16, 1996; Ginsburg wrote the opinion; Thomas, Rehnquist, and Scalia dissented.

States cannot prevent someone from appealing a parental termination order solely because of inability to pay for a transcript of the proceeding.

The ruling backed the right of a Mississippi woman, Melissa Brooks, to contest a lower court decision terminating her rights to her two young children. The Mississippi Supreme Court refused to hear her appeal because she could not pay the $2,352.36 needed to prepare the 950-page transcript of the trial and other materials.

In a 6–3 decision, the Court said that denying an appeal in a parental termination proceeding solely because of indigency violated rights to due process and equal protection. " . . . [W]e place decrees forever terminating parental rights in the category of cases in which the State may not 'bolt the door to equal justice,'" Ginsburg wrote, quoting from a 1956 decision that similarly prohibited states from denying an appeal in felony cases because of an inability to pay for a transcript.

Ginsburg followed the 1956 ruling, *Griffin v. Illinois,* in using both the Due Process and Equal Protection Clauses of the Fourteenth Amendment as a basis for the ruling. Four justices joined Ginsburg's opinion. In an opinion concurring in the judgment, Kennedy said he would have based the ruling solely on the Due Process Clause.

In a dissenting opinion, Thomas warned that the ruling would result in "greater demands on the State to provide assistance to would-be appellants in all manner of civil cases. . . ." He called for overruling the 1956 decision and a later decision that extended the same rule to minor criminal cases. Scalia joined all of Thomas's dissent; Rehnquist joined part of the opinion, but not the section calling for overruling the prior decisions.

Caterpillar Inc. v. Lewis, decided by a 9–0 vote, December 10, 1996; Ginsburg wrote the opinion.

A Kentucky construction worker lost a bid to get a new trial in state court despite a federal judge's erroneous interim ruling that his personal injury suit belonged in federal court because of diversity of citizenship.

In a complex civil procedure ruling, the Court ruled that the earlier incorrect ruling did not require setting aside the federal court verdict in the case as long as the requirements for diversity of citizenship jurisdiction existed at the time of trial.

"Once a diversity case has been tried in federal court," Ginsburg wrote in the unanimous opinion, "considerations of finality, efficiency, and economy become overwhelming."

Class Actions

Amchem Products, Inc. v. Windsor, decided by a 6–2 vote, June 25, 1997; Ginsburg wrote the opinion; Breyer and Stevens dissented in part; O'Connor did not participate.

The Court refused to revive a $1.3 billion class-action settlement for hundreds of thousands of asbestos-exposure claims, saying that the proposed class was too big and the issues too disparate to permit class action treatment.

The ruling upheld a decision by the Third U.S. Circuit Court of Appeals on a massive class-action settlement that was negotiated by plaintiffs' lawyers and attorneys for twenty asbestos manufacturers and approved by a lower federal court in Philadelphia. The proposed settlement would have provided specified payments to all individuals who had not yet filed an asbestos-exposure suit but who had been exposed, or their family members exposed, to asbestos through their jobs. In its ruling, the appeals court said the suit did not meet the requirements for certification as a class action under Rule 23 of the Federal Rules of Civil Procedure that "common issues" predominate over other questions and that the named plaintiffs would "adequately represent" the interests of the entire class.

By a 6–2 vote, the Court agreed. Ginsburg began by saying that the appeals court was wrong to disregard the importance of settlement in deciding whether to certify the class action. But she continued by saying that the appeals court's opinion "amply demonstrates why—with or without a settlement on the table—the sprawling class . . . does not satisfy Rule 23's requirements."

In a mostly dissenting opinion, Breyer said he agreed with the majority that settlement is "relevant" to class certification, but faulted Ginsburg for taking a too-critical view of the settlement. " . . . [T]he need for settlement in this mass tort case, with hundreds of thousands of lawsuits, is greater than the Court's opinion suggests," he wrote. Stevens joined the dissent; O'Connor recused herself. *(See story, pp. 62–66; excerpts, pp. 176–190.)*

False Claims

Hughes Aircraft Co. v. United States ex rel. Schumer, decided by a 9–0 vote, June 16, 1997; Thomas wrote the opinion.

The Court refused to give retroactive effect to a law easing the rules for so-called "*qui tam*" actions—suits brought by a private individual to recover money from someone who submitted a false claim to the government.

The ruling limited the effect of a 1986 law designed to make it easier for "whistleblowers" to use the rarely-invoked procedure, which allows a private party to sue on behalf of the government and to share in any recovery. Previously, the law barred a *qui tam* action if the government had any prior information or evidence about the claim; the 1986 amendment allowed a *qui tam* claim as long as the government had not publicly disclosed any information in its possession. The Ninth U.S. Circuit Court of Appeals ruled that the 1986 law applied retroactively to permit a suit brought by a former Hughes Aircraft Co. engineer, who claimed the company defrauded the government between 1982 and 1984 on a cost-plus contract to develop a radar system for a new bomber.

In a unanimous decision, the Court held that the law could not be applied to claims that arose before it was enacted. "Nothing in the 1986 amendment evidences a clear intent by Congress that it be applied retroactively,"

Thomas wrote. The decision left unresolved other issues the company raised to try to narrow the scope of the law.

Criminal Law and Procedure

Appeals

Johnson v. United States, decided by a 9–0 vote, May 12, 1997; Rehnquist wrote the opinion.

A Florida woman convicted of perjury before a federal grand jury during a drug investigation failed to win a new trial despite a jury instruction that was held after trial to be erroneous.

The woman, whose boyfriend was under investigation for cocaine trafficking, was found guilty of lying about the source of around $100,000 she invested in home improvement. Evidence at trial showed that the money came from her boyfriend. In appealing the conviction, the woman sought to take advantage of the Court's 1995 decision, *United States v. Gaudin*, that requires a jury rather than a judge to decide whether a false statement is "material" in perjury cases. But the Eleventh U.S. Circuit Court of Appeals said the error—which the woman did not raise at trial—did not affect "substantial rights" because of the "overwhelming" evidence that the woman's testimony was material to the grand jury probe.

In a unanimous decision, the Court agreed, but on slightly different grounds. Even if the error affected the woman's rights, Rehnquist wrote, no reversal was required because the defect did not result in a "miscarriage of justice."

Capital Punishment

Greene v. Georgia, decided by a 9–0 vote, December 16, 1996; *per curiam* (unsigned) opinion.

State appellate courts need not defer to trial judges' rulings on disqualifying potential jurors in capital punishment cases.

The Court summarily ruled that the Georgia Supreme Court misapplied a 1985 precedent in rejecting a death row inmate's claim that a trial judge improperly excused five potential jurors for expressing reservations about capital punishment.

In its ruling, the Georgia high court cited a 1985 decision, *Wainwright v. Witt*, as requiring appellate courts to defer to trial judges' rulings on the jurors' potential bias. But the Court said the 1985 ruling concerned federal judges' power in habeas corpus cases and did not require state appellate courts to adopt the same limitation in reviewing state cases.

Contempt of Court

Pounders, Judge, Superior Court of California, Los Angeles County v. Watson,
decided by a 7–2 vote, June 27, 1997; *per curiam* (unsigned) opinion; Stevens
and Breyer dissented.

The Court summarily upheld a summary contempt of court citation
against a Los Angeles defense attorney for violating a judge's instruction not
to comment on the sentence her client faced if convicted.

The attorney, Penelope Watson, was held in contempt by Judge William
S. Pounders after asking her client, one of several defendants in a murder
case, whether he faced a possible life sentence. Pounders, who had previously admonished Watson's co-counsel not to raise the issue, summarily held
Watson in contempt. In a federal habeas corpus proceeding, Watson claimed
she was entitled to a separate hearing before being held in contempt. A
federal district court rejected her plea, but the Ninth U.S. Court of Appeals
granted the petition on the ground that her conduct was "not so disruptive
as to justify summary contempt procedure."

Ruling on the case without oral argument, the Court held that a "pattern of repeated violations" is not required for a judge to summarily impose
a contempt of court citation.

In a dissenting opinion, Stevens, joined by Breyer, said that the case
should have been set for argument.

Criminal Offenses

United States v. Lanier, decided by a 9–0 vote, March 31, 1997; Souter
wrote the opinion.

The Court revived the federal prosecution of a former Tennessee judge
for allegedly violating constitutional rights of five women by sexually assaulting them in his chambers.

The ruling reversed a decision by the Sixth U.S. Circuit Court of Appeals to set aside the 1992 conviction of the former judge, David Lanier, who
had been found guilty of sexually assaulting five women on seven separate
occasions. Lanier was charged under a Reconstruction-era civil rights statute known as Section 242 that makes it unlawful for anyone acting "under
color of law" to "willfully" deprive a person of "any rights . . . protected by
the Constitution or laws of the United States." Lanier, a member of a politically influential family, was never charged in state court.

At the federal court trial, the judge instructed the jury that the right to
be free from sexual battery was a right protected by the Constitution for
purposes of the law. In a 6–5 decision reversing the conviction, however, the
appeals court held that the public had no notice that section 242 covered
sexual assault crimes.

In a unanimous but limited decision, the Court held that the appellate court had applied the wrong standard in determining whether the law applied to sexual assault. Souter said the appeals court was wrong to interpret the Court's 1945 decision, *Screws v. United States*, as limiting section 242 to offenses already recognized by the Court itself or "fundamentally similar" conduct. That standard, Souter said, was "unnecessarily high." Instead, he concluded, section 242 could be applied "if, but only if, in the light of pre-existing law the unlawfulness [under the Constitution is] apparent."

The ruling returned the case to the appeals court for evaluation under that standard.

United States v. O'Hagan, decided by 6–3, 7–2, and 9–0 votes, June 25, 1997; Ginsburg wrote the opinion; Thomas, Rehnquist, and Scalia dissented in part.

Federal securities law prohibits someone from using inside information to trade in a company's stock even if the individual does not work for the company or owe it any legal duty.

The ruling upheld the convictions of a Minneapolis lawyer, James O'Hagan, who made $3.4 million in profits by trading in securities of a company that was being taken over by another company that his law firm briefly represented. O'Hagan was convicted of securities fraud, fraudulent trading in connection with a tender offer, and mail fraud. But the Eighth U.S. Circuit Court of Appeals reversed all the convictions.

The appeals court held that in insider trading cases the government could not prosecute someone for "misappropriating" information unless the individual owed a duty of loyalty to the company whose stock was being traded. It also held that the Securities and Exchange Commission had exceeded its statutory authority in prohibiting anyone from trading stock during a tender offer on the basis of nonpublic information. Finally, it reversed the mail fraud counts because they depended on the other charges as the indictment was structured.

The Court reinstated the convictions in a critical victory for the government's expansive theories of insider trading liability. Writing for the majority, Ginsburg said that the government's "misappropriation theory" met the statutory definition of "deceptive" conduct "in connection with" securities transactions because O'Hagan deceived his law firm by using confidential information for securities trading. She said the tender-offer rule was "a proper exercise of the Commission's prophylactic power" to prevent securities fraud. And, on that basis, she said the mail fraud convictions were also valid.

In the main dissent, Thomas, joined by Rehnquist, said he would reverse the convictions for securities fraud and fraudulent tender-offer trading. Thomas said that the misappropriation theory "fails to provide a consistent and coherent" interpretation for imposing liability and agreed with O'Hagan that the tender-offer rule went beyond the SEC's statutory authority. But he voted to uphold the mail-fraud convictions. Separately, Scalia voted to reverse the securities fraud convictions, saying the law could not be expanded beyond cases involving deception of someone involved in buying or selling securities. But Scalia joined the rest of Ginsburg's opinion upholding the other convictions. *(See story, pp. 66–70; excerpts, pp. 190–204.)*

United States v. Wells, decided by an 8–1 vote, February 26, 1997; Souter wrote the opinion; Stevens dissented.

The Court eased the requirements for a conviction under a federal law that prohibits making false statements to a federally insured bank.

In a nearly unanimous decision, the Court held that the statute does not require prosecutors to prove that a false statement was a "material" factor in inducing a bank to make a loan. Souter said that by its text the statute applied to "any" false statement, with no requirement for what he termed "influential significance."

The decision vacated a ruling by the Eighth U.S. Circuit Court of Appeals reversing the convictions of two Missouri men for making false statements in connection with business loans. Most federal courts to rule on the issue had interpreted the statute to include a materiality requirement. Stevens, in a lone dissent, complained the ruling would allow convictions for "immaterial falsehoods."

Evidence

Old Chief v. United States, decided by a 5–4 vote, January 7, 1997; Souter wrote the opinion; O'Connor, Rehnquist, Scalia, and Thomas dissented.

A defendant charged under a law prohibiting possession of a firearm by a felon may prevent the government from offering specific evidence about his previous offense by stipulating to his prior conviction.

The ruling upheld an argument by a defendant, Johnny Lynn Old Chief, convicted under the firearm possession statute in connection with what the Court called "a fracas involving at least one gunshot." Before trial, Old Chief offered to stipulate that he had previously been convicted of a felony included in the statute. But the judge allowed the government to introduce the record of the conviction, which showed Old Chief had been found guilty of assault and given a five-year prison sentence.

In a closely divided decision, the Court ruled the judge had abused his discretion by allowing the government to introduce the evidence over the defendant's objection. Souter said that even though the nature of Old Chief's prior conviction was "relevant," it created a "risk of unfair prejudice."

Writing for the dissenters, O'Connor said, "I cannot agree that it 'unfairly' prejudices a defendant for the Government to prove his prior conviction with evidence that reveals the name or basic nature of his past crime."

Guilty Pleas

United States v. Hyde, decided by a 9–0 vote, May 27, 1997; Rehnquist wrote the opinion.

A defendant has no absolute right to withdraw a guilty plea after a judge has accepted the plea but before the judge approves a plea agreement between the defense and prosecution.

The ruling backed the government in reinstating a guilty plea by a California man facing a maximum thirty-year prison sentence for several fraud counts. The defendant pleaded guilty in open court, but sought to withdraw the plea before the judge accepted the plea bargain—in which the government promised to take no position on a specific sentence. The judge refused to allow the defendant to withdraw the plea. But the Ninth U.S. Circuit Court of Appeals said he could withdraw the plea because it was "inextricably bound together" with the plea agreement.

In a unanimous opinion, the Court said the appeals court was wrong. "Guilty pleas can be accepted while plea agreements are deferred," Rehnquist wrote, pointing to a provision in the Federal Rules of Criminal Procedure, "and the acceptance of the two can be separated in time." The appeals court's holding, Rehnquist added, "would degrade the otherwise serious act of pleading guilty into something akin to a move in a game of chess."

Habeas Corpus

Bracy v. Gramley, Warden, decided by a 9–0 vote, June 9, 1997; Rehnquist wrote the opinion.

A convicted triple murderer in Illinois was given a chance to prove that he should have a new trial because of alleged bias by the corrupt judge who presided over his trial.

The inmate, William Bracy, was convicted of an execution-style triple murder in a trial before then-Judge Thomas J. Maloney. Maloney himself was convicted of taking bribes as a result of a federal investigation of judicial corruption in state courts in Chicago. Bracy contended in his federal habeas corpus petition that Maloney displayed bias against him in his trial in order to deflect suspicion about his handling of two other murder cases in which the judge had shown favoritism toward defendants in exchange for bribes. A federal district court judge and the Seventh U.S. Circuit Court of Appeals both denied Maloney a chance to gather evidence to support his claim.

In a unanimous decision, the Court held that Bracy had made a sufficient factual showing to establish "good cause" for discovery as required by federal rules governing habeas corpus cases. Rehnquist described Maloney as "thoroughly steeped in corruption," but also stressed that Bracy had pointed to specific evidence indicating that the judge was "actually biased" against him in his own case.

California v. Roy, decided by a 9–0 vote, November 4, 1996; *per curiam* (unsigned) opinion.

Federal courts hearing habeas corpus challenges by state inmates should apply a relaxed standard in determining whether an error at trial is "harmless" and does not require a new trial.

The unanimous decision reversed a decision by the Ninth U.S. Circuit Court of Appeals granting a new trial to a California inmate convicted of robbery and first-degree murder. The inmate's habeas corpus petition complained of an erroneous jury instruction at his trial. The federal district court ruled the error was harmless, but the Ninth U.S. Circuit Court of Appeals said the mistake could not be excused unless the jury would "necessarily" have reached the same verdict with the correct instruction.

In an unsigned opinion issued without hearing argument, the Court said the appeals court should have used a less strict test: whether the error had a "substantial and injurious effect" on the jury's verdict.

Lambrix v. Singletary, Secretary, Florida Department of Corrections, decided by a 5–4 vote, May 12, 1997; Scalia wrote the opinion; Stevens, O'Connor, Ginsburg, and Breyer dissented.

The Court said an earlier decision regarding defective jury instructions in capital sentencing procedures could not be applied retroactively in federal habeas corpus cases.

The earlier decision, *Espinosa v. Florida* (1992), held that a defective jury instruction taints a judge's decision to impose the death penalty in states where the judge is required to give great weight to the jury's recommendation. A Florida death row inmate convicted in a 1983 murder sought to use the new ruling to gain a new trial. But the Eleventh U.S. Circuit Court of Appeals said the ruling should not be applied retroactively.

In a 5–4 decision, the Court agreed. Scalia said that *Espinosa* announced a "new rule of law" that, under the Court's 1989 decision *Teague v. Lane*, was not to be applied retroactively.

Writing for the dissenters, Stevens said "there was nothing new about *Espinosa*'s holding that the jury plays a central role in Florida's capital sentencing scheme."

Lindh v. Murphy, Warden, decided by a 5–4 vote, June 23, 1997; Souter wrote the opinion; Rehnquist, Scalia, Kennedy, and Thomas dissented.

Newly enacted provisions limiting state inmates' ability to challenge their convictions in federal court do not apply to cases pending when the law went into effect.

The ruling limited the scope of the Antiterrorism and Effective Death Penalty Act of 1996, which contained a variety of new restrictions on federal habeas corpus petitions in capital and noncapital cases. The law specified that some provisions were to apply to pending capital cases, but was silent on whether the rest of the law was retroactive. Federal appeals courts split on the issue. The Court agreed to resolve the conflict in a ruling by the Seventh U.S. Circuit Court of Appeals. The appeals court applied one of the law's provisions—barring consideration of claims not ruled on in state courts—to reject a habeas petition by a Wisconsin inmate convicted of noncapital murder.

By a 5–4 vote, the Court held the law did not apply to the "general run" of cases pending when it took effect. "The statute reveals Congress's intent to apply the amendments . . . only to such cases as were filed after the statute's enactments," Souter wrote.

Writing for the dissenters, Rehnquist said the Court's precedents "strongly suggest that, absent congressional direction otherwise, we should apply [the provision] to pending cases."

O'Dell v. Netherland, Warden, decided by a 5–4 vote, June 19, 1997; Thomas wrote the opinion; Stevens, Souter, Ginsburg, and Breyer dissented.

The Court limited the ability of death row inmates to invalidate their sentences through federal habeas corpus petitions by invoking a 1995 decision regarding jury instructions in capital cases.

The ruling rejected the habeas corpus petition of a Virginia man, Joseph O'Dell, sentenced to death for a 1985 rape-murder. O'Dell sought a new sentencing hearing on the basis of the Court's 1995 decision, *Simmons v. South Carolina*, which required judges in some capital cases to tell jurors about the option of sentencing a defendant to life imprisonment without possibility of parole. The Fourth U.S. Circuit Court of Appeals rejected the petition, ruling that *Simmons* was a "new" rule that could not be used by defendants convicted before the decision.

By a 5–4 vote, the Court agreed. Thomas reviewed precedents existing at the time of O'Dell's sentencing, in 1988, and concluded that a "reasonable" judge would not have anticipated the ruling in *Simmons* requiring jurors to be told about the life-without-parole sentencing option. He also rejected O'Dell's argument that he was entitled to an exception to the bar against invoking new rulings in habeas corpus cases because the rule had a fundamental effect on the fairness of the proceeding.

Writing for the four dissenters, Stevens contended that *Simmons* "applied a fundamental principle that is as old as the adversary system itself." He also said the ruling had been "quite clearly articulated" by the Court in two earlier opinions.

Prisons and Jails

Lynce v. Mathis, Superintendent, Tomoka Correctional Institution, decided by a 9–0 vote, February 19, 1997; Stevens wrote the opinion.

A Florida law retroactively canceling early release credits awarded inmates to alleviate prison overcrowding violated the Constitution's Ex Post Facto Clause.

The ruling reinstated a habeas corpus petition filed by a Florida man sentenced in 1986 to twenty-two years for attempted murder but released in 1992 on the basis of "early release credits" aimed at easing overcrowding in the state's prisons. Authorities rearrested the man under a 1992 law that retroactively nullified the credits for inmates sentenced for murder or attempted murder. Two lower federal courts rejected the inmate's habeas corpus petition aimed at winning his release.

In a unanimous decision, the Court said the action violated the Ex Post Facto Clause, which prohibits some governmental actions that have retroactive effects. Stevens said that the Florida law "disadvantaged" the inmate and that the state legislature's original motivation for awarding the early release credit was "not relevant" to his claim.

In a partial concurring opinion, Thomas, joined by Scalia, said the ruling applied only to credits "already earned and used," not to the availability of future release credits.

Young v. Harper, decided by a 9–0 vote, March 18, 1997; Thomas wrote the opinion.

An Oklahoma inmate released under a "preparole" program aimed at relieving prison overcrowding had a due process right to a hearing before being reincarcerated.

The decision upheld a ruling by the Tenth U.S. Circuit Court of Appeals granting a habeas corpus petition filed by inmate Ernest Harper, who had been released under the overcrowding relief plan in 1990 after serving fifteen years of a life sentence for two murders. Harper claimed that the state violated his due process rights by reincarcerating him without a hearing five months after the governor denied his application for normal parole.

In a unanimous opinion, Thomas said Harper's case was governed by the Court's 1972 decision, *Morrissey v. Brewer*, requiring a hearing in parole matters. Rejecting Oklahoma's argument that the early-release plan did not require a hearing because it was comparable to a transfer between different prisons, Thomas said the program "differed from parole in name alone."

Search and Seizure

Maryland v. Wilson, decided by a 7–2 vote, February 19, 1997; Rehnquist wrote the opinion; Stevens and Kennedy dissented.

When making a traffic stop, police may order a passenger as well as the driver to get out of the car pending completion of the stop.

The decision extended the Court's 1977 ruling, *Pennsylvania v. Mimms*, that allowed police to order a driver out of an automobile in order to protect the officer's safety. Maryland courts, ruling in a case where police found a quantity of drugs after ordering a passenger to exit, said the same rule did not apply to passengers.

In a 7–2 decision, the Court disagreed. Rehnquist said that passengers as well as drivers could be "possible sources of harm to the officer" during a traffic stop. Rehnquist acknowledged that the passenger's liberty interest is greater because the passenger is not responsible for the traffic offense. But he said ordering the passenger out of the car would prevent access to any weapons inside and "as a practical matter" was a minimal intrusion since "the passengers are already stopped by virtue of the stop of the vehicle."

In a dissent, Stevens said the ruling expanded "the power of the State to make an initial seizure of persons who are not even suspected of having violated the law." Kennedy joined Stevens's opinion and wrote a brief separate dissent, saying the decision "puts tens of millions of passengers at risk of arbitrary control by the police."

Ohio v. Robinette, decided by an 8–1 vote, November 18, 1996; Rehnquist wrote the opinion; Stevens dissented in part.

The Fourth Amendment does not require police in a routine traffic stop to tell a motorist he is free to go before asking permission to search his vehicle.

The decision set aside a ruling by the Ohio Supreme Court that relied on both the state and federal constitutions in imposing the so-called "first-tell-then-ask" rule. The court's ruling had set aside the drug conviction of a motorist, Robert Robinette. A deputy sheriff had stopped Robinette for speeding and, after writing a citation, asked for permission to search his car. The search yielded a quantity of marijuana.

In reversing the Ohio court, the Court said that the deputy's actions did not violate the Fourth Amendment's prohibition against "unreasonable" searches. Rehnquist said it would be "unrealistic to require police officers to always inform detainees that they are free to go before a consent to search may be deemed voluntary."

All of the justices agreed on the holding, but in an opinion concurring in the judgment Ginsburg stressed that the Ohio court could adopt the rule again if it was based solely on the state constitution. In a partial dissent, Stevens said the Ohio court properly set aside the conviction on the ground that Robinette was being unlawfully detained after the officer finished writing the ticket.

Richards v. Wisconsin, decided by a 9–0 vote, April 28, 1997; Stevens wrote the opinion.

The Court refused to allow a blanket exception for drug cases to its general rule requiring police to knock and announce their identity before executing a search warrant at a residence.

The ruling said the Wisconsin Supreme Court was wrong to carve out a broad exception to the Court's 1995 decision limiting no-knock searches, *Wilson v. Arkansas*. The Wisconsin court said the interests of protecting officers' safety and preventing the destruction of evidence justified no-knock searches in felony drug cases.

In a unanimous and fairly brief decision, the Court rejected the drug-case exception. Stevens said the Wisconsin court's decision was based on "considerable overgeneralization." In addition, he said, if categorical exceptions were allowed, the general knock-and-announce rule "would be meaningless."

The Court nonetheless upheld the conviction challenged in the case, holding that police had adequate grounds for their unannounced entry into a motel room occupied by a suspected drug dealer. And in a significant footnote, Stevens said police could "exercise their independent judgment" in deciding whether a no-knock search was justified even if the magistrate who issued the search warrant refused to authorize one.

Sentencing

United States v. Gonzales, decided by a 7–2 vote, March 3, 1997; O'Connor wrote the opinion; Stevens and Breyer dissented.

The mandatory five-year federal sentence for using a gun in connection with a drug-related crime must be served after rather than at the same time as any state prison term.

The 7–2 decision reversed a ruling by the Tenth U.S. Circuit Court of Appeals, which—alone among federal appeals courts to rule on the issue—said federal judges could order the gun-related enhancement to run simultaneously with a state sentence.

Writing for the majority, O'Connor said the federal statute's provision prohibiting the gun-related sentence from running concurrently with "any other term of imprisonment" applied both to state or federal sentences. "Congress did not add any language limiting the breadth of [the word 'any'], and so we must read [the section] as referring to all 'term[s] of imprisonment,' including those imposed by state courts," she wrote.

The dissenting justices argued that the section applied only to other federal sentences, not to state terms.

United States v. LaBonte, decided by a 6–3 vote, May 27, 1997; Thomas wrote the opinion; Breyer, Stevens, and Ginsburg dissented.

The Court required the federal Sentencing Commission to increase the maximum possible sentences for repeat drug or violent crime offenders.

The ruling backed the government's plea to throw out a Sentencing Commission guideline interpreting a statutory provision requiring sentences for a third drug or violent felony to be set "at or near the maximum term authorized." The commission guideline prescribed sentences based on the penalties for the underlying offenses without regard to sentence enhancements provided for repeat offenders. The First U.S. Circuit Court of Appeals, ruling in three consolidated cases involving repeat drug offenders, upheld the commission's rule.

In a unanimous decision, the Court held the guideline was inconsistent with "the plain and unambiguous language" of the sentencing law. "Congress surely did not establish enhanced penalties for repeat offenders," Thomas wrote, "only to have the Commission render them a virtual nullity."

Writing for the dissenters, Breyer said the statutory language was "ambiguous" and the commission's guideline "a permissible construction of the language." Before joining the Court, Breyer helped write the law setting up the Sentencing Commission and served as one of its original members.

United States v. Watts, decided by a 7–2 vote, January 6, 1997; *per curiam* (unsigned) opinion; Stevens and Kennedy dissented.

A federal judge, in sentencing a defendant, may consider charges of which the defendant has been acquitted if the prosecution proves the defendant probably committed the offenses.

The ruling, issued without hearing argument, reversed decisions by separate panels of the Ninth U.S. Circuit Court of Appeals in two drug cases. In one case, a federal judge in Hawaii gave a maximum, thirty-three-month sentence to a defendant, Cheryl Putra, who had been convicted of selling one ounce of cocaine but acquitted of a separate five-ounce sale on the same day. In the other case, a judge in Los Angeles extended Vernon Watts's eighteen-year sentence by about four years after Watts was convicted on drug dealing charges but acquitted of using a gun during the transaction. In both cases, appellate panels said judges could not consider offenses that juries had rejected by returning acquittals on those counts.

In its unsigned decision, the Court said the "blanket prohibition" imposed by the appellate rulings ignored "the broad discretion" allowed to sentencing courts in considering information about a defendant and the lower standard of proof for the prosecution in introducing such information. "We therefore hold," the Court wrote, "that a jury's verdict of acquittal does not prevent the sentencing court from considering conduct underlying the acquitted charge, so long as that conduct has been proved by a preponderance of the evidence."

Scalia and Breyer wrote separate concurrences, disagreeing whether the Sentencing Commission had the power to change the ruling: Breyer said yes, Scalia said no.

In separate dissents, Stevens disagreed with the holding, Kennedy with the summary procedure. Stevens said it was "repugnant" to hold that "a charge that cannot be sustained by proof beyond a reasonable doubt may give rise to the same punishment as if it had been proved." Kennedy said that the ruling "raises concerns about undercutting the verdict of acquittal" and that the case should have been scheduled for full argument.

Sexual Offenders

Kansas v. Hendricks, decided by a 5–4 vote, June 23, 1997; Thomas wrote the opinion; Breyer, Stevens, Souter, and Ginsburg dissented.

States can confine violent sexual predators in mental institutions after they complete their prison sentences without violating their rights.

The ruling upheld a 1994 Kansas law establishing a civil commitment procedure for anyone who had been convicted of or charged with a sexually violent offense and who suffers from "a mental abnormality or personality disorder" that makes the person "likely to engage" in similar acts in the future. The law was challenged by Leroy Hendricks, a recidivist pedophile, who was ordered held in a mental hospital in 1994 after completing a prison term of about ten years for "indecent liberties" with two young boys. The Kansas Supreme Court ruled the law violated substantive due process on the ground that a "mental abnormality" did not constitute a "mental illness" permitting civil commitment. The state asked the Court to review the conviction. Hendricks then also asked the Court to review two questions that the Kansas court did not reach: whether the law violated the constitutional prohibitions against successive punishments or retroactive punishment.

The Court rejected Hendricks's due process claim by a nearly unanimous vote but divided 5–4 on the retroactive punishment issue. Writing for the majority, Thomas said the requirement to find "future dangerousness" based on a "mental abnormality" or "personality disorder" was "consistent with" other civil commitment laws upheld in the past. He also concluded that the law was civil, not criminal, based on a number of factors. He cited the law's disavowal of "any punitive intent," procedural safeguards, segregation of offenders from general prison population, availability of treatment "if possible," and "immediate release" upon a showing that the individual was no longer dangerous or mentally impaired. On that basis, he said the law did not violate the Double Jeopardy Clause's prohibition against successive punishments or the Ex Post Facto Clause's ban on retroactive punishment.

In a brief concurrence, Kennedy cautioned against allowing a civil commitment procedure to become "a mechanism for retribution or general deterrence."

In a limited dissent, Breyer also found that the law satisfied due process requirements, but concluded that Hendricks's confinement amounted to unconstitutional retroactive punishment. Citing the lack of evidence of treatment for Hendricks, Breyer said the confinement was "basically punitive" and violated the Ex Post Facto Clause because the law "changed the legal consequences that attached to Hendricks's earlier crimes." Stevens and Souter joined all of Breyer's opinion; Ginsburg joined only the retroactive punishment section, but did not write separately to explain her views on the due process claim. *(See story, pp. 58–61; excerpts, pp. 204–215.)*

Election Law

Ballot Access

Timmons, Acting Director, Ramsey County Department of Property Records and Revenue v. Twin Cities Area New Party, decided by a 6–3 vote, April 28, 1997; Rehnquist wrote the opinion; Stevens, Souter, and Ginsburg dissented.

States may enact laws prohibiting candidates from being listed on the ballot by more than one political party.

The ruling rejected a challenge by a minor party to a Minnesota law comparable to so-called anti-fusion statutes enacted in about forty states. The Twin Cities Area New Party challenged the law after election officials in 1994 rejected its petition to list as its candidate for state legislature an incumbent representative also running as the Democratic-Farmer-Labor Party's candidate. The party challenged the law as an unconstitutional infringement of its rights of political association under the First Amendment. A federal district court judge rejected the challenge, but the Eighth U.S. Circuit Court of Appeals agreed with the party that the law was invalid.

In a 6–3 decision, the Court held that the law did not violate the First Amendment. Rehnquist said that the burdens imposed on the party's associational rights were "not severe" and were justified by the "weighty valid state interests in ballot integrity and political stability."

In a dissenting opinion, Stevens said the state's claimed interests in preventing voter confusion, ballot manipulation, and intraparty factionalism were unconvincing. He also rejected the majority's argument that the law was needed to protect the two-party system. Ginsburg joined Stevens's opinion; Souter joined most of the opinion, but left open the question whether fusion laws could be justified to protect the two-party system.

Redistricting and Reapportionment

Abrams v. Johnson, decided by a 5–4 vote, June 19, 1997; Kennedy wrote the opinion; Breyer, Stevens, Souter, and Ginsburg dissented.

The Court upheld a lower court's decision to adopt a congressional redistricting plan for Georgia that created only one majority-black district.

The ruling was the Court's second decision on redistricting plans adopted after Georgia gained a congressional seat as a result of the 1990 census. In the first ruling, *Miller v. Johnson* (1995), the Court struck down a plan with three majority-black districts. *(See* Supreme Court Yearbook, 1994–1995, *pp. 32–36.)* After the Georgia legislature could not agree on a new plan, the three-judge federal district court drew its own map with one majority-black district. A group of black voters and the Justice Department, which had backed plans with two majority-black districts, appealed the ruling. They argued that the court improperly failed to follow policies of the state legislature and that the court-ordered plan violated the federal Voting Rights Act by "diluting" the voting strength of minority voters.

By the same 5–4 vote as in its first ruling in the case, the Court upheld the court-drawn redistricting. Writing for the majority, Kennedy said that the lower court "acted well within its discretion in deciding it could not draw two majority-black districts without engaging in racial gerrymandering." He also rejected the Voting Rights Act challenge, saying that black voters were not "sufficiently compact" to require creation of a second majority-black district.

Writing for the dissenters, Breyer said the court-ordered plan "departs dramatically from the Georgia Legislature's preference" for two majority-black districts. He said the ruling would "unreasonably restrict legislators' use of race" in drawing district lines and increase the risk of "judicial entanglement" in the redistricting process.

Lawyer v. Department of Justice, decided by a 5–4 vote, June 25, 1997; Souter wrote the opinion; Scalia, O'Connor, Kennedy, and Thomas dissented.

The Court upheld a lower federal court's decision to approve a redrawn Florida legislative district without first ruling the original districting plan unconstitutional or allowing the legislature itself to revise the plan.

The ruling left in place a state senatorial district with about a 36 percent black voting-age population that included predominantly black parts of Tampa and St. Petersburg. An earlier plan drawn by the Florida Supreme Court created a district with about a 45 percent black voting-age population that stretched into parts of two neighboring counties. White voters filed a federal court suit challenging that plan under the Court's decisions limiting racially motivated redistricting. The revised plan was drawn up in settlement negotiations, approved by lawyers for each chamber of the Florida legislature and the state's attorney general, and then ordered adopted by the lower court. But one white voter among the original plaintiffs challenged the redrawn district as racially motivated and the court's procedure in adopting it.

By a 5–4 vote, the Court held that the lower court was not required to rule on the constitutionality of the original plan or to give the full legislature an opportunity to redraw the district map before implementing its own plan. Souter said that the state "had selected its opportunity by entering into the settlement agreement" and that there were "no reasons . . . to burden its exercise of choice by requiring a formal adjudication of unconstitutionality." Souter also said the redrawn district was constitutional because traditional districting principles had not been improperly subordinated to considerations of race.

Writing for the four dissenters, Scalia called the ruling an "unprecedented intrusion upon state sovereignty" because the lower court never ruled the challenged plan invalid and never gave the legislature an opportunity to "remedy whatever unconstitutional features it contained."

Voting Rights

Foreman v. Dallas County, Texas, decided by a 9–0 vote, June 27, 1997; *per curiam* (unsigned) opinion.

The Court summarily ordered additional proceedings to determine whether Dallas County should have sought Justice Department approval under the Voting Rights Act to change its method of appointing election precinct judges.

The decision set aside a ruling by a three-judge court that the Voting Rights Act's preclearance requirement did not apply to a move by the County Commission in 1996 to appoint only Republicans as election judges. African-American and Hispanic voters who had previously served as election judges filed suit challenging the move, but the county argued the changes were "discretionary" and not covered by the federal law.

In an unsigned opinion issued without hearing oral argument, the Court said the ruling was inconsistent with its precedents requiring preclearance for "informal as well as formal changes." The decision returned the case for further evidence on the method of appointing electing judges as of 1972, when Texas became subject to the Voting Rights Act.

Lopez v. Monterey County, California, decided by a 9–0 vote, November 6, 1996; O'Connor wrote the opinion.

A federal court may not order a change in voting procedure in a jurisdiction covered by the Voting Rights Act's requirement to preclear such changes with either the Justice Department or the federal district court in Washington.

The unanimous ruling reversed a decision by a three-judge federal court to put into effect for a 1995 election a racially-drawn districting plan for municipal courts in Monterey County, California. The county crafted the plan as an interim solution to a suit by Latino residents. They claimed that the creation of a countywide municipal court many years earlier should have been precleared under the Voting Rights Act because it reduced Latinos' voting strength.

Writing for the Court, O'Connor said the lower court was wrong to circumvent the preclearance provision. Congress sought to prevent voting rights discrimination, she said, "by giving exclusive authority to pass on the discriminatory effect or purpose of an election to the Attorney General and to the District Court for the District of Columbia."

The ruling left unsettled the underlying issues in the case: whether the court consolidation did violate the Voting Rights Act and, if so, whether the county's decision to create Latino majorities in three out of four judicial districts was consistent with the Court's recent rulings limiting the use of race in drawing district lines.

Reno, Attorney General v. Bossier Parish School Board, decided by a 7–2 vote, May 12, 1997; O'Connor wrote the opinion; Stevens and Souter dissented in part.

The Court limited the impact of the federal Voting Rights Act provision requiring localities with a history of discrimination to obtain prior approval before making any change in voting practices or procedures.

By a 7–2 vote, the Court held that a locality can be denied preclearance under section 5 of the act only if the proposed change leaves minority group voters worse off in voting rights. Preclearance cannot be denied, O'Connor wrote for the majority, solely because the new electoral procedure violates a broader Voting Rights Act provision—section 2—that prohibits "dilution" of minority groups' voting strength.

The complex ruling came in a dispute over redistricting school board seats in Bossier Parish, Louisiana, following the 1990 census. The parish's governing body adopted a school board districting plan that—like the previous lines—included no majority-black districts. After the local NAACP challenged the plan on grounds it violated section 2 of the Voting Rights Act, Attorney General Janet Reno refused to preclear the plan under section 5. In a split ruling, however, a three-judge federal district court in Washington ruled that Reno was wrong to deny preclearance and that evidence of "vote dilution" could not be considered in a section 5 case.

In her opinion, O'Connor said section 5 was "designed to combat only those effects that are retrogressive." But she also said the evidence of vote dilution "may be relevant to establish a jurisdiction's intent to retrogress." On that basis, she said, the case should be returned to the lower court for further consideration.

Four justices agreed with O'Connor's opinion in full. In a partial concurrence, Breyer, joined by Ginsburg, argued the Court should also have held that preclearance could be denied if a jurisdiction intentionally diluted minority voting strength.

In a dissenting opinion, Stevens, joined by Souter, agreed on remanding the case, but disagreed with the limits on preclearance. The majority's ruling, Stevens wrote, "would allow the Attorney General of the United States to place her stamp of approval on a state action that is in clear violation of federal law."

Young v. Fordice, Governor of Mississippi, decided by a 9–0 vote, March 31, 1997; Breyer wrote the opinion.

Mississippi was required under the Voting Rights Act to obtain prior approval for its decision to adopt a simplified voting registration system for federal elections but not for state and local balloting.

The state acted in response to the 1993 National Voter Registration Act—the so-called motor voter law—which required states to adopt a variety of steps to make it easier for people to register to vote. Mississippi election officials adopted new registration procedures, but the Mississippi legislature killed a bill to recognize the simplified registration for state and local elections. A group of voters and the U.S. Justice Department then sued the state on the ground that it should have obtained preclearance for the move under the 1965 Voting Rights Act. But a three-judge federal district court said that the state had obtained preclearance for the federal procedures and that preclearance was not required to leave existing state procedures in place.

In a unanimous decision, the Court disagreed. The dual system, Breyer wrote, "contains numerous examples of new, significantly different administrative practices . . . the kind of discretionary, nonministerial changes that call for federal [Voting Rights Act] review."

Environmental Law

Endangered Species

Bennett v. Spear, decided by a 9–0 vote, March 19, 1997; Scalia wrote the opinion.

The Endangered Species Act allows any person, not just environmentalists, to go to court to challenge regulatory actions not only for underenforcement of the law but also for overenforcement.

The decision reinstated a suit by two Oregon ranchers and a pair of irrigation districts contesting an action by the U.S. Fish and Wildlife Service to list as endangered two species of fish found in federally operated reservoirs along the California-Oregon border. They contended that the action led the Bureau of Reclamation, which manages the reservoirs, to reduce private water allotments in one year by about 80 percent. But the Ninth U.S. Circuit Court of Appeals upheld a lower court's dismissal of the suit, saying the plaintiffs were outside the "zone of interests" protected by the 1973 species protection law.

In a unanimous opinion, the Court held the law's provision allowing "any person" to bring suit to require compliance with the law gave the plaintiffs legal standing to go to court. " . . . [T]here is no textual basis for saying that [the act's] expansion of standing requirements applies to environmentalists alone," Scalia wrote. The ruling also said the plaintiffs could challenge enforcement of the law under the Administrative Procedure Act, which imposes procedural requirements before any "final agency action" can be taken.

Family Law

Child Support Enforcement

Blessing, Director, Arizona Department of Economic Security v. Freestone, decided by a 9–0 vote, April 21, 1997; O'Connor wrote the opinion.

The Court barred a broad class-action suit aimed at forcing Arizona to improve its compliance with a federal child-support enforcement law. But it returned the case to lower federal courts to consider the validity of more limited claims.

The ruling came in a federal civil rights suit filed by five Arizona mothers who claimed the state was violating their rights by failing to collect child support owed them by out-of-state fathers. A federal law, Title IV-D of the Social Security Act, required states to establish a jointly funded child support enforcement program. The Secretary of Health and Human Services was allowed to reduce federal funding if a state did not "substantially comply" with the provisions of the law.

A federal district court judge dismissed the women's suit, ruling that the law did not create individual rights enforceable in federal court. But the Ninth U.S. Circuit Court of Appeals disagreed and reinstated the suit.

In a unanimous opinion, the Court held that the law does not give individuals a federal right to force a state to substantially comply with its provisions. "Far from creating an *individual* entitlement to services," O'Connor wrote, "the standard is simply a yardstick for the Secretary to measure the *systemwide* performance of a State's Title IV-D program." But O'Connor said some provisions of the law might be specific enough to create rights enforceable in federal court.

In a concurring opinion, Scalia, joined by Kennedy, said he would leave open the possibility of barring any suits by mothers to enforce the law.

Federal Government

Federal Regulation

Dunn v. Commodity Futures Trading Commission, decided by a 9–0 vote, February 25, 1997; Stevens wrote the opinion.

The Commodity Futures Trading Commission has no authority to regulate over-the-counter trading in options to buy or sell foreign currency.

The unanimous decision interpreted a provision of a 1974 law that generally expanded the agency's regulatory authority but exempted from its jurisdiction any "transactions in foreign currency." Two lower federal courts, ruling in an enforcement action brought by the agency against a foreign currency trader and three trading firms, held that the exemption did not apply to options trading.

Writing for the Court, Stevens said it was "plain that foreign currency options are 'transactions in foreign currency' within the meaning of the statute."

Glickman, Secretary of Agriculture v. Wileman Brothers & Elliott, Inc., decided by a 5–4 vote, June 25, 1997; Stevens wrote the opinion; Souter, Rehnquist, Scalia, and Thomas dissented.

The federal government can require agricultural producers to pay the costs of industrywide generic advertising programs without violating the First Amendment's protections for freedom of speech.

The ruling upheld a generic advertising program for California peaches, plums, and nectarines approved by a majority of growers under the authority of a New Deal–era law, the federal Agricultural Marketing Agreement Act. A number of fruit growers, processors, and handlers challenged the marketing agreement on a variety of grounds, including a First Amendment claim that the scheme violated their rights to be free from "compelled speech." The Ninth U.S. Circuit Court of Appeals agreed that the plan violated the First Amendment.

In a closely divided ruling, the Court disagreed and upheld the generic advertising program. Stevens said the marketing orders did not warrant heightened First Amendment scrutiny because they "impose no restraint on the freedom of any producer to communicate any message to any audience," "do not compel any person to engage in any actual or symbolic speech," and "do not compel the producers to endorse or to finance any political or ideological views." On that basis, he said the arrangement was "a species of economic regulation" entitled to "the same strong presumption of validity that we accord to other policy judgments made by Congress."

In a dissenting opinion, Souter said the scheme amounted to "coerced subsidies for speech" and could not be justified under the Court's three-part test for judging restrictions on commercial speech. He said the generic advertising did not relate to a substantial governmental interest, did not directly advance that interest, and was not narrowly tailored. Rehnquist and Scalia joined all of Souter's opinion; Thomas joined most of the opinion, but said he would use a stricter test to determine the validity of the program.

Printz, Sheriff/Coroner, Ravalli County, Montana v. United States, decided by a 5–4 vote, June 27, 1997; Scalia wrote the opinion; Stevens, Souter, Ginsburg, and Breyer dissented.

The federal government cannot require state or local law enforcement officials to conduct background checks on prospective gun purchasers.

The ruling—an important victory for states' rights advocates and gun control opponents—struck down a provision of the Brady Handgun Violence Prevention Act. The 1993 law established a five-day waiting period to purchase a handgun and, pending completion of a nationwide "instant-check system," required local law enforcement officers to determine the prospective gun purchaser's eligibility to own the weapon. Sheriffs in Arizona and Montana won rulings from federal district courts striking the law down as an unconstitutional federal regulatory command to state and local officials. But the Ninth U.S. Circuit Court of Appeals, in a consolidated decision in the two cases, upheld the law.

By a 5–4 vote, the Court ruled the background-check requirement exceeded federal powers. " . . . [T]he Federal Government may not compel the States to implement, by legislation or executive action, federal regulatory programs," Scalia wrote. He declined to rule on the constitutionality of the five-day waiting period, saying the sheriffs were not the proper parties to raise the issue.

O'Connor and Thomas added brief concurrences. O'Connor said the ruling did not necessarily nullify "purely ministerial reporting requirements" imposed on state or local officials under Congress's power to regulate interstate commerce. Thomas said he believed that the federal regulatory scheme might be unconstitutional under the Second Amendment's "right-to-bear-arms" provision, at least as to intrastate gun transactions.

Writing for the four dissenters, Stevens called the law "more comparable to a statute requiring local police officers to report the identity of missing children . . . than to an offensive federal command to a sovereign state." Souter wrote an additional dissent; so did Breyer, joined by Stevens. *(See story, pp. 45–49; excerpts, pp. 273–290.)*

Freedom of Information

Bibles, Director, Oregon Bureau of Land Management v. Oregon Natural Desert Association, decided by a 9–0 vote, February 18, 1997; *per curiam* (unsigned) opinion.

The federal Bureau of Land Management did not have to comply with a conservation group's Freedom of Information Act request to turn over its mailing list of people who receive BLM information and publications.

The decision summarily reversed a ruling by the Ninth U.S. Circuit Court of Appeals that would have allowed the Oregon Natural Desert Association access to the list. The group said it wanted to send people on the list information to counter what it termed the agency's "propaganda."

In a brief, unsigned opinion, the Court said the appeals court was wrong to recognize a public interest in providing the additional information to people on the bureau's list. Citing its 1994 decision, *Department of Defense v. Federal Labor Relations Authority*, the Court said "the only relevant public interest" in weighing freedom of information requests is "the extent to which disclosure of the information would shed light on an agency's performance of its statutory duties."

Military

Edmond v. United States, decided by a 9–0 vote, May 19, 1997; Scalia wrote the opinion.

The Court rejected a challenge to the method of appointment of civilian judges on the Coast Guard Court of Criminal Appeals.

The ruling came in six consolidated cases challenging the appointment of the civilian judges on the appellate tribunal by the Secretary of Transportation rather than by the president. The defendants, convicted of various offenses by courts-martial and their convictions affirmed by the appeals court, claimed that the Constitution required the appellate judge to be nominated by the president and confirmed by the Senate.

In a unanimous decision, the Court said the appellate judges were "inferior officers" under the Constitution and Congress could give the power to appoint them to the head of a department instead of the president. Scalia stressed that the judges, despite their "significant authority," work under the supervision of the general counsel of the Department of Transportation and their decisions are reviewed by the U.S. Court of Appeals for the Armed Forces. ". . . [T]he judges of the Court of Criminal Appeals have no power to render a final decision on behalf of the United States unless permitted to do so by other executive officers," Scalia wrote.

Native Americans

Babbitt, Secretary of the Interior v. Youpee, decided by an 8–1 vote, January 21, 1997; Ginsburg wrote the opinion; Stevens dissented.

The Court struck down a federal law prohibiting Native Americans who own small parcels of land within reservations from passing down the property to their heirs.

The ruling struck down a second attempt by Congress to reduce the fractionation of lands on reservations. The Indian Land Consolidation Act, originally passed in 1983, provided that certain small parcels of property within reservations would pass to the tribe upon the owner's death. The law was immediately challenged as an unconstitutional interference with property rights, and Congress in 1984 slightly reduced the impact of the law to try to meet the objections. Three years later, the Court in *Hodel v. Irving* struck down the original law, but made no ruling on the revised statute.

In the new decision, the Court said the revisions did not cure the constitutional problems. The amended law "severely restricts the right of an individual to direct the descent of his property," Ginsburg wrote.

In a lone dissent, Stevens said, "The federal government's interest in minimizing the fractionated ownership of Indian lands—and thereby paving the way to the productive development of their property—is strong enough to justify the legislative remedy created" by the law.

Strate, Associate Tribal Judge, Tribal Court of the Three Affiliated Tribes of the Fort Berthold Indian Reservation v. A-1 Contractors, decided by a 9–0 vote, April 28, 1997; Ginsburg wrote the opinion.

Tribal courts ordinarily do not have jurisdiction over civil suits involving non-tribe members arising from automobile accidents on state highways that cross Indian reservations.

The ruling barred a tribal court on the Fort Berthold Indian Reservation in North Dakota from trying a suit brought by a non-Indian plaintiff against the driver and owner of a gravel truck after a collision in November 1990. The accident occurred on a portion of state highway constructed on a right-of-way that crosses the reservation. The company that owned the truck brought suit in federal court to contest the tribal court's jurisdiction, and two lower federal courts ruled in its favor.

In a unanimous decision, the Court agreed that the tribal court did not have jurisdiction over the suit. Tribal courts ordinarily do not have civil authority over non-members, Ginsburg wrote. Traffic accident cases do not fall within an exception, she continued, because they are "not necessary to protect tribal self-government" or "crucial to the political integrity, the economic security, or the health or welfare" of the tribe.

Separation of Powers

Clinton v. Jones, decided by a 9–0 vote, May 27, 1997; Stevens wrote the opinion.

The president is not entitled to an automatic stay during his term in office of proceedings in a civil lawsuit relating to private, unofficial conduct that occurred before his election.

The ruling came in a politically charged federal civil rights lawsuit brought by Paula Corbin Jones, a former Arkansas state employee, who accused President Clinton of an unwanted sexual advance while he was governor. A federal district court judge ruled that discovery could proceed in the case, but that any trial would be deferred until after Clinton left office. The Eighth U.S. Circuit Court of Appeals, however, rejected any delay in the proceedings, including discovery. Clinton's private attorney and the Justice Department asked the Court to overturn that ruling.

In a unanimous decision, the Court held that the separation of powers doctrine gives the president no "categorical immunity" in civil lawsuits involving conduct unrelated to his office. "Like every other citizen," Stevens wrote, Jones "has a right to an orderly disposition of her claims."

Stevens discounted the possibility that proceedings in private litigation would create an "unacceptable burden on the President's time and energy." In Jones's case, Stevens said the lower court's original stay was an abuse of discretion because it took "no account whatever of [her] interest in bringing the case to trial."

Breyer concurred in the judgment, but did not join Stevens's opinion. In a lengthy separate opinion, Breyer agreed that the Constitution did not require "automatic temporary immunity" for the presidency in private civil lawsuits. But he contended that the Constitution "forbids a federal judge in such a case to interfere with the President's discharge of his public duties." *(See story, pp. 40–45; excerpts, pp. 168–176.)*

Raines, Director, Office of Management and Budget v. Byrd, decided by a 7–2 vote, June 26, 1997; Rehnquist wrote the opinion; Stevens and Breyer dissented.

The Court dismissed a lawsuit by members of Congress challenging the Line Item Veto Act and sharply curtailed the ability of lawmakers to bring similar constitutional suits in the future.

The ruling—the Court's first direct holding on the issue of "legislative standing"—left unsettled the constitutionality of the 1996 act allowing the president to "cancel" individual spending items or limited tax breaks after signing a bill into law. A federal district court judge had ruled the measure unconstitutional as intruding on Congress's lawmaking powers. The Clinton administration defended the law's constitutionality, but also argued the lawmakers had no standing to raise the issue in court because they had suffered no personal injury.

By a 7–2 vote, the Court agreed the lawmakers had no legal standing to bring the case. Rehnquist said the lawmakers "have alleged no injury to themselves as individuals" and the "institutional injury" they claimed was "wholly abstract and widely dispersed."

In a separate concurring opinion, Souter said the legal standing issue was "fairly debatable." He said he was "resolving doubts" on the issue in part to avoid intervening in "a power contest" between Congress and the president. Ginsburg joined Souter's opinion as well as Rehnquist's.

In a dissenting opinion, Stevens argued that the lawmakers had standing because the measure denied all members of Congress the opportunity to vote on what he called "the truncated measure that survives the exercise of the President's cancellation authority." For the same reason, he said, the act was unconstitutional. Breyer also said he would recognize standing, but expressed no opinion on the act's constitutionality.

First Amendment

Church and State

Agostini v. Felton, decided by a 5–4 vote, June 23, 1997; O'Connor wrote the opinion; Souter, Stevens, Ginsburg, and Breyer dissented.

Public school teachers can provide remedial educational services to disadvantaged students at church-affiliated schools without violating the constitutional prohibition against governmental establishment of religion.

The decision, in a New York City case, overturned a twelve-year-old precedent in the face of a significant procedural obstacle. The Court in 1985 voted 5–4 in *Aguilar v. Felton* to bar the use of federal funds to pay public school teachers for providing remedial services at parochial schools. The city responded by setting up mobile trailers adjacent to many parochial schools to provide the services off-site. The city continued to complain about the decision as the costs of those arrangements mounted. Meanwhile, the Court issued two rulings in 1986 and 1993 somewhat weakening the limits on governmental aid to students at church-affiliated schools. In addition, five justices specifically called for reconsidering *Aguilar* in a 1994 decision.

Citing those factors, the city returned to federal court, using a rule of federal civil procedure—Rule 60(b)—to ask that the injunction limiting its use of the federal funds be dissolved. A lower federal court and the Second U.S. Circuit Court of Appeals both held that they had no authority under Rule 60(b) to disregard a Supreme Court precedent.

By a 5–4 vote, the Court held the city could use the federal funds to provide services on a neutral basis to disadvantaged children on the premises of parochial schools under safeguards to prevent improper aid to religion. O'Connor, one of the dissenters in *Aguilar*, said the city's program "does not result in governmental indoctrination; define its recipients by reference to religion; or create an excessive entanglement."

On the procedural issue, O'Connor said that the Court's reconsideration of the city's case could be justified by the effect of the two other church-school aid rulings—*Witters v. Washington Department of Services for the Blind* (1986) and *Zobrest v. Catalina Foothills School District* (1993). The effect of those rulings, she said, was that *Aguilar* was "no longer good law."

Dissenting justices sharply challenged both the substantive and the procedural basis for the ruling. On the substantive issue, Souter said the ruling would "authorize direct state aid to religious institutions on an unparalleled scale, in violation of the Establishment Clause's central prohibition against religious subsidies by the government." Stevens and Ginsburg joined all of Souter's opinion; Breyer joined most of it.

In a separate dissent, Ginsburg criticized the Court's decision to take up the issue in the New York City case. She said the ruling "bends Rule 60(b) to a purpose—allowing an 'anytime' rehearing in this case—unrelated to the governance of district court proceedings to which the rule . . . is directed." Stevens, Souter, and Breyer joined her opinion. *(See story, pp. 54–57; excerpts, pp. 215–230.)*

City of Boerne v. Flores, Archbishop of San Antonio, decided by a 6–3 vote, June 25, 1997; Kennedy wrote the opinion; O'Connor, Souter, and Breyer dissented.

Congress exceeded its power in passing a law, the Religious Freedom Restoration Act, that sharply restricted the power of states to enforce laws that have an incidental effect on religious practices.

The 1993 law provided that a state could not enforce a law that burdened religious practices unless the measure had a "compelling governmental interest" and was "the least restrictive means" of furthering that interest. Congress passed the law after the Court in a 1990 decision, *Employment Div., Dept. of Human Resources of Oregon v. Smith,* set a laxer standard for judging laws that burdened religious practices.

A Roman Catholic pastor in the small Texas city of Boerne cited the 1993 law in contesting the city's refusal, on historic preservation grounds, to allow an addition to its small, seventy-year-old church. A federal district court ruled the law unconstitutional, but the Fifth U.S. Circuit Court of Appeals disagreed and upheld the measure.

The Court struck down the statute by a 6–3 vote. Kennedy said the law sought to broadly override state and local laws by attempting to make "a substantive change in constitutional protections" as determined by the Court. On that basis, he concluded, "RFRA contradicts vital principles necessary to maintain separation of powers and the federal balance." Four justices joined Kennedy's opinion in full; Scalia joined all but a part discussing the drafting of the Fourteenth Amendment.

Stevens wrote a short concurring opinion, terming the law an improper establishment of religion. Scalia also wrote a concurring opinion, defending the *Smith* decision.

Three justices dissented on grounds that the *Smith* ruling should be reconsidered. In the main dissent, O'Connor agreed with the majority that Congress had no power to redefine constitutional protections. But she argued that *Smith* had "harmed religious liberty" and called for a reargument to consider whether to overrule it. Breyer joined most of O'Connor's opinion, but specified in a separate dissent that he was expressing no view on Congress's power to define substantive constitutional provisions. Souter wrote a short dissent, saying he also favored reconsidering the *Smith* decision. *(See story, pp. 49–54; excerpts, pp. 231–242.)*

Freedom of Speech

Reno, Attorney General v. American Civil Liberties Union, decided by 9–0 and 7–2 votes, June 26, 1997; Stevens wrote the opinion; O'Connor and Rehnquist dissented in part.

A new federal law aimed at limiting access by minors to sexually oriented material on the Internet violated the First Amendment by suppressing constitutionally protected speech for adults.

The ruling struck down the Communications Decency Act, enacted as part of a broad telecommunications law rewrite in 1996. The law made it a crime to knowingly transmit an obscene or indecent message or image to a minor. The act also made it a crime to knowingly send a "patently offensive" message or image to a specific person under the age of eighteen or to display the message or image in a manner available to minors. An array of First Amendment advocates and Internet user groups challenged the law immediately after its enactment. A special three-judge court in Philadelphia agreed the law was unconstitutional; the Clinton administration asked the Court to review the ruling.

In a mostly unanimous decision, the Court agreed the law violated free speech rights. Stevens cited what he called the law's "many ambiguities" in concluding that it "effectively suppresses a large amount of speech that adults have a constitutional right to receive and to address to one another." He also said that the law was not "narrowly tailored" as required by the First Amendment because there were "less restrictive alternatives" available to limit minors' access to sexual material, such as "tagging" sexually oriented material or setting up different regulations for web sites containing such material than for the rest of the Internet.

In a partial dissent, O'Connor, joined by Rehnquist, agreed that the law was "overbroad" because it covered "all communications between adults and minors, regardless of how many adults might be part of the audience. . . ." But she said she would uphold the prohibition against transmitting indecent or patently offensive material in cases where "the party initiating the communication knows that all of the recipients are minors." *(See story, pp. 35–40; excerpts, pp. 243–258.)*

Telecommunications

Turner Broadcasting System, Inc. v. Federal Communications Commission, decided by a 5–4 vote, March 31, 1997; Kennedy wrote the opinion; O'Connor, Scalia, Thomas, and Ginsburg dissented.

The federal law requiring cable television systems to carry the signals of local broadcast stations does not violate the First Amendment.

The ruling upholding the so-called "must-carry" provisions of a 1992 cable television law was a victory for broadcasters and a setback for cable operators and programmers. Cable operators challenged the law as an unconstitutional infringement on their editorial freedom; broadcasters called the statute necessary to ensure viewer access to local stations and to prevent anticompetitive actions by cable operators. A special three-judge federal court upheld the law, but the Court in 1994 ordered a new hearing to weigh the justifications of the law under a heightened "intermediate scrutiny" standard. *(See* Supreme Court Yearbook, 1993–1994, *pp. 52–55.)* The three-judge court again upheld the law.

In a narrowly divided decision, the Court held the law satisfied the intermediate-scrutiny standard because it served an important governmental interest without burdening more speech than necessary to serve that interest. Kennedy said Congress had "an independent interest in preserving a multiplicity of broadcasters" to ensure households without cable access to information and entertainment. He also said Congress had adequate information to conclude that the must-carry provisions were necessary because of "a real threat to local broadcasting's economic health." Finally, he said evidence indicated that the "vast majority" of cable systems had not been significantly affected by the provisions.

Breyer concurred with most of the ruling, but rejected Kennedy's reliance on an anticompetitive rationale.

O'Connor led the same four dissenters who had called for striking the law down in the Court's first ruling. She said the ruling used an "inappropriately lenient level of scrutiny" and exhibited "an extraordinary and unwarranted deference for congressional judgments. . . ." *(See story, pp. 70–73; excerpts, pp. 151–168.)*

Immigration Law

Immigration and Naturalization Service v. Yang, decided by a 9–0 vote, November 13, 1996; Scalia wrote the opinion.

Immigration authorities have discretion to use an immigrant's fraud in entering the United States as grounds for deporting the immigrant despite a general policy of disregarding such conduct in deportation hearings.

The unanimous decision backed the Immigration and Naturalization Service's effort to deport a former Taiwanese resident, Yueh-Shaio Yang, who along with his wife executed a complex, fraudulent scheme to enter the United States years earlier. The INS moved to deport Yang after learning of the scheme in 1992. But the Ninth U.S. Circuit Court of Appeals said Yang was entitled to a waiver of deportation because of the agency's general policy of disregarding "entry fraud or misrepresentation" in deportation proceedings.

Writing for the Court, Scalia said the appeals court was wrong to require the INS to follow the policy. "The 'entry fraud' exception being . . . a rule of the INS's own invention, the INS is entitled, within reason, to define that exception as it pleases," Scalia wrote.

Individual Rights

Abortion

Lambert, Gallatin County Attorney v. Wicklund, decided by a 9–0 vote, March 31, 1997; *per curiam* (unsigned) opinion.

The Court reinstituted Montana's parental notice abortion law, saying that a federal appeals court misapplied prior rulings in striking down the statute.

The Montana law prohibited physicians from performing abortions on a minor unless one or both parents were notified at least forty-eight hours in advance, but allowed a court to waive the requirement if notification was "not in the best interests" of the minor. The Ninth U.S. Circuit Court of Appeals held the judicial bypass procedure was too narrow, saying the test should have been whether an abortion was in the minor's best interests.

In a decision issued without oral argument in the case, the Court said the appeals court misinterpreted its prior rulings on parental notification provisions. ". . . [R]equiring a minor to show that parental notification is not in her best interests is equivalent to a judicial bypass procedure requiring a minor to show that abortion without notification is in her best interests," the unsigned opinion stated.

In a separate opinion, Stevens, joined by Ginsburg and Breyer, disagreed with the interpretation that the law required a minor to prove both that an abortion was in her best interest and that parental notification was not. That issue, he wrote, "is best left to another day."

Mazurek, Attorney General of Montana v. Armstrong, decided by a 6–3 vote, June 19, 1997; *per curiam* (unsigned) opinion; Stevens, Ginsburg, and Breyer dissented.

The Court allowed Montana to enforce a state law requiring abortions to be performed only by a licensed physician.

The summary ruling—issued without hearing argument—overturned a ruling by the Ninth U.S. Circuit Court of Appeals that had enjoined enforcement of the 1995 law. The appeals court held that the plaintiffs challenging the law—including the only physician's assistant who had been assisting in performing abortions before enactment of the law—were entitled to a preliminary injunction because they had shown "a fair chance of success" on the merits of their claim.

By a 6–3 vote, the Court said the appeals court ruling was "clearly erroneous under our precedents." The unsigned opinion pointed to a number of rulings, including the 1992 decision in *Planned Parenthood of Southeastern Pa. v. Casey*, as upholding the right of states to adopt physician-only abortion statutes. The opinion also noted that some forty other states had similar laws.

Writing for the three dissenters, Stevens argued the case did not have "sufficient importance to justify review of the merits at this preliminary stage of the proceedings."

Schenck v. Pro-Choice Network of Western New York, decided by 6–3 and 8–1 votes, February 19, 1997; Rehnquist wrote the opinion; Scalia, Kennedy, and Thomas dissented in part; Breyer dissented in part.

The Court upheld a federal judge's injunction ordering anti-abortion demonstrators to stay at least fifteen feet away from entrances to abortion clinics. But it struck down part of the order establishing a "floating buffer zone" around patients and clinic staff as they approached or left the clinics.

The split ruling came in a suit brought by abortion clinics in western New York after a campaign of aggressive demonstrations by anti-abortion groups that included physical blockades and what the Court called "in your face" confrontations with clinic patients and staff. A federal judge issued a temporary restraining order in 1990 and a preliminary injunction in 1992 that set up a fifteen-foot "fixed buffer zone" around clinic entrances, doorways, and driveways. The injunction also required demonstrators to maintain the same fifteen-foot distance—a so-called "floating bubble"—from patients and staff entering or leaving the clinics.

A three-judge federal appeals initially struck down the injunction by a 2–1 vote. But, on a rehearing, the full Second U.S. Circuit Court of Appeals upheld the injunction by a 10–2 vote. The defendants asked the Court to review the ruling, contending that it went beyond the restrictions on anti-abortion demonstrations permitted under the Court's 1994 ruling in a similar case, *Madsen v. Women's Health Center, Inc.*

Applying the *Madsen* ruling, the Court said the floating buffer zones were improper because they "burden more speech than is necessary to serve the relevant government interests." Rehnquist said that with a limited exception for two "sidewalk counselors" permitted within the floating zone, the injunction prevented demonstrators "from communicating a message from a normal conversational distance or handing leaflets to people entering or leaving the clinics who are walking on the public sidewalks."

By contrast, Rehnquist said the fixed buffer zone was "necessary to ensure that people and vehicles trying to enter or exit the clinic property or clinic parking lots can do so."

Three justices—Scalia, Kennedy, and Thomas—voted to overturn the injunction in its entirety. Writing for the three, who also dissented in the *Madsen* decision, Scalia said the new opinion "makes a destructive inroad upon First Amendment law."

Separately, Breyer said he would uphold all of the injunction, which he said had been misinterpreted by the other justices. Breyer said the injunction did not in fact set up a floating bubble, but he also suggested a moving buffer zone might be justifiable in some circumstances. In a footnote in his opinion, Rehnquist said Breyer "misreads the record" in the case.

Assisted Suicide

Vacco, Attorney General of New York v. Quill, decided by a 9–0 vote, June 26, 1997; Rehnquist wrote the opinion.

Washington v. Glucksberg, decided by a 9–0 vote, June 26, 1997; Rehnquist wrote the opinion.

State laws prohibiting physicians from assisting a terminally ill patient to commit suicide do not violate the patients' or the physicians' rights to due process or equal protection of the laws.

The unanimous decisions in two separate cases rejected rulings by federal appeals courts that barred the enforcement of laws banning physician-assisted suicide for the terminally ill. The laws were challenged in New York and Washington by doctors and by several individuals with terminal illnesses. In the New York case, the Second U.S. Circuit Court of Appeals ruled the assisted-suicide ban violated equal protection because some terminally ill patients could hasten their death by refusing life-sustaining medical treatment. In the Washington case, the Ninth U.S. Circuit Court of Appeals ruled the ban placed an undue burden on the exercise of a constitutionally protected liberty interest. Both states asked the Court to review the rulings; the Clinton administration joined in urging the laws be upheld.

Writing for the Court in both cases, Rehnquist said both laws were constitutional. In the New York case, Rehnquist said "the distinction between assisting suicide and withdrawing life-sustaining treatment" was "both important and logical" and "certainly rational." In the Washington case, Rehnquist said that the "asserted 'right' to assistance in committing suicide" was "not a fundamental liberty interest protected by the Due Process Clause" and that the state had "unquestionably important and legitimate interests" in banning assisted suicide. Those interests, he said, included preservation of human life; protecting the integrity and ethics of the medical profession; protecting vulnerable groups, such as the poor, the elderly, and disabled persons, from abuse, neglect, or mistakes; and avoiding "the path to voluntary and perhaps even involuntary euthanasia."

Despite the unanimous vote, five justices wrote separate concurring opinions distancing themselves to varying degrees from Rehnquist's opinion. O'Connor concurred in Rehnquist's opinion, but stressed that the opposing parties agreed that the laws still allowed physicians to prescribe pain-killing medication to alleviate suffering even to the point of hastening death. Ginsburg and Breyer both said they concurred with O'Connor's opinion, but not with the Court's. Stevens and Souter wrote longer opinions concurring in the judgment, but suggesting that the ruling would not bar similar constitutional claims in different cases in the future. *(See story, pp. 28–35; excerpts, pp. 258–264.)*

Damage Suits

Board of County Commissioners of Bryan County, Oklahoma v. Brown, decided by a 5–4 vote, April 28, 1997; O'Connor wrote the opinion; Souter, Stevens, Ginsburg, and Breyer dissented.

The Court made it harder for victims of police brutality to recover damages in federal civil rights suits from municipal governments for inadequately screening or training law enforcement officers.

The decision threw out an $818,000 jury award won by a Texas woman, Jill Brown, who was severely injured after a Bryan County, Oklahoma, reserve deputy sheriff arrested her in 1991 following a high-speed automobile chase. The deputy, Stacy Burns, was hired at the age of twenty-one by the county sheriff, his great-uncle, despite a lengthy criminal record, including charges of reckless driving, resisting arrest, and assault. A federal court jury held the county liable for the injuries after ruling the sheriff's "hiring policy" amounted to "deliberate indifference to [Brown's] constitutional needs." The Fifth U.S. Circuit Court of Appeals upheld the verdict, rejecting the county's argument that liability could not be imposed on the basis of a single hiring decision.

In a closely divided decision, the Court held that the evidence was insufficient to meet the standard for municipal liability established in prior rulings. A municipality can be held liable for inadequate prehiring scrutiny of an employee's background, O'Connor wrote, only if "deprivation of a third party's federally protected right" was the "plainly obvious consequence" of the hiring.

Dissenting justices criticized the majority's reading of the facts of the case and the law. In one of the dissenting opinions, Souter, joined by Stevens and Breyer, said the ruling created a "newly-demanding standard of fault" that would be virtually impossible to meet. In a separate opinion, Breyer went further and called for re-examining precedents that ruled out automatically holding a municipality liable for constitutional violations by its employees. Stevens and Ginsburg joined his opinion.

Edwards v. Balisok, decided by a 9–0 vote, May 19, 1997; Scalia wrote the opinion.

The Court barred a Washington state prison inmate's effort to use a federal civil rights suit to obtain damages for what he claimed was a wrongful disciplinary decision to take away thirty days of "good-time credit."

The unanimous ruling relied on a 1994 precedent that limited prison inmates' use of so-called section 1983 suits—named after the section of the U.S. code in which the provision appears. In that ruling, the Court held that an inmate cannot bring a section 1983 suit claiming an illegal conviction or sentence unless a state or federal court had already ruled the conviction or sentence invalid. The suit by the Washington inmate posed the question whether the ruling also applied to prison disciplinary hearings.

In a unanimous opinion, the Court extended the earlier ruling and barred the inmate's plea for damages. Scalia said the inmate's allegations of bias by the prison disciplinary officer "necessarily imply the invalidity of the punishment imposed."

Johnson v. Fankell, decided by a 9–0 vote, June 9, 1997; Stevens wrote the opinion.

Public officials named as defendants in a federal civil rights suit filed in state court have no federal right to a preliminary appeal from a ruling denying qualified immunity.

The ruling came in a suit brought against Idaho Liquor Dispensary officials by a former state employee who claimed she was wrongfully discharged. The officials claimed immunity from suit on the ground that their actions did not violate "clearly established" rights. After the state trial judge rejected the plea, the Idaho Supreme Court refused to consider the officials' "interlocutory appeal," saying the ruling was not a final order. The officials then asked the Court to review the decision, saying that they would have been entitled to a pretrial appeal in federal court.

Unanimously, the Court held that the defendants had no federal right to an interlocutory appeal on the immunity issue. Stevens said the federal procedural right "simply does not apply in a nonfederal forum."

McMillian v. Monroe County, Alabama, decided by a 5–4 vote, June 2, 1997; Rehnquist wrote the opinion; Ginsburg, Stevens, Souter, and Breyer dissented.

Alabama sheriffs are state rather than county policymakers for purposes of determining their liability in federal court suits for violating an individual's constitutional rights.

The ruling—a setback for civil rights groups—came in a suit by a Alabama man, Walter McMillian, who was released from prison in 1993 after winning reversal of a murder conviction six years earlier. McMillian charged Monroe County Sheriff Tom Tate among others with violating his constitutional rights by withholding evidence and intimidating him into giving a false confession. Two lower federal courts, applying the Court's 1978 decision *Monell v. New York City Department of Social Services*, held that the county could not be held liable because Tate was a state rather than county policymaker.

The Court agreed in a closely divided decision ostensibly limited to Alabama law. Rehnquist cited provisions of the Alabama constitution, state law, and state supreme court rulings in concluding that sheriffs function as state officials rather than county officials. He stressed that the ruling did not contradict rulings by federal courts designating sheriffs in other states as local officials. "There is no inconsistency created by court decisions that declare sheriffs to be county officers in one State, and not in another," he wrote.

Writing for the four dissenters, Ginsburg sharply disagreed. "Alabama law defining the office of sheriff indicates that the sheriff acts within and for the county when setting and implementing law enforcement policy," she wrote. But she also said that the ruling appeared to be limited to Alabama and "does little to alter" local government liability for constitutional violations "in most jurisdictions."

Richardson v. McKnight, decided by a 5–4 vote, June 23, 1997; Breyer wrote the opinion; Scalia, Rehnquist, Kennedy, and Thomas dissented.

Private prison guards do not have special legal protection from federal civil rights suits brought by inmates for alleged excessive use of force or other mistreatment.

The ruling upheld a preliminary ruling by the Sixth U.S. Circuit Court of Appeals in an excessive force suit brought by two Tennessee inmates against guards employed at a privately-run correctional center. The guards sought to dismiss the suit on the ground that they were entitled to the same legal protection—"qualified immunity"—accorded to prison guards at state-run facilities. The appeals court rejected the argument.

By a 5–4 vote, the Court also refused to grant the private guards qualified immunity from federal civil rights suits. Breyer said that there was no historic recognition of immunity for private prison guards and that policy reasons for granting such protection to state employees did not apply to private guards. "Ordinary competitive pressures," Breyer wrote, would suffice to "help private firms adjust their behavior in response to the incentives that tort suits provide."

Writing for the dissenters, Scalia said the effect of the ruling would be to "artificially raise the cost of privatizing prisons." ". . . [I]t is likely," he concluded, "that taxpayers and prisoners will suffer as a consequence."

The ruling returned the case to lower courts for further proceedings. Breyer noted that the guards might be entitled to a special "good faith" defense against the suit.

Drug Testing

Chandler v. Miller, Governor of Georgia, decided by an 8–1 vote, April 15, 1997; Ginsburg wrote the opinion; Rehnquist dissented.

A Georgia law requiring drug testing for candidates for major state offices was held unconstitutional as an unreasonable search under the Fourth Amendment.

The 1990 law—the only one of its kind among the states—required candidates for governor and other executive offices, state legislator, and state court judgeships to submit to a urinalysis drug test sometime prior to thirty days before an election. A number of Libertarian Party candidates, including the party's nominee for lieutenant governor, Walker Chandler, challenged the law in 1994 as a violation of the Fourth Amendment. But a federal district court judge refused to block enforcement of the law before the 1994 election, and the Eleventh U.S. Circuit Court of Appeals upheld the statute, in a 2–1 decision, afterward.

In a nearly unanimous decision, the Court ruled that the state had not presented sufficient grounds for an exception to the normal rule against suspicionless searches. The state showed "no evidence of a drug problem" among its officials, Ginsburg wrote, and the law would not be effective anyway because candidates themselves chose the time for the drug test. "However well-meant, the candidate drug test Georgia has devised diminishes personal privacy for a symbol's sake," Ginsburg concluded. "The Fourth Amendment shields society against such state action."

In a lone dissent, Rehnquist said the state was entitled to take preventive action against drug use. ". . . [S]urely the State need not wait for a drug addict, or one inclined to use drugs illegally, to run for or actually become Governor before it installs a prophylactic mechanism," he wrote.

Job Discrimination

Robinson v. Shell Oil Co., decided by a 9–0 vote, February 18, 1997; Thomas wrote the opinion.

Federal civil rights law prohibits employers from giving an unfavorable job reference about a former employee in retaliation for filing a job discrimination complaint.

The ruling reinstated a suit filed by Charles Robinson, a former Shell Oil Co. salesman, who claimed the company provided an unfavorable reference because of a job discrimination complaint he filed after he was fired from his position. Robinson claimed the company's action violated the provision of the Civil Rights Act that prohibits discrimination against any "employees" or "applicants for employment." But the Fourth U.S. Circuit Court of Appeals, in a 7–5 decision, agreed with the company's argument that the antiretaliation provision could be invoked only by current, not former, employees.

In a unanimous decision, the Court disagreed. Thomas explained that despite ambiguity in the specific provision, the law elsewhere used the word "employees" to apply to former as well as current workers. In addition, he said, extending the antiretaliation provision to former employees served the statute's "primary purpose" of "maintaining unfettered access to statutory remedial mechanisms."

Walters v. Metropolitan Educational Enterprises, Inc., decided by a 9–0 vote, January 14, 1997; Scalia wrote the opinion.

The Court slightly eased the test used to determine whether small businesses have enough employees to be covered by the federal anti–job discrimination law.

Title VII of the Civil Rights Act of 1964 applies to any employer that "has fifteen or more employees for each working day in each of twenty or more calendar weeks in the current or preceding calendar year." The Seventh U.S. Circuit Court of Appeals interpreted that provision to count employees only on days on which they performed their work or were counted for their absence. The appeals court ruling had the effect of dismissing a retaliatory discharge suit brought by a former employee of a Chicago-based encyclopedia sales company.

In a unanimous decision reinstating the suit, the Court adopted what it called the "payroll method" for counting number of employees: "whether the employer has an employment relationship with the individual on the day in question." Scalia said the payroll method "represents the fair reading of the statutory language," while the alternative urged by the employer— counting the number of employees actually paid on each working day— would entail "an incredibly complex and expensive factual inquiry."

Official English

Arizonans for Official English v. Arizona, decided by a 9–0 vote, March 3, 1997; Ginsburg wrote the opinion.

The Court sidestepped a ruling on a free speech challenge to a state ballot initiative requiring all governmental actions to be conducted in English.

The decision ordered the dismissal of a suit by a former Arizona state employee seeking to invalidate the "official English" initiative narrowly approved by the state's voters in 1988. Two lower federal courts had ruled the measure invalid as an infringement of the bilingual state worker's First Amendment rights. The employee left her state job two months after winning the first of those rulings from a federal district court judge in Phoenix.

On appeal, the state sought to have the suit dismissed as moot because the plaintiff no longer worked for the government. But the Ninth U.S. Circuit Court of Appeals held that the woman still had a claim for nominal damages and, by a 7–5 vote, upheld the lower court's ruling striking down the measure.

Unanimously, the Court held that the case should have been dismissed. The plaintiff "lacked a still vital claim for prospective relief" after she resigned from her state job, Ginsburg wrote, and her plea for nominal damages "could not genuinely revive her case."

Ginsburg bluntly criticized both federal courts for not allowing the Arizona Supreme Court to rule on the meaning of the ballot measure before ruling on its constitutionality. She noted that the state attorney general had issued an interpretation narrowing the scope of the ballot measure. But Ginsburg stressed that the Court was expressing no opinion on the correct interpretation of the ballot measure or its constitutionality.

Labor Law

Overtime

Auer v. Robbins, decided by a 9–0 vote, February 19, 1997; Scalia wrote the opinion.

Public employees can be treated as salaried workers and denied overtime pay as long as they are not normally subjected to pay deductions for disciplinary reasons.

The ruling rejected an effort by St. Louis police officers to broaden their eligibility for overtime pay. The Labor Department had previously held that employers could deny workers overtime pay only if they were not subject to disciplinary deductions. The St. Louis officers sought overtime pay after a sergeant was docked for disciplinary reasons, but the Eighth U.S. Circuit Court of Appeals rejected the plea, saying the case was a "one-time incident."

The Court unanimously agreed, upholding the position taken by the Labor Department in a brief submitted at the justices' request. The department said the "no disciplinary deductions" test should apply only when there was an actual practice or significant likelihood of docking employees for infractions. Scalia said the department's position "avoids the imposition of massive and unanticipated overtime liability" in situations in which disciplinary deductions are unlikely to be invoked against salaried employees.

Pensions and Benefits

Boggs v. Boggs, decided by 7–2 and 5–4 votes, June 2, 1997; Kennedy wrote the opinion; Breyer and O'Connor dissented, joined in part by Rehnquist and Ginsburg.

The federal pension protection law overrides state community property law so as to prevent a spouse from controlling the disposition of proceeds of a pension plan or other retirement benefits.

The ruling came in a factually complex dispute between a Louisiana woman who was the second wife of a retired telephone company employee and the three sons of the man's first marriage. The three sons claimed a share of Isaac Boggs's pension and retirement benefits under the will that their mother, Dorothy Boggs, left at her death in 1979. They contended that Louisiana's community property law gave their mother an interest in their father's pension benefits that she could pass to her heirs.

Sandra Boggs, Isaac's second wife, claimed that the federal pension protection law known as ERISA gave her the right to Isaac's retirement benefits after his death in 1989. A federal district court and the Fifth U.S. Circuit Court of Appeals both rejected her argument. Sandra Boggs, supported by the Justice Department, then asked the Court to review the case and reverse the appellate decision.

In a 5–4 ruling, the Court agreed that ERISA preempts state community property law. Kennedy said the pension protection law, as enacted in 1978 and significantly amended by the Retirement Equity Act in 1984, reflected "Congress's concern for surviving spouses" of retirees. Community property laws, he said, could conflict with that purpose. "ERISA's solicitude for the economic security of surviving spouses," Kennedy wrote, "would be undermined by allowing a predeceasing spouse's heirs and legatees to have a community property interest in the survivor's annuity."

Writing for the dissenters, Breyer acknowledged that ERISA guaranteed a surviving spouse some interest in pension benefits, but argued that the law did not require nullification of Dorothy Boggs's community property interest. "Congress did not intend ERISA to pre-empt" community property law, he said, "at least not . . . where a first wife's bequest need not prevent a second wife from obtaining precisely those benefits that ERISA specifically set aside for her."

O'Connor joined Breyer's opinion in full; Rehnquist and Ginsburg did not join the section dealing with the major issue in the case: Sandra Boggs's surviving spouse's right to Isaac Boggs's monthly annuity. They did not write separately to explain their views.

Community property laws, which generally give a husband and a wife equal rights to property accumulated during their marriage, were on the books in nine states. The Fifth Circuit's ruling applied to two of those states: Louisiana and Texas. The Ninth U.S. Circuit Court of Appeals had reached the opposite result in a separate case; its ruling applied in five community property states, including the largest: California.

Inter-Modal Rail Employees Association v. Atchison, Topeka & Santa Fe Railway Co., decided by a 9–0 vote, May 12, 1997; O'Connor wrote the opinion.

The federal pension security law prohibits an employer from firing a worker for the purpose of taking away health or welfare benefits.

The ruling reinstated a suit by Los Angeles railyard workers who were terminated after the Atchison, Topeka & Santa Fe Railway contracted out work previously done by a subsidiary company. The workers claimed the move violated a provision of the federal Employee Retirement Income Security Act (ERISA) that prohibits firing an employee "for the purpose of interfering with the attainment of any right to which [the worker] may become entitled under the [company's employee benefits] plan." A federal appeals court ruled the workers could sue over their vested pension rights, but not over health and welfare benefits.

In a unanimous decision, the Court said the workers could proceed with both prongs of the suit. O'Connor said the appeals court ruling was "contradicted by the plain language" of the ERISA provision. Employers are free to unilaterally change health and welfare benefits, O'Connor acknowledged, but they must follow formal procedures in doing so and cannot "informally amend their plans one participant at a time."

Prevailing Wage Laws

California Division of Labor Standards Enforcement v. Dillingham Construction, N.A., Inc., decided by a 9–0 vote, February 18, 1997; Thomas wrote the opinion.

State prevailing wage laws are not preempted by the federal law governing employee benefit plans.

The decision marked another effort by the Court to define the extent that the federal Employee Retirement Income Security Act (ERISA) overrides state laws affecting employee benefits. The Ninth U.S. Circuit Court of Appeals had ruled that ERISA preempted a California law requiring public works contractors to pay prevailing wages to all employees except for trainees enrolled in an approved apprenticeship program.

Unanimously, the Court disagreed. Quoting the act's preemption provision, Thomas said that California's regulation of apprenticeship programs did not "relate to" or have a "connection with" benefit plans subject to ERISA. The law "does not bind ERISA plans to anything," Thomas said.

In a concurring opinion, Scalia, joined by Ginsburg, said the Court had failed "to bring clarity" to the preemption issue in the fourteen cases it had decided on the question since ERISA's enactment in 1974. He said the act's "relate to" criterion was so broad as to be "illusory" and argued the Court should instead apply ordinary principles of preemption to such disputes.

Public Employees

Gilbert, President, East Stroudsburg University v. Homar, decided by a 9–0 vote, June 9, 1997; Scalia wrote the opinion.

A public employee arrested for a crime has no constitutional right to a hearing before being suspended without pay.

The ruling overturned a decision by the Third U.S. Circuit Court of Appeals in favor of a Pennsylvania state college police officer who was suspended without pay after an arrest on drug charges that were later dismissed. The appeals court said the Due Process Clause required the state university to provide the officer with notice and an opportunity for hearing before his pay was suspended.

In a unanimous decision, the Court disagreed. The purpose of a prior hearing, Scalia wrote, "would be to assure that there are reasonable grounds to support the suspension without pay. But here that has already been assured by the arrest and the filing of charges."

Remedies

Metro-North Commuter Railroad Co. v. Buckley, decided by 9–0 and 7–2 votes, June 23, 1997; Breyer wrote the opinion; Ginsburg and Stevens dissented in part.

Railway workers cannot recover damages under federal law for emotional distress resulting from exposure to toxic substances such as asbestos if they show no physical symptoms of disease. The ruling also tentatively rejected a railway worker's effort to recover the costs of medical monitoring resulting from his exposure to asbestos.

The decision came in a test case brought by a New York pipefitter, Michael Buckley, employed by the Metro-North Commuter Railroad Co. to maintain the pipes in the steam tunnels of New York City's Grand Central Terminal. Buckley sued under the Federal Employees' Liability Act, a 1907 law that provides tort remedies for railway employees for workplace injuries. Metro-North admitted that Buckley had been negligently exposed to asbestos for at least two years, but argued he was not entitled to damages for emotional distress because he showed no symptoms of disease. The company also opposed his effort to recover medical monitoring costs. A federal district court ruled in favor of the railroad, but the Second U.S. Circuit Court of Appeals reversed and held that Buckley had stated an adequate claim on both points.

By a 7–2 vote, the Court held that Buckley's emotional distress claim was legally insufficient under the railway workers' law. Breyer acknowledged that the Court in 1994 interpreted the law to permit recovery for emotional distress after a physical impact. But physical impact, he said, "does not include a simple physical contact with a substance that might cause a disease at a substantially later time. . . ."

On the second point, Breyer said that Buckley was not entitled to a lump-sum recovery for the costs of medical monitoring. In both parts of the decision, Breyer stressed that recognition of "unlimited and unpredictable liability" could diminish the likelihood of recovery by seriously injured workers at a later date.

In a largely dissenting opinion, Ginsburg, joined by Stevens, said that Buckley's exposure to asbestos qualified as a "physical impact" but that his emotional distress claim failed because he had not presented "objective evidence of severe emotional distress." On the medical costs, she said that Buckley should be able to recover and added that Breyer's opinion appeared to leave open the possibility of awarding costs in some form other than a one-time payment, such as a court-supervised fund.

Workers' Compensation

Harbor Tug & Barge Co. v. Papai, decided by a 6–3 vote, May 12, 1997; Kennedy wrote the opinion; Stevens, Ginsburg, and Breyer dissented.

The Court made it harder for some harbor workers to take advantage of the federal law governing injuries to seamen instead of the less generous law governing injuries to longshore workers.

By a 6–3 vote, the Court held that harbor workers who take short-term assignments on a number of boats with different owners ordinarily do not qualify as seamen under the federal Jones Act. That law allows an injured seaman to sue in court for open-ended damages. Longshore workers, by contrast, receive scheduled compensation for injuries under a different federal law, the Longshore and Harbor Workers' Compensation Act.

The decision barred a Jones Act suit by a California harbor worker injured while painting parts of a tugboat in navigation. He claimed he qualified as a seaman because he worked for a number of boats that hired workers from the same union hall and because most of his work was done on boats in navigation.

Writing for the majority, Kennedy said a harbor worker must work for a single boat or a group of commonly-owned boats to qualify as a seaman. Stevens, writing for the dissenters, argued that the worker's status should be determined "by the character of the work for the group of vessel owners that used the same union agent to make selections from the same pool of employees."

Ingalls Shipbuilding, Inc. v. Director, Office of Workers' Compensation Programs, Department of Labor, decided by 9–0 and 7–2 votes, February 18, 1997; O'Connor wrote the opinion; Scalia and Thomas dissented in part.

The Court allowed the surviving spouse of a shipyard worker who died from workplace exposure to asbestos to seek workers' compensation benefits despite a settlement her husband reached with the asbestos manufacturer and suppliers before his death.

The somewhat complex ruling rejected an argument by the shipbuilding company that the widow had forfeited her right to the statutory death benefits by failing to obtain its approval to the settlements. The law requires a person "entitled to compensation" to obtain the employer's written approval of any settlement with third parties.

Writing for the Court, O'Connor said that the requirement did not apply to the woman because she was not "entitled to compensation" while her husband was still alive. All justices agreed on this part of the decision. O'Connor stressed that the company might be entitled to an offset for any amounts her husband received in the settlements.

In a second holding, the Court said that the director of the workers' compensation office has standing to appear in court when employers challenge decisions by the Benefits Review Board, the administrative agency that adjudicates workers' compensation claims. Scalia, joined by Thomas, dissented, saying the board was the proper party in such cases.

Metropolitan Stevedore Co. v. Rambo, decided by a 6–3 vote, June 19, 1997; Souter wrote the opinion; O'Connor, Scalia, and Thomas dissented.

A longshore worker can receive nominal compensation for a workplace injury that has the potential for affecting future earnings even if it does not hurt his earning capacity at present.

The ruling favored a California man, John Rambo, who suffered a partial permanent disability as a result of an injury to his leg and back while doing longshore work for Metropolitan Stevedore Co. After being awarded benefits under the federal Longshore and Harbor Workers' Compensation

Act, he got a new job as a crane operator, earning considerably more than in his previous work. The Court, in a 1995 decision, held that Rambo's benefits should be reduced because of his new economic condition even though his physical condition was unchanged. On remand, the Ninth U.S. Circuit Court of Appeals held that Rambo was still entitled to nominal compensation because his injury could affect his earnings in the future.

By a 6–3 vote, the Court agreed. ". . . [A] worker is entitled to nominal compensation," Souter wrote, "when his work-related injury has not diminished his wage-earning capacity under current circumstances, but there is a significant potential that the injury will cause diminished capacity under future conditions." The worker has the burden of proof on the issue, Souter added.

Writing for the dissenters, O'Connor argued that the law "does not permit an [administrative law judge] to award purely nominal benefits in order to guard against the possibility of a future drop in earning power."

Property Law
Land Use Regulation

Suitum v. Tahoe Regional Planning Agency, decided by a 9–0 vote, May 27, 1997; Souter wrote the opinion.

A California woman won the right to a trial of her suit for compensation because of a regulatory scheme that barred her from building on a Lake Tahoe-area lot.

The ruling—a victory for property rights groups—overturned decisions by two lower federal courts that had blocked Bernadine Suitum from an immediate trial of her suit against the bistate Tahoe Regional Planning Agency. The agency's plan for limiting development around Lake Tahoe, which lies on the border between California and Nevada, compensated landowners by allotting "transferable development rights" that they could sell to other property owners in the area. Suitum filed a federal court suit claiming the regulations deprived her of all valuable use of her property. Two lower federal courts said the case was not "ripe"—ready for trial—because Suitum had not first tried to sell the development rights allotted to her.

In a unanimous decision, the Court disagreed. Souter said the agency's determination that Suitum could not build on her lot was a "final action" for purposes of satisfying the ripeness doctrine. The agency, Souter said, had "no discretion to exercise" over her right to use the land or to obtain development rights.

In a concurring opinion, Scalia, joined by O'Connor and Thomas, said the discussion of the development rights was unnecessary. The development rights, Scalia said, had "no bearing upon whether there has been a 'final decision' concerning the extent to which the plaintiff's land use has been constrained."

States

Boundary Disputes

United States v. Alaska, decided by 9–0 vote and 6–3 votes, June 19, 1997; O'Connor wrote the opinion; Thomas, Rehnquist, and Scalia dissented in part.

The Court sided with the United States and against Alaska in an eighteen-year-old dispute over ownership of oil- and natural gas-rich submerged lands off the state's Arctic coast.

The case began in 1979 when the federal government filed an original claim with the Court seeking to establish title to the lands in order to sell mineral leases for lands in the Beaufort Sea, off the state's northeastern coast. Alaska filed a counterclaim for title to submerged coastal lands within the National Petroleum Reserve in the northwestern part of the state and the Arctic National Wildlife Refuge in the northeast. A "special master" appointed by the Court to hold hearings and make recommendations ruled in favor of the United States on most of the issues, but found that Alaska owned the coastal lands within the wildlife refuge. Alaska and the United States each filed "exceptions" to the recommendations.

In a detailed opinion, the Court sided with the United States on each of the points. The justices divided 6–3 on the two major disputes but were unanimous on two other issues. O'Connor said that the federal government had retained ownership of submerged lands off the petroleum reserve's coast at the time of Alaskan statehood in 1957. She also said the government retained ownership of lands off the coast of the wildlife refuge because the U.S. Fish and Wildlife Service had a pending application to create a federal refuge as of 1957.

In a partial dissent, Thomas, joined by Rehnquist and Scalia, sided with Alaska on those two issues. Thomas said that the United States made no "express retention" of coastal lands within the petroleum reserve either when the reserve was created in 1923 or when Alaska became a state in 1957. And he argued that the state owned the wildlife refuge coastal lands because the wildlife refuge had not yet been created.

All justices joined O'Connor's opinion on two other points. First, she limited the state's ownership of lands off the coast of barrier islands to a three-mile belt from each individual island; Alaska wanted to link the islands for purposes of establishing a baseline for measuring the three-mile belt, thus encircling more of the submerged lands between islands. Second, she rejected Alaska's claim that a sand and gravel bar known as Dinkum

Sands was an island for purposes of establishing state ownership of the adjacent submerged lands.

The ruling meant that the federal government would get some $1 billion in mineral lease payments held in escrow during the dispute. The ruling also cheered environmentalists, who believed the federal government would do a better job than the state protecting the environmentally fragile areas off the wildlife refuge coast.

Immunity

Idaho v. Coeur d'Alene Tribe of Idaho, decided by a 5–4 vote, June 23, 1997; Kennedy wrote the main opinion; O'Connor wrote a concurring opinion; Souter, Stevens, Ginsburg, and Breyer dissented.

The Court rejected on state immunity grounds an Indian tribe's effort to bring a federal court suit to settle a property dispute between the tribe and the state of Idaho.

The ruling stemmed from a suit against Idaho officials by the Coeur d'Alene Tribe over ownership of the submerged lands below Lake Coeur d'Alene, which lies to the north of the most populated part of the tribe's reservation. The tribe claimed ownership based on executive orders and congressional action dating to 1873, but the state disputed the claim. In federal court, the state argued that the suit was barred by the Eleventh Amendment, which generally prohibits private suits against states in federal court. The tribe claimed the suit was authorized under the Court's 1908 decision, *Ex parte Young*, which allows federal court suits against state officials for an injunction against future violations of federally protected rights. The suit was dismissed by a lower federal court but reinstated by the Ninth U.S. Circuit Court of Appeals.

In a fractured ruling, the Court rejected the suit, but stopped short of a substantial narrowing of the important doctrine permitting federal court actions aginst state officials. Writing for a five-justice majority, Kennedy said the suit was "the functional equivalent of a quiet title action" and was barred because it "implicates special sovereignty interests" of the state. But in a different section of the opinion, Kennedy went further and proposed that a case-by-case balancing test of state interests be used to test all suits brought under *Ex parte Young*. Only Rehnquist joined that part of the opinion.

In a concurring opinion, O'Connor, joined by Scalia and Thomas, explicitly rejected Kennedy's approach. "The principal opinion replaces a straightforward inquiry . . . with a vague balancing test . . . ," she wrote.

Writing for the four dissenters, Souter said the suit should have been allowed. The tribe, he wrote, "claims that officers of the State of Idaho are acting to regulate land that belongs to the Tribe under federal law" and was seeking "declaratory and injunctive relief to halt the regulation as an ongoing violation of that law." But he also expressed satisfaction that O'Connor's "controlling opinion" rejected Kennedy's approach of case-by-case balancing in *Ex parte Young* suits.

Regents of the University of California v. Doe, decided by a 9–0 vote, February 19, 1997; Stevens wrote the opinion.

An arm of state government is immune from suit in federal court even if the federal government has agreed by contract to indemnify it for any judgment.

The unanimous decision barred a federal court suit by a New York scientist who said the federally funded Lawrence Livermore National Laboratory at the University of California in Berkeley broke an agreement to hire him. A federal district court dismissed the suit, brought on grounds of diversity of citizenship, saying the state university enjoyed sovereign immunity under the Eleventh Amendment. But the Ninth U.S. Circuit Court of Appeals reinstated the suit, saying that the laboratory's sovereign immunity was negated by the federal government's promise to indemnify it for any judgments.

In a brief and unanimous opinion, the Court said the indemnification provision had no effect on the state's immunity. "The Eleventh Amendment protects the State from the risk of adverse judgments," Stevens wrote, "even though the State may be indemnified by a third party."

Taxation

Arkansas v. Farm Credit Services of Central Arkansas, decided by a 9–0 vote, June 2, 1997; Kennedy wrote the opinion.

Farm credit associations established under federal law cannot use a federal court suit to contest imposition of a state tax.

The ruling dismissed on jurisdictional grounds a suit brought by four production credit associations (PCAs) in Arkansas seeking to win a broad exemption from state property and income taxes. A federal district court judge and the Eighth U.S. Circuit Court of Appeals both ruled that the PCAs were entitled to the exemption because the federal law providing for their creation designates them as "instrumentalities" of the federal government.

In a unanimous decision, the Court ruled that the suit did not belong in federal court because of the Tax Injunction Act, which generally bars federal court suits seeking to block state taxes. The anti-injunction act does not block federal court suits by the federal government, but Kennedy said the PCAs had to file in state court because they "do not have or exercise power analogous to that of . . . any of the departments of regulatory agencies of the United States."

Camps Newfound/Owatonna, Inc. v. Town of Harrison, decided by a 5–4 vote, May 19, 1997; Stevens wrote the opinion; Scalia, Rehnquist, Thomas, and Ginsburg dissented.

States cannot deny a tax exemption to a nonprofit organization solely because it primarily serves people from outside the state.

The ruling struck down a Maine law that provided a property tax exemption for charitable organizations only if most of their clients were state residents. The law was challenged by a camp operated by the Christian Science Church that primiarily served youngsters from outside Maine. A state court judge ruled that the tax exemption violated the U.S. Constitution's protection for interstate commerce. But the state's highest court upheld the measure, saying it treated all charities alike and had only "incidental effects on interstate commerce."

In a narrowly divided decision, the Court ruled the measure unconstitutional under the so-called Dormant Commerce Clause, a court-made doctrine that limits the ability of states to impose economic burdens on businesses engaged in interestate commerce. "We see no reason," Stevens wrote for the majority, "why the nonprofit character of an enterprise should exclude it from the coverage of either the affirmative or the negative aspect of the Commerce Clause."

Stevens rejected alternative arguments in defense of the tax exemption offered by the town where the camps were located. He said the differential tax treatment could not be justified as a tax subsidy targeted to charities that serve in-state residents or as a governmental decision to purchase services from such organizations.

The ruling drew two lengthy dissenting opinions. In the first, Scalia said Maine's "narrow tax exemption" had "nothing to do with economic protectionism" but was designed only to "compensate" private charities for serving state residents. Rehnquist, Thomas, and Ginsburg joined his opinion. In the second of the dissents, Thomas went further and attacked the Court's entire line of Dormant Commerce Clause cases, saying they had "no basis in the text of the Constitution" and had proved "virtually unworkable in application." Rehnquist and Scalia, but not Ginsburg, joined his opinion.

The Maine law was apparently unique in the country. But the case attracted friend-of-the-court briefs from a variety of charitable organizations that warned against allowing states to deny tax exemptions to groups that serve national audiences.

De Buono, New York Commissioner of Health v. NYSA-ILA Medical and Clinical Services Fund, decided by a 7–2 vote, June 2, 1997; Stevens wrote the opinion; Scalia and Thomas dissented on jurisdictional grounds.

The federal law regulating employee benefit plans does not prevent states from taxing hospitals or clinics owned by benefit plans.

The ruling rejected an effort by a longshore workers' benefits plan that owned two medical clinics in New York to escape a state tax on health care facilities. The Second U.S. Circuit Court of Appeals ruled that the broad preemption provision in the federal Employee Retirement Income Security

Act (ERISA) blocked the state from imposing the levy on facilities owned by pension funds.

The Court disagreed. Writing for seven justices, Stevens said New York's tax was not "the type of state law that Congress intended ERISA to supersede."

Scalia, joined by Thomas, dissented, but only on jurisdictional grounds. He argued that the Court needed to hear additional arguments on whether the federal Tax Injunction Act barred the benefit plan from using a federal court suit to try to block the tax.

General Motors Corp. v. Tracy, Tax Commissioner of Ohio, decided by an 8–1 vote, February 18, 1997; Souter wrote the opinion; Stevens dissented.

States may impose a sales tax on unregulated out-of-state natural gas producers and marketers even if regulated natural gas utilities within the state are exempt from the levy.

The ruling rejected an argument by General Motors Corp. that the Ohio tax scheme—a product of the partial deregulation of the natural gas market—amounted to unconstitutional discrimination against interstate commerce. GM, which bought all of its natural gas for its Ohio plants from unregulated out-of-state suppliers, unsuccessfully challenged the differential treatment in Ohio courts.

In a nearly unanimous decision, the Court declined to upset the system. Souter said Ohio was entitled to exempt the local utilities because their "singular role" in serving a "captive market" of residential customers meant they were "dissimilar" from natural gas marketers serving larger industrial customers. He noted that Congress could exercise its power over interstate commerce to change the tax scheme if it wanted.

In a lone dissent, Stevens said the potential impact of denying the utilities a "discriminatory tax advantage" was not "a sufficient justification" for the scheme.

Torts

Racketeering

Klehr v. A.O. Smith Corp., decided by a 9–0 vote, June 19, 1997; Breyer wrote the opinion.

The Court rejected an expansive ruling for setting the deadline for bringing a federal civil racketeering suit. But the decision failed to resolve a conflict among lower courts on three other possible methods of deciding when a plaintiff must file a suit brought under the Racketeer Influenced and Corrupt Organizations Act (RICO).

The ruling upheld the dismissal of a RICO suit filed in 1993 by Minnesota dairy farmers Marvin and Mary Klehr against the manufacturer of a silo that they bought in 1974 to store cattle feed. The couple claimed that the feed rotted because the silo malfunctioned and that the manufacturer concealed the problem through misrepresentations. A federal district court judge and the Eighth U.S. Circuit Court of Appeals both ruled the couple had waited too long to bring the suit. The Court agreed to review the case to try to settle a conflict between four different approaches for deciding what date to use to determine whether a RICO suit was filed within the four-year statute of limitations.

In a limited ruling, the Court rejected the broadest of the four rulings on the issue: a rule adopted by the Third Circuit that allowed a plaintiff to bring suit within four years after "the last predicate act" that was part of the alleged pattern of racketeering. Breyer said that approach "lengthens the limitations period dramatically." But Breyer said the Klehrs' case did not require the Court to settle which of three other rules should be adopted.

In a partial concurring opinion, Scalia, joined by Thomas, complained that the ruling left "reduced but unresolved the well-known split in authority that prompted us to take this case." Scalia contended the Court should have adopted the narrowest rule for calculating the statute of limitations: a rule that starts the four-year deadline at the time of the first injury to the plaintiff.

4 *Preview of the 1997–1998 Term*

Sharon Taxman and Debra Williams were both in their ninth year of teaching business education at Piscataway High School in central New Jersey in 1989 when the township's school board found it had to lay one of them off because of declining enrollment. In previous layoff situations, the school board had used random selection systems to choose between teachers with equal seniority. But the school board decided to use a different criterion to decide this time. In the interest of racial diversity, the board fired Taxman because she was white and Williams was black.

The layoff came as Taxman was worried about paying for her teenaged son's college education. She also felt the reason for the board's decision was wrong, legally and morally. So she filed a complaint with the Equal Employment Opportunity Commission (EEOC), charging that the firing amounted to racial discrimination in employment in violation of Title VII of the Civil Rights Act of 1964. A federal judge eventually agreed and approved a jury award totaling about $144,000 in back pay and interest.

Taxman was rehired four years later, taking a classroom adjacent to Williams—who remained the only black among fourteen teachers in the high school's business department. But the case continued and, eight years after the original layoff, reached the Supreme Court. The school board asked the Court to overturn both the award and a broadly written appeals court decision that barred racial diversity as a basis for affirmative action policies.

The justices' decision to hear the case in the 1997–1998 term set the stage for another Court ruling on the contentious issue of affirmative action for racial minorities and women. Critics of affirmative action hoped the Court would draw a sharp line against the use of race as a factor in employment decisions by government or even private employers. (*Piscataway Township Board of Education v. Taxman*)

The Piscataway case was one of forty-seven disputes that the justices put on the Court's calendar before taking their summer recess. The figure roughly equaled the number of cases, forty-six, the Court had carried over a year earlier. But the issues for the coming year appeared to be less momentous.

Apart from the affirmative action case, the other cases appeared unlikely to generate the same kind of banner headlines produced by the Court's end-of-term rulings in June 1997. As always, however, the cases presented an

Note: The Piscataway School Board voted on November 20, as this book was going to press, to pay Sharon Taxman $433,500 to settle her racial discrimination suit. Her attorney said he and the school board's lawyer would ask the Supreme Court to drop its consideration of the case. Critics of affirmative action were disappointed but voiced confidence that the Court would continue to narrow the use of racial preferences. "Civil rights groups have temporarily delayed the inevitable," said Clint Bolick, litigation director for the Institute for Justice.

array of unsettled legal questions and at least the potential for unanticipated developments.

In one case, for example, the Court was being asked to decide whether
its sexual harassment rulings applied to conduct between people of the same
sex. While many observers expected the Court to say yes, critics of the previous rulings hoped the justices would use the case to narrow those decisions.
In another case, the justices were to review a military appeals court's decision to open the door to possible use of polygraph tests in courts-martial.
The Court was generally expected to maintain the ban on lie detector tests,
but a ruling the other way could send shock waves through state and federal
criminal justice systems.

In line with their practice of the last five years, the justices also added
cases to the calendar in the week preceding the start of the new term. But
the ten cases the justices agreed to review on September 29 were also less
than overwhelming. Among the most interesting was a boundary dispute
between the states of New York and New Jersey over ownership of Ellis Island, the historic gateway for millions of immigrants to America that lies in
New York harbor between the two states. The case had both symbolic and
financial significance: the island offered the potential for commercial development and historic preservation that could draw tourism revenues. (*New
Jersey v. New York*)

Along with a death penalty case from California the justices agreed to
review in August, the new cases brought the total number on the Court's
calendar to fifty-eight as the new term began on October 6. The justices
would continue adding cases after they reconvened, with cases accepted by
January likely to be decided during the 1997–1998 term.

Affirmative Action

The Piscataway case reached the Court as political and legal trends were
going against the use of racial preferences. California voters in November
1996 approved a state ballot initiative banning the use of racial preferences
in government contracting, public employment, and state college and university admissions. The Court itself had issued a ruling in 1995 narrowing
the scope for racial preferences in government contracting and, in a series
of decisions since 1993, had backed challenges to the use of race in legislative and congressional redistricting.

The Court in the 1970s and '80s, however, had permitted both private
and public employers to adopt affirmative action policies to remedy past
discrimination against racial minorities and women. It had also opened the
door, in its controversial *Bakke* decision in 1978, for colleges and universities
to adopt admissions policies aimed at promoting racial diversity. But the
Court also issued rulings in the 1980s limiting the enforcement of affirma-

tive action policies by public employers if they resulted in layoffs of non-minority employees.

Critics of affirmative action viewed the Piscataway case as an ideal context for dramatizing the costs of racial preferences in human as well as policy terms. Both teachers had been scarred by the episode. Taxman, the white teacher, declined to give media interviews, but her attorney described her as depressed by the long-simmering controversy. For her part, Williams complained that the school board was wrong to have used race as the only criterion at the time of the layoff. "I don't want minority students to feel I'm there because of my color," she told a *USA Today* reporter.

Sharon Taxman

Piscataway itself appeared to present none of the usual justifications for remedial use of affirmative action. The suburban township (population 47,000) was racially integrated, and the school system's 6,200 students were also racially mixed: about 50 percent white, 30 percent African-American, 10 percent Asian, and 5 percent Hispanic. The school system had no history of racial discrimination, and the teaching staff reflected the racial mix in the district's population.

Still, the school board defended its decision to keep Williams as the only black teacher in the high school's business department as unexceptionable. "The importance of diversity in the educational environment was so obvious," the school board's lawyer, David B. Rubin, commented. "It is a very, very

Debra Williams

culturally diverse community, and the folks in the school administration believe that contributes to the educational experience. We believe the same principles apply to the faculty."

But Taxman's attorney mocked the school board's concern with the racial composition of one single department. "They're arguing that the business department wouldn't have had a diverse faculty," Stephen Klausner said. "I don't buy that." Williams "taught keyboarding," Klausner continued. "How much ethnic diversity can you give on the keyboard?"

The school board made no headway with its argument in the lower courts. U.S. District Court Judge Maryanne Trump Barry ruled in September 1993 that Supreme Court precedents did not permit the board to adopt an affirmative action plan solely to promote racial diversity among the faculty. On appeal, the Third U.S. Circuit Court of Appeals agreed. "Although we applaud the goal of racial diversity," Judge Walter K. Stapleton wrote for the 8–3 majority in August 1996, "we cannot agree that Title VII permits an employer to advance that goal through non-remedial discriminatory measures."

By the time the case reached the appeals court, it had become a political hot potato for the Clinton administration. Initially, the Justice Department under President George Bush's administration had supported Taxman, filing suit on her behalf in 1991 after the EEOC found probable cause in her claim. Under Clinton, however, the Justice Department sought to change positions and side with the school board. The appeals court refused to let the government change sides, but allowed it to withdraw from the suit.

After the school board asked the Court to review the case in April 1997, administration lawyers debated what position to take. In June, the government urged the Court not to hear the case, saying it was "not an appropriate vehicle" to decide the issue of non-remedial affirmative action. After the justices agreed to review the case on their last day before the summer recess, administration lawyers crafted a new position.

In a brief filed in late August, the solicitor general's office said the school board had not proved a need for using race in its decision to fire Taxman. "A simple desire to promote diversity for its own sake . . . is not a permissible basis for taking race into account," the brief stated. Still, the administration argued, school systems in some circumstances could show "a compelling interest in obtaining the educational benefits of a racially diverse faculty at each of its schools" and could justify the use of race as "one factor" in making assignment or transfer decisions.

The government's latest shift prompted snide comments from supporters and critics of affirmative action. Christopher Hansen, a staff attorney with the American Civil Liberties Union, called the brief a "double flip-flop." Douglas Kmiec, a conservative law professor at Notre Dame University, quipped: "Which way did the government go? It went Pis-cat-a-way."

The school board did draw support from an array of civil rights organizations, which filed ten friend-of-the-court briefs urging the justices to allow employers to consider racial diversity as one goal in fashioning affirmative action policies. On the opposite side, conservative legal groups were working on briefs urging the Court to uphold the appeals court ruling and limit the use of racial preferences to cases carefully designed to remedy past discrimination. While some groups were expected to limit their arguments to government employers, others were planning to urge the Court to bar voluntary affirmative action plans by private employers as well.

Civil rights supporters braced for an adverse ruling in the case. "This Court has not been looking favorably on affirmative action plans," said Theodore Shaw, associate director of the NAACP Legal Defense and Educational Fund. "And these facts involving a layoff situation are already difficult."

Critics of affirmative action, on the other hand, were voicing confidence. "We believe that the Supreme Court has spoken repeatedly and convincingly that past discrimination is the only possible justification for race-conscious governmental action," said Clint Bolick, vice president of the Institute of Justice.

Many Court-watchers were predicting, however, that the decision might be narrower than critics of affirmative action hoped or supporters feared. In particular, these observers noted that Justice O'Connor, who often cast the decisive vote in affirmative action cases, had a penchant for carefully qualified rulings rather than sweeping legal pronouncements. And they noted that a decade earlier O'Connor had carefully skirted a ruling on the use of race to promote diversity among school faculties.

O'Connor had voted with the 5–4 majority in the Court's 1986 decision, *Wygant v. Jackson Board of Education*, in invalidating an Ohio school district's policy that protected some recently hired black teachers from layoffs. But in a separate opinion, she stressed that the board had justified its policy only on grounds of remedying general societal discrimination, not on grounds of promoting a diverse teaching staff. For that reason, she said, "I do not believe it necessary to discuss the magnitude of that interest or its applicability in this case."

Following are some of the other major cases on the Court's calendar as it began its 1997–1998 term:

Business Law

Credit unions. Federally chartered credit unions asked the Court to throw out a major legal victory won by commercial banks seeking to limit the expansion of their rival financial institutions.

The federal appeals court in Washington struck down an expansive interpretation of the 1934 law governing federal credit unions. The law limited membership in federal credit unions to "groups having a common bond of occupation or association." The National Credit Union Administration (NCUA) in 1982 revised its interpretation of that provision to permit credit unions to include unrelated occupational groups.

A group of North Carolina banks, backed by the American Banking Association, filed suit in 1990 seeking to block the NCUA from allowing the North Carolina-based AT&T Family Federal Credit Union to expand to include employees of various small businesses in North Carolina and Virginia. The federal appeals court in Washington ruled in favor of the banks.

Both the NCUA and the credit unions' trade association urged the Court to overturn the decision. The regulatory agency said the decision "threatens the survival of many existing federal credit unions around the country" and could cause "extreme disruption in the credit union industry." But the banks argued the agency had misinterpreted the federal law. "NCUA cites nothing showing that Congress intended that a single credit union could string to-gether multiple common bonds," their brief read. (*National Credit Union Administration v. First National Bank & Trust Co.*; *AT&T Family Federal Credit Union v. First National Bank & Trust Co.*)

Vertical price fixing. Major business groups and the Justice Department joined in urging the Court to overturn a thirty-year-old precedent that made it per se illegal for suppliers to establish price ceilings for their dealers.

The issue arose in an antitrust suit filed by a former Chicago-area ser-vice station dealer against an oil distributor. The dealer charged that his contract with the distributor effectively set a maximum resale price by pro-viding that the distributor would recoup any additional profits if the dealer charged more than the "suggested" retail price. The federal appeals court in Chicago said the suit was valid under the Court's 1968 decision, *Albrecht v. Herald Tribune Co.*, that so-called vertical price fixing agreements between manufacturers or suppliers and their dealers are per se illegal. But the appeals court also strongly criticized the decision and said it should be overruled.

An array of business groups, including the National Association of Manu-facturers and the American Petroleum Institute, joined the oil company in urging the Court to review the case. In a supporting brief, the Justice De-partment and the Federal Trade Commission called for an easing of the rule against maximum vertical price fixing, arguing that such agreements can sometimes serve "the pro-competitive purpose of limiting a dealer's ability to exploit market power." But thirty-three states joined in a brief calling for the per se ban to be retained. They warned that maximum resale price agree-ments were likely to pressure "weaker retailers," "cause price rigidity," and make it harder to detect agreements to establish minimum prices. (*State Oil Co. v. Khan*)

Courts and Procedure

Expert testimony. The Court agreed to decide how strictly federal appeals courts should review lower court decisions on admitting or excluding scien-tific testimony at trials.

The hotly contested issue stemmed from the Court's 1993 decision, *Daubert v. Merrell Dow Pharmaceuticals, Inc.*, that required federal judges to determine the scientific basis of expert testimony before allowing it to be used at trial. Federal appeals courts had divided on what standard they should use in reviewing lower court decisions under the new rule. Lawyers in tort cases also were divided: plaintiffs' attorneys generally wanted appeals courts to exercise more oversight, while lawyers for insurers and business interests favored a more deferential approach.

In the case the Court agreed to review, a federal judge in Georgia excluded expert testimony that attorneys for Robert and Karen Joiner wanted to present to try to show that Robert, an electrician, had contracted lung cancer as a result of exposure to chemicals in electric transformers. The judge then granted summary judgment to the three companies named as defendants: General Electric Co. and Westinghouse Corp, which manufactured the transformers, and Monsanto Co., which allegedly made the chemical. But the federal appeals court for Georgia reversed. It held that appellate courts should exercise "stringent" review of decisions to bar expert testimony and that, under that standard, the judge had made a mistake.

In asking the Court to review the case, the three companies said trial judges should have "broad discretion" in ruling on the admissibility of expert testimony. They also said the appeals court was wrong to apply a "double standard" of reviewing decisions to exclude testimony more strictly than rulings to allow evidence. The U.S. Chamber of Commerce and other business groups as well as the Justice Department backed their appeal. But plaintiffs' groups argued that the trial judge had gone too far in excluding the testimony. "The Court should take this opportunity," the plaintiffs' group Trial Lawyers for Public Justice wrote in a supporting brief, "to re-emphasize the limited nature of the trial judge's gatekeeping function." (*General Electric Co. v. Joiner*)

"Whistleblower" testimony. The children of a woman killed in a fiery automobile crash challenged a court-enforced agreement preventing a former General Motors engineer from testifying against the company in product liability suits.

The children had won a $11.3 million jury award against GM in federal court in Missouri after using testimony from the former engineer, Ronald Elwell, in the trial. GM had sought to block the testimony because Elwell had previously agreed—for an undisclosed amount of money—to an injunction issued by a Michigan state court judge barring him from testifying against GM in product liability suits except under subpoena. The federal appeals court in St. Louis ordered a new trial, saying the trial judge was required to enforce the Michigan court's injunction under the constitutional provision requiring courts in one state to give "full faith and credit" to orders issued by courts in another state.

Contesting the decision, attorneys for the accident victim's children said the ruling "would provide wrongdoers with a blueprint for purchasing the silence of potentially vital witnesses." But GM's lawyers denied the company was "trying to buy the silence of a whistleblower" and insisted the plaintiffs should have challenged the injunction against Elwell's testimony in the Michigan court instead of the federal court in Missouri. (*Baker v. General Motors Corp.*)

Attorney trust accounts. The Court took up a constitutional challenge to a program operating in virtually every state that pooled funds from small trust accounts held by lawyers to help fund legal services for the poor.

The program—known by the acronym IOLTA for "Interest on Lawyer Trust Accounts"—had been promoted by private and mandatory bar groups since the mid-1970s to supplement other funding for legal aid. Supporters said that by pooling nominal trust accounts that would not earn interest if maintained separately, the plan cost clients nothing but provided legal aid programs with significant funding, about $96 million in 1995.

The conservative Washington Legal Foundation challenged the programs and, after being rebuffed by a number of state and federal courts, won a ruling from the federal appeals court in Texas that clients had a "cognizable property interest" in the interest earned on the trust funds. The administrators of the Texas program, backed by the American Bar Association and an array of other bar groups, urged the Court to overturn the ruling. They argued the IOLTA programs "did not alter . . . expectations of lawyers or clients with regard to the ability to earn interest on lawyers' client trust accounts." (*Phillips v. Washington Legal Foundation*)

Criminal Law and Procedure

Lie detector tests. The government asked the Court to reinstate a rule in military courts completely banning the use of polygraph tests as evidence.

The Court of Appeals for the Armed Forces invalidated the ban on lie detector tests by a 3–2 vote in a case involving a serviceman convicted of a variety of charges, including use of drugs. The serviceman denied the drug charge and took a lie detector test, which indicated no deception. But the court-martial refused to allow his lawyers to try to lay a foundation for introducing the results as evidence. In its ruling, the appeals court agreed with the serviceman's lawyers that the total ban was an arbitrary limitation on his Sixth Amendment right to present a defense.

The government described lie detector tests as "a scientific technique whose reliability and helpfulness are widely questioned" and contended the appeals court ruling conflicted with "a longstanding rule followed in state and federal civilian courts." But the defense lawyers called the blanket exclusion "arbitrary and unreasonable." "It cannot be determined in a vacuum," they wrote, "that polygraph evidence, in all cases, under all circumstances, is confusing, a waste of time, and unreliable." (*United States v. Scheffer*)

Double jeopardy. Three former Oklahoma bankers who were civilly fined for improper insider loans asked the Court to bar the government from criminally prosecuting them for the same transactions.

John Hudson served as chairman and Larry Baresel and Jack Butler Rackley served as officers or directors of several small Oklahoma banks during the 1980s. After federal bank regulators charged them with making insider loans, they agreed to pay fines totaling about $44,000. When the government indicted them in 1992 for the same offenses, they claimed the prosecution violated the Double Jeopardy Clause. The federal appeals court for Oklahoma rejected the claim. It ruled that the fines amounted to a "remedial" sanction because they were not "overwhelmingly disproportionate" to the government's "damages" as measured by the cost of the civil proceeding.

In urging reversal, attorneys for the three men said the fines were "plainly punitive" and barred a subsequent criminal case. The government defended the prosecution, but joined in urging the Court to review the case. It said lower courts needed "guidance" on the question of when "monetary penalties imposed under civil regulatory enforcement schemes trigger double jeopardy scrutiny." (*Hudson v. United States*)

No-knock searches. The government asked the Court to reject a federal appeals court rule requiring special evidence of danger before police can cause property damage in executing a no-knock search warrant.

The Ninth U.S. Circuit Court of Appeals in California applied the rule in suppressing two weapons seized from a defendant's garage after police broke in through a window while searching for a prison escapee. The officers had cited the danger of violence in obtaining a warrant authorizing a no-knock search, but the appeals court said they needed more specific evidence to justify an entry with property damage.

The government said the Ninth Circuit's rule was "disruptive to law enforcement" and "increases the risk of harm faced by officers executing warrants." But the defendant's attorneys argued that the knock-and-announce rule protected both property and people. "Failure to comply with the strict requirements of the knock-and-announce principle," the defense lawyers said, "has caused, and continues to cause, many more deaths to officers and civilians than the reverse." (*United States v. Ramirez*)

Capital punishment. A Virginia death row inmate sought to have his sentence overturned because the jury was given no instructions on the use of mitigating evidence in deciding whether to impose the death penalty.

Douglas Buchanan was convicted of capital murder for the 1987 killings of his father, stepmother, and two stepbrothers. Although Virginia law lists mitigating factors to consider in a death penalty case, the judge's instructions did not cite them or give the jury any other guidance on the issue. Buchanan filed a federal habeas corpus petition seeking to overturn the death sentence, but a lower court judge and the federal appeals court for Virginia both rejected his plea.

In seeking review, Buchanan's lawyers argued that the failure to give the jury instructions on mitigating evidence "turned the sentencing proceeding into an unregulated, arbitrary free-for-all." But lawyers for the state insisted that Buchanan's lawyers had been allowed to present and argue the mitigating evidence. ". . . [T]he Constitution clearly did not require that instructions provide any further explanation of the concept of mitigation," the state's lawyers said. (*Buchanan v. Angelone*)

Executive clemency. The Ohio parole authority asked to overturn a federal appeals court decision that held due process protections applied to state executive clemency procedures in death penalty cases.

Ohio revised its executive clemency procedures in 1994 to require the state's clemency review board to gather information on and offer an opportunity for an interview to a death row inmate shortly after the end of his state court appeals. Eugene Woodard, sentenced to death for a 1990 robbery-murder, challenged the procedure in federal court. He argued that he was forced to choose between seeking clemency or challenging his sentence through post-conviction procedures; that choice, he said, violated his right to due process and his right to remain silent. A federal district judge rejected the plea, but the federal appeals court for Ohio held that the clemency procedures must meet some due process requirements and ordered the judge to reconsider the case.

In asking the Court to review the case, the state's attorneys argued the decision "threatens to undo decades of precedent concerning the wide discretion available to the States in establishing executive clemency procedures." But the Ohio public defender's office argued that clemency was "an integral part" of the capital punishment process and "some level of due process protection" was required. (*Ohio Adult Parole Authority v. Woodard*)

Election Law

Advocacy groups. The Federal Election Commission asked the Court to overturn a ruling that could force political advocacy groups to disclose the amounts and the recipients of campaign contributions.

The ruling by the federal appeals court in Washington came in a citizen suit challenging the FEC's refusal to define the American Israel Public Affairs Committee (AIPAC) as a "political committee" subject to campaign disclosure requirements. The plaintiffs were all critics of the influential pro-Israeli lobbying group. The FEC ruled that AIPAC did not have to disclose the amounts or the beneficiaries of its campaign contributions because they were not the group's "major purpose." But the appeals court, in a 9–2 ruling, said the commission was misreading federal election law and Court precedents interpreting the statute.

In seeking to overturn the ruling, the FEC argued the decision would place "substantial burdens on organizations engaged primarily in issue advocacy." The commission also said the plaintiffs had no legal standing to bring the suit. In response, the group that brought the suit argued that "a dual-purpose organization" should not be exempted from campaign disclosure requirements "simply because election spending is its 'minor' purpose." (*Federal Election Commission v. Akins*)

Louisiana open primary. The Court agreed to decide the legality of Louisiana's system allowing members of Congress to be elected by winning a majority of votes in a primary open to candidates of any party.

State officials sought to overturn a federal appeals court decision striking down the "open primary" election as conflicting with a federal law that sets congressional elections on the first Tuesday after the first Monday in November. Louisiana's law—enacted in 1978 and the only such law in the country—provided that no election need be held in November if a candidate won a majority in a primary open to all candidates held in early October.

In their suit attacking the system, four one-time congressional candidates—three Republicans and one independent—said the procedure "directly conflicts" with federal law. But state officials defended the Louisiana procedure, arguing that the federal law did not require states to hold a "contested election" in November. (*Foster v. Love*)

Environmental Law

"Right-to-know" suits. An array of industry groups urged the Court to bar citizen suits for past violations of a federal law requiring public disclosure of the use of toxic chemicals.

The issue arose in a suit brought by an environmental group against a Chicago steel-finishing company under the Emergency Planning and Community Right-to-Know Act of 1986. The law required companies using toxic chemicals to file reports with local, state, or federal officials listing the substances and amount held on site or released into the environment. The act authorized enforcement suits by "any citizen," but required 60-days' advance notice of the suit to the defendant. The plaintiff could recover a civil penalty of up to $25,000 per violation plus the cost of litigation, including attorneys' fees.

The Steel Company, a small steel-finishing company in Chicago's industrial section, claimed it had no knowledge of the law, but filed the necessary information in 1991 after receiving an intent-to-sue notification from Citizens for a Better Environment. A federal district court judge dismissed the suit, saying Congress did not intend to allow recovery for "historical violations" of the law. But a federal appeals court reinstated the action.

Trade associations representing the steel, chemical, petroleum and timber industries joined the company in urging the Court to bar suits for past violations if they are corrected before the suit reaches court. But the Clinton administration sided with the environmental group. Citizen suits would be "a futile gesture," the administration argued, if companies "could avoid suit altogether by delaying their filings . . . until they received a citizen's notice of suit." (*The Steel Co. v. Citizens for a Better Environment*)

Landmark preservation. The city of Chicago brought a landmark preservation dispute to the Court in an effort to have the case tried in federal rather than state court.

The city's landmark commission had refused to give the International College of Surgeons a permit to demolish two historic, lakeshore mansions to make way for construction of a 40-story luxury condominium tower. The surgeons' group contested the action in state court in a suit raising both state and federal law claims. The city used the federal "removal" procedure to have the case tried in federal court, which upheld the city's action. But the federal appeals court in Chicago ruled the case belonged in state court.

The legal question seemed technical: whether an appeal of a local administrative agency amounted to a "civil action" for purposes of the federal removal statute. But two groups normally opposed to each other—the National Trust for Historic Preservation and Defenders of Property Rights—both called for overturning the decision. Each group contended it was important for litigants in landmark preservation cases to have access to federal courts. (*City of Chicago v. International College of Surgeons*)

Federal Government

Federal employees. The government asked the Court to rule that federal workers charged with misconduct on the job can be disciplined for making false statements when they deny the accusations in official investigations.

The Court of Appeals for the Federal Circuit, citing "procedural due process concerns," ruled in June 1996 that an agency could not bring a "falsification" charge on the basis of an employee's "denial of another charge or of underlying facts relating to that other charge." The ruling affected six federal workers facing various misconduct charges who had all denied the accusations when questioned by investigators.

In seeking review, the Office of Personnel Management contended the decision "threatens to do substantial damage to the ethical underpinnings of the civil service." But the employees argued that allowing a separate charge for falsification in such cases would have the effect of "chilling an employee's right to respond." "In essence," lawyers for one of the employees said, "even minor charges would become removal offenses." (*King v. Erickson*)

Native Americans. The state of Alaska sought to overturn a ruling that it said could grant sovereign "Indian country" status to vast areas of the state occupied by native tribes.

Alaskan officials argued that Indian country status was barred by the Alaskan Native Claims Settlement Act, a 1971 law that extinguished historic Indian titles to land in exchange for a cash payment and new political arrangements. But a remote village occupied by some 350 Athabaskan Indians won a ruling from the Ninth U.S. Circuit Court of Appeals recognizing the village as Indian country.

In seeking review, the state said the appeals court ruling could result in granting Indian country status to as much as 40 million acres of land—comparable to the total acreage of Indian country lands in the lower forty-eight states. Lawyers for the Native American Rights Fund argued the 1971 law did not bar Indian country status in the state. But they also said the ruling would apply only to the handful of villages that opted out of the act. (*Alaska v. Native Village of Venetie Tribal Government*)

First Amendment

Public television. Public television stations sought to overturn a federal appeals court decision that threatened their ability to sponsor campaign debates unless they invited all legally qualified candidates to participate.

Ralph Forbes, a perennial candidate for Arkansas state offices, challenged the refusal of the state's public television network to include him in a debate among candidates in a 1992 congressional race. After a long court fight, Forbes won a ruling from the federal appeals court for Arkansas that the debate amounted to a "limited public forum" and the state-owned network had no legally sufficient reason for excluding him.

The trade association for public television stations, the Federal Communications Commission, and the federal Commission on Presidential Debates joined in calling for the decision to be overturned. The FCC said the ruling could "discourage many [public TV] broadcasters from sponsoring political debates at all." But Forbes won backing from Ross Perot's campaign organization and the Green Party as well as the American Civil Liberties Union. "The inevitable consequence of a decision by government broadcasters" to exclude a qualified candidate from a debate, the ACLU warned, "will be to diminish that candidate's viability" and "distort the democratic process." (*Arkansas Educational Television Commission v. Forbes*)

Immigration Law

Citizenship for illegitimate children. The adult daughter of a Filipina woman and a U.S. serviceman challenged the constitutionality of an immigration law establishing barriers to citizenship for illegitimate children of American fathers.

Immigration law bestowed citizenship automatically on a child born out of wedlock to an American mother and a foreign father. But the illegitimate child of an American father could gain U.S. citizenship only if the father acknowledged paternity before the child reached the age of eighteen.

Lorelyn Penero Miller, who was denied citizenship because her father acknowledged paternity only after she turned twenty-one, argued the distinction violated equal protection because it had "no rational basis." But the government said the differential treatment was justified because of the difficulty of proof of paternity and the absence of close ties between fathers and their illegitimate children. (*Miller v. Albright*)

Individual Rights

Same-sex sexual harassment. The Court agreed to decide whether federal civil rights law allowed a worker to recover damages for sexual harassment by someone of the same sex.

The issue reached the Court in a case brought by a former oil drilling rig worker in Louisiana who claimed male coworkers taunted, assaulted, and threatened to rape him. Joseph Oncale claimed that his employer, Sundowner Offshore Services, Inc., did nothing to stop the harassment and that he was forced to quit in November 1991 after three months on the job. The company denied the allegations, but also argued that the federal anti–job discrimination law—Title VII of the Civil Rights Act of 1964—did not cover sexual harassment by someone of the same sex. The Fifth U.S. Circuit Court of Appeals agreed; other federal appeals courts were divided on the issue.

In urging the Court to review the case, Oncale's attorneys argued that "[n]either a man nor a woman can be required . . . to run a gauntlet of sexual abuse, as a condition of employment." The Clinton administration also contended that the federal law applied to sexual harassment "without regard to the gender of the harasser or the victim." But lawyers for the company—noting that Oncale could sue under state law—said that his argument "trivializes Title VII's important purpose" and "ignores [its] limited scope." (*Oncale v. Sundowner Offshore Services, Inc.*)

Police chases. The Court agreed to review a federal appeals court ruling that law enforcement agencies said improperly exposed police officers to liability in damage suits arising from high-speed auto chases.

The ruling stemmed from the death of a California teenager, Philip Lewis, who was a passenger on a motorcycle involved in a high-speed pursuit by a Sacramento County sheriff's deputy. The boy's parents filed a federal court suit claiming the deputy violated their son's rights to substantive due process under the Fourteenth Amendment. A federal district court judge, applying Court precedents, said the deputy was entitled to qualified immunity because the law governing liability for police chases was not clear at the time of the accident. But the federal appeals court for California reinstated the suit.

In seeking to overturn the decision, lawyers for the deputy said the ruling conflicted with Court rulings limiting constitutional claims for due process violations to governmental actions that "shock the conscience." In a friend-of-the-court brief, three local governments in California went further and urged that police chase suits be limited to intentional actions that violated the Fourth Amendment. But lawyers for the boy's parents said that the deputy's attorneys were misreading the Court's precedents and that the restriction advocated by the local governments was "shocking." (*County of Sacramento v. Lewis*)

Damage suits. The Court agreed to hear three separate cases stemming from damage suits brought against local officials under federal civil rights laws.

A deputy district attorney in Seattle asked the Court to rule that prosecutors are absolutely immune from suit when they obtain arrest warrants against a suspect. Prosecutor Lynne Kalina was sued by a former burglary suspect, who claimed she violated his civil rights by submitting a false affidavit in court to get an arrest warrant against him. Although prosecutors have absolute immunity in court proceedings, the Ninth U.S. Circuit Court of Appeals ruled that they enjoy only "qualified immunity" in obtaining arrest warrants. The Justice Department, prosecutors' groups, and more than thirty states joined Kalina in urging the Court to overturn the decision. (*Kalina v. Fletcher*)

Two city officials in Fall River, Massachusetts, asked the Court to overturn a jury verdict against them in a suit brought by a former head of the city's health and human services department for voting to abolish her department. Janet Scott-Harris claimed that the two officials—Mayor Daniel Bogan and Councillor Marilyn Roderick—initiated the city council's decision to abolish her agency and her job in retaliation for her complaining about racial slurs made about her by another city employee. The federal appeals court in Boston rejected the officials' plea that they were entitled to absolute legislative immunity for the adoption of the ordinance. (*Bogan v. Scott-Harris*)

Finally, in a case from the District of Columbia, convicted murderer Leonard Crawford-El sought to overturn a federal appeals court ruling that set a high barrier for damage suits against public officials for retaliation for exercising First Amendment rights. Crawford-El claimed he was transferred to a prison in Washington State and personal property was withheld from him because of comments he made to the *Washington Post* about overcrowding in the District of Columbia prison. But the federal appeals court for the District of Columbia said prison officials were entitled to dismissal on grounds of qualified immunity unless Crawford-El could prove unconstitutional intent by "clear and convincing evidence." (*Crawford-El v. Britton*)

Labor Law

Employer polling. Business groups urged the Court to disapprove a National Labor Relations Board (NLRB) policy limiting the right of employers to poll workers to determine their support for an existing union.

The NLRB found an Allentown, Pennsylvania, truck dealership guilty of an unfair labor practice for polling its thirty-two workers in February 1991 to see whether the machinists' union local representing the employees still had majority support. The company said it conducted the survey because comments from several workers raised doubts about the union's backing. But the NLRB said that employers could conduct such polls only if they first had "objective evidence" to indicate that a union had lost majority support. Despite the results of the poll—which showed a 19–13 majority against retaining the union—a federal appeals court upheld the sanction against the truck dealership.

Defending the policy, the NLRB argued that employer-sponsored polling creates a "state of turbulence" by "periodically compelling the union to re-establish its majority." But in a brief backing the dealership, the U.S. Chamber of Commerce said the NLRB policy was irrational. "An employer, in other words, is free to poll its employees," the Chamber's brief read, "but only when it already knows the results of that poll." (*Allentown Mack Sales and Service, Inc. v. National Labor Relations Board*)

Appendix

Opinion Excerpts   151

How the Court Works   291

Brief Biographies   303

Glossary of Legal Terms   320

United States Constitution   326

Opinion Excerpts

Following are excerpts from some of the most important rulings of the Supreme Court's 1996–1997 term. They appear in the order in which they were announced. Footnotes and legal citations are omitted.

No. 95-992

Turner Broadcasting System, Inc., et al., Appellants
v. Federal Communications Commission et al.

On appeal from the United States District Court
for the District of Columbia

[March 31, 1997]

JUSTICE KENNEDY delivered the opinion of the Court, except as to a portion of Part II-A-1.

Sections 4 and 5 of the Cable Television Consumer Protection and Competition Act of 1992 require cable television systems to dedicate some of their channels to local broadcast television stations. Earlier in this case, we held the so-called "must-carry" provisions to be content-neutral restrictions on speech, subject to intermediate First Amendment scrutiny under *United States v. O'Brien* (1968). A plurality of the Court considered the record as then developed insufficient to determine whether the provisions were narrowly tailored to further important governmental interests, and we remanded the case to the District Court for the District of Columbia for additional factfinding.

On appeal from the District Court's grant of summary judgment for appellees, the case now presents the two questions left open during the first appeal: First, whether the record as it now stands supports Congress' predictive judgment that the must-carry provisions further important governmental interests; and second, whether the provisions do not burden substantially more speech than necessary to further those interests. We answer both questions in the affirmative, and conclude the must-carry provisions are consistent with the First Amendment.

I

An outline of the Cable Act, Congress' purposes in adopting it, and the facts of the case are set out in detail in our first opinion, *Turner Broadcasting System, Inc. v. FCC* (1994) (*Turner*), and a more abbreviated summary will suffice here. Soon after Congress enacted the Cable Television Consumer Protection and Competition Act of 1992 (Cable Act), appellants brought suit against the United States and the Federal Communications Commission (both referred to here as the Government) in the United States District Court for the District of Columbia, challenging the constitutionality of the must-carry provisions under the First Amendment. The three-judge District Court, in a divided opinion, granted summary judgment for the Government and intervenor-defendants. A majority of the court sustained the must-carry provisions under the intermediate standard of scrutiny set forth in *United States v. O'Brien* concluding the must-carry provisions were content-neutral "industry-specific antitrust and fair trade" legislation narrowly tailored to preserve local broadcasting beset by monopoly power in most cable systems, growing concentration in the cable industry, and concomitant risks of programming decisions driven by anticompetitive policies. (1993).

On appeal, we agreed with the District Court that must-carry does not "distinguish favored speech from disfavored speech on the basis of the ideas or views expressed," but is a content-neutral regulation designed "to prevent cable operators from exploiting their economic power to the detriment of broadcasters," and "to ensure that all Americans, especially those unable to subscribe to cable, have access to free television programming—whatever its content." We held that, under the intermediate level of scrutiny applicable to content-neutral regulations, must-carry would be sustained if it were shown to further an important or substantial governmental interest unrelated to the suppression of free speech, provided the incidental restrictions did not "burden substantially more speech than is necessary to further" those interests. (Quoting *Ward v. Rock Against Racism* (1989)). Although we "ha[d] no difficulty concluding" the interests must-carry was designed to serve were important in the abstract, a four-Justice plurality concluded genuine issues of material fact remained regarding whether "the economic health of local broadcasting is in genuine jeopardy and need of the protections afforded by must-carry," and whether must-carry "'burden[s] substantially more speech than is necessary to further the government's legitimate interests.'" JUSTICE STEVENS would have found the statute valid on the record then before us; he agreed to remand the case to ensure a judgment of the Court, and the case was returned to the District Court for further proceedings.

The District Court oversaw another 18 months of factual development on remand "yielding a record of tens of thousands of pages" of evidence, comprised of materials acquired during Congress' three years of pre-enactment hearings, as well as additional expert submissions, sworn declarations and testimony, and industry documents obtained on remand. Upon consideration of the expanded record, a divided panel of the District Court again granted summary judgment to appellees. (1995). [Summary of district court opinions omitted.]

This direct appeal followed. We noted probable jurisdiction (1996), and we now affirm.

II

We begin where the plurality ended in *Turner*, applying the standards for intermediate scrutiny enunciated in *O'Brien*. A content-neutral regulation will be sustained under the First Amendment if it advances important governmental interests unrelated to the suppression of free speech and does not burden substantially more speech than necessary to further those interests. As noted in *Turner*, must-carry was designed to serve "three interrelated interests: (1) preserving the benefits of free, over-the-air local broadcast television, (2) promoting the widespread dissemination of information from a multiplicity of sources, and (3) promoting fair competition in the market for television programming." We decided then, and now reaffirm, that each of those is an important governmental interest. . . . Forty percent of American households continue to rely on over-the-air signals for television programming. Despite the growing importance of cable television and alternative technologies, "'broadcasting is demonstrably a principal source of information and entertainment for a great part of the Nation's population.'" [Quoting *Turner.*] We have identified a corresponding "governmental purpose of the highest order" in ensuring public access to "a multiplicity of information sources." And it is undisputed the Government has an interest in "eliminating restraints on fair competition . . . , even when the individuals or entities subject to particular regulations are engaged in expressive activity protected by the First Amendment."

On remand, and again before this Court, both sides have advanced new interpretations of these interests in an attempt to recast them in forms "more readily proven." The Government downplays the importance of showing a risk to the broadcast industry as a whole and suggests the loss of even a few broadcast stations "is a matter of critical importance." Taking the opposite approach, appellants argue Congress' interest in preserving broadcasting is not implicated unless it is shown the industry as a whole would fail without must-carry and suggest Congress' legitimate interest in "assuring that the public has access to a multiplicity of information sources" extends only as far as preserving "a minimum amount of television broadcast service."

These alternative formulations are inconsistent with Congress' stated interests in enacting must-carry. The congressional findings do not reflect concern that, absent must-carry, "a few voices" would be lost from the television marketplace. In explicit factual findings, Congress expressed clear concern that the "marked shift in market share from broadcast television to cable television services" resulting from increasing market penetration by cable services, as well as the expanding horizontal concentration and vertical integration of cable operators, combined to give cable systems the incentive and ability to delete, reposition, or decline carriage to local broadcasters in an attempt to favor affiliated cable programmers. . . .

At the same time, Congress was under no illusion that there would be a complete disappearance of broadcast television nationwide in the absence of must-carry. Congress recognized broadcast programming (and network programming in particular) "remains the most popular programming on cable systems." . . . Congress was concerned not that broadcast television would disappear in its entirety without must-carry, but that without it, "significant numbers of broadcast stations will be refused carriage on cable systems," and those "broadcast stations denied carriage will either deteriorate to a substantial degree or fail altogether." . . .

Nor do the congressional findings support appellants' suggestion that legitimate legislative goals would be satisfied by the preservation of a rump broadcasting industry providing a minimum of broadcast service to Americans without cable. . . . [T]he Cable Act's findings reflect a concern that congressional action was necessary to prevent "a reduction in the number of media voices available to consumers." Congress identified a specific interest in "ensuring [the] continuation" of "the local origination of [broadcast] programming" . . . and found must-carry necessary "to serve the goals" of the original Communications Act of 1934 of "providing a fair, efficient, and equitable distribution of broadcast services." . . .

Although Congress set no definite number of broadcast stations sufficient for these purposes, the Cable Act's requirement that all cable operators with more than

12 channels set aside one-third of their channel capacity for local broadcasters refutes the notion that Congress contemplated preserving only a bare minimum of stations. . . .

The dissent proceeds on the assumption that must-carry is designed solely to be (and can only be justified as) a measure to protect broadcasters from cable operators' anticompetitive behavior. Federal policy, however, has long favored preserving a multiplicity of broadcast outlets regardless of whether the conduct that threatens it is motivated by anticompetitive animus or rises to the level of an antitrust violation. . . . Broadcast television is an important source of information to many Americans. Though it is but one of many means for communication, by tradition and use for decades now it has been an essential part of the national discourse on subjects across the whole broad spectrum of speech, thought, and expression. . . . Congress has an independent interest in preserving a multiplicity of broadcasters to ensure that all households have access to information and entertainment on an equal footing with those who subscribe to cable.

A

On our earlier review, we were constrained by the state of the record to assessing the importance of the Government's asserted interests when "viewed in the abstract." The expanded record now permits us to consider whether the must-carry provisions were designed to address a real harm, and whether those provisions will alleviate it in a material way. We turn first to the harm or risk which prompted Congress to act. The Government's assertion that "the economic health of local broadcasting is in genuine jeopardy and in need of the protections afforded by must-carry" rests on two component propositions: First, "significant numbers of broadcast stations will be refused carriage on cable systems" absent must-carry. Second, "the broadcast stations denied carriage will either deteriorate to a substantial degree or fail altogether."

In reviewing the constitutionality of a statute, "courts must accord substantial deference to the predictive judgments of Congress." . . . We owe Congress' findings deference in part because the institution "is far better equipped than the judiciary to 'amass and evaluate the vast amounts of data' bearing upon" legislative questions. . . . This principle has special significance in cases, like this one, involving congressional judgments concerning regulatory schemes of inherent complexity and assessments about the likely interaction of industries undergoing rapid economic and technological change. . . . We owe Congress' findings an additional measure of deference out of respect for its authority to exercise the legislative power. Even in the realm of First Amendment questions where Congress must base its conclusions upon substantial evidence, deference must be accorded to its findings as to the harm to be avoided and to the remedial measures adopted for that end, lest we infringe on traditional legislative authority to make predictive judgments when enacting nationwide regulatory policy.

1

We have no difficulty in finding a substantial basis to support Congress' conclusion that a real threat justified enactment of the must-carry provisions. We examine first the evidence before Congress and then the further evidence presented to the District Court on remand to supplement the congressional determination.

As to the evidence before Congress, there was specific support for its conclusion that cable operators had considerable and growing market power over local video programming markets. Cable served at least 60 percent of American households in 1992, and evidence indicated cable market penetration was projected to grow beyond 70 percent. As Congress noted, cable operators possess a local monopoly over cable households. Only one percent of communities are served by more than one cable system. Even in communities with two or more cable systems, in the typical case each system has a local monopoly over its subscribers. Cable operators thus exercise "control over most (if not all) of the television programming that is channeled into the subscriber's home. . . . [and] can thus silence the voice of competing speakers with a mere flick of the switch." [*Turner*]

Evidence indicated the structure of the cable industry would give cable operators increasing ability and incentive to drop local broadcast stations from their systems, or reposition them to a less-viewed channel. Horizontal concentration was increasing as a small number of multiple system operators (MSO's) acquired large numbers of cable systems nationwide. The trend was accelerating, giving the MSO's increasing market power. In 1985, the 10 largest MSO's controlled cable systems serving slightly less than 42 percent of all cable subscribers; by 1989, the figure was nearly 54 percent.

Vertical integration in the industry also was increasing. As Congress was aware, many MSO's owned or had affiliation agreements with cable programmers. Evidence indicated that before 1984 cable operators had equity interests in 38 percent of cable programming networks. In the late 1980's, 64 percent of new cable programmers were held in vertical ownership. Congress concluded that "vertical integration gives cable operators the incentive and ability to favor their affiliated programming services." . . .

. . . The reasonableness of Congress' conclusion was borne out by the evidence on remand, which also reflected cable industry favoritism for integrated programmers. . . .

In addition, evidence before Congress, supplemented on remand, indicated that cable systems would have incentives to drop local broadcasters in favor of other programmers less likely to compete with them for audience and advertisers. Independent local broadcasters tend to be the closest substitutes for cable programs, because their programming tends to be similar, and because both primarily target the same type of advertiser: those interested in cheaper (and more frequent) ad spots than are typically available on network affiliates. The ability of broadcast stations to compete for advertising is greatly increased by cable carriage, which increases viewership substantially. With expanded viewership, broadcast presents a more competitive medium for television advertising. Empirical studies indicate that cable-carried broadcasters so enhance competition for advertising that even modest increases in the numbers of broadcast stations carried on cable are correlated with significant decreases in advertising revenue to cable systems. Empirical evidence also indicates that demand for premium cable services (such as pay-per-view) is reduced when a cable system carries more independent broadcasters. Thus, operators stand to benefit by dropping broadcast stations.

Cable systems also have more systemic reasons for seeking to disadvantage broadcast stations: Simply stated, cable has little interest in assisting, through carriage, a competing medium of communication. As one cable-industry executive put it, "'our job is to promote cable television, not broadcast television.'" . . . The incentive to subscribe to cable is lower in markets with many over-the-air viewing options. . . . Congress could therefore reasonably conclude that cable systems would drop broadcasters in favor of programmers—even unaffiliated ones—less likely to compete with them for audience and advertisers. . . .

The dissent contends Congress could not reasonably conclude cable systems would engage in such predation because cable operators, whose primary source of revenue is subscriptions, would not risk dropping a widely viewed broadcast station in order to capture advertising revenues. However, if viewers are faced with the choice of sacrificing a handful of broadcast stations to gain access to dozens of cable channels (plus network affiliates), it is likely they would still subscribe to cable even if they would prefer the dropped television stations to the cable programming that replaced them. . . .

It was more than a theoretical possibility in 1992 that cable operators would take actions adverse to local broadcasters; indeed, significant numbers of broadcasters had already been dropped. [Kennedy noted a study in 1988 that showed 280 out of 912 responding broadcast stations had been dropped or denied carriage in 1,533 instances.] . . .

Substantial evidence demonstrated that absent must-carry the already "serious" problem of noncarriage would grow worse because "additional local broadcast signals will be deleted, repositioned, or not carried." The record included anecdotal evidence showing the cable industry was acting with restraint in dropping broadcast stations in an effort to discourage reregulation. There was also substantial evidence that advertising revenue would be of increasing importance to cable operators as subscribership growth began to flatten, providing a steady, increasing incentive to deny carriage to local broadcasters in an effort to capture their advertising revenue. . . .

Additional evidence developed on remand supports the reasonableness of Congress' predictive judgment. Approximately 11 percent of local broadcasters were not carried on the typical cable system in 1989. The figure had grown to even more significant proportions by 1992. . . .

The evidence on remand also indicated that the growth of cable systems' market power proceeded apace. The trend towards greater horizontal concentration continued. . . . By 1994, the 10 largest MSO's controlled 63 percent of cable systems, a figure projected to have risen to 85 percent by the end of 1996. MSO's began to gain control of as many cable systems in a given market as they could, in a trend known as "clustering." Cable systems looked increasingly to advertising (and especially local advertising) for revenue growth, and cable systems had increasing incentives to drop local broadcasters in favor of cable programmers (whether affiliated or not). The vertical integration of the cable industry also continued, so by 1994, MSO's serving about 70 percent of the Nation's cable subscribers held equity interests in cable programmers. . . .

This is not a case in which we are called upon to give our best judgment as to the likely economic consequences of certain financial arrangements or business structures, or to assess competing economic theories and predictive judgments, as we would in a case arising, say, under the antitrust laws. . . . The issue before us is whether, given conflicting views of the probable development of the television industry, Congress had substantial evidence for making the judgment that it did. We need not put our imprimatur on Congress' economic theory in order to validate the reasonableness of its judgment.

2

The harm Congress feared was that stations dropped or denied carriage would be at a "serious risk of financial difficulty" and would "deteriorate to a substantial degree or fail altogether." Congress had before it substantial evidence to support its conclusion. Congress was advised the viability of a broadcast station depends to a material extent on its ability to secure cable carriage. . . . Empirical research in the record before Congress confirmed the "'direct correlation [between] size in audience and station [advertising] revenues,'" and that viewership was in turn heavily dependent on cable carriage.

Considerable evidence, consisting of statements compiled from dozens of broadcasters who testified before Congress and the FCC, confirmed that broadcast stations had fallen into bankruptcy, curtailed their broadcast operations, and suffered serious reductions in operating revenues as a result of adverse carriage decisions by cable systems. The record also reflected substantial evidence that stations without cable carriage encountered severe difficulties obtaining financing for operations, reflecting the financial markets' judgment that the prospects are poor for broadcasters unable to secure carriage. . . . We hold Congress could conclude from the substantial body of evidence before it that "absent legislative action, the free local off-air broadcast system is endangered." . . .

To be sure, the record also contains evidence to support a contrary conclusion. Appellants (and the dissent in the District Court) make much of the fact that the number of broadcast stations and their advertising revenue continued to grow during the period without must-carry, albeit at a diminished rate. Evidence introduced on remand indicated that only 31 broadcast stations actually went dark during the period without must-carry (one of which failed after a tornado destroyed its transmitter), and during the same period some 263 new stations signed on the air. New evidence appellants produced on remand indicates the average cable system voluntarily carried local broadcast stations accounting for about 97 percent of television ratings in noncable households. Appellants, as well as the dissent in the District Court, contend that in light of such evidence, it is clear "the must-carry law is not necessary to assure the economic viability of the broadcast system as a whole."

This assertion misapprehends the relevant inquiry. The question is not whether Congress, as an objective matter, was correct to determine must-carry is necessary to prevent a substantial number of broadcast stations from losing cable carriage and suffering significant financial hardship. Rather, the question is whether the legislative conclusion was reasonable and supported by substantial evidence in the record before Congress. In making that determination, we are not to "re-weigh the evidence de novo, or to replace Congress' factual predictions with our own." Rather, we are simply to determine if the standard is satisfied. If it is, summary judgment for defendants-appellees is appropriate regardless of whether the evidence is in conflict. . . .

We think it apparent must-carry serves the Government's interests "in a direct and effective way." [*Ward.*] Must-carry ensures that a number of local broadcasters retain cable carriage, with the concomitant audience access and advertising revenues needed to support a multiplicity of stations. Appellants contend that even were this so, must-carry is broader than necessary to accomplish its goals. We turn to this question.

B

The second portion of the *O'Brien* inquiry concerns the fit between the asserted interests and the means chosen to advance them. Content-neutral regulations do not pose the same "inherent dangers to free expression" that content-based regulations do, and thus are subject to a less rigorous analysis, which affords the Government latitude in designing a regulatory solution. Under intermediate scrutiny, the Government may employ the means of its choosing " 'so long as the . . . regulation promotes a substantial governmental interest that would be achieved less effectively absent the regulation,' " and does not " 'burden substantially more speech than is necessary to further' " that interest.

The must-carry provisions have the potential to interfere with protected speech in two ways. First, the provisions restrain cable operators' editorial discretion in creating programming packages by "reduc[ing] the number of channels over which [they] exercise unfettered control." Second, the rules "render it more difficult for cable programmers to compete for carriage on the limited channels remaining."

Appellants say the burden of must-carry is great, but the evidence adduced on remand indicates the actual effects are modest. Significant evidence indicates the vast majority of cable operators have not been affected in a significant manner by must-carry. Cable operators have been able to satisfy their must-carry obligations 87 percent of the time using previously unused channel capacity; 94.5 percent of the 11,628 cable systems nationwide have not had to drop any programming in order to fulfill their must-carry obligations; the remaining 5.5 percent have had to drop an average of only 1.22 services from their programming; and cable operators nationwide carry 99.8 percent of the programming they carried before enactment of must-carry. . . . Appellees contend the burdens of must-carry will soon diminish as cable channel capacity increases, as is occurring nationwide.

We do not understand appellants to dispute in any fundamental way the accuracy of those figures, only their significance. They note national averages fail to account for greater crowding on certain (especially urban) cable systems and contend that half of all cable systems, serving two-thirds of all cable subscribers, have no available capacity. Appellants argue that the rate of growth in cable programming outstrips cable operators' creation of new channel space, that the rate of cable growth is lower than claimed, and that must-carry infringes First Amendment rights now irrespective of future growth. Finally, they say that regardless of the percentage of channels occupied, must-carry still represents "thousands of real and individual infringements of speech."

While the parties' evidence is susceptible of varying interpretations, a few definite conclusions can be drawn about the burdens of must-carry. It is undisputed that broadcast stations gained carriage on 5,880 channels as a result of must-carry. While broadcast stations occupy another 30,006 cable channels nationwide, this carriage does not represent a significant First Amendment harm to either system operators or cable programmers because those stations were carried voluntarily before 1992, and even appellants represent that the vast majority of those channels would continue to be carried in the absence of any legal obligation to do so. The 5,880 channels occupied by added broadcasters represent the actual burden of the regulatory scheme. Appellants concede most of those stations would be dropped in the absence of must-carry, so the figure approximates the benefits of must-carry as well.

Because the burden imposed by must-carry is congruent to the benefits it affords, we conclude must-carry is narrowly tailored to preserve a multiplicity of broadcast stations for the 40 percent of American households without cable. . . .

Appellants say the must-carry provisions are overbroad because they require carriage in some instances when the Government's interests are not implicated: the must-carry rules prohibit a cable system operator from dropping a broadcaster "even if the operator has no anticompetitive motives, and even if the broadcaster that would have to be dropped . . . would survive without cable access." [*Turner*] (O'CONNOR, J., dissenting). We are not persuaded that either possibility is so prevalent that must-carry is substantially overbroad. . . . [C]able systems serving 70 percent of subscribers are vertically integrated with cable programmers, so anticompetitive motives may be implicated in a majority of systems' decisions not to carry broadcasters. Some broadcasters will opt for must-carry although they would not suffer serious financial harm in its absence. . . . Even on the doubtful assumption that a narrower but still practicable must-carry rule could be drafted to exclude all instances in which the Government's interests are not implicated, our cases establish that content-neutral regulations are not "invalid simply because there is some imaginable alternative that might be less burdensome on speech."

Appellants posit a number of alternatives in an effort to demonstrate a less-restrictive means to achieve the Government's aims. . . . Our precedents establish that when evaluating a content-neutral regulation which incidentally burdens speech, we will not invalidate the preferred remedial scheme because some alternative solution is marginally less intrusive on a speaker's First Amendment interests. . . .

In any event, after careful examination of each of the alternatives suggested by appellants, we cannot conclude that any of them is an adequate alternative to must-carry for promoting the Government's legitimate interests.

[Kennedy described and rejected five alternatives: (1) a more limited set of must-carry rules; (2) the use of input selector or "A/B" switches, which, in combination with antennas, would permit viewers to switch between cable and broadcast input; (3) a leased-access regime, under which both broadcasters and cable programmers would have equal access to cable channels at regulated rates; (4) a system of subsidies for financially weak stations; or (5) a system of antitrust enforcement or an administrative complaint procedure to protect broadcasters from cable operators' anticompetitive conduct.

[In rejecting the more limited must-carry rules, Kennedy said that Congress had made "a deliberate . . . choice to adopt the present levels of protection, to which this Court must defer." Congress had also considered the use of A/B switches, Kennedy said, and determined it be "not feasible" because of "technical shortcomings and lack of consumer acceptance." The leased-access option, he continued, would not be effective and would defeat Congress's purpose by imposing costs on small broadcasters. Subsidies, Kennedy said, would "serve a different purpose than must-carry" and would require an "elaborate administrative structure" that could involve the government in "making content-based determinations about programming." Finally, Congress could have concluded that antitrust enforcement or an administrative complaint procedure would be "inadequate substitutes" for must-carry because of "the considerable expense and delay inherent in antitrust litigation" and "the great disparities in wealth and sophistication between the average independent broadcast station and average cable system operator."]

There is a final argument made by appellants that we do not reach. Appellant Time Warner Entertainment raises in its brief a separate First Amendment challenge to a subsection of the Cable Act that requires carriage on unfilled must-carry channels of low power broadcast stations if the FCC determines that the station's programming "would address local news and informational needs which are not being adequately served by full power television broadcast stations because of the geographic distance of such full power stations from the low power station's community of license." [Kennedy said the issue received "only the most glancing" attention from the parties, both before the district court and in briefs and arguments before the Court. "Even if the issue is 'fairly included' in the broadly worded question presented," Kennedy concluded, "it is tangential to the main issue, and prudence dictates that we not decide this question based on such scant argumentation."]

III

Judgments about how competing economic interests are to be reconciled in the complex and fast-changing field of television are for Congress to make. Those judgments "cannot be ignored or undervalued simply because [appellants] cas[t] [their] claims under the umbrella of the First Amendment." Appellants' challenges to must-carry reflect little more than disagreement over the level of protection broadcast stations are to be afforded and how protection is to be attained. We cannot displace Congress' judgment respecting content-neutral regulations with our own, so long as its policy is grounded on reasonable factual findings supported by evidence that is substantial for a legislative determination. Those requirements were met in this case, and in these circumstances the First Amendment requires nothing more. The judgment of the District Court is affirmed.

It is so ordered.

JUSTICE STEVENS, concurring.

As JUSTICE KENNEDY clearly explains, the policy judgments made by Congress in the enactment of legislation that is intended to forestall the abuse of monopoly power are entitled to substantial deference. That is true even when the attempt to protect an economic market imposes burdens on communication. . . . If this statute regulated the content of speech rather than the structure of the market, our task would be quite different. Though I write to emphasize this important point, I fully concur in the Court's thorough opinion.

JUSTICE BREYER, concurring in part.

I join the opinion of the Court except insofar as Part II-A-1 relies on an anticompetitive rationale. . . . Whether or not the statute does or does not sensibly compensate for some significant market defect, it undoubtedly seeks to provide over-the-air viewers who *lack* cable with a rich mix of over-the-air programming by guaranteeing the over-the-air stations that provide such programming with the extra dollars that an additional cable audience will generate. I believe that this purpose—to assure the over-the-air public "access to a multiplicity of information sources,"—provides sufficient basis for rejecting appellants' First Amendment claim.

I do not deny that the compulsory carriage that creates the "guarantee" extracts a serious First Amendment price. It interferes with the protected interests of the cable operators to choose their own programming; it prevents displaced cable program providers from obtaining an audience; and it will sometimes prevent some cable viewers from watching what, in its absence, would have been their preferred set of programs. This "price" amounts to a "suppression of speech."

But there are important First Amendment interests on the other side as well. The statute's basic noneconomic purpose is to prevent too precipitous a decline in the quality and quantity of programming choice for an ever-shrinking non-cable-subscribing segment of the public. This purpose reflects what "has long been a basic tenet of national communications policy," namely that "the widest possible dissemination of information from diverse and antagonistic sources is essential to the welfare of the public." . . .

With important First Amendment interests on both sides of the equation, the key question becomes one of proper fit. That question, in my view, requires a reviewing court to determine both whether there are significantly less restrictive ways to achieve Congress' over-the-air programming objectives, and also to decide whether the statute, in its effort to achieve those objectives, strikes a reasonable balance between potentially speech-restricting and speech-enhancing consequences. The majority's opinion analyzes and evaluates those consequences, and I agree with its conclusions in respect to both of these matters.

In particular, I note (and agree) that a cable system, physically dependent upon the availability of space along city streets, at present (perhaps less in the future) typically faces little competition, that it therefore constitutes a kind of bottleneck that controls the range of viewer choice (whether or not it uses any consequent economic power for economically predatory purposes), and that *some* degree—at least a limited degree—of governmental intervention and control through regulation can prove appropriate when justified under [*United States v.*] *O'Brien* [(1968)] (at least when not "content based"). I also agree that, without the statute, cable systems would likely carry significantly fewer over-the-air stations, that station revenues would therefore decline, and that the quality of over-the-air programming on such stations would almost inevitably suffer. I agree further that the burden the statute imposes upon the cable system, potential cable programmers, and cable viewers, is limited and will diminish as typical cable system capacity grows over time.

Finally, I believe that Congress could reasonably conclude that the statute will help the typical over-the-air viewer (by maintaining an expanded range of choice) more than it will hurt the typical cable subscriber (by restricting cable slots otherwise available for preferred programming). . . . In these circumstances, I do not believe the First Amendment dictates a result that favors the cable viewers' interests.

These and other similar factors discussed by the majority, lead me to agree that the statute survives "intermediate scrutiny," whether or not the statute is properly tailored to Congress' purely economic objectives.

JUSTICE O'CONNOR, with whom JUSTICE SCALIA, JUSTICE THOMAS, and JUSTICE GINSBURG join, dissenting.

In sustaining the must-carry provisions of the Cable Television Protection and Competition Act of 1992 against a First Amendment challenge by cable system operators and cable programmers, the Court errs in two crucial respects. First, the

Court disregards one of the principal defenses of the statute urged by appellees on remand: that it serves a substantial interest in preserving "diverse," "quality" programming that is "responsive" to the needs of the local community. The course of this litigation on remand and the proffered defense strongly reinforce my view that the Court adopted the wrong analytic framework in the prior phase of this case. [*Turner Broadcasting System, Inc. v. FCC* (1994) (*Turner*) (O'CONNOR, J., concurring in part and dissenting in part).] Second, the Court misapplies the "intermediate scrutiny" framework it adopts. Although we owe deference to Congress' predictive judgments and its evaluation of complex economic questions, we have an independent duty to identify with care the Government interests supporting the scheme, to inquire into the reasonableness of congressional findings regarding its necessity, and to examine the fit between its goals and its consequences. The Court fails to discharge its duty here.

I

I did not join those portions of the principal opinion in *Turner* holding that the must-carry provisions of the Cable Act are content neutral and therefore subject to intermediate First Amendment scrutiny. . . .

Much of the principal opinion [in this case] treats the must-carry provisions as a species of antitrust regulation enacted by Congress in response to a perceived threat that cable system operators would otherwise engage in various forms of anticompetitive conduct resulting in harm to broadcasters. The Court recognizes that appellees cannot show an anticompetitive threat to broadcast television simply by demonstrating that "a few" broadcast stations would be forced off the air in the absence of must-carry. . . . The notion that Congress premised the must-carry provisions upon a far graver threat to the structure of the local broadcast system than the loss of "a few" stations runs through virtually every passage in the principal *Turner* opinion that discusses the Government interests the provisions were designed to serve. . . . Ostensibly adopting this framework, the Court now asks whether Congress could reasonably have thought the must-carry regime necessary to prevent a "*significant* reduction in the multiplicity of broadcast programming sources available to noncable households." (emphasis added).

I fully agree that promoting fair competition is a legitimate and substantial Government goal. But the Court nowhere examines whether the breadth of the must-carry provisions comports with a goal of preventing anticompetitive harms. . . .

. . . As discussed below, the must-carry provisions cannot be justified as a narrowly tailored means of addressing anticompetitive behavior. As a result, the Court's inquiry into whether must-carry would prevent a "significant reduction in the multiplicity of broadcast programming sources" collapses into an analysis of an ill-defined and generalized interest in maintaining broadcast stations, wherever they might be threatened and whatever their viewership. . . . Must-carry is . . . justified as a way of preserving viewers' access to a Spanish or Chinese language station or of preventing an independent station from adopting a home-shopping format. Undoubtedly, such goals are reasonable and important, and the stations in question may well be worthwhile targets of Government subsidies. But appellees' characterization of must-carry as a means of protecting these stations, like the Court's explicit concern for promoting "'community self-expression'" and the "'local origination of broadcast programming,'" reveals a content-based preference for broadcast programming.

This justification of the regulatory scheme is, in my view, wholly at odds with the *Turner* Court's premise that must-carry is a means of preserving "access to free television programming—*whatever its content.*" (emphasis added).

I do not read JUSTICE BREYER's opinion—which analyzes the must-carry rules in part as a "speech-enhancing" measure designed to ensure a "rich mix" of over-the-air programming—to treat the content of over-the-air programming as irrelevant to whether the Government's interest in promoting it is an important one. The net result appears to be that five Justices of this Court *do not* view must-carry as a narrowly tailored means of serving a substantial governmental interest in preventing anticompetitive behavior; and that five Justices of this Court *do* see the significance of the content of over-the-air programming to the Government's and appellees' efforts to defend the law. Under these circumstances, the must-carry provisions should be subject to strict scrutiny, which they surely fail.

II

The principal opinion goes to great lengths to avoid acknowledging that preferences for "quality," "diverse," and "responsive" local programming underlie the must-carry scheme, although the partial concurrence's reliance on such preferences is explicit. I take the principal opinion at its word and evaluate the claim that the threat of anticompetitive behavior by cable operators supplies a content-neutral basis for sustaining the statute. It does not. . . .

A

The principal opinion devotes substantial discussion to the structure of the cable industry. As of 1992, cable already served 60 percent of American households. . . .

. . . Because I remain convinced that the statute is not a measured response to congressional concerns about monopoly power, in my view the principal opinion's discussion on this point is irrelevant. But even if it were relevant, it is incorrect.

1

The *Turner* plurality recognized that Congress' interest in curtailing anticompetitive behavior is substantial "in the abstract." The principal opinion now concludes that substantial evidence supports the congressional judgment that cable operators have incentives to engage in significant anticompetitive behavior. It appears to accept two related arguments on this point: first, that vertically integrated cable operators prefer programming produced by their affiliated cable programming networks to broadcast programming; and second, that potential advertising revenues supply cable system operators, whether affiliated with programmers or not, with incentives to prefer cable programming to broadcast programming.

To support the first proposition, the principal opinion states that "[e]xtensive testimony" before Congress showed that in fact operators do have incentives to favor vertically integrated programmers. This testimony . . . is primarily that of persons appearing before Congress on behalf of the private appellees in this case. It is appropriate to regard the testimony of interested persons with a degree of skepticism when our task is to engage in "'independent judgment of the facts bearing on an issue of constitutional law.'" Moreover, even accepting as reasonable Congress' conclusion that cable operators have incentives to favor affiliated programmers, Congress has already limited the number of channels on a cable system that can be occupied by affiliated programmers. Once a cable system operator reaches that cap, it can no longer bump a broadcaster in favor of an affiliated programmer. If Congress were concerned that broadcasters favored too many affiliated programmers, it could simply adjust the cap. Must-carry simply cannot be justified as a response to the allegedly "substantial" problem of vertical integration.

The second argument, that the quest for advertising revenue will supply cable operators with incentives to drop local broadcasters, takes two forms. First, some cable programmers offer blank slots within a program into which a cable operator can insert advertisements; appellees argue that "[t]he opportunity to sell such advertising gives cable programmers an additional value to operators above broadcast stations. . . ." But that "additional value" arises only because the must-carry provisions *require* cable operators to carry broadcast signals without alteration. Judge Williams was correct in noting that the Government cannot have "a 'substantial interest' in remedying a competitive distortion that arises entirely out of a detail in its own purportedly remedial legislation." Second, appellees claim that since cable operators compete directly with broadcasters for some advertising revenue, operators will profit if they can drive broadcasters out of the market and capture their advertising revenue. Even if the record before Congress included substantial evidence that "advertising revenue would be of increasing importance to cable operators as subscribership growth began to flatten," it does not necessarily follow that Congress could reasonably find that the quest for advertising revenues supplies cable operators with incentives to engage in predatory behavior, or that must-carry is a reasonable response to such incentives. There is no dispute that a cable system depends primarily upon its subscriber base for revenue. A cable operator is therefore unlikely to drop a widely viewed station in order to capture advertising revenues. . . .

2

Under the standard articulated by the *Turner* plurality, the conclusion that must-carry serves a substantial governmental interest depends upon the "essential propositio[n]" that, without must-carry, "significant numbers of broadcast stations will be refused carriage on cable systems." In analyzing whether this undefined standard is satisfied, the Court focuses almost exclusively on raw numbers of stations denied carriage or "repositioned"—that is, shifted out of their traditional channel positions.

The Court begins its discussion of evidence of adverse carriage decisions with the 1988 study sponsored by the Federal Communications Commission. But in *Turner*, the plurality criticized this very study, noting that it did not indicate the time frame within which carriage denials occurred or whether the stations were later restored to their positions. . . .

In canvassing the additional evidence offered on remand, the Court focuses on the suggestion of one of appellees' experts that the 1988 FCC survey underestimated the number of drops of broadcast stations in the non-must-carry era. The data do not indicate which of these stations would now qualify for mandatory carriage. . . . Without some further analysis, I do not see how the Court can, in the course of its independent scrutiny on a question of constitutional law, deem Congress' judgment "reasonable."

In any event, the larger problem with the Court's approach is that neither the FCC study nor the additional evidence on remand canvassed by the Court says anything about the broadcast markets in which adverse carriage decisions take place. The Court accepts Congress' stated concern about preserving the availability of a "multiplicity" of broadcast stations, but apparently thinks it sufficient to evaluate that concern in the abstract, without considering how much local service is already available in a given broadcast market. . . .

Nor can we evaluate whether must-carry is necessary to serve an interest in preserving broadcast stations without examining the value of the stations protected by the must-carry scheme to viewers in noncable households. . . . The only analysis in the record of the relationship between carriage and noncable viewership favors the appellants. A 1991 study by Federal Trade Commission staff concluded that most cable systems voluntarily carried broadcast stations with any reportable ratings in noncable households and that most instances of noncarriage involved "relatively remote (and duplicated) network stations, or local stations that few viewers watch." . . .

3

I turn now to the evidence of harm to broadcasters denied carriage or repositioned. The Court remanded for a determination whether broadcast stations denied carriage would be at "'serious risk of financial difficulty'" and would "'deteriorate to a substantial degree or fail altogether.'" The *Turner* plurality noted that there was no evidence that "local broadcast stations have fallen into bankruptcy, turned in their broadcast licenses, curtailed their broadcast operations, or suffered a serious reduction in operating revenues" because of adverse carriage decisions. The record on remand does not permit the conclusion, at the summary judgment stage, that Congress could reasonably have predicted serious harm to a significant number of stations in the absence of must-carry.

The purported link between an adverse carriage decision and severe harm to a station depends on yet another untested premise. Even accepting the conclusion that a cable system operator has a monopoly over cable services to the home, it does not necessarily follow that the operator also has a monopoly over all video services to cabled households. Cable subscribers using an input selector switch and an antenna can receive broadcast signals. Widespread use of such switches would completely eliminate any cable system "monopoly" over sources of video input. Growing use of direct-broadcast satellite television also tends to undercut the notion that cable operators have an inevitable monopoly over video services entering cable households. . . .

The Court concludes that the evidence on remand meets the threshold of harm established in *Turner*. The Court begins with the "[c]onsiderable evidence" that broadcast stations denied carriage have fallen into bankruptcy. . . . The "considerable evidence" relied on by the Court consists of repeated references to the bankruptcies of the same 23 commercial independent stations—apparently, new stations. . . .

The Court also claims that the record on remand reflects "considerable evidence" of stations curtailing their broadcast operations or suffering reductions in operating revenues. Most of the anecdotal accounts of harm on which the Court relies are sharply disputed. . . . Congress' reasonable conclusions are entitled to deference. . . . Nevertheless, in the course of our independent review, we cannot ignore sharp conflicts in the record that call into question the reasonableness of Congress' findings.

Moreover, unlike other aspects of the record on remand, the station-specific accounts cited by the Court do permit an evaluation of trends in the various broadcast markets . . . in which carriage denials allegedly caused harm. . . . [A]ll but one of the commercial broadcast stations cited as claiming a curtailment in operations or a decline in revenue was broadcasting within [a broadcast market] that experienced net growth, or at least no net reduction, in the number of commercial broadcast stations operating during the non-must-carry era. . . .

. . . The principal opinion disavows a need to closely scrutinize the logic of the regulatory scheme at issue on the ground that it "need not put [its] imprimatur on Congress' economic theory in order to validate the reasonableness of its judgment." That approach trivializes the First Amendment issue at stake in this case. A highly dubious economic theory has been advanced as the "substantial interest" supporting a First Amendment burden on cable operators and cable programmers. In finding that must-carry serves a substantial interest, the principal opinion necessarily accepts that theory. The partial concurrence does not, but neither does it articulate what threat to the availability of a "multiplicity" of broadcast stations would exist in a perfectly competitive market.

B

I turn now to the second portion of the *O'Brien* inquiry, which concerns the fit between the Government's asserted interests and the means chosen to advance them. The Court observes that "broadcast stations gained carriage on 5,880 channels as a result of must-carry," and recognizes that this forced carriage imposes a burden on cable system operators and cable programmers.

. . . [T]he Court's leap to the conclusion that must-carry "is narrowly tailored to preserve a multiplicity of broadcast stations" is nothing short of astounding. The Court's logic is circular. Surmising that most of the 5,880 channels added by the regulatory scheme would be dropped in its absence, the Court concludes that the figure also approximates the "benefit" of must-carry. Finding the scheme's burden "congruent" to the benefit it affords, the Court declares the statute narrowly tailored. The Court achieves this result, however, only by equating the *effect* of the statute—requiring cable operators to add 5,880 stations—with the governmental *interest* sought to be served. . . . The "evi[l] the Government seeks to eliminate" is not the failure of cable operators to carry *these 5,880 stations*. Rather, to read the first half of the principal opinion, the "evil" is *anticompetitive behavior* by cable operators. As a factual matter, we do not know whether these stations were not carried because of anticompetitive impulses. . . .

In my view, the statute is not narrowly tailored to serve a substantial interest in preventing anticompetitive conduct. I do not understand Justice Breyer to disagree with this conclusion. . . . Congress has commandeered up to one third of each cable system's channel capacity for the benefit of local broadcasters, without any regard for whether doing so advances the statute's alleged goals. To the extent that Congress was concerned that anticompetitive impulses would lead vertically integrated operators to prefer those programmers in which the operators have an ownership stake, the Cable Act is overbroad, since it does not impose its requirements solely on such operators. . . .

Finally, I note my disagreement with the Court's suggestion that the availability of less-speech-restrictive alternatives is never relevant to *O'Brien*'s narrow tailoring inquiry. The *Turner* Court remanded this case in part because a plurality concluded that "judicial findings concerning the availability and efficacy of constitutionally acceptable less restrictive means of achieving the Government's asserted interests" were lacking in the original record. The Court's present position on this issue is puzzling.

Our cases suggest only that we have not interpreted the narrow tailoring inquiry to "require elimination of all less restrictive alternatives." Put another way, we have refrained from imposing a least-restrictive-means requirement in cases involving intermediate First Amendment scrutiny. It is one thing to say that a regulation need not be the least-speech-restrictive means of serving an important governmental objective. It is quite another to suggest, as I read the majority to do here, that the availability of less-speech-restrictive alternatives cannot establish or confirm that a regulation is substantially broader than necessary to achieve the Government's goals. . . .

. . . [I]n this case it is plain without reference to any alternatives that the must-carry scheme is "substantially broader than necessary" to serve the only governmental interest that the principal opinion fully explains—preventing unfair competition. If Congress truly sought to address anticompetitive behavior by cable system operators, it passed the wrong law. . . . Nevertheless, the availability of less restrictive alternatives—a leased-access regime and subsidies—reinforces my conclusion that the must-carry provisions are overbroad. [Discussion of alternatives omitted.]

III

Finally, I note my disagreement with the Court's decision to sidestep a question reserved in *Turner*, fairly included within the question presented here; and argued by one of the appellants: whether the must-carry rules requiring carriage of low power stations survive constitutional scrutiny. A low power station qualifies for carriage only if the Federal Communications Commission determines that the station's programming "would address local news and informational needs which are not being adequately served by full power television broadcast stations because of the geographic distance of such full power stations from the low power station's community of license." As the *Turner* Court noted, "this aspect of §4 appears to single out certain low-power broadcasters for special benefits on the basis of content." Because I believe that the must-carry provisions fail even intermediate scrutiny, it is clear that they would fail scrutiny under a stricter content-based standard. . . .

IV

In sustaining the must-carry provisions of the Cable Act, the Court ignores the main justification of the statute urged by appellees and subjects restrictions on expressive activity to an inappropriately lenient level of scrutiny. The principal opinion then misapplies the analytic framework it chooses, exhibiting an extraordinary and unwarranted deference for congressional judgments, a profound fear of delving into complex economic matters, and a willingness to substitute untested assumptions for evidence. In light of gaps in logic and evidence, it is improper to conclude, at the summary judgment stage, that the must-carry scheme serves a significant governmental interest "in a direct and effective way." Moreover, because the undisputed facts demonstrate that the must-carry scheme is plainly not narrowly tailored to serving the only governmental interest the principal opinion fully explains and embraces—preventing anticompetitive behavior—appellants are entitled to summary judgment in their favor.

JUSTICE BREYER disavows the principal opinion's position on anticompetitive behavior, and instead treats the must-carry rules as a "speech-enhancing" measure designed to ensure access to "quality" programming for noncable households. Neither the principal opinion nor the partial concurrence explains the nature of the alleged threat to the availability of a "multiplicity of broadcast programming sources," if that threat does not arise from cable operators' anticompetitive conduct. Such an approach makes it impossible to discern whether Congress was addressing a problem that is "real, not merely conjectural," and whether must-carry addresses the problem in a "direct and material way." [Quoting *Turner* (plurality opinion).]

I therefore respectfully dissent, and would reverse the judgment below.

□□□

No. 95-1853

William Jefferson Clinton, Petitioner
v. Paula Corbin Jones

On writ of certiorari to the United States Court
of Appeals for the Eighth Circuit

[May 27, 1997]

JUSTICE STEVENS delivered the opinion of the Court.

This case raises a constitutional and a prudential question concerning the Office of the President of the United States. Respondent, a private citizen, seeks to recover damages from the current occupant of that office based on actions allegedly taken before his term began. The President submits that in all but the most exceptional cases the Constitution requires federal courts to defer such litigation until his term ends and that, in any event, respect for the office warrants such a stay. Despite the force of the arguments supporting the President's submissions, we conclude that they must be rejected.

I

Petitioner, William Jefferson Clinton, was elected to the Presidency in 1992, and re-elected in 1996. His term of office expires on January 20, 2001. In 1991 he was the Governor of the State of Arkansas. Respondent, Paula Corbin Jones, is a resident of California. In 1991 she lived in Arkansas, and was an employee of the Arkansas Industrial Development Commission.

On May 6, 1994, she commenced this action in the United States District Court for the Eastern District of Arkansas by filing a complaint naming petitioner and Danny Ferguson, a former Arkansas State Police officer, as defendants. The complaint alleges two federal claims, and two state law claims over which the federal court has jurisdiction because of the diverse citizenship of the parties. As the case comes to us, we are required to assume the truth of the detailed—but as yet untested—factual allegations in the complaint.

Those allegations principally describe events that are said to have occurred on the afternoon of May 8, 1991, during an official conference held at the Excelsior Hotel in Little Rock, Arkansas. The Governor delivered a speech at the conference; respondent—working as a state employee—staffed the registration desk. She alleges that Ferguson persuaded her to leave her desk and to visit the Governor in a business suite at the hotel, where he made "abhorrent" [quoting from complaint] sexual advances that she vehemently rejected. She further claims that her superiors at work subsequently dealt with her in a hostile and rude manner, and changed her duties to punish her for rejecting those advances. Finally, she alleges that after petitioner was elected President, Ferguson defamed her by making a statement to a reporter that implied she had accepted petitioner's alleged overtures, and that various persons authorized to speak for the President publicly branded her a liar by denying that the incident had occurred.

Respondent seeks actual damages of $75,000, and punitive damages of $100,000. Her complaint contains four counts. The first charges that petitioner, acting under color of state law, deprived her of rights protected by the Constitution, in violation of 42 U. S. C. §1983. The second charges that petitioner and Ferguson engaged in a conspiracy to violate her federal rights, also actionable under federal law. See 42 U. S. C. §1985. The third is a state common-law claim for intentional infliction of emotional distress, grounded primarily on the incident at the hotel. The fourth count, also based on state law, is for defamation, embracing both the comments allegedly made to the press by Ferguson and the statements of petitioner's agents. Inasmuch as the legal sufficiency of the claims has not yet been challenged, we assume, without deciding, that each of the four counts states a cause of action as a matter of law. With the exception of the last charge, which arguably may involve conduct within the outer perimeter of the President's official responsibilities, it is perfectly clear that the alleged misconduct of petitioner was unrelated to any of his official duties as President of the United States and, indeed, occurred before he was elected to that office.

II

In response to the complaint, petitioner promptly advised the District Court that he intended to file a motion to dismiss on grounds of Presidential immunity, and requested the court to defer all other pleadings and motions until after the immunity issue was resolved. Relying on our cases holding that immunity questions should be decided at the earliest possible stage of the litigation, our recognition of the "'singular importance of the President's duties,'" (quoting *Nixon v. Fitzgerald* (1982)), and the fact that the question did not require any analysis of the allegations of the complaint, the court granted the request. [1994] Petitioner thereupon filed a motion "to dismiss . . . without prejudice and to toll any statutes of limitation [that may be applicable] until he is no longer President, at which time the plaintiff may refile the instant suit." Extensive submissions were made to the District Court by the parties and the Department of Justice.

The District Judge denied the motion to dismiss on immunity grounds and ruled that discovery in the case could go forward, but ordered any trial stayed until the end of petitioner's Presidency. (1994). . . .

Both parties appealed. A divided panel of the Court of Appeals affirmed the denial of the motion to dismiss, but because it regarded the order postponing the trial until the President leaves office as the "functional equivalent" of a grant of temporary immunity, it reversed that order. (1996). . . .

III

The President, represented by private counsel, filed a petition for certiorari. The Solicitor General, representing the United States, supported the petition, arguing that the decision of the Court of Appeals was "fundamentally mistaken" and created "serious risks for the institution of the Presidency." In her brief in opposition to certiorari, respondent argued that this "one-of-a-kind case is singularly inappropriate" for the exercise of our certiorari jurisdiction because it did not create any conflict among the Courts of Appeals, it "does not pose any conceivable threat to the functioning of the Executive Branch," and there is no precedent supporting the President's position.

While our decision to grant the petition expressed no judgment concerning the merits of the case, it does reflect our appraisal of its importance. The representations made on behalf of the Executive Branch as to the potential impact of the precedent established by the Court of Appeals merit our respectful and deliberate consideration. . . .

IV

Petitioner's principal submission—that "in all but the most exceptional cases," the Constitution affords the President temporary immunity from civil damages litigation arising out of events that occurred before he took office—cannot be sustained on the basis of precedent.

Only three sitting Presidents have been defendants in civil litigation involving their actions prior to taking office. Complaints against Theodore Roosevelt and Harry Truman had been dismissed before they took office; the dismissals were affirmed after their respective inaugurations. Two companion cases arising out of an automobile accident were filed against John F. Kennedy in 1960 during the Presidential campaign. After taking office, he unsuccessfully argued that his status as Commander in Chief gave him a right to a stay under the Soldiers' and Sailors' Civil Relief Act of 1940. The motion for a stay was denied by the District Court, and the matter was settled out of court. Thus, none of those cases sheds any light on the constitutional issue before us.

The principal rationale for affording certain public servants immunity from suits for money damages arising out of their official acts is inapplicable to unofficial conduct. In cases involving prosecutors, legislators, and judges we have repeatedly explained that the immunity serves the public interest in enabling such officials to perform their designated functions effectively without fear that a particular decision may give rise to personal liability. . . . That rationale provided the principal basis for our holding that a former President of the United States was "entitled to absolute immunity from damages liability predicated on his official acts" [*Fitzgerald*]. Our central concern was to avoid rendering the President "unduly cautious in the discharge of his official duties."

This reasoning provides no support for an immunity for unofficial conduct. As we explained in *Fitzgerald*, "the sphere of protected action must be related closely to the immunity's justifying purposes." Because of the President's broad responsibilities, we recognized in that case an immunity from damages claims arising out of official acts extending to the "outer perimeter of his authority." But we have never suggested that the President, or any other official, has an immunity that extends beyond the scope of any action taken in an official capacity. . . .

Moreover, when defining the scope of an immunity for acts clearly taken within an official capacity, we have applied a functional approach. . . . Hence, for example, a judge's absolute immunity does not extend to actions performed in a purely administrative capacity. As our opinions have made clear, immunities are grounded in "the nature of the function performed, not the identity of the actor who performed it."

Petitioner's effort to construct an immunity from suit for unofficial acts grounded purely in the identity of his office is unsupported by precedent.

V

We are also unpersuaded by the evidence from the historical record to which petitioner has called our attention. [Remainder of section omitted.]

VI

Petitioner's strongest argument supporting his immunity claim is based on the text and structure of the Constitution. He does not contend that the occupant of the Office of the President is "above the law," in the sense that his conduct is entirely immune from judicial scrutiny. The President argues merely for a postponement of the judicial proceedings that will determine whether he violated any law. His argument is grounded in the character of the office that was created by Article II of the Constitution, and relies on separation of powers principles that have structured our constitutional arrangement since the founding.

As a starting premise, petitioner contends that he occupies a unique office with powers and responsibilities so vast and important that the public interest demands that he devote his undivided time and attention to his public duties. He submits that—given the nature of the office—the doctrine of separation of powers places limits on the authority of the Federal Judiciary to interfere with the Executive Branch that would be transgressed by allowing this action to proceed.

We have no dispute with the initial premise of the argument. . . .

It does not follow, however, that separation of powers principles would be violated by allowing this action to proceed. . . .

. . . [I]n this case there is no suggestion that the Federal Judiciary is being asked to perform any function that might in some way be described as "executive." Respondent is merely asking the courts to exercise their core Article III jurisdiction to decide cases and controversies. Whatever the outcome of this case, there is no possibility that the decision will curtail the scope of the official powers of the Executive Branch. The litigation of questions that relate entirely to the unofficial conduct of the individual who happens to be the President poses no perceptible risk of misallocation of either judicial power or executive power.

Rather than arguing that the decision of the case will produce either an aggrandizement of judicial power or a narrowing of executive power, petitioner contends that—as a by-product of an otherwise traditional exercise of judicial power—burdens will be placed on the President that will hamper the performance of his official duties. We have recognized that "[e]ven when a branch does not arrogate power to itself . . . the separation-of-powers doctrine requires that a branch not impair another in the performance of its constitutional duties." *Loving v. United States* (1996). As a factual matter, petitioner contends that this particular case—as well as the potential additional litigation that an affirmance of the Court of Appeals judgment might spawn—may impose an unacceptable burden on the President's time and energy, and thereby impair the effective performance of his office.

Petitioner's predictive judgment finds little support in either history or the relatively narrow compass of the issues raised in this particular case. As we have already noted, in the more than 200-year history of the Republic, only three sitting Presidents have been subjected to suits for their private actions. If the past is any indicator, it seems unlikely that a deluge of such litigation will ever engulf the Presidency. As for the case at hand, if properly managed by the District Court, it appears to us highly unlikely to occupy any substantial amount of petitioner's time.

Of greater significance, petitioner errs by presuming that interactions between the Judicial Branch and the Executive, even quite burdensome interactions, necessarily rise to the level of constitutionally forbidden impairment of the Executive's ability to perform its constitutionally mandated functions. . . . The fact that a federal court's exercise of its traditional Article III jurisdiction may significantly burden the time and attention of the Chief Executive is not sufficient to establish a violation of the Constitution. Two long-settled propositions . . . support that conclusion.

First, we have long held that when the President takes official action, the Court has the authority to determine whether he has acted within the law. . . .

Second, it is also settled that the President is subject to judicial process in appropriate circumstances. Although Thomas Jefferson apparently thought otherwise, Chief Justice Marshall, when presiding in the treason trial of Aaron Burr, ruled that a subpoena *duces tecum* could be directed to the President. . . . We unequivocally and emphatically endorsed Marshall's position when we held that President Nixon was obligated to comply with a subpoena commanding him to produce certain tape recordings of his conversations with his aides. *United States v. Nixon* (1974). . . .

. . . If the Judiciary may severely burden the Executive Branch by reviewing the legality of the President's official conduct, and if it may direct appropriate process to the President himself, it must follow that the federal courts have power to determine the legality of his unofficial conduct. The burden on the President's time and energy that is a mere by-product of such review surely cannot be considered as onerous as the direct burden imposed by judicial review and the occasional invalidation of his official actions. We therefore hold that the doctrine of separation of powers does not require federal courts to stay all private actions against the President until he leaves office.

The reasons for rejecting such a categorical rule apply as well to a rule that would require a stay "in all but the most exceptional cases." Indeed, if the Framers of the Constitution had thought it necessary to protect the President from the burdens of private litigation, we think it far more likely that they would have adopted a categorical rule than a rule that required the President to litigate the question whether a specific case belonged in the "exceptional case" subcategory. In all events, the question whether a specific case should receive exceptional treatment is more appropriately the subject of the exercise of judicial discretion than an interpretation of the Constitution. Accordingly, we turn to the question whether the

District Court's decision to stay the trial until after petitioner leaves office was an abuse of discretion.

VII

The Court of Appeals described the District Court's discretionary decision to stay the trial as the "functional equivalent" of a grant of temporary immunity. Concluding that petitioner was not constitutionally entitled to such an immunity, the court held that it was error to grant the stay. Although we ultimately conclude that the stay should not have been granted, we think the issue is more difficult than the opinion of the Court of Appeals suggests.

Strictly speaking the stay was not the functional equivalent of the constitutional immunity that petitioner claimed, because the District Court ordered discovery to proceed. Moreover, a stay of either the trial or discovery might be justified by considerations that do not require the recognition of any constitutional immunity. . . . Although we have rejected the argument that the potential burdens on the President violate separation of powers principles, those burdens are appropriate matters for the District Court to evaluate in its management of the case. The high respect that is owed to the office of the Chief Executive, though not justifying a rule of categorical immunity, is a matter that should inform the conduct of the entire proceeding, including the timing and scope of discovery.

Nevertheless, we are persuaded that it was an abuse of discretion for the District Court to defer the trial until after the President leaves office. Such a lengthy and categorical stay takes no account whatever of the respondent's interest in bringing the case to trial. The complaint was filed within the statutory limitations period—albeit near the end of that period—and delaying trial would increase the danger of prejudice resulting from the loss of evidence, including the inability of witnesses to recall specific facts, or the possible death of a party.

The decision to postpone the trial was, furthermore, premature. The proponent of a stay bears the burden of establishing its need. In this case, at the stage at which the District Court made its ruling, there was no way to assess whether a stay of trial after the completion of discovery would be warranted. Other than the fact that a trial may consume some of the President's time and attention, there is nothing in the record to enable a judge to assess the potential harm that may ensue from scheduling the trial promptly after discovery is concluded. We think the District Court may have given undue weight to the concern that a trial might generate unrelated civil actions that could conceivably hamper the President in conducting the duties of his office. If and when that should occur, the court's discretion would permit it to manage those actions in such fashion (including deferral of trial) that interference with the President's duties would not occur. But no such impingement upon the President's conduct of his office was shown here.

VIII

We add a final comment on two matters that are discussed at length in the briefs: the risk that our decision will generate a large volume of politically motivated harassing and frivolous litigation, and the danger that national security concerns might prevent the President from explaining a legitimate need for a continuance.

We are not persuaded that either of these risks is serious. Most frivolous and vexatious litigation is terminated at the pleading stage or on summary judgment, with little if any personal involvement by the defendant. Moreover, the availability of sanctions provides a significant deterrent to litigation directed at the President in his unofficial capacity for purposes of political gain or harassment. History indicates that the likelihood that a significant number of such cases will be filed is remote. Although scheduling problems may arise, there is no reason to assume that the District Courts will be either unable to accommodate the President's needs or unfaithful to the tradition—especially in matters involving national security—of giving "the utmost deference to Presidential responsibilities." . . . In short, we have confidence in the ability of our federal judges to deal with both of these concerns.

If Congress deems it appropriate to afford the President stronger protection, it may respond with appropriate legislation. . . . If the Constitution embodied the rule that the President advocates, Congress, of course, could not repeal it. But our holding today raises no barrier to a statutory response to these concerns.

The Federal District Court has jurisdiction to decide this case. Like every other citizen who properly invokes that jurisdiction, respondent has a right to an orderly disposition of her claims. Accordingly, the judgment of the Court of Appeals is affirmed.

It is so ordered.

JUSTICE BREYER, concurring in the judgment.

I agree with the majority that the Constitution does not automatically grant the President an immunity from civil lawsuits based upon his private conduct. Nor does the "doctrine of separation of powers . . . require federal courts to stay" virtually "all private actions against the President until he leaves office." Rather, as the Court of Appeals stated, the President cannot simply rest upon the claim that a private civil lawsuit for damages will "interfere with the constitutionally assigned duties of the Executive Branch . . . without detailing any specific responsibilities or explaining how or the degree to which they are affected by the suit." (1996). To obtain a postponement the President must "bea[r] the burden of establishing its need."

In my view, however, once the President sets forth and explains a conflict between judicial proceeding and public duties, the matter changes. At that point, the Constitution permits a judge to schedule a trial in an ordinary civil damages action (where postponement normally is possible without overwhelming damage to a plaintiff) only within the constraints of a constitutional principle—a principle that forbids a federal judge in such a case to interfere with the President's discharge of his public duties. I have no doubt that the Constitution contains such a principle applicable to civil suits, based upon Article II's vesting of the entire "executive Power" in a single individual, implemented through the Constitution's structural separation of powers, and revealed both by history and case precedent.

I recognize that this case does not require us now to apply the principle specifically, thereby delineating its contours; nor need we now decide whether lower courts are to apply it directly or categorically through the use of presumptions or rules of administration. Yet I fear that to disregard it now may appear to deny it. I also fear that the majority's description of the relevant precedents de-emphasizes the extent to which they support a principle of the President's independent authority to control his own time and energy. . . . Further, if the majority is wrong in predicting the future infrequency of private civil litigation against sitting Presidents, acknowledgement and future delineation of the constitutional principle will prove a practically necessary institutional safeguard. For these reasons, I think it important to explain how the Constitution's text, history, and precedent support this principle of judicial noninterference with Presidential functions in ordinary civil damages actions.

I

The Constitution states that the "executive Power shall be vested in a President." U. S. Const., Art. II, §1. This constitutional delegation means that a sitting President is unusually busy, that his activities have an unusually important impact upon the lives of others, and that his conduct embodies an authority bestowed by the entire American electorate. He (along with his constitutionally subordinate Vice President) is the only official for whom the entire Nation votes, and is the only elected officer to represent the entire Nation both domestically and abroad.

This constitutional delegation means still more. Article II makes a single President responsible for the actions of the Executive Branch in much the same way that the entire Congress is responsible for the actions of the Legislative Branch, or the entire Judiciary for those of the Judicial Branch. It thereby creates a constitutional equivalence between a single President, on the one hand, and many legislators, or judges, on the other. . . .

For present purposes, this constitutional structure means that the President is not like Congress, for Congress can function as if it were whole, even when up to half of its members are absent. It means that the President is not like the Judiciary, for judges often can designate other judges, *e.g.*, from other judicial circuits, to sit even should an entire court be detained by personal litigation. It means that, unlike Congress, which is regularly out of session, the President never adjourns.

More importantly, these constitutional objectives explain why a President . . . cannot delegate ultimate responsibility or the active obligation to supervise that goes with it. And the related constitutional equivalence between President, Congress, and the Judiciary, means that judicial scheduling orders in a private civil case must not only take reasonable account of, say, a particularly busy schedule, or a job on which others critically depend, or an underlying electoral mandate. They must also reflect the fact that interference with a President's ability to carry out his public responsibilities is constitutionally equivalent to interference with the ability of the entirety of Congress, or the Judicial Branch, to carry out their public obligations.

II [OMITTED]

III

The majority points to the fact that private plaintiffs have brought civil damage lawsuits against a sitting President only three times in our Nation's history; and it relies upon the threat of sanctions to discourage, and "the court's discretion" to manage, such actions so that "interference with the President's duties would not occur." I am less sanguine. . . .

I concede the possibility that district courts, supervised by the Courts of Appeals and perhaps this Court, might prove able to manage private civil damage actions against sitting Presidents without significantly interfering with the discharge of Presidential duties—at least if they manage those actions with the constitutional problem in mind. Nonetheless, predicting the future is difficult, and I am skeptical. Should the majority's optimism turn out to be misplaced, then, in my view, courts will have to develop administrative rules applicable to such cases (including postponement rules of the sort at issue in this case) in order to implement the basic constitutional directive. A Constitution that separates powers in order to prevent one branch of Government from significantly threatening the workings of another could not grant a single judge more than a very limited power to second guess a President's reasonable determination (announced in open court) of his scheduling needs, nor could it permit the issuance of a trial scheduling order that would significantly interfere with the President's discharge of his duties—in a private civil damage action the trial of which might be postponed without the plaintiff suffering enormous harm. . . . I agree with the majority's determination that a constitutional defense must await a more specific showing of need; I do not agree with what I believe to be an understatement of the "danger." And I believe that ordinary case-management principles are unlikely to prove sufficient to deal with private civil lawsuits for damages unless supplemented with a constitutionally based requirement that district courts schedule proceedings so as to avoid significant interference with the President's ongoing discharge of his official responsibilities.

IV

This case is a private action for civil damages in which, as the District Court here found, it is possible to preserve evidence and in which later payment of interest can compensate for delay. The District Court in this case determined that the Constitution required the postponement of trial during the sitting President's term. It may well be that the trial of this case cannot take place without significantly interfering with the President's ability to carry out his official duties. Yet, I agree with the majority that there is no automatic temporary immunity and that the President should have to provide the District Court with a reasoned explanation of why the immunity is needed; and I also agree that, in the absence of that explanation, the court's postponement of the trial date was premature. For those reasons, I concur in the result.

□□□

No. 96-270

Amchem Products, Inc., et al., Petitioners
v. George Windsor et al.

On writ of certiorari to the United States Court
of Appeals for the Third Circuit

[June 25, 1997]

JUSTICE GINSBURG delivered the opinion of the Court.

This case concerns the legitimacy under Rule 23 of the Federal Rules of Civil Procedure of a class-action certification sought to achieve global settlement of current and future asbestos-related claims. The class proposed for certification potentially encompasses hundreds of thousands, perhaps millions, of individuals tied together by this commonality: each was, or some day may be, adversely affected by past exposure to asbestos products manufactured by one or more of 20 companies. Those companies, defendants in the lower courts, are petitioners here.

The United States District Court for the Eastern District of Pennsylvania certified the class for settlement only, finding that the proposed settlement was fair and that representation and notice had been adequate. That court enjoined class members from separately pursuing asbestos-related personal-injury suits in any court, federal or state, pending the issuance of a final order. The Court of Appeals for the Third Circuit vacated the District Court's orders, holding that the class certification failed to satisfy Rule 23's requirements in several critical respects. We affirm the Court of Appeals' judgment.

I

A

The settlement-class certification we confront evolved in response to an asbestos-litigation crisis. A United States Judicial Conference Ad Hoc Committee on Asbestos Litigation, appointed by THE CHIEF JUSTICE in September 1990, described facets of the problem in a 1991 report:

> "[This] is a tale of danger known in the 1930s, exposure inflicted upon millions of Americans in the 1940s and 1950s, injuries that began to take their toll in the 1960s, and a flood of lawsuits beginning in the 1970s. On the basis of past and current filing data, and because of a latency period that may last as long as 40 years for some asbestos related diseases, a continuing stream of claims can be expected. The final toll of asbestos related injuries is unknown. Predictions have been made of 200,000 asbestos disease deaths before the year 2000 and as many as 265,000 by the year 2015.
>
> "The most objectionable aspects of asbestos litigation can be briefly summarized: dockets in both federal and state courts continue to grow; long delays are routine; trials are too long; the same issues are litigated over and over; transaction costs exceed the victims' recovery by nearly two to one; exhaustion of assets threatens and distorts the process; and future claimants may lose altogether."

Real reform, the report concluded, required federal legislation creating a national asbestos dispute-resolution scheme. . . . As recommended by the Ad Hoc Committee, the Judicial Conference of the United States urged Congress to act. To this date, no congressional response has emerged.

In the face of legislative inaction, the federal courts—lacking authority to replace state tort systems with a national toxic tort compensation regime—endeavored to work with the procedural tools available to improve management of federal asbestos litigation. Eight federal judges, experienced in the superintendence of asbestos cases, urged the Judicial Panel on Multidistrict Litigation (MDL Panel), to consolidate in a single district all asbestos complaints then pending in federal courts. Accepting the recommendation, the MDL Panel transferred all asbestos cases then filed, but not yet on trial in federal courts to a single district, the United States

District Court for the Eastern District of Pennsylvania; pursuant to the transfer order, the collected cases were consolidated for pretrial proceedings before Judge Weiner. The order aggregated pending cases only; no authority resides in the MDL Panel to license for consolidated proceedings claims not yet filed.

B

After the consolidation, attorneys for plaintiffs and defendants formed separate steering committees and began settlement negotiations. Ronald L. Motley and Gene Locks—later appointed, along with Motley's law partner Joseph F. Rice, to represent the plaintiff class in this action—co-chaired the Plaintiffs' Steering Committee. Counsel for the Center for Claims Resolution (CCR), the consortium of 20 former asbestos manufacturers now before us as petitioners, participated in the Defendants' Steering Committee. Although the MDL order collected, transferred, and consolidated only cases already commenced in federal courts, settlement negotiations included efforts to find a "means of resolving . . . future cases." . . .

In November 1991, the Defendants' Steering Committee made an offer designed to settle all pending and future asbestos cases by providing a fund for distribution by plaintiffs' counsel among asbestos-exposed individuals. The Plaintiffs' Steering Committee rejected this offer, and negotiations fell apart. CCR, however, continued to pursue "a workable administrative system for the handling of future claims."

To that end, CCR counsel approached the lawyers who had headed the Plaintiffs' Steering Committee in the unsuccessful negotiations, and a new round of negotiations began; that round yielded the mass settlement agreement now in controversy. At the time, the former heads of the Plaintiffs' Steering Committee represented thousands of plaintiffs with then-pending asbestos-related claims—claimants the parties to this suit call "inventory" plaintiffs. CCR indicated in these discussions that it would resist settlement of inventory cases absent "some kind of protection for the future." . . .

Settlement talks thus concentrated on devising an administrative scheme for disposition of asbestos claims not yet in litigation. In these negotiations, counsel for masses of inventory plaintiffs endeavored to represent the interests of the anticipated future claimants, although those lawyers then had no attorney-client relationship with such claimants.

Once negotiations seemed likely to produce an agreement purporting to bind potential plaintiffs, CCR agreed to settle, through separate agreements, the claims of plaintiffs who had already filed asbestos-related lawsuits. In one such agreement, CCR defendants promised to pay more than $200 million to gain release of the claims of numerous inventory plaintiffs. After settling the inventory claims, CCR, together with the plaintiffs' lawyers CCR had approached, launched this case, exclusively involving persons outside the MDL Panel's province—plaintiffs without already pending lawsuits.

C

The class action thus instituted was not intended to be litigated. Rather, within the space of a single day, January 15, 1993, the settling parties—CCR defendants and the representatives of the plaintiff class described below—presented to the District Court a complaint, an answer, a proposed settlement agreement, and a joint motion for conditional class certification.

The complaint identified nine lead plaintiffs, designating them and members of their families as representatives of a class comprising all persons who had not filed an asbestos-related lawsuit against a CCR defendant as of the date the class action commenced, but who (1) had been exposed—occupationally or through the occupational exposure of a spouse or household member—to asbestos or products containing asbestos attributable to a CCR defendant, or (2) whose spouse or family member had been so exposed. Untold numbers of individuals may fall within this description. . . . The complaint delineated no subclasses; all named plaintiffs were designated as representatives of the class as a whole.

The complaint invoked the District Court's diversity jurisdiction and asserted various state-law claims for relief, including (1) negligent failure to warn, (2) strict liability, (3) breach of express and implied warranty, (4) negligent infliction of emotional distress, (5) enhanced risk of disease, (6) medical monitoring, and (7) civil conspiracy. Each plaintiff requested unspecified damages in excess of $100,000. CCR defendants' answer denied the principal allegations of the complaint and asserted 11 affirmative defenses.

A stipulation of settlement accompanied the pleadings; it proposed to settle, and to preclude nearly all class members from litigating against CCR companies, all claims not filed before January 15, 1993, involving compensation for present and future asbestos-related personal injury or death. An exhaustive document exceeding 100 pages, the stipulation presents in detail an administrative mechanism and a schedule of payments to compensate class members who meet defined asbestos-exposure and medical requirements. The stipulation describes four categories of compensable disease: mesothelioma; lung cancer; certain "other cancers" (colon-rectal, laryngeal, esophageal, and stomach cancer); and "non-malignant conditions" (asbestosis and bilateral pleural thickening). Persons with "exceptional" medical claims—claims that do not fall within the four described diagnostic categories—may in some instances qualify for compensation, but the settlement caps the number of "exceptional" claims CCR must cover.

For each qualifying disease category, the stipulation specifies the range of damages CCR will pay to qualifying claimants. Payments under the settlement are not adjustable for inflation. Mesothelioma claimants—the most highly compensated category—are scheduled to receive between $20,000 and $200,000. . . .

Compensation above the fixed ranges may be obtained for "extraordinary" claims. But the settlement places both numerical caps and dollar limits on such claims. The settlement also imposes "case flow maximums," which cap the number of claims payable for each disease in a given year.

Class members are to receive no compensation for certain kinds of claims, even if otherwise applicable state law recognizes such claims. Claims that garner no compensation under the settlement include claims by family members of asbestos-exposed individuals for loss of consortium, and claims by so-called "exposure-only" plaintiffs for increased risk of cancer, fear of future asbestos-related injury, and medical monitoring. "Pleural" claims, which might be asserted by persons with asbestos-related plaques on their lungs but no accompanying physical impairment, are also excluded. Although not entitled to present compensation, exposure-only claimants and pleural claimants may qualify for benefits when and if they develop a compensable disease and meet the relevant exposure and medical criteria. Defendants forgo defenses to liability, including statute of limitations pleas.

Class members, in the main, are bound by the settlement in perpetuity, while CCR defendants may choose to withdraw from the settlement after ten years. A small number of class members—only a few per year—may reject the settlement and pursue their claims in court. Those permitted to exercise this option, however, may not assert any punitive damages claim or any claim for increased risk of cancer. Aspects of the administration of the settlement are to be monitored by the AFL-CIO and class counsel. Class counsel are to receive attorneys' fees in an amount to be approved by the District Court.

D

On January 29, 1993, as requested by the settling parties, the District Court conditionally certified, under Federal Rule of Civil Procedure 23(b)(3), an encompassing opt-out class. The certified class included persons occupationally exposed to defendants' asbestos products, and members of their families, who had not filed suit as of January 15. Judge Weiner appointed Locks, Motley, and Rice as class counsel, noting that "[t]he Court may in the future appoint additional counsel if it is deemed necessary and advisable." At no stage of the proceedings, however, were additional counsel in fact appointed. Nor was the class ever divided into subclasses. In a separate order, Judge Weiner assigned to Judge Reed, also of the Eastern District of Pennsylvania, "the task of conducting fairness proceedings and of determining whether the proposed settlement is fair to the class." Various class members raised objections to the settlement stipulation, and Judge Weiner granted the objectors full rights to participate in the subsequent proceedings.

In preliminary rulings, Judge Reed held that the District Court had subject-matter jurisdiction (1993), and he approved the settling parties' elaborate plan for giving notice to the class (1993). The court-approved notice informed recipients that they could exclude themselves from the class, if they so chose, within a three-month opt-out period.

Objectors raised numerous challenges to the settlement. They urged that the settlement unfairly disadvantaged those without currently compensable conditions in that it failed to adjust for inflation or to account for changes, over time, in medical understanding. They maintained that compensation levels were intolerably low in comparison to awards available in tort litigation or payments received by the inventory plaintiffs. And they objected to the absence of any compensation for certain claims, for example, medical monitoring, compensable under the tort law of several States. Rejecting these and all other objections, Judge Reed concluded that the settlement terms were fair and had been negotiated without collusion. He also found that adequate notice had been given to class members and that final class certification under Rule 23(b)(3) was appropriate. (1994).

[Detailed summary of district court's rulings omitted.]

The objectors appealed. The United States Court of Appeals for the Third Circuit vacated the certification, holding that the requirements of Rule 23 had not been satisfied. [*Georgine v. Amchem Products, Inc.* (1996).]

E

[Ginsburg summarized what she called the Court of Appeals' "long, heavily detailed" opinion. She said that the court held that the requirements of Rule 23(a) and (b)(3) must be met "without taking into account the settlement" but that the court nevertheless "closely considered the terms of the settlement as it examined aspects of the case under Rule 23 criteria." The court found that the suit did not satisfy the "predominance" requirement because of "the number of uncommon issues in this humongous class action." The suit also did not meet the "adequacy of representation" requirement, the appeals court ruled, because of "serious intraclass conflicts"— in particular, the divergence of interests between plaintiffs already afflicted with an asbestos-related disease and plaintiffs without manifest injury (exposure-only plaintiffs). Finally, the appeals court also rejected the District Court's assessment of the superiority of the class action.]

We granted certiorari (1996) and now affirm.

II

Objectors assert in this Court, as they did in the District Court and Court of Appeals, an array of jurisdictional barriers. Most fundamentally, they maintain that the settlement proceeding instituted by class counsel and CCR is not a justiciable case or controversy within the confines of Article III of the Federal Constitution. In the main, they say, the proceeding is a nonadversarial endeavor to impose on countless individuals without currently ripe claims an administrative compensation regime binding on those individuals if and when they manifest injuries. . . .

. . . [T]he Third Circuit declined to reach these issues because they "would not exist but for the [class action] certification." We agree. . . . We therefore follow the path taken by the Court of Appeals, mindful that Rule 23's requirements must be interpreted in keeping with Article III constraints, and with the Rules Enabling Act, which instructs that rules of procedure "shall not abridge, enlarge or modify any substantive right.". . .

III

To place this controversy in context, we briefly describe the characteristics of class actions for which the Federal Rules provide. Rule 23, governing federal-court class actions, stems from equity practice and gained its current shape in an innovative 1966 revision. Rule 23(a) states four threshold requirements applicable to all class actions: (1) numerosity (a "class [so large] that joinder of all members is impracticable"); (2) commonality ("questions of law or fact common to the class"); (3) typicality (named parties' claims or defenses "are typical . . . of the class"); and (4) adequacy of representation (representatives "will fairly and adequately protect the interests of the class").

In addition to satisfying Rule 23(a)'s prerequisites, parties seeking class certification must show that the action is maintainable under Rule 23(b)(1), (2), or (3). Rule 23(b)(1) covers cases in which separate actions by or against individual class members would risk establishing "incompatible standards of conduct for the party opposing the class," Fed. Rule Civ. Proc. 23(b)(1)(A), or would "as a practical matter be dispositive of the interests" of nonparty class members "or substantially impair or impede their ability to protect their interests," Fed. Rule Civ. Proc. 23(b)(1)(B). . . .

In the 1966 class-action amendments, Rule 23(b)(3), the category at issue here, was "the most adventuresome" innovation. Rule 23(b)(3) added to the complex-litigation arsenal class actions for damages designed to secure judgments binding all class members save those who affirmatively elected to be excluded. . . .

. . . To qualify for certification under Rule 23(b)(3), a class must meet two requirements beyond the Rule 23(a) prerequisites: Common questions must "predominate over any questions affecting only individual members"; and class resolution must be "superior to other available methods for the fair and efficient adjudication of the controversy." . . .

While the text of Rule 23(b)(3) does not exclude from certification cases in which individual damages run high, the Advisory Committee had dominantly in mind vindication of "the rights of groups of people who individually would be without effective strength to bring their opponents into court at all." . . .

To alert class members to their right to "opt out" of a (b)(3) class, Rule 23 instructs the court to "direct to the members of the class the best notice practicable under the circumstances, including individual notice to all members who can be identified through reasonable effort." Fed. Rule Civ. Proc. 23(c)(2). . . .

No class action may be "dismissed or compromised without [court] approval," preceded by notice to class members. Fed. Rule Civ. Proc. 23(e). . . .

In the decades since the 1966 revision of Rule 23, class action practice has become ever more "adventuresome" as a means of coping with claims too numerous to secure their "just, speedy, and inexpensive determination" one by one. The development reflects concerns about the efficient use of court resources and the conservation of funds to compensate claimants who do not line up early in a litigation queue.

Among current applications of Rule 23(b)(3), the "settlement only" class has become a stock device. . . . Although all Federal Circuits recognize the utility of Rule 23(b)(3) settlement classes, courts have divided on the extent to which a proffered settlement affects court surveillance under Rule 23's certification criteria.

In [*In re General Motors Corp. Pick-Up Truck Fuel Tank Products Liability Litigation* (1995)] and in the instant case, the Third Circuit held that a class cannot be certified for settlement when certification for trial would be unwarranted. Other courts have held that settlement obviates or reduces the need to measure a proposed class against the enumerated Rule 23 requirements. [Citation of cases omitted.]

A proposed amendment to Rule 23 would expressly authorize settlement class certification, in conjunction with a motion by the settling parties for Rule 23(b)(3) certification, "even though the requirements of subdivision (b)(3) might not be met for purposes of trial." In response to the publication of this proposal, voluminous public comments—many of them opposed to, or skeptical of, the amendment—were received by the Judicial Conference Standing Committee on Rules of Practice and Procedure. The Committee has not yet acted on the matter. We consider the certification at issue under the rule as it is currently framed.

IV

We granted review to decide the role settlement may play, under existing Rule 23, in determining the propriety of class certification. The Third Circuit's opinion stated that each of the requirements of Rule 23(a) and (b)(3) "must be satisfied without taking into account the settlement." That statement, petitioners urge, is incorrect.

We agree with petitioners to this limited extent: settlement is relevant to a class certification. The Third Circuit's opinion bears modification in that respect. But the Court of Appeals in fact did not ignore the settlement; instead, that court homed in on settlement terms in explaining why it found the absentees' interests inadequately represented. The Third Circuit's close inspection of the settlement in that regard was altogether proper.

Confronted with a request for settlement-only class certification, a district court need not inquire whether the case, if tried, would present intractable management problems, for the proposal is that there be no trial. But other specifications of the rule—those designed to protect absentees by blocking unwarranted or overbroad class definitions—demand undiluted, even heightened, attention in the settlement context. Such attention is of vital importance, for a court asked to certify a settlement class will lack the opportunity, present when a case is litigated, to adjust the class, informed by the proceedings as they unfold.

And, of overriding importance, courts must be mindful that the rule as now composed sets the requirements they are bound to enforce. . . . Courts are not free to amend a rule outside the process Congress ordered. . . .

Rule 23(e), on settlement of class actions, reads in its entirety: "A class action shall not be dismissed or compromised without the approval of the court, and notice of the proposed dismissal or compromise shall be given to all members of the class in such manner as the court directs." This prescription was designed to function as an additional requirement, not a superseding direction, for the "class action" to which Rule 23(e) refers is one qualified for certification under Rule 23(a) and (b). . . . Subdivisions (a) and (b) focus court attention on whether a proposed class has sufficient unity so that absent members can fairly be bound by decisions of class representatives. That dominant concern persists when settlement, rather than trial, is proposed.

The safeguards provided by the Rule 23(a) and (b) class-qualifying criteria, we emphasize, are not impractical impediments—checks shorn of utility—in the settlement class context. First, the standards set for the protection of absent class members serve to inhibit appraisals of the chancellor's foot kind—class certifications dependent upon the court's gestalt judgment or overarching impression of the settlement's fairness.

Second, if a fairness inquiry under Rule 23(e) controlled certification, eclipsing Rule 23(a) and (b), and permitting class designation despite the impossibility of litigation, both class counsel and court would be disarmed. Class counsel confined to settlement negotiations could not use the threat of litigation to press for a better offer, and the court would face a bargain proffered for its approval without benefit of adversarial investigation.

Federal courts, in any case, lack authority to substitute for Rule 23's certification criteria a standard never adopted—that if a settlement is "fair," then certification is proper. Applying to this case criteria the rulemakers set, we conclude that the Third Circuit's appraisal is essentially correct. Although that court should have acknowledged that settlement is a factor in the calculus, a remand is not warranted on that account. The Court of Appeals' opinion amply demonstrates why—with or without a settlement on the table—the sprawling class the District Court certified does not satisfy Rule 23's requirements.

A

We address first the requirement of Rule 23(b)(3) that "[common] questions of law or fact . . . predominate over any questions affecting only individual members." The District Court concluded that predominance was satisfied based on two factors: class members' shared experience of asbestos exposure and their common "interest in receiving prompt and fair compensation for their claims, while minimizing the risks and transaction costs inherent in the asbestos litigation process as it occurs presently in the tort system." The settling parties also contend that the settlement's fairness is a common question, predominating over disparate legal issues that might be pivotal in litigation but become irrelevant under the settlement.

The predominance requirement stated in Rule 23(b)(3), we hold, is not met by the factors on which the District Court relied. The benefits asbestos-exposed persons might gain from the establishment of a grand-scale compensation scheme is a matter fit for legislative consideration, but it is not pertinent to the predominance inquiry. . . .

The Rule 23(b)(3) predominance inquiry tests whether proposed classes are sufficiently cohesive to warrant adjudication by representation. The inquiry appropriate under Rule 23(e), on the other hand, protects unnamed class members "from unjust or unfair settlements affecting their rights when the representatives become fainthearted before the action is adjudicated or are able to secure satisfaction of their individual claims by a compromise." But it is not the mission of Rule 23(e) to assure the class cohesion that legitimizes representative action in the first place. If a common interest in a fair compromise could satisfy the predominance requirement of Rule 23(b)(3), that vital prescription would be stripped of any meaning in the settlement context.

The District Court also relied upon this commonality: "The members of the class have all been exposed to asbestos products supplied by the defendants. . . ." Even if Rule 23(a)'s commonality requirement may be satisfied by that shared experience, the predominance criterion is far more demanding. Given the greater number of questions peculiar to the several categories of class members, and to individuals within each category, and the significance of those uncommon questions, any overarching dispute about the health consequences of asbestos exposure cannot satisfy the Rule 23(b)(3) predominance standard. . . .

No settlement class called to our attention is as sprawling as this one. . . . Even mass tort cases arising from a common cause or disaster may, depending upon the circumstances, satisfy the predominance requirement. The Advisory Committee for the 1966 revision of Rule 23, it is true, noted that "mass accident" cases are likely to present "significant questions, not only of damages but of liability and defenses of liability, . . . affecting the individuals in different ways." And the Committee advised that such cases are "ordinarily not appropriate" for class treatment. But the text of the rule does not categorically exclude mass tort cases from class certification, and district courts, since the late 1970s, have been certifying such cases in increasing number. The Committee's warning, however, continues to call for caution when individual stakes are high and disparities among class members great. As the Third Circuit's opinion makes plain, the certification in this case does not follow the counsel of caution. That certification cannot be upheld, for it rests on a conception of Rule 23(b)(3)'s predominance requirement irreconcilable with the rule's design.

B

Nor can the class approved by the District Court satisfy Rule 23(a)(4)'s requirement that the named parties "will fairly and adequately protect the interests of the class." The adequacy inquiry under Rule 23(a)(4) serves to uncover conflicts of interest between named parties and the class they seek to represent. . . .

As the Third Circuit pointed out, named parties with diverse medical conditions sought to act on behalf of a single giant class rather than on behalf of discrete subclasses. In significant respects, the interests of those within the single class are not aligned. Most saliently, for the currently injured, the critical goal is generous immediate payments. That goal tugs against the interest of exposure-only plaintiffs in ensuring an ample, inflation-protected fund for the future. . . .

The disparity between the currently injured and exposure-only categories of plaintiffs, and the diversity within each category are not made insignificant by the District Court's finding that petitioners' assets suffice to pay claims under the settlement. Although this is not a "limited fund" case certified under Rule 23(b)(1)(B), the terms of the settlement reflect essential allocation decisions designed to confine compensation and to limit defendants' liability. For example, as earlier described, the settlement includes no adjustment for inflation; only a few claimants per year can opt out at the back end; and loss-of-consortium claims are extinguished with no compensation.

The settling parties, in sum, achieved a global compromise with no structural assurance of fair and adequate representation for the diverse groups and individuals affected. . . . The Third Circuit found no assurance here—either in the terms of the settlement or in the structure of the negotiations—that the named plaintiffs operated under a proper understanding of their representational responsibilities. That assessment, we conclude, is on the mark.

C

Impediments to the provision of adequate notice, the Third Circuit emphasized, rendered highly problematic any endeavor to tie to a settlement class persons with no perceptible asbestos-related disease at the time of the settlement. Many persons in the exposure-only category, the Court of Appeals stressed, may not even know of their exposure, or realize the extent of the harm they may incur. Even if they fully appreciate the significance of class notice, those without current afflictions may not have the information or foresight needed to decide, intelligently, whether to stay in or opt out.

Family members of asbestos-exposed individuals may themselves fall prey to disease or may ultimately have ripe claims for loss of consortium. Yet large numbers of people in this category—future spouses and children of asbestos victims—could not be alerted to their class membership. And current spouses and children of the occupationally exposed may know nothing of that exposure.

Because we have concluded that the class in this case cannot satisfy the requirements of common issue predominance and adequacy of representation, we need not rule, definitively, on the notice given here. In accord with the Third Circuit, however, we recognize the gravity of the question whether class action notice sufficient under the Constitution and Rule 23 could ever be given to legions so unselfconscious and amorphous.

V

The argument is sensibly made that a nationwide administrative claims processing regime would provide the most secure, fair, and efficient means of compensating victims of asbestos exposure. Congress, however, has not adopted such a solution. And Rule 23, which must be interpreted with fidelity to the Rules Enabling Act and applied with the interests of absent class members in close view, cannot carry the large load CCR, class counsel, and the District Court heaped upon it. As this case exemplifies, the rulemakers' prescriptions for class actions may be endangered by "those who embrace [Rule 23] too enthusiastically just as [they are by] those who approach [the rule] with distaste." . . .

* * *

For the reasons stated, the judgment of the Court of Appeals for the Third Circuit is

Affirmed.

JUSTICE O'CONNOR took no part in the consideration or decision of this case.

JUSTICE BREYER, with whom JUSTICE STEVENS joins, concurring in part and dissenting in part.

Although I agree with the Court's basic holding that "settlement is relevant to a class certification," I find several problems in its approach that lead me to a different conclusion. First, I believe that the need for settlement in this mass tort case, with hundreds of thousands of lawsuits, is greater than the Court's opinion suggests. Second, I would give more weight than would the majority to settlement-related issues for purposes of determining whether common issues predominate. Third, I am uncertain about the Court's determination of adequacy of representation, and do not believe it appropriate for this Court to second-guess the District Court on the matter without first having the Court of Appeals consider it. Fourth, I am uncertain about the tenor of an opinion that seems to suggest the settlement is unfair. And fifth, in the absence of further review by the Court of Appeals, I cannot accept the majority's suggestions that "notice" is inadequate.

These difficulties flow from the majority's review of what are highly fact-based, complex, and difficult matters, matters that are inappropriate for initial review before this Court. The law gives broad leeway to district courts in making class certification decisions, and their judgments are to be reviewed by the Court of Appeals only for abuse of discretion. . . . Accordingly, I do not believe that we should in effect set aside the findings of the District Court. That court is far more familiar with the issues and litigants than is a court of appeals or are we, and therefore has "broad power and discretion . . . with respect to matters involving the certification" of class actions. . . .

I do not believe that we can rely upon the Court of Appeals' review of the District Court record, for that review, and its ultimate conclusions, are infected by a legal error. . . . There is no evidence that the Court of Appeals at any point considered the settlement as something that would help the class meet Rule 23. I find, moreover, the fact-related issues presented here sufficiently close to warrant further detailed appellate court review under the correct legal standard. And I shall briefly explain why this is so.

I

First, I believe the majority understates the importance of settlement in this case. Between 13 and 21 million workers have been exposed to asbestos in the workplace—over the past 40 or 50 years—but the most severe instances of such exposure probably occurred three or four decades ago. This exposure has led to several hundred thousand lawsuits, about 15% of which involved claims for cancer and about 30% for asbestosis. About half of the suits have involved claims for pleural thickening and plaques—the harmfulness of which is apparently controversial. . . . Some of those who suffer from the most serious injuries, however, have received little or no compensation. . . . These lawsuits have taken up more than 6% of all federal civil filings in one recent year, and are subject to a delay that is twice that of other civil suits. . . .

. . . [T]he settlement before us is unusual in terms of its importance, both to many potential plaintiffs and to defendants, and with respect to the time, effort, and expenditure that it reflects. All of which leads me to be reluctant to set aside the District Court's findings without more assurance than I have that they are wrong. I cannot obtain that assurance through comprehensive review of the record because that is properly the job of the Court of Appeals and that court, understandably, but as we now hold, mistakenly, believed that settlement was not a relevant (and, as I would say, important) consideration.

Second, the majority, in reviewing the District Court's determination that common "issues of fact and law predominate," says that the predominance "inquiry trains on the legal or factual questions that qualify each class member's case as a genuine controversy, questions that preexist any settlement." I find it difficult to interpret this sentence in a way that could lead me to the majority's conclusion. If the majority means that these pre-settlement questions are what matters, then how does it reconcile its statement with its basic conclusion that "settlement is relevant" to class certification, or with the numerous lower court authority that says that settlement is not only relevant, but important?

Nor do I understand how one could decide whether common questions "predominate" in the abstract without looking at what is likely to be at issue in the proceedings that will ensue, namely, the settlement. . . . How can a court make a contextual judgment of the sort that Rule 23 requires without looking to what proceedings will follow? Such guideposts help it decide whether, in light of common concerns and differences, certification will achieve Rule 23's basic objective—"economies of time, effort, and expense." . . .

The majority may mean that the District Court gave too much weight to the settlement. But I am not certain how it can reach that conclusion. It cannot rely upon the Court of Appeals, for that court gave no positive weight at all to the settlement. Nor can it say that the District Court relied solely on "a common interest in a fair compromise," for the District Court did not do so. Rather, it found the settlement relevant because it explained the importance of the class plaintiffs' common features and common interests. . . . That is to say, the settlement underscored the importance of (a) the common fact of exposure, (b) the common interest in receiving some compensation for certain rather than running a strong risk of no compensation, and (c) the common interest in avoiding large legal fees, other transaction costs, and delays.

Of course, as the majority points out, there are also important differences among class members. Different plaintiffs were exposed to different products for different times; each has a distinct medical history and a different history of smoking; and many cases arise under the laws of different States. The relevant question, however, is *how much* these differences matter in respect to the legal proceedings that lie ahead. Many, if not all, toxic tort class actions involve plaintiffs with such differences. And the differences in state law are of diminished importance in respect to a proposed settlement in which the defendants have waived all defenses and agreed to compensate all those who were injured.

These differences might warrant subclasses, though subclasses can have problems of their own. . . . Or these differences may be too serious to permit an effort at group settlement. This kind of determination, as I have said, is one that the law commits to the discretion of the district court—reviewable for abuse of discretion by a court of appeals. I believe that we are far too distant from the litigation itself to reweigh the fact-specific Rule 23 determinations and to find them erroneous without the benefit of the Court of Appeals first having restudied the matter with today's legal standard in mind.

Third, the majority concludes that the "representative parties" will not "fairly and adequately protect the interests of the class." It finds a serious conflict between plaintiffs who are now injured and those who may be injured in the future because "for the currently injured, the critical goal is generous immediate payments," a goal that "tugs against the interest of exposure-only plaintiffs in ensuring an ample, inflation-protected fund for the future."

I agree that there is a serious problem, but it is a problem that often exists in toxic tort cases. . . . And it is a problem that potentially exists whenever a single defendant injures several plaintiffs, for a settling plaintiff leaves fewer assets available for the others. With class actions, at least, plaintiffs have the consolation that a district court, thoroughly familiar with the facts, is charged with the responsibility of ensuring that the interests of no class members are sacrificed.

But this Court cannot easily safeguard such interests through review of a cold record. . . . The majority's use of the lack of an inflation adjustment as evidence of inadequacy of representation for future plaintiffs is one example of this difficulty. An inflation adjustment might not be as valuable as the majority assumes if most plaintiffs are old and not worried about receiving compensation decades from now. There are, of course, strong arguments as to its value. But that disagreement is one that this Court is poorly situated to resolve.

Further, certain details of the settlement that are not discussed in the majority opinion suggest that the settlement may be of greater benefit to future plaintiffs than the majority suggests. The District Court concluded that future plaintiffs receive a "significant value" from the settlement due to variety of its items that benefit future plaintiffs, such as: (1) tolling the statute of limitations so that class members "will no longer be forced to file premature lawsuits or risk their claims being time-barred"; (2) waiver of defenses to liability; (3) payment of claims, if and when members become sick, pursuant to the settlement's compensation standards, which avoids "the uncertainties, long delays and high transaction costs [including attorney's fees] of the tort system"; (4) "some assurance that there will be funds available if and when they get sick," based on the finding that each defendant "has shown an ability to fund the payment of all qualifying claims" under the settlement; and (5) the right to additional compensation if cancer develops (many settlements for plaintiffs with noncancerous conditions bar such additional claims). For these reasons, and others, the District Court found that the distinction between present and future plaintiffs was "illusory."

I do not know whether or not the benefits are more or less valuable than an inflation adjustment. But I can certainly recognize an argument that they are. . . . The difficulties inherent in both knowing and understanding the vast number of relevant individual fact-based determinations here counsel heavily in favor of deference to district court decisionmaking in Rule 23 decisions. Or, at the least, making certain that appellate court review has taken place with the correct standard in mind.

Fourth, I am more agnostic than is the majority about the basic fairness of the settlement. The District Court's conclusions rested upon complicated factual findings that are not easily cast aside. It is helpful to consider some of them, such as its determination that the settlement provided "fair compensation . . . while reducing the delays and transaction costs endemic to the asbestos litigation process" and that "the proposed class action settlement is superior to other available methods for the fair and efficient resolution of the asbestos-related personal injury claims of class members." . . . Indeed, the settlement has been endorsed as fair and reasonable by the AFL-CIO (and its Building and Construction Trades Department), which represents a " 'substantial percentage' " of class members, and which has a role in monitoring implementation of the settlement. I do not intend to pass judgment upon the settlement's fairness, but I do believe that these matters would have to be explored in far greater depth before I could reach a conclusion about fairness. And that task, as I have said, is one for the Court of Appeals.

Finally, I believe it is up to the District Court, rather than this Court, to review the legal sufficiency of notice to members of the class. The District Court found that the plan to provide notice was implemented at a cost of millions of dollars and included hundreds of thousands of individual notices, a wide-ranging television and print campaign, and significant additional efforts by 35 international and national unions to notify their members. Every notice emphasized that an individual did not currently have to be sick to be a class member. And in the end, the District Court was "confident" that Rule 23 and due process requirements were satisfied because, as a result of this "extensive and expensive notice procedure," "over six million" individuals "received actual notice materials," and "millions more" were reached by the media campaign. Although the majority, in principle, is reviewing a Court of Appeals' conclusion, it seems to me that its opinion might call into question the fact-related determinations of the District Court. To the extent that it does so, I disagree, for such findings cannot be so quickly disregarded. And I do not think that our precedents permit this Court to do so.

II

The issues in this case are complicated and difficult. The District Court might have been correct. Or not. Subclasses might be appropriate. Or not. I cannot tell. And I do not believe that this Court should be in the business of trying to make these fact-based determinations. That is a job suited to the district courts in the first instance, and the courts of appeal on review. But there is no reason in this case to believe that the Court of Appeals conducted its prior review with an understanding that the settlement could have constituted a reasonably strong factor in favor of class certification. For this reason, I would provide the courts below with an opportunity to analyze the factual questions involved in certification by vacating the judgment, and remanding the case for further proceedings.

□□□

No. 96-842

United States, Petitioner v. James Herman O'Hagan

On writ of certiorari to the United States Court
of Appeals for the Eighth Circuit

[June 25, 1997]

JUSTICE GINSBURG delivered the opinion of the Court.

This case concerns the interpretation and enforcement of §10(b) and §14(e) of the Securities Exchange Act of 1934, and rules made by the Securities and Exchange Commission pursuant to these provisions, Rule 10b-5 and Rule 14e-3(a). Two prime questions are presented. The first relates to the misappropriation of material, nonpublic information for securities trading; the second concerns fraudulent practices in the tender offer setting. In particular, we address and resolve these issues: (1) Is a person who trades in securities for personal profit, using confidential information misappropriated in breach of a fiduciary duty to the source of the information, guilty of violating §10(b) and Rule 10b-5? (2) Did the Commission exceed its rulemaking authority by adopting Rule 14e-3(a), which proscribes trading on undisclosed information in the tender offer setting, even in the absence of a duty to disclose? Our answer to the first question is yes, and to the second question, viewed in the context of this case, no.

I

Respondent James Herman O'Hagan was a partner in the law firm of Dorsey & Whitney in Minneapolis, Minnesota. In July 1988, Grand Metropolitan PLC (Grand Met), a company based in London, England, retained Dorsey & Whitney as local counsel to represent Grand Met regarding a potential tender offer for the common stock of the Pillsbury Company, headquartered in Minneapolis. Both Grand Met and Dorsey & Whitney took precautions to protect the confidentiality of Grand Met's tender offer plans. O'Hagan did no work on the Grand Met representation. Dorsey & Whitney withdrew from representing Grand Met on September 9, 1988. Less than a month later, on October 4, 1988, Grand Met publicly announced its tender offer for Pillsbury stock.

On August 18, 1988, while Dorsey & Whitney was still representing Grand Met, O'Hagan began purchasing call options for Pillsbury stock. Each option gave him the right to purchase 100 shares of Pillsbury stock by a specified date in September 1988. Later in August and in September, O'Hagan made additional purchases of Pillsbury call options. By the end of September, he owned 2,500 unexpired Pillsbury options, apparently more than any other individual investor. O'Hagan also purchased, in September 1988, some 5,000 shares of Pillsbury common stock, at a price just under $39 per share. When Grand Met announced its tender offer in October, the price of Pillsbury stock rose to nearly $60 per share. O'Hagan then sold his Pillsbury call options and common stock, making a profit of more than $4.3 million.

The Securities and Exchange Commission (SEC or Commission) initiated an investigation into O'Hagan's transactions, culminating in a 57-count indictment. The indictment alleged that O'Hagan defrauded his law firm and its client, Grand Met, by using for his own trading purposes material, nonpublic information regarding Grand Met's planned tender offer. According to the indictment, O'Hagan used the profits he gained through this trading to conceal his previous embezzlement and conversion of unrelated client trust funds. O'Hagan was charged with 20 counts of mail fraud, in violation of 18 U. S. C. §1341; 17 counts of securities fraud, in violation of §10(b) of the Securities Exchange Act of 1934 (Exchange Act) and SEC Rule 10b-5 (1996); 17 counts of fraudulent trading in connection with a tender offer, in violation of §14(e) of the Exchange Act and SEC Rule 14e-3(a); and 3 counts of violating federal money laundering statutes. A jury convicted O'Hagan on all 57 counts, and he was sentenced to a 41-month term of imprisonment.

A divided panel of the Court of Appeals for the Eighth Circuit reversed all of O'Hagan's convictions (1996). Liability under §10(b) and Rule 10b-5, the Eighth Circuit held, may not be grounded on the "misappropriation theory" of securities fraud on which the prosecution relied. The Court of Appeals also held that Rule 14e-3(a)—which prohibits trading while in possession of material, nonpublic information relating to a tender offer—exceeds the SEC's §14(e) rulemaking authority because the rule contains no breach of fiduciary duty requirement. The Eighth Circuit further concluded that O'Hagan's mail fraud and money laundering convictions rested on violations of the securities laws, and therefore could not stand once the securities fraud convictions were reversed. Judge Fagg, dissenting, stated that he would recognize and enforce the misappropriation theory, and would hold that the SEC did not exceed its rulemaking authority when it adopted Rule 14e-3(a) without requiring proof of a breach of fiduciary duty.

Decisions of the Courts of Appeals are in conflict on the propriety of the misappropriation theory under §10(b) and Rule 10b-5 and on the legitimacy of Rule 14e-3(a) under §14(e). We granted certiorari (1997) and now reverse the Eighth Circuit's judgment.

II

We address first the Court of Appeals' reversal of O'Hagan's convictions under §10(b) and Rule 10b-5. . . . [T]he Eighth Circuit rejected the misappropriation theory as a basis for §10(b) liability. We hold . . . that criminal liability under §10(b) may be predicated on the misappropriation theory.

A

In pertinent part, §10(b) of the Exchange Act provides:

"It shall be unlawful for any person, directly or indirectly, by the use of any means or instrumentality of interstate commerce or of the mails, or of any facility of any national securities exchange—

. . . .

"(b) To use or employ, in connection with the purchase or sale of any security registered on a national securities exchange or any security not so registered, any manipulative or deceptive device or contrivance in contravention of such rules and regulations as the [Securities and Exchange] Commission may prescribe as necessary or appropriate in the public interest or for the protection of investors." 15 U. S. C. §78j(b).

The statute thus proscribes (1) using any deceptive device (2) in connection with the purchase or sale of securities, in contravention of rules prescribed by the Commission. The provision, as written, does not confine its coverage to deception of a purchaser or seller of securities; rather, the statute reaches any deceptive device used "in connection with the purchase or sale of any security."

Pursuant to its §10(b) rulemaking authority, the Commission has adopted Rule 10b-5, which, as relevant here, provides:

"It shall be unlawful for any person, directly or indirectly, by the use of any means or instrumentality of interstate commerce, or of the mails or of any facility of any national securities exchange,

"(a) To employ any device, scheme, or artifice to defraud, [or]

. . . .

"(c) To engage in any act, practice, or course of business which operates or would operate as a fraud or deceit upon any person,

"in connection with the purchase or sale of any security."

Liability under Rule 10b-5, our precedent indicates, does not extend beyond conduct encompassed by §10(b)'s prohibition. . . .

Under the "traditional" or "classical theory" of insider trading liability, §10(b) and Rule 10b-5 are violated when a corporate insider trades in the securities of his corporation on the basis of material, nonpublic information. Trading on such information qualifies as a "deceptive device" under §10(b), we have affirmed, because "a relationship of trust and confidence [exists] between the shareholders of a corporation and those insiders who have obtained confidential information by reason of their position with that corporation." *Chiarella v. United States* (1980). That relationship, we recognized, "gives rise to a duty to disclose [or to abstain from trading] because of the 'necessity of preventing a corporate insider from . . . tak[ing] unfair advantage of . . . uninformed . . . stockholders.'" The classical theory applies not only to officers, directors, and other permanent insiders of a corporation, but also to attorneys, accountants, consultants, and others who temporarily become fiduciaries of a corporation. See *Dirks v. SEC* (1983).

The "misappropriation theory" holds that a person commits fraud "in connection with" a securities transaction, and thereby violates §10(b) and Rule 10b-5, when he misappropriates confidential information for securities trading purposes, in breach of a duty owed to the source of the information. Under this theory, a fiduciary's undisclosed, self-serving use of a principal's information to purchase or sell securities, in breach of a duty of loyalty and confidentiality, defrauds the principal of the exclusive use of that information. In lieu of premising liability on a fiduciary relationship between company insider and purchaser or seller of the company's stock, the misappropriation theory premises liability on a fiduciary-turned-trader's deception of those who entrusted him with access to confidential information.

The two theories are complementary, each addressing efforts to capitalize on nonpublic information through the purchase or sale of securities. The classical theory targets a corporate insider's breach of duty to shareholders with whom the insider transacts; the misappropriation theory outlaws trading on the basis of nonpublic information by a corporate "outsider" in breach of a duty owed not to a trading party, but to the source of the information. The misappropriation theory is thus designed to "protec[t] the integrity of the securities markets against abuses by 'outsiders' to a corporation who have access to confidential information that will affect th[e] corporation's security price when revealed, but who owe no fiduciary or other duty to that corporation's shareholders."

In this case, the indictment alleged that O'Hagan, in breach of a duty of trust and confidence he owed to his law firm, Dorsey & Whitney, and to its client, Grand Met, traded on the basis of nonpublic information regarding Grand Met's planned tender offer for Pillsbury common stock. This conduct, the Government charged, constituted a fraudulent device in connection with the purchase and sale of securities.

B

We agree with the Government that misappropriation, as just defined, satisfies §10(b)'s requirement that chargeable conduct involve a "deceptive device or contrivance" used "in connection with" the purchase or sale of securities. We observe, first, that misappropriators, as the Government describes them, deal in deception. A fiduciary who "[pretends] loyalty to the principal while secretly converting the principal's information for personal gain" "dupes" or defrauds the principal.

We addressed fraud of the same species in *Carpenter v. United States* (1987), which involved the mail fraud statute's proscription of "any scheme or artifice to defraud," 18 U. S. C. §1341. Affirming convictions under that statute, we said in *Carpenter* that an employee's undertaking not to reveal his employer's confidential information "became a sham" when the employee provided the information to his co-conspirators in a scheme to obtain trading profits. A company's confidential information, we recognized in *Carpenter*, qualifies as property to which the company has a right of exclusive use. The undisclosed misappropriation of such information, in violation of a fiduciary duty, the Court said in *Carpenter*, constitutes fraud akin to embezzlement—"'the fraudulent appropriation to one's own use of the money or goods entrusted to one's care by another.'" *Carpenter*'s discussion of the fraudulent misuse of confidential information, the Government notes, "is a particularly apt source of guidance here, because [the mail fraud statute] (like Section 10(b)) has long been held to require deception, not merely the breach of a fiduciary duty."

Deception through nondisclosure is central to the theory of liability for which the Government seeks recognition. As counsel for the Government stated in explanation of the theory at oral argument: "To satisfy the common law rule that a trustee may not use the property that [has] been entrusted [to] him, there would have to be consent. To satisfy the requirement of the Securities Act that there be no deception, there would only have to be disclosure." . . .

The misappropriation theory advanced by the Government is consistent with *Santa Fe Industries, Inc. v. Green* (1977), a decision underscoring that §10(b) is not an all-purpose breach of fiduciary duty ban; rather, it trains on conduct involving manipulation or deception. In contrast to the Government's allegations in this case, in *Santa Fe Industries*, all pertinent facts were disclosed by the persons charged with violating §10(b) and Rule 10b-5; therefore, there was no deception through nondisclosure to which liability under those provisions could attach. Similarly, full disclosure forecloses liability under the misappropriation theory: Because the deception essential to the misappropriation theory involves feigning fidelity to the source of information, if the fiduciary discloses to the source that he plans to trade on the nonpublic information, there is no "deceptive device" and thus no §10(b) violation—although the fiduciary-turned-trader may remain liable under state law for breach of a duty of loyalty.

We turn next to the §10(b) requirement that the misappropriator's deceptive use of information be "in connection with the purchase or sale of [a] security." This element is satisfied because the fiduciary's fraud is consummated, not when the fiduciary gains the confidential information, but when, without disclosure to his principal, he uses the information to purchase or sell securities. The securities transaction and the breach of duty thus coincide. This is so even though the person or entity defrauded is not the other party to the trade, but is, instead, the source of the nonpublic information. . . . A misappropriator who trades on the basis of material, nonpublic information, in short, gains his advantageous market position through deception; he deceives the source of the information and simultaneously harms members of the investing public.

The misappropriation theory targets information of a sort that misappropriators ordinarily capitalize upon to gain no-risk profits through the purchase or sale of securities. Should a misappropriator put such information to other use, the statute's prohibition would not be implicated. The theory does not catch all conceivable forms of fraud involving confidential information; rather, it catches fraudulent means of capitalizing on such information through securities transactions.

The Government notes another limitation on the forms of fraud §10(b) reaches: "The misappropriation theory would not . . . apply to a case in which a person defrauded a bank into giving him a loan or embezzled cash from another, and then used the proceeds of the misdeed to purchase securities. In such a case, the Government states, "the proceeds would have value to the malefactor apart from their use in a securities transaction, and the fraud would be complete as soon as the money was obtained." In other words, money can buy, if not anything, then at least many things; its misappropriation may thus be viewed as sufficiently detached from a subsequent securities transaction that §10(b)'s "in connection with" requirement would not be met.

The dissent's charge that the misappropriation theory is incoherent because information, like funds, can be put to multiple uses misses the point. The Exchange Act was enacted in part "to insure the maintenance of fair and honest markets," and there is no question that fraudulent uses of confidential information fall within §10(b)'s prohibition if the fraud is "in connection with" a securities transaction. It is hardly remarkable that a rule suitably applied to the fraudulent uses of certain kinds of information would be stretched beyond reason were it applied to the fraudulent use of money.

The dissent does catch the Government in overstatement. Observing that money can be used for all manner of purposes and purchases, the Government urges that confidential information of the kind at issue derives its value only from its utility in securities trading. . . . . Substitute "ordinarily" for "only," and the Government is on the mark.

Our recognition that the Government's "only" is an overstatement has provoked the dissent to cry "new theory." But the very case on which the dissent relies, *Motor Vehicle Mfrs. Assn. of United States, Inc. v. State Farm Mut. Automobile Ins. Co.* (1983), shows the extremity of that charge. In *State Farm*, we reviewed an agency's rescission of a rule under the same "arbitrary and capricious" standard by which the promulgation of a rule under the relevant statute was to be judged; in our decision concluding that the agency had not adequately explained its regulatory action, we cautioned that a "reviewing court should not attempt itself to make up for such deficiencies." Here, by contrast, Rule 10b-5's promulgation has not been challenged; we consider only the Government's charge that O'Hagan's alleged fraudulent conduct falls within the prohibitions of the rule and §10(b). In this context, we acknowledge simply that, in defending the Government's interpretation of the rule and statute in this Court, the Government's lawyers have pressed a solid point too far, something lawyers, occasionally even judges, are wont to do.

The misappropriation theory comports with §10(b)'s language, which requires deception "in connection with the purchase or sale of any security," not deception of an identifiable purchaser or seller. The theory is also well-tuned to an animating purpose of the Exchange Act: to insure honest securities markets and thereby promote investor confidence. . . . Although informational disparity is inevitable in the securities markets, investors likely would hesitate to venture their capital in a market where trading based on misappropriated nonpublic information is unchecked by law. An investor's informational disadvantage vis-à-vis a misappropriator with material, nonpublic information stems from contrivance, not luck; it is a disadvantage that cannot be overcome with research or skill. . . .

In sum, considering the inhibiting impact on market participation of trading on misappropriated information, and the congressional purposes underlying §10(b), it makes scant sense to hold a lawyer like O'Hagan a §10(b) violator if he works for a law firm representing the target of a tender offer, but not if he works for a law firm representing the bidder. The text of the statute requires no such result. The misappropriation at issue here was properly made the subject of a §10(b) charge because it meets the statutory requirement that there be "deceptive" conduct "in connection with" securities transactions.

C

The Court of Appeals rejected the misappropriation theory primarily on two grounds. First, as the Eighth Circuit comprehended the theory, it requires neither misrepresentation nor nondisclosure. As we just explained, however, deceptive nondisclosure is essential to the §10(b) liability at issue. Concretely, in this case, "it [was O'Hagan's] failure to disclose his personal trading to Grand Met and Dorsey, in breach of his duty to do so, that ma[de] his conduct 'deceptive' within the meaning of [§]10(b)."

Second and "more obvious," the Court of Appeals said, the misappropriation theory is not moored to §10(b)'s requirement that "the fraud be 'in connection with the purchase or sale of any security.'" According to the Eighth Circuit, three of our decisions reveal that §10(b) liability cannot be predicated on a duty owed to the source of nonpublic information: *Chiarella v. United States* (1980); *Dirks v. SEC* (1983);

and *Central Bank of Denver, N. A. v. First Interstate Bank of Denver, N. A.* (1994). . . . We read the statute and our precedent differently, and note again that §10(b) refers to "the purchase or sale of any security," not to identifiable purchasers or sellers of securities.

[Ginsburg summarized and analyzed the three decisions. In *Chiarella*, the Court reversed the conviction under §10(b) and Rule 10b-5 of a printer who used nonpublic information from documents he handled to buy shares of companies targeted for takeover bids. Ginsburg said the Court held that Chiarella could not be convicted solely for failing to disclose the information to shareholders of the target company before trading in the shares. But she said the ruling "expressly left open the misappropriation theory before us today." In *Dirks*, the Court set aside the SEC's censure of an investment analyst for passing on nonpublic information gained from a former corporate insider to clients and other investors. That ruling, Ginsburg said, also "left room for application of the misappropriation theory in cases like the one we confront. . . ." Finally, Ginsburg said that the most recent of the decisions, *Central Bank*, dealt only with aiding-and-abetting liability under §10(b) and Rule 10b-5 in civil cases and did not address the scope of §d Rule 10b-5 in criminal prosecutions.]

In sum, the misappropriation theory, as we have examined and explained it in this opinion, is both consistent with the statute and with our precedent. Vital to our decision that criminal liability may be sustained under the misappropriation theory, we emphasize, are two sturdy safeguards Congress has provided regarding scienter. To establish a criminal violation of Rule 10b-5, the Government must prove that a person "willfully" violated the provision. Furthermore, a defendant may not be imprisoned for violating Rule 10b-5 if he proves that he had no knowledge of the rule. O'Hagan's charge that the misappropriation theory is too indefinite to permit the imposition of criminal liability, thus fails not only because the theory is limited to those who breach a recognized duty. In addition, the statute's "requirement of the presence of culpable intent as a necessary element of the offense does much to destroy any force in the argument that application of the [statute]" in circumstances such as O'Hagan's is unjust.

The Eighth Circuit erred in holding that the misappropriation theory is inconsistent with §10(b). The Court of Appeals may address on remand O'Hagan's other challenges to his convictions under §10(b) and Rule 10b-5.

III

We consider next the ground on which the Court of Appeals reversed O'Hagan's convictions for fraudulent trading in connection with a tender offer, in violation of §14(e) of the Exchange Act and SEC Rule 14e-3(a). A sole question is before us as to these convictions: Did the Commission, as the Court of Appeals held, exceed its rulemaking authority under §14(e) when it adopted Rule 14e-3(a) without requiring a showing that the trading at issue entailed a breach of fiduciary duty? We hold that the Commission, in this regard and to the extent relevant to this case, did not exceed its authority.

The governing statutory provision, §14(e) of the Exchange Act, reads in relevant part:

"It shall be unlawful for any person . . . to engage in any fraudulent, deceptive, or manipulative acts or practices, in connection with any tender offer. . . . The

[SEC] shall, for the purposes of this subsection, by rules and regulations define, and prescribe means reasonably designed to prevent, such acts and practices as are fraudulent, deceptive, or manipulative."

Section 14(e)'s first sentence prohibits fraudulent acts in connection with a tender offer. This self-operating proscription was one of several provisions added to the Exchange Act in 1968 by the Williams Act. The section's second sentence delegates definitional and prophylactic rulemaking authority to the Commission. Congress added this rulemaking delegation to §14(e) in 1970 amendments to the Williams Act.

Through §14(e) and other provisions on disclosure in the Williams Act, Congress sought to ensure that shareholders "confronted by a cash tender offer for their stock [would] not be required to respond without adequate information." . . .

Relying on §14(e)'s rulemaking authorization, the Commission, in 1980, promulgated Rule 14e-3(a). That measure provides:

"(a) If any person has taken a substantial step or steps to commence, or has commenced, a tender offer (the 'offering person'), it shall constitute a fraudulent, deceptive or manipulative act or practice within the meaning of section 14(e) of the [Exchange] Act for any other person who is in possession of material information relating to such tender offer which information he knows or has reason to know is nonpublic and which he knows or has reason to know has been acquired directly or indirectly from:
"(1) The offering person,
"(2) The issuer of the securities sought or to be sought by such tender offer, or
"(3) Any officer, director, partner or employee or any other person acting on behalf of the offering person or such issuer, to purchase or sell or cause to be purchased or sold any of such securities or any securities convertible into or exchangeable for any such securities or any option or right to obtain or to dispose of any of the foregoing securities, unless within a reasonable time prior to any purchase or sale such information and its source are publicly disclosed by press release or otherwise."

As characterized by the Commission, Rule 14e-3(a) is a "disclose or abstain from trading" requirement. . . .

In the Eighth Circuit's view, because Rule 14e-3(a) applies whether or not the trading in question breaches a fiduciary duty, the regulation exceeds the SEC's §14(e) rulemaking authority. . . .

. . . [W]e agree with the United States that Rule 14e-3(a), as applied to cases of this genre, qualifies under §14(e) as a "means reasonably designed to prevent" fraudulent trading on material, nonpublic information in the tender offer context. A prophylactic measure, because its mission is to prevent, typically encompasses more than the core activity prohibited. . . . We hold, accordingly, that under §14(e), the Commission may prohibit acts, not themselves fraudulent under the common law or §10(b), if the prohibition is "reasonably designed to prevent . . . acts and practices [that] are fraudulent."

Because Congress has authorized the Commission, in §14(e), to prescribe legislative rules, we owe the Commission's judgment "more than mere deference or weight." Therefore, in determining whether Rule 14e-3(a)'s "disclose or abstain from trading" requirement is reasonably designed to prevent fraudulent acts, we must accord the Commission's assessment "controlling weight unless [it is] arbitrary, capricious, or manifestly contrary to the statute." *Chevron U. S. A. Inc. v. Natural Resources Defense Council, Inc.* (1984). In this case, we conclude, the Commission's assessment is none of these. . . .

The United States emphasizes that Rule 14e-3(a) reaches trading in which "a breach of duty is likely but difficult to prove." "Particularly in the context of a tender offer," as the Tenth Circuit recognized, "there is a fairly wide circle of people with confidential information," [*SEC v.*] *Peters* [(1992)], notably, the attorneys, investment bankers, and accountants involved in structuring the transaction. The availability of that information may lead to abuse. . . . Individuals entrusted with nonpublic information, particularly if they have no long-term loyalty to the issuer, may find the temptation to trade on that information hard to resist in view of "the very large short-term profits potentially available [to them]."

. . .[I]t is a fair assumption that trading on the basis of material, nonpublic information will often involve a breach of a duty of confidentiality to the bidder or target company or their representatives. The SEC, cognizant of the proof problem that could enable sophisticated traders to escape responsibility, placed in Rule 14e-3(a) a "disclose or abstain from trading" command that does not require specific proof of a breach of fiduciary duty. That prescription, we are satisfied, applied to this case, is a "means reasonably designed to prevent" fraudulent trading on material, nonpublic information in the tender offer context. . . . Therefore, insofar as it serves to prevent the type of misappropriation charged against O'Hagan, Rule 14e-3(a) is a proper exercise of the Commission's prophylactic power under §14(e).

IV

Based on its dispositions of the securities fraud convictions, the Court of Appeals also reversed O'Hagan's convictions . . . for mail fraud. . . . [T]he Court of Appeals said [that] the indictment was so structured that the mail fraud charges could not be disassociated from the securities fraud charges, and absent any securities fraud, "there was no fraud upon which to base the mail fraud charges."

. . . We need not linger over this matter, for our rulings on the securities fraud issues require that we reverse the Court of Appeals judgment on the mail fraud counts as well.

O'Hagan, we note, attacked the mail fraud convictions in the Court of Appeals on alternate grounds; his other arguments, not yet addressed by the Eighth Circuit, remain open for consideration on remand.

* * *

The judgment of the Court of Appeals for the Eighth Circuit is reversed, and the case is remanded for further proceedings consistent with this opinion.

It is so ordered.

JUSTICE SCALIA, concurring in part and dissenting in part.

I join Parts I, III, and IV of the Court's opinion. I do not agree, however, with Part II of the Court's opinion, containing its analysis of respondent's convictions under §10(b) and Rule 10b-5.

I do not entirely agree with JUSTICE THOMAS's analysis of those convictions either, principally because it seems to me irrelevant whether the Government's theory of why respondent's acts were covered is "coherent and consistent." . . . In point of fact, respondent's actions either violated §10(b) and Rule 10b-5, or they did not—regardless of the reasons the Government gave. And it is for us to decide.

While the Court's explanation of the scope of §10(b) and Rule 10b-5 would be entirely reasonable in some other context, it does not seem to accord with the principle of lenity we apply to criminal statutes. . . . In light of that principle, it seems to me that the unelaborated statutory language: "[t]o use or employ in connection with the purchase or sale of any security . . . any manipulative or deceptive device or contrivance," §10(b), must be construed to require the manipulation or deception of a party to a securities transaction.

JUSTICE THOMAS, with whom THE CHIEF JUSTICE joins, concurring in the judgment in part and dissenting in part.

Today the majority upholds respondent's convictions for violating §10(b) of the Securities Exchange Act of 1934, and Rule 10b-5 promulgated thereunder, based upon the Securities and Exchange Commission's "misappropriation theory." Central to the majority's holding is the need to interpret §10(b)'s requirement that a deceptive device be "use[d] or employ[ed], in connection with the purchase or sale of any security." Because the Commission's misappropriation theory fails to provide a coherent and consistent interpretation of this essential requirement for liability under §10(b), I dissent.

The majority also sustains respondent's convictions under §14(e) of the Securities Exchange Act, and Rule 14e-3(a) promulgated thereunder, regardless of whether respondent violated a fiduciary duty to anybody. I dissent too from that holding because, while §14(e) does allow regulations prohibiting nonfraudulent acts as a prophylactic against certain fraudulent acts, neither the majority nor the Commission identifies any relevant underlying fraud against which Rule 14e-3(a) reasonably provides prophylaxis. With regard to the respondent's mail fraud convictions, however, I concur in the judgment of the Court.

I

I do not take issue with the majority's determination that the undisclosed misappropriation of confidential information by a fiduciary can constitute a "deceptive device" within the meaning of §10(b). Nondisclosure where there is a pre-existing duty to disclose satisfies our definitions of fraud and deceit for purposes of the securities laws.

Unlike the majority, however, I cannot accept the Commission's interpretation of when a deceptive device is "use[d] . . . in connection with" a securities transaction. Although the Commission and the majority at points seem to suggest that any relation to a securities transaction satisfies the "in connection with" requirement of §10(b), both ultimately reject such an overly expansive construction and require a more integral connection between the fraud and the securities transaction. The majority states, for example, that the misappropriation theory applies to undisclosed misappropriation of confidential information "for securities trading purposes." . . . The Commission goes further, and argues that the misappropriation theory satisfies the "in connection with" requirement because it "depends on an *inherent* connection between the deceptive conduct and the purchase or sale of a security" (emphasis added). . . .

The Commission's construction of the relevant language in §10(b), and the incoherence of that construction, become evident as the majority attempts to describe why the fraudulent theft of information falls under the Commission's misappropriation theory, but the fraudulent theft of money does not. The majority correctly notes that confidential information "qualifies as property to which the company has a right of exclusive use." It then observes that the "undisclosed misappropriation of such information, in violation of a fiduciary duty, . . . constitutes fraud akin to embezzlement—the fraudulent appropriation to one's own use of the money or goods entrusted to one's care by another." So far the majority's analogy to embezzlement is well taken, and adequately demonstrates that undisclosed misappropriation can be a fraud on the source of the information.

What the embezzlement analogy does not do, however, is explain how the relevant fraud is "use[d] or employ[ed], in connection with" a securities transaction. And when the majority seeks to distinguish the embezzlement of funds from the embezzlement of information, it becomes clear that neither the Commission nor the majority has a coherent theory regarding §10(b)'s "in connection with" requirement.

Turning first to why embezzlement of information supposedly meets the "in connection with" requirement, the majority asserts that the requirement

> "is satisfied because the fiduciary's fraud is consummated, not when the fiduciary gains the confidential information, but when, without disclosure to his principal, he uses the information to purchase or sell securities. The securities transaction and the breach of duty thus coincide."

The majority later notes . . . the Government's contention that the embezzlement of funds used to purchase securities would not fall within the misappropriation theory. The misappropriation of funds used for a securities transaction is not covered by its theory, the Government explains, because "the proceeds would have value to the malefactor apart from their use in a securities transaction, and the fraud would be complete as soon as the money was obtained." . . .

My understanding of the Government's proffered theory of liability, and its construction of the "in connection with" requirement, is confirmed by the Government's explanation during oral argument:

> "[Court]: What if I appropriate some of my client's money in order to buy stock?
>
> . . . .
>
> "[Court]: Have I violated the securities laws?
> "[Counsel]: I do not think that you have.
> "[Court]: Why not? Isn't that in connection with the purchase of securit[ies] just as much as this one is?
> "[Counsel]: It's not just as much as this one is, because in this case it is the use of the information that enables the profits, pure and simple. There would be no opportunity to engage in profit—
> "[Court]: Same here. I didn't have the money. The only way I could buy this stock was to get the money.

. . . .

"[Counsel]: The difference . . . is that once you have the money you can do anything you want with it. In a sense, the fraud is complete at that point, and then you go on and you can use the money to finance any number of other activities, but *the connection is far less close than in this case, where the only value of this information for personal profit for respondent was to take it and profit in the securities markets by trading on it.*

. . . .

"[Court]: So what you're saying is, is in this case the misappropriation can only be of relevance, or is of substantial relevance, is with reference to the purchase of securities.

"[Counsel]: Exactly.

"[Court]: When you take money out of the accounts you can go to the racetrack, or whatever.

"[Counsel]: That's exactly right, and because of that difference, [there] can be no doubt that this kind of misappropriation of property is in connection with the purchase or sale of securities.

"Other kinds of misappropriation of property may or may not, but this is a unique form of fraud, unique to the securities markets, in fact, because *the only way in which respondent could have profited through this information is by either trading on it or by tipping somebody else to enable their trades.*" (emphases added).

As the above exchange demonstrates, the relevant distinction is not that the misappropriated information was used for a securities transaction (the money example met that test), but rather that it could only be used for such a transaction. . . .

Once the Government's construction of the misappropriation theory is accurately described and accepted—along with its implied construction of §10(b)'s "in connection with" language—that theory should no longer cover cases, such as this one, involving fraud on the source of information where the source has no connection with the other participant in a securities transaction. It seems obvious that the undisclosed misappropriation of confidential information is not necessarily consummated by a securities transaction. In this case, for example, upon learning of Grand Met's confidential takeover plans, O'Hagan could have done any number of things with the information: He could have sold it to a newspaper for publication; he could have given or sold the information to Pillsbury itself; or he could even have kept the information and used it solely for his personal amusement, perhaps in a fantasy stock trading game.

Any of these activities would have deprived Grand Met of its right to "exclusive use" of the information and, if undisclosed, would constitute "embezzlement" of Grand Met's informational property. Under *any* theory of liability, however, these activities would not violate §10(b). . . . That O'Hagan actually did use the information to purchase securities is thus no more significant here than it is in the case of embezzling money used to purchase securities. . . .

The majority makes no attempt to defend the misappropriation theory as set forth by the Commission. Indeed, the majority implicitly concedes the indefensibility of the Commission's theory by acknowledging that alternative uses of misappropriated information exist that do not violate the securities laws and then dismissing the Government's repeated explanations of its misappropriation theory as mere "overstatement." Having rejected the Government's description of its theory, the majority then engages in the "imaginative" exercise of constructing its own misappropriation theory from whole cloth. Thus, we are told, if we merely "[s]ubstitute 'ordinarily' for 'only'" when describing the degree of connectedness between a misappropriation and a securities transaction, the Government would have a winner. . . .

I need not address the coherence, or lack thereof, of the majority's new theory, for it suffers from a far greater, and dispositive, flaw: It is not the theory offered by the Commission. Indeed, as far as we know from the majority's opinion, this new theory has never been proposed by the Commission, much less adopted by rule or otherwise. . . .

Whether the majority's new theory has merit, we cannot possibly tell on the record before us. . . . We simply do not know what would or would not be covered by such a requirement, and hence cannot evaluate whether the requirement embodies a consistent and coherent interpretation of the statute. Moreover, persons subject to this new theory, such as respondent here, surely could not and cannot regulate their behavior to comply with the new theory because, until today, the theory has never existed. In short, the majority's new theory is simply not presented by this case, and cannot form the basis for upholding respondent's convictions.

. . . [T]he majority also points to various policy considerations underlying the securities laws, such as maintaining fair and honest markets, promoting investor confidence, and protecting the integrity of the securities markets. But the repeated reliance on such broad-sweeping legislative purposes reaches too far and is misleading in the context of the misappropriation theory. It reaches too far in that, regardless of the overarching purpose of the securities laws, it is not illegal to run afoul of the "purpose" of a statute, only its letter. The majority's approach is misleading in this case because it glosses over the fact that the supposed threat to fair and honest markets, investor confidence, and market integrity comes not from the supposed fraud in this case, but from the mere fact that the information used by O'Hagan was nonpublic. . . .

The majority's statement that a "misappropriator who trades on the basis of material, nonpublic information, in short, *gains his advantageous market position through deception; he deceives the source of the information and simultaneously harms members of the investing public,*" (emphasis added), thus focuses on the wrong point. Even if it is true that trading on nonpublic information hurts the public, it is true whether or not there is any deception of the source of the information. Moreover, as we have repeatedly held, use of nonpublic information to trade is not itself a violation of §10(b). Rather, it is the use of fraud "in connection with" a securities transaction that is forbidden. Where the relevant element of fraud has no impact on the integrity of the subsequent transactions as distinct from the nonfraudulent element of using nonpublic information, one can reasonably question whether the fraud was used in connection with a securities transaction. And one can likewise question whether removing that aspect of fraud, though perhaps laudable, has anything to do with the confidence or integrity of the market. . . .

II

I am also of the view that O'Hagan's conviction for violating Rule 14e-3(a) cannot stand. . . .

The Commission offers two grounds in defense of Rule 14e-3(a). First, it argues that §14(e) delegates to the Commission the authority to "define" fraud differently than that concept has been defined by this Court, and that Rule 14e-3(a) is a valid exercise of that "defining" power. Second, it argues that §14(e) authorizes the Commission to "prescribe means reasonably designed to prevent" fraudulent acts, and that Rule 14e-3(a) is a prophylactic rule that may prohibit nonfraudulent acts as a means of preventing fraudulent acts that are difficult to detect or prove.

The majority declines to reach the Commission's first justification, instead sustaining Rule 14e-3(a) on the ground that

> "under §14(e), the Commission may prohibit acts, not themselves fraudulent under the common law or §10(b), if the prohibition is 'reasonably designed to prevent . . . acts and practices [that] are fraudulent.' "

According to the majority, prohibiting trading on nonpublic information is necessary to prevent such supposedly hard-to-prove fraudulent acts and practices as trading on information obtained from the buyer in breach of a fiduciary duty, and possibly "warehousing," whereby the buyer tips allies prior to announcing the tender offer and encourages them to purchase the target company's stock.

I find neither of the Commission's justifications for Rule 14e-3(a) acceptable in misappropriation cases. With regard to the Commission's claim of authority to redefine the concept of fraud, I agree with the Eighth Circuit that the Commission misreads the relevant provision of §14(e). . . .

Turning to the Commission's second justification for Rule 14e-3(a), although I can agree with the majority that §14(e) authorizes the Commission to prohibit nonfraudulent acts as a means reasonably designed to prevent fraudulent ones, I cannot agree that Rule 14e-3(a) satisfies this standard. . . .

. . . In order to be a valid prophylactic regulation, Rule 14e-3(a) must be reasonably designed not merely to prevent any fraud, but to prevent persons from engaging in "fraudulent, deceptive, or manipulative acts or practices, *in connection with* any tender offer." 15 U. S. C. §78n(e) (emphasis added). . . . Even assuming that a person misappropriating information from the bidder commits fraud on the bidder, the Commission has provided no coherent or consistent explanation as to why such fraud is "in connection with" a tender offer. . . .

. . .[T]he majority notes with seeming approval the Commission's justification of Rule 14e-3(a) "as a means necessary and proper to assure the efficacy of Williams Act protections." . . .

While enhancing the overall efficacy of the Williams Act may be a reasonable goal, it is not one that may be pursued through §14(e), which limits its grant of rulemaking authority to the prevention of fraud, deceit, and manipulation. As we have held in the context of §10(b), "not every instance of financial unfairness constitutes fraudulent activity." Because, in the context of misappropriation cases, Rule 14e-3(a) is not a means "reasonably designed" to prevent persons from engaging in fraud "in connection with" a tender offer, it exceeds the Commission's authority under §14(e), and respondent's conviction for violation of that Rule cannot be sustained.

III

With regard to respondent's convictions on the mail-fraud counts, my view is that it may be sustained regardless of whether respondent may be convicted of the securities fraud counts. . . .

. . . I do not think the wording of the indictment in the current case requires a finding of securities fraud in order to find mail fraud. Certainly the jury instructions do not make the mail-fraud count dependent on the securities fraud counts. Rather, the counts were simply predicated on the same *factual* basis, and just because those facts are legally insufficient to constitute securities fraud does not make them legally insufficient to constitute mail fraud. I therefore concur in the judgment of the Court as it relates to respondent's mail-fraud convictions.

□□□

Nos. 95-1649 and 95-9075

Kansas, Petitioner v. Leroy Hendricks

Leroy Hendricks, Petitioner v. Kansas

On writs of certiorari to the Supreme Court of Kansas

[June 23, 1997]

JUSTICE THOMAS delivered the opinion of the Court.

In 1994, Kansas enacted the Sexually Violent Predator Act, which establishes procedures for the civil commitment of persons who, due to a "mental abnormality" or a "personality disorder," are likely to engage in "predatory acts of sexual violence." The State invoked the Act for the first time to commit Leroy Hendricks, an inmate who had a long history of sexually molesting children, and who was scheduled for release from prison shortly after the Act became law. Hendricks challenged his commitment on, *inter alia,* "substantive" due process, double jeopardy, and *ex post facto* grounds. The Kansas Supreme Court invalidated the Act, holding that its pre-commitment condition of a "mental abnormality" did not satisfy what the court perceived to be the "substantive" due process requirement that involuntary civil commitment must be predicated on a finding of "mental illness." (1996). The State of Kansas petitioned for certiorari. Hendricks subsequently filed a cross-petition in which he reasserted his federal double jeopardy and *ex post facto* claims. We granted certiorari on both the petition and the cross-petition (1996) and now reverse the judgment below.

I

A

The Kansas Legislature enacted the Sexually Violent Predator Act (Act) in 1994 to grapple with the problem of managing repeat sexual offenders. Although Kansas already had a statute addressing the involuntary commitment of those defined as "mentally ill," the legislature determined that existing civil commitment procedures were inadequate to confront the risks presented by "sexually violent predators." . . .

As a result, the Legislature found it necessary to establish "a civil commitment procedure for the long-term care and treatment of the sexually violent predator." The Act defined a "sexually violent predator" as:

"any person who has been convicted of or charged with a sexually violent offense and who suffers from a mental abnormality or personality disorder which makes the person likely to engage in the predatory acts of sexual violence."

A "mental abnormality" was defined, in turn, as a "congenital or acquired condition affecting the emotional or volitional capacity which predisposes the person to commit sexually violent offenses in a degree constituting such person a menace to the health and safety of others."

As originally structured, the Act's civil commitment procedures pertained to: (1) a presently confined person who, like Hendricks, "has been convicted of a sexually violent offense" and is scheduled for release; (2) a person who has been "charged with a sexually violent offense" but has been found incompetent to stand trial; (3) a person who has been found "not guilty by reason of insanity of a sexually violent offense"; and (4) a person found "not guilty" of a sexually violent offense because of a mental disease or defect.

The initial version of the Act, as applied to a currently confined person such as Hendricks, was designed to initiate a specific series of procedures. The custodial agency was required to notify the local prosecutor 60 days before the anticipated release of a person who might have met the Act's criteria. The prosecutor was then obligated, within 45 days, to decide whether to file a petition in state court seeking the person's involuntary commitment. If such a petition were filed, the court was to determine whether "probable cause" existed to support a finding that the person was a "sexually violent predator" and thus eligible for civil commitment. Upon such a determination, transfer of the individual to a secure facility for professional evaluation would occur. After that evaluation, a trial would be held to determine beyond a reasonable doubt whether the individual was a sexually violent predator. If that determination were made, the person would then be transferred to the custody of the Secretary of Social and Rehabilitation Services (Secretary) for "control, care and treatment until such time as the person's mental abnormality or personality disorder has so changed that the person is safe to be at large."

In addition to placing the burden of proof upon the State, the Act afforded the individual a number of other procedural safeguards. In the case of an indigent person, the State was required to provide, at public expense, the assistance of counsel and an examination by mental health care professionals. The individual also received the right to present and crossexamine witnesses, and the opportunity to review documentary evidence presented by the State.

Once an individual was confined, the Act required that "[t]he involuntary detention or commitment . . . shall conform to constitutional requirements for care and treatment." Confined persons were afforded three different avenues of review: First, the committing court was obligated to conduct an annual review to determine whether continued detention was warranted. Second, the Secretary was permitted, at any time, to decide that the confined individual's condition had so changed that release was appropriate, and could then authorize the person to petition for release. Finally, even without the Secretary's permission, the confined person could at any time file a release petition. If the court found that the State could no longer satisfy its burden under the initial commitment standard, the individual would be freed from confinement.

B

In 1984, Hendricks was convicted of taking "indecent liberties" with two 13-year-old boys. After serving nearly 10 years of his sentence, he was slated for release to a halfway house. Shortly before his scheduled release, however, the State filed a petition in state court seeking Hendricks' civil confinement as a sexually violent predator. On August 19, 1994, Hendricks appeared before the court with counsel and moved to dismiss the petition on the grounds that the Act violated various federal constitutional provisions. Although the court reserved ruling on the Act's constitutionality, it concluded that there was probable cause to support a finding that Hendricks was a sexually violent predator, and therefore ordered that he be evaluated at the Larned State Security Hospital.

Hendricks subsequently requested a jury trial to determine whether he qualified as a sexually violent predator. During that trial, Hendricks' own testimony revealed a chilling history of repeated child sexual molestation and abuse, beginning in 1955 when he exposed his genitals to two young girls. At that time, he pleaded guilty to indecent exposure. Then, in 1957, he was convicted of lewdness involving a young girl and received a brief jail sentence. In 1960, he molested two young boys while he worked for a carnival. After serving two years in prison for that offense, he was paroled, only to be rearrested for molesting a 7-year-old girl. Attempts were made to treat him for his sexual deviance, and in 1965 he was considered "safe to be at large," and was discharged from a state psychiatric hospital.

Shortly thereafter, however, Hendricks sexually assaulted another young boy and girl—he performed oral sex on the 8-year-old girl and fondled the 11-year-old boy. He was again imprisoned in 1967, but refused to participate in a sex offender treatment program, and thus remained incarcerated until his parole in 1972. Diagnosed as a pedophile, Hendricks entered into, but then abandoned, a treatment program. He testified that despite having received professional help for his pedophilia, he continued to harbor sexual desires for children. Indeed, soon after his 1972 parole, Hendricks began to abuse his own stepdaughter and stepson. He forced the children to engage in sexual activity with him over a period of approximately four years. Then, as noted above, Hendricks was convicted of "taking indecent liberties" with two adolescent boys after he attempted to fondle them. As a result of that conviction, he was once again imprisoned, and was serving that sentence when he reached his conditional release date in September 1994.

Hendricks admitted that he had repeatedly abused children whenever he was not confined. He explained that when he "get[s] stressed out," he "can't control the urge" to molest children. Although Hendricks recognized that his behavior harms children, and he hoped he would not sexually molest children again, he stated that the only sure way he could keep from sexually abusing children in the future was "to die." Hendricks readily agreed with the state physician's diagnosis that he suffers from pedophilia and that he is not cured of the condition; indeed, he told the physician that "treatment is bull—."

The jury unanimously found beyond a reasonable doubt that Hendricks was a sexually violent predator. The trial court subsequently determined, as a matter of state law, that pedophilia qualifies as a "mental abnormality" as defined by the Act, and thus ordered Hendricks committed to the Secretary's custody.

Hendricks appealed, claiming, among other things, that application of the Act to him violated the Federal Constitution's Due Process, Double Jeopardy, and *Ex Post Facto* Clauses. The Kansas Supreme Court accepted Hendricks' due process claim. The court declared that in order to commit a person involuntarily in a civil proceeding, a State is required by "substantive" due process to prove by clear and convincing evidence that the person is both (1) mentally ill and (2) a danger to himself or to others. The court then determined that the Act's definition of "mental abnormality" did not satisfy what it perceived to be this Court's "mental illness" requirement in the civil commitment context. As a result, the court held that "the Act violates Hendricks' substantive due process rights."

The majority did not address Hendricks' *ex post facto* or double jeopardy claims. The dissent, however, considered each of Hendricks' constitutional arguments and rejected them.

II

A

Kansas argues that the Act's definition of "mental abnormality" satisfies "substantive" due process requirements. We agree. . . . States have in certain narrow circumstances provided for the forcible civil detainment of people who are unable to control their behavior and who thereby pose a danger to the public health and safety. . . . We have consistently upheld such involuntary commitment statutes provided the confinement takes place pursuant to proper procedures and evidentiary standards. It thus cannot be said that the involuntary civil confinement of a limited subclass of dangerous persons is contrary to our understanding of ordered liberty.

The challenged Act unambiguously requires a finding of dangerousness either to one's self or to others as a prerequisite to involuntary confinement. . . . The statute thus requires proof of more than a mere predisposition to violence; rather, it requires evidence of past sexually violent behavior and a present mental condition that creates a likelihood of such conduct in the future if the person is not incapacitated. . . .

A finding of dangerousness, standing alone, is ordinarily not a sufficient ground upon which to justify indefinite involuntary commitment. We have sustained civil commitment statutes when they have coupled proof of dangerousness with the proof of some additional factor, such as a "mental illness" or "mental abnormality." . . . The Kansas Act is plainly of a kind with these other civil commitment statutes: It requires a finding of future dangerousness, and then links that finding to the existence of a "mental abnormality" or "personality disorder" that makes it difficult, if not impossible, for the person to control his dangerous behavior. . . .

Hendricks nonetheless argues that our earlier cases dictate a finding of "mental illness" as a prerequisite for civil commitment. . . . He then asserts that a "mental abnormality" is not equivalent to a "mental illness" because it is a term coined by the Kansas Legislature, rather than by the psychiatric community. Contrary to Hendricks' assertion, the term "mental illness" is devoid of any talismanic significance. . . .

Indeed, we have never required State legislatures to adopt any particular nomenclature in drafting civil commitment statutes. Rather, we have traditionally left

to legislators the task of defining terms of a medical nature that have legal significance. As a consequence, the States have, over the years, developed numerous specialized terms to define mental health concepts. Often, those definitions do not fit
precisely with the definitions employed by the medical community. . . .

To the extent that the civil commitment statutes we have considered set forth
criteria relating to an individual's inability to control his dangerousness, the Kansas
Act sets forth comparable criteria and Hendricks' condition doubtless satisfies those
criteria. The mental health professionals who evaluated Hendricks diagnosed him
as suffering from pedophilia, a condition the psychiatric profession itself classifies
as a serious mental disorder. [Citing 1 American Psychiatric Association, Treatments
of Psychiatric Disorders, 617–633 (1989), among other sources.] Hendricks even
conceded that, when he becomes "stressed out," he cannot "control the urge" to
molest children. This admitted lack of volitional control, coupled with a prediction
of future dangerousness, adequately distinguishes Hendricks from other dangerous
persons who are perhaps more properly dealt with exclusively through criminal
proceedings. Hendricks' diagnosis as a pedophile, which qualifies as a "mental abnormality" under the Act, thus plainly suffices for due process purposes.

B

We granted Hendricks' cross-petition to determine whether the Act violates
the Constitution's double jeopardy prohibition or its ban on *ex post facto* lawmaking.
The thrust of Hendricks' argument is that the Act establishes criminal proceedings;
hence confinement under it necessarily constitutes punishment. . . . We are unpersuaded by Hendricks' argument that Kansas has established criminal proceedings.

The categorization of a particular proceeding as civil or criminal "is first of all
a question of statutory construction." We must initially ascertain whether the legislature meant the statute to establish "civil" proceedings. If so, we ordinarily defer to
the legislature's stated intent. Here, Kansas' objective to create a civil proceeding is
evidenced by its placement of the Sexually Violent Predator Act within the Kansas
probate code, instead of the criminal code, as well as its description of the Act as
creating a "*civil commitment procedure*" (emphasis added). Nothing on the face of the
statute suggests that the legislature sought to create anything other than a civil commitment scheme designed to protect the public from harm.

Although we recognize that a "civil label is not always dispositive," we will reject
the legislature's manifest intent only where a party challenging the statute provides
"the clearest proof" that "the statutory scheme [is] so punitive either in purpose or
effect as to negate [the State's] intention" to deem it "civil." . . . Hendricks, however,
has failed to satisfy this heavy burden.

As a threshold matter, commitment under the Act does not implicate either of
the two primary objectives of criminal punishment: retribution or deterrence. The
Act's purpose is not retributive because it does not affix culpability for prior criminal conduct. Instead, such conduct is used solely for evidentiary purposes, either to
demonstrate that a "mental abnormality" exists or to support a finding of future
dangerousness. . . . In addition, the Kansas Act does not make a criminal conviction
a prerequisite for commitment—persons absolved of criminal responsibility may
nonetheless be subject to confinement under the Act. . . .

Moreover, unlike a criminal statute, no finding of scienter is required to commit an individual who is found to be a sexually violent predator; instead, the com-

mitment determination is made based on a "mental abnormality" or "personality disorder" rather than on one's criminal intent. . . .

Nor can it be said that the legislature intended the Act to function as a deterrent. Those persons committed under the Act are, by definition, suffering from a "mental abnormality" or a "personality disorder" that prevents them from exercising adequate control over their behavior. Such persons are therefore unlikely to be deterred by the threat of confinement. And the conditions surrounding that confinement do not suggest a punitive purpose on the State's part. The State has represented that an individual confined under the Act is not subject to the more restrictive conditions placed on state prisoners, but instead experiences essentially the same conditions as any involuntarily committed patient in the state mental institution. . . .

Hendricks focuses on his confinement's potentially indefinite duration as evidence of the State's punitive intent. That focus, however, is misplaced. Far from any punitive objective, the confinement's duration is instead linked to the stated purposes of the commitment, namely, to hold the person until his mental abnormality no longer causes him to be a threat to others. . . . If, at any time, the confined person is adjudged "safe to be at large," he is statutorily entitled to immediate release.

Furthermore, commitment under the Act is only *potentially* indefinite. The maximum amount of time an individual can be incapacitated pursuant to a single judicial proceeding is one year. If Kansas seeks to continue the detention beyond that year, a court must once again determine beyond a reasonable doubt that the detainee satisfies the same standards as required for the initial confinement. . . .

Hendricks next contends that the State's use of procedural safeguards traditionally found in criminal trials makes the proceedings here criminal rather than civil. . . . The numerous procedural and evidentiary protections afforded here demonstrate that the Kansas Legislature has taken great care to confine only a narrow class of particularly dangerous individuals, and then only after meeting the strictest procedural standards. That Kansas chose to afford such procedural protections does not transform a civil commitment proceeding into a criminal prosecution.

Finally, Hendricks argues that the Act is necessarily punitive because it fails to offer any legitimate "treatment." Without such treatment, Hendricks asserts, confinement under the Act amounts to little more than disguised punishment. Hendricks' argument assumes that treatment for his condition is available, but that the State has failed (or refused) to provide it. The Kansas Supreme Court, however, apparently rejected this assumption, explaining:

> "It is clear that the overriding concern of the legislature is to continue the segregation of sexually violent offenders from the public. Treatment with the goal of reintegrating them into society is incidental, at best. The record reflects that treatment for sexually violent predators is all but nonexistent. The legislature concedes that sexually violent predators are not amenable to treatment under [the existing Kansas involuntary commitment statute]. If there is nothing to treat under [that statute], then there is no mental illness. In that light, the provisions of the Act for treatment appear somewhat disingenuous."

It is possible to read this passage as a determination that Hendricks' condition was *untreatable* under the existing Kansas civil commitment statute, and thus the Act's sole purpose was incapacitation. . . .

Accepting the Kansas court's apparent determination that treatment is not possible for this category of individuals does not obligate us to adopt its legal conclusions. We have already observed that, under the appropriate circumstances and when accompanied by proper procedures, incapacitation may be a legitimate end of the civil law. Accordingly, the Kansas court's determination that the Act's "overriding concern" was the continued "segregation of sexually violent offenders" is consistent with our conclusion that the Act establishes civil proceedings. . . . [W]e have never held that the Constitution prevents a State from civilly detaining those for whom no treatment is available, but who nevertheless pose a danger to others. A State could hardly be seen as furthering a "punitive" purpose by involuntarily confining persons afflicted with an untreatable, highly contagious disease. . . . Similarly, it would be of little value to require treatment as a precondition for civil confinement of the dangerously insane when no acceptable treatment existed. To conclude otherwise would obligate a State to release certain confined individuals who were both mentally ill and dangerous simply because they could not be successfully treated for their afflictions. . . .

Alternatively, the Kansas Supreme Court's opinion can be read to conclude that Hendricks' condition is treatable, but that treatment was not the State's "overriding concern" and that no treatment was being provided (at least at the time Hendricks was committed). . . . Even if we accept this determination that the provision of treatment was not the Kansas Legislature's "overriding" or "primary" purpose in passing the Act, this does not rule out the possibility that an ancillary purpose of the Act was to provide treatment, and it does not require us to conclude that the Act is punitive. . . .

Although the treatment program initially offered Hendricks may have seemed somewhat meager, it must be remembered that he was the first person committed under the Act. That the State did not have all of its treatment procedures in place is thus not surprising. What is significant, however, is that Hendricks was placed under the supervision of the Kansas Department of Health and Social and Rehabilitative Services, housed in a unit segregated from the general prison population and operated not by employees of the Department of Corrections, but by other trained individuals. And, before this Court, Kansas declared "[a]bsolutely" that persons committed under the Act are now receiving in the neighborhood of "31.5 hours of treatment per week."

Where the State has "disavowed any punitive intent"; limited confinement to a small segment of particularly dangerous individuals; provided strict procedural safeguards; directed that confined persons be segregated from the general prison population and afforded the same status as others who have been civilly committed; recommended treatment if such is possible; and permitted immediate release upon a showing that the individual is no longer dangerous or mentally impaired, we cannot say that it acted with punitive intent. We therefore hold that the Act does not establish criminal proceedings and that involuntary confinement pursuant to the Act is not punitive. Our conclusion that the Act is nonpunitive thus removes an essential prerequisite for both Hendricks' double jeopardy and *ex post facto* claims.

1

The Double Jeopardy Clause provides: "[N]or shall any person be subject for the same offence to be twice put in jeopardy of life or limb." Although generally understood to preclude a second prosecution for the same offense, the Court has also interpreted this prohibition to prevent the State from "punishing twice, or attempting a second time to punish criminally, for the same offense." *Witte v. United States* (1995). Hendricks argues that, as applied to him, the Act violates double jeopardy principles because his confinement under the Act, imposed after a conviction and a term of incarceration, amounted to both a second prosecution and a second punishment for the same offense. We disagree.

Because we have determined that the Kansas Act is civil in nature, initiation of its commitment proceedings does not constitute a second prosecution. . . . Moreover, as commitment under the Act is not tantamount to "punishment," Hendricks' involuntary detention does not violate the Double Jeopardy Clause, even though that confinement may follow a prison term. . . . If an individual otherwise meets the requirements for involuntary civil commitment, the State is under no obligation to release that individual simply because the detention would follow a period of incarceration. . . .

2

Hendricks' *ex post facto* claim is similarly flawed. The *Ex Post Facto* Clause, which "'forbids the application of any new punitive measure to a crime already consummated,'" has been interpreted to pertain exclusively to penal statutes. As we have previously determined, the Act does not impose punishment; thus, its application does not raise *ex post facto* concerns. Moreover, the Act clearly does not have retroactive effect. Rather, the Act permits involuntary confinement based upon a determination that the person currently both suffers from a "mental abnormality" or "personality disorder" and is likely to pose a future danger to the public. To the extent that past behavior is taken into account, it is used, as noted above, solely for evidentiary purposes. Because the Act does not criminalize conduct legal before its enactment, nor deprive Hendricks of any defense that was available to him at the time of his crimes, the Act does not violate the *Ex Post Facto* Clause.

III

We hold that the Kansas Sexually Violent Predator Act comports with due process requirements and neither runs afoul of double jeopardy principles nor constitutes an exercise in impermissible *ex post facto* lawmaking. Accordingly, the judgment of the Kansas Supreme Court is reversed.

It is so ordered.

JUSTICE KENNEDY, concurring.

I join the opinion of the Court in full and add these additional comments. . . .

Notwithstanding its civil attributes, the practical effect of the Kansas law may be to impose confinement for life. At this stage of medical knowledge, although future treatments cannot be predicted, psychiatrists or other professionals engaged in treating pedophilia may be reluctant to find measurable success in treatment even after a long period and may be unable to predict that no serious danger will come from release of the detainee.

A common response to this may be, "A life term is exactly what the sentence should have been anyway," or, in the words of a Kansas task force member, "So be it."

The point, however, is not how long Hendricks and others like him should serve a criminal sentence. With his criminal record, after all, a life term may well have been the only sentence appropriate to protect society and vindicate the wrong. The concern instead is whether it is the criminal system or the civil system which should make the decision in the first place. If the civil system is used simply to impose punishment after the State makes an improvident plea bargain on the criminal side, then it is not performing its proper function. These concerns persist whether the civil confinement statute is put on the books before or after the offense. We should bear in mind that while incapacitation is a goal common to both the criminal and civil systems of confinement, retribution and general deterrence are reserved for the criminal system alone.

On the record before us, the Kansas civil statute conforms to our precedents. If, however, civil confinement were to become a mechanism for retribution or general deterrence, or if it were shown that mental abnormality is too imprecise a category to offer a solid basis for concluding that civil detention is justified, our precedents would not suffice to validate it.

JUSTICE BREYER, with whom JUSTICES STEVENS and SOUTER join, and with whom JUSTICE GINSBURG joins as to Parts II and III, dissenting.

I agree with the majority that the Kansas Act's "definition of 'mental abnormality'" satisfies the "substantive" requirements of the Due Process Clause. Kansas, however, concedes that Hendricks' condition is treatable; yet the Act did not provide Hendricks (or others like him) with any treatment until after his release date from prison and only inadequate treatment thereafter. These, and certain other, special features of the Act convince me that it was not simply an effort to commit Hendricks civilly, but rather an effort to inflict further punishment upon him. The *Ex Post Facto* Clause therefore prohibits the Act's application to Hendricks, who committed his crimes prior to its enactment.

I

I begin with the area of agreement. . . .

A

In my view, the Due Process Clause permits Kansas to classify Hendricks as a mentally ill and dangerous person for civil commitment purposes. I agree with the majority that the Constitution gives States a degree of leeway in making this kind of determination. But, because I do not subscribe to all of its reasoning, I shall set forth three sets of circumstances that, taken together, convince me that Kansas has acted within the limits that the Due Process Clause substantively sets.

First, the psychiatric profession itself classifies the kind of problem from which Hendricks suffers as a serious mental disorder. . . .

Second, Hendricks' abnormality does not consist simply of a long course of antisocial behavior, but rather it includes a specific, serious, and highly unusual inability to control his actions. . . .

Third, Hendricks' mental abnormality also makes him dangerous. Hendricks "has been convicted of . . . a sexually violent offense," and a jury found that he "suffers from a mental abnormality . . . which makes" him "likely to engage" in similar "acts of sexual violence" in the future. . . .

B

The Kansas Supreme Court also held that the Due Process Clause requires a State to provide treatment to those whom it civilly confines (as "mentally ill" and "dangerous"). . . .

This case does not require us to consider whether the Due Process Clause *always* requires treatment—whether, for example, it would forbid civil confinement of an *untreatable* mentally ill, dangerous person. To the contrary, Kansas argues that pedophilia is an "abnormality" or "illness" that can be treated. . . . Hence the legal question before us is whether the Clause forbids Hendricks' confinement unless Kansas provides him with treatment *that it concedes is available.* . . .

II

Kansas' 1994 Act violates the Federal Constitution's prohibition of "any . . . *ex post facto* Law" if it "inflicts" upon Hendricks "a greater punishment" than did the law "annexed to" his "crime[s]" when he "committed" those crimes in 1984. The majority . . . finds the Act is not "punitive." With respect to that basic question, I disagree with the majority.

Certain resemblances between the Act's "civil commitment" and traditional criminal punishments are obvious. Like criminal imprisonment, the Act's civil commitment amounts to "secure" confinement and "incarceration against one's will." . . . In addition, a basic objective of the Act is incapacitation. . . .

Moreover, the Act, like criminal punishment, imposes its confinement (or sanction) only upon an individual who has previously committed a criminal offense. . . . And the Act imposes that confinement through the use of persons (county prosecutors), procedural guarantees (trial by jury, assistance of counsel, psychiatric evaluations), and standards ("beyond a reasonable doubt") traditionally associated with the criminal law.

These obvious resemblances by themselves, however, are not legally sufficient to transform what the Act calls "civil commitment" into a criminal punishment. . . . Nor does the fact that criminal behavior triggers the Act make the critical difference. . . . Neither is the presence of criminal law-type procedures determinative. . . .

If these obvious similarities cannot by themselves prove that Kansas' "civil commitment" statute is criminal, neither can the word "civil" written into the statute by itself prove the contrary. . . . [W]hen a State believes that treatment does exist, and then couples that admission with a legislatively required delay of such treatment until a person is at the end of his jail term (so that further incapacitation is therefore necessary), such a legislative scheme begins to look punitive. . . .

Several important treatment-related factors—factors of a kind that led the five-member *Allen* [*v. Illinois* (1986)] majority to conclude that the Illinois' legislature's purpose was primarily civil, not punitive—in this case suggest precisely the opposite. First, the State Supreme Court here . . . has held that treatment is not a significant objective of the Act. The Kansas court wrote that the Act's purpose is "segregation of sexually violent offenders," with "treatment" a matter that was "incidental at best." . . .

The record provides support for the Kansas court's conclusion. The court found that, as of the time of Hendricks' commitment, the State had not funded treatment, it had not entered into treatment contracts, and it had little, if any, qualified treatment staff. . . .

Second, the Kansas statute insofar as it applies to previously convicted offenders, such as Hendricks, commits, confines, and treats those offenders after they have served virtually their entire criminal sentence. That time-related circumstance seems deliberate. The Act explicitly defers diagnosis, evaluation, and commitment proceedings until a few weeks prior to the "anticipated release" of a previously convicted offender from prison. But why, one might ask, does the Act not commit and require treatment of sex offenders sooner, say soon after they begin to serve their sentences? . . .

Third, the statute, at least as of the time Kansas applied it to Hendricks, did not require the committing authority to consider the possibility of using less restrictive alternatives, such as postrelease supervision, halfway houses, or other methods that *amici* supporting Kansas here have mentioned. The laws of many other States require such consideration. . . .

Fourth, the laws of other States confirm, through comparison, that Kansas' "civil commitment" objectives do not require the statutory features that indicate a punitive purpose. I have found 17 States with laws that seek to protect the public from mentally abnormal, sexually dangerous individuals through civil commitment or other mandatory treatment programs. Ten of those statutes, unlike the Kansas statute, begin treatment of an offender soon after he has been apprehended and charged with a serious sex offense. Only seven, like Kansas, delay "civil" commitment (and treatment) until the offender has served his criminal sentence (and this figure includes the Acts of Minnesota and New Jersey, both of which generally do not delay treatment). Of these seven, however, six (unlike Kansas) require consideration of less restrictive alternatives. [Citations omitted.] Only one State other than Kansas, namely Iowa, both delays civil commitment (and consequent treatment) and does not explicitly consider less restrictive alternatives. But the law of that State applies prospectively only, thereby avoiding *ex post facto* problems. . . .

. . . [W]hen a State decides offenders can be treated and confines an offender to provide that treatment, but then refuses to provide it, the refusal to treat while a person is fully incapacitated begins to look punitive.

The majority suggests that this is the very case I say it is not, namely a case of a mentally ill person who is untreatable. . . . [The Kansas Supreme Court], however, did not find that Hendricks was untreatable; it found that he was untreated—quite a different matter. . . .

The majority suggests in the alternative that recent evidence shows that Kansas is now providing treatment. That evidence comes from two sources. First, a statement by the Kansas Attorney General at oral argument that those committed under the Act are now receiving treatment. And second, in a footnote, a Kansas trial judge's statement, in a state habeas proceeding nearly one year after Hendricks was committed, that Kansas is providing treatment. I do not see how either of these statements can be used to justify the validity of the Act's application to Hendricks at the time he filed suit. . . .

III

To find that the confinement the Act imposes upon Hendricks is "punishment" is to find a violation of the *Ex Post Facto* Clause. Kansas does not deny that the 1994 Act changed the legal consequences that attached to Hendricks' earlier crimes, and in a way that significantly "disadvantage[d] the offender."

To find a violation of that Clause here, however, is not to hold that the Clause prevents Kansas, or other States, from enacting dangerous sexual offender statutes. A statute that operates prospectively, for example, does not offend the *Ex Post Facto* Clause. Neither does it offend the *Ex Post Facto* Clause for a State to sentence offenders to the fully authorized sentence, to seek consecutive, rather than concurrent, sentences, or to invoke recidivism statutes to lengthen imprisonment. Moreover, a statute that operates retroactively, like Kansas' statute, nonetheless does not offend the Clause *if the confinement that it imposes is not punishment*—if, that is to say, the legislature does not simply add a later criminal punishment to an earlier one.

The statutory provisions before us do amount to punishment primarily because, as I have said, the legislature did not tailor the statute to fit the nonpunitive civil aim of treatment, which it concedes exists in Hendricks' case. The Clause in these circumstances does not stand as an obstacle to achieving important protections for the public's safety; rather it provides an assurance that, where so significant a restriction of an individual's basic freedoms is at issue, a State cannot cut corners. Rather, the legislature must hew to the Constitution's liberty-protecting line.

I therefore would affirm the judgment below.

Nos. 96-552 and 96-553

Rachel Agostini, et al., Petitioners
v. Betty-Louise Felton et al.

Chancellor, Board of Education of the
City of New York, et al., Petitioners
v. Betty-Louise Felton et al.

On writs of certiorari to the United States Court
of Appeals for the Second Circuit

[June 23, 1997]

JUSTICE O'CONNOR delivered the opinion of the Court.

In *Aguilar v. Felton* (1985), this Court held that the Establishment Clause of the First Amendment barred the city of New York from sending public school teachers into parochial schools to provide remedial education to disadvantaged children pursuant to a congressionally mandated program. On remand, the District Court for the Eastern District of New York entered a permanent injunction reflecting our ruling. Twelve years later, petitioners—the parties bound by that injunction—seek relief from its operation. Petitioners maintain that Aguilar cannot be squared with our intervening Establishment Clause jurisprudence and ask that we explicitly recognize what our more recent cases already dictate: *Aguilar* is no longer good law. We agree with petitioners that *Aguilar* is not consistent with our subsequent Establishment Clause decisions and further conclude that, on the facts presented here, petitioners are entitled under Federal Rule of Civil Procedure 60(b)(5) to relief from the operation of the District Court's prospective injunction.

I

In 1965, Congress enacted Title I of the Elementary and Secondary Education Act of 1965 to "provid[e] full educational opportunity to every child regardless of economic background." Toward that end, Title I channels federal funds, through the States, to "local educational agencies" (LEA's). The LEA's spend these funds to provide remedial education, guidance, and job counseling to eligible students. . . . An eligible student is one (i) who resides within the attendance boundaries of a public school located in a low-income area and (ii) who is failing, or is at risk of failing, the State's student performance standards. Title I funds must be made available to all eligible children, regardless of whether they attend public schools, and the services provided to children attending private schools must be "equitable in comparison to services and other benefits for public school children."

An LEA providing services to children enrolled in private schools is subject to a number of constraints that are not imposed when it provides aid to public schools. Title I services may be provided only to those private school students eligible for aid, and cannot be used to provide services on a "school-wide" basis. In addition, the LEA must retain complete control over Title I funds; retain title to all materials used to provide Title I services; and provide those services through public employees or other persons independent of the private school and any religious institution. The Title I services themselves must be "secular, neutral, and nonideological," and must "supplement, and in no case supplant, the level of services" already provided by the private school.

Petitioner Board of Education of the City of New York (Board), an LEA, first applied for Title I funds in 1966 and has grappled ever since with how to provide Title I services to the private school students within its jurisdiction. Approximately 10% of the total number of students eligible for Title I services are private school students. Recognizing that more than 90% of the private schools within the Board's jurisdiction are sectarian, the Board initially arranged to transport children to public schools for after-school Title I instruction. But this enterprise was largely unsuccessful. Attendance was poor, teachers and children were tired, and parents were concerned for the safety of their children. The Board then moved the after-school instruction onto private school campuses, as Congress had contemplated when it enacted Title I. After this program also yielded mixed results, the Board implemented the plan we evaluated in *Aguilar v. Felton*.

That plan called for the provision of Title I services on private school premises during school hours. Under the plan, only public employees could serve as Title I instructors and counselors. Assignments to private schools were made on a voluntary basis and without regard to the religious affiliation of the employee or the wishes of the private school. . . .

Before any public employee could provide Title I instruction at a private school, she would be given a detailed set of written and oral instructions emphasizing the secular purpose of Title I and setting out the rules to be followed to ensure that this purpose was not compromised. [Specification of instructions omitted.] To ensure compliance with these rules, a publicly employed field supervisor was to attempt to make at least one unannounced visit to each teacher's classroom every month.

In 1978, six federal taxpayers—respondents here—sued the Board in the District Court for the Eastern District of New York. Respondents sought declaratory and injunctive relief, claiming that the Board's Title I program violated the Establishment Clause. The District Court permitted the parents of a number of parochial school students who were receiving Title I services to intervene as codefendants. The District Court granted summary judgment for the Board, but the Court of Appeals for the Second Circuit reversed. While noting that the Board's Title I program had "done so much good and little, if any, detectable harm," the Court of Appeals nevertheless held that *Meek v. Pittenger* (1975) and *Wolman v. Walter* (1977) compelled it to declare the program unconstitutional. In a 5–4 decision, this Court affirmed on the ground that the Board's Title I program necessitated an "excessive entanglement of church and state in the administration of [Title I] benefits." On remand, the District Court permanently enjoined the Board

> "from using public funds for any plan or program under [Title I] to the extent that it requires, authorizes or permits public school teachers and guidance counselors to provide teaching and counseling services on the premises of sectarian schools within New York City."

The Board, like other LEA's across the United States, modified its Title I program so it could continue serving those students who attended private religious schools. Rather than offer Title I instruction to parochial school students at their schools, the Board reverted to its prior practice of providing instruction at public school sites, at leased sites, and in mobile instructional units (essentially vans converted into classrooms) parked near the sectarian school. The Board also offered computer-aided instruction, which could be provided "on premises" because it did not require public employees to be physically present on the premises of a religious school.

It is not disputed that the additional costs of complying with *Aguilar*'s mandate are significant. Since the 1986–1987 school year, the Board has spent over $100 million providing computer-aided instruction, leasing sites and mobile instructional units, and transporting students to those sites. Under the Secretary of Education's regulations, those costs "incurred as a result of implementing alternative delivery systems to comply with the requirements of *Aguilar v. Felton*" and not paid for with other state or federal funds are to be deducted from the federal grant before the Title I funds are distributed to any student. These "*Aguilar* costs" thus reduce the amount of Title I money an LEA has available for remedial education, and LEA's have had to cut back on the number of students who receive Title I benefits. From Title I funds available for New York City children between the 1986–1987 and the 1993–1994 school years, the Board had to deduct $7.9 million "off-the-top" for compliance with *Aguilar*. When *Aguilar* was handed down, it was estimated that some 20,000 economically disadvantaged children in the city of New York and some 183,000 children nationwide would experience a decline in Title I services. . . .

In October and December of 1995, petitioners—the Board and a new group of parents of parochial school students entitled to Title I services—filed motions in the

District Court seeking relief under Federal Rule of Civil Procedure 60(b) from the permanent injunction entered by the District Court on remand from our decision in *Aguilar.* Petitioners argued that relief was proper under Rule 60(b)(5) and our decision in *Rufo v. Inmates of Suffolk County Jail* (1992), because the "decisional law [had] changed to make legal what the [injunction] was designed to prevent." Specifically, petitioners pointed to the statements of five Justices in *Board of Ed. of Kiryas Joel Village School Dist. v. Grumet* (1994) calling for the overruling of *Aguilar.* The District Court denied the motion. The District Court recognized that petitioners, "at bottom," sought "a procedurally sound vehicle to get the [propriety of the injunction] back before the Supreme Court," and concluded that the "the Board ha[d] properly proceeded under Rule 60(b) to seek relief from the injunction." Despite its observations that "the landscape of Establishment Clause decisions has changed," and that "[t]here may be good reason to conclude that *Aguilar*'s demise is imminent," the District Court denied the Rule 60(b) motion on the merits because *Aguilar*'s demise had "not yet occurred." The Court of Appeals for the Second Circuit "affirmed substantially for the reasons stated in" the District Court's opinion. We granted certiorari (1997) and now reverse.

II

The question we must answer is a simple one: Are petitioners entitled to relief from the District Court's permanent injunction under Rule 60(b)? Rule 60(b)(5), the subsection under which petitioners proceeded below, states:

> "On motion and upon such terms as are just, the court may relieve a party . . . from a final judgment [or] order . . . [when] it is no longer equitable that the judgment should have prospective application."

In *Rufo v. Inmates of Suffolk County Jail,* we held that it is appropriate to grant a Rule 60(b)(5) motion when the party seeking relief from an injunction or consent decree can show "a significant change either in factual conditions or in law." . . .

Petitioners point to three changes in the factual and legal landscape that they believe justify their claim for relief under Rule 60(b)(5). They first contend that the exorbitant costs of complying with the District Court's injunction constitute a significant factual development warranting modification of the injunction. Petitioners also argue that there have been two significant legal developments since *Aguilar* was decided: a majority of Justices have expressed their views that *Aguilar* should be reconsidered or overruled; and *Aguilar* has in any event been undermined by subsequent Establishment Clause decisions, including *Witters v. Washington Dept. of Servs. for Blind* (1986), *Zobrest v. Catalina Foothills School Dist.* (1993), and *Rosenberger v. Rector and Visitors of Univ. of Va.* (1995).

Respondents counter that, because the costs of providing Title I services offsite were known at the time *Aguilar* was decided, and because the relevant case law has not changed, the District Court did not err in denying petitioners' motions. . . .

We agree with respondents that petitioners have failed to establish the significant change in factual conditions required by *Rufo.* Both petitioners and this Court were, at the time *Aguilar* was decided, aware that additional costs would be incurred if Title I services could not be provided in parochial school classrooms. . . . That these predictions of additional costs turned out to be accurate does not constitute a change in factual conditions warranting relief under Rule 60(b)(5). . . .

We also agree with respondents that the statements made by five Justices in *Kiryas Joel* do not, in themselves, furnish a basis for concluding that our Establishment Clause jurisprudence has changed. [Discussion of case omitted.]. . . [T]he question of *Aguilar*'s propriety was not before us. The views of five Justices that the case should be reconsidered or overruled cannot be said to have effected a change in Establishment Clause law.

In light of these conclusions, petitioners' ability to satisfy the prerequisites of Rule 60(b)(5) hinges on whether our later Establishment Clause cases have so undermined *Aguilar* that it is no longer good law. We now turn to that inquiry.

III

A

In order to evaluate whether *Aguilar* has been eroded by our subsequent Establishment Clause cases, it is necessary to understand the rationale upon which *Aguilar*, as well as its companion case, *School Dist. of Grand Rapids v. Ball* (1985), rested.

[Discussion of *Ball*, which struck down a "Shared Time" program for public school teachers to teach supplemental courses on the premises of church-affiliated schools, and further discussion of *Aguilar* omitted.]

Distilled to essentials, the Court's conclusion that the Shared Time program in *Ball* had the impermissible effect of advancing religion rested on three assumptions: (i) any public employee who works on the premises of a religious school is presumed to inculcate religion in her work; (ii) the presence of public employees on private school premises creates a symbolic union between church and state; and (iii) any and all public aid that directly aids the educational function of religious schools impermissibly finances religious indoctrination, even if the aid reaches such schools as a consequence of private decisionmaking. Additionally, in *Aguilar* there was a fourth assumption: that New York City's Title I program necessitated an excessive government entanglement with religion because public employees who teach on the premises of religious schools must be closely monitored to ensure that they do not inculcate religion.

B

Our more recent cases have undermined the assumptions upon which *Ball* and *Aguilar* relied. To be sure, the general principles we use to evaluate whether government aid violates the Establishment Clause have not changed since *Aguilar* was decided. For example, we continue to ask whether the government acted with the purpose of advancing or inhibiting religion, and the nature of that inquiry has remained largely unchanged. . . . Likewise, we continue to explore whether the aid has the "effect" of advancing or inhibiting religion. What has changed since we decided *Ball* and *Aguilar* is our understanding of the criteria used to assess whether aid to religion has an impermissible effect.

1

As we have repeatedly recognized, government inculcation of religious beliefs has the impermissible effect of advancing religion. Our cases subsequent to *Aguilar* have, however, modified in two significant respects the approach we use to assess indoctrination. First, we have abandoned the presumption erected in *Meek* and *Ball* that the placement of public employees on parochial school grounds inevitably results in the impermissible effect of state-sponsored indoctrination or constitutes a symbolic union between government and religion. In *Zobrest v. Catalina Foothills School Dist.* (1993), we examined whether the [Individuals with Disabilities Education Act (IDEA)] was constitutional as applied to a deaf student who sought to bring his state-employed sign-language interpreter with him to his Roman Catholic high school. We held that this was permissible, expressly disavowing the notion that "the Establishment Clause [laid] down [an] absolute bar to the placing of a public employee in a sectarian school." . . . We refused to presume that a publicly employed interpreter would be pressured by the pervasively sectarian surroundings to inculcate religion by "add[ing] to [or] subtract[ing] from" the lectures translated. . . . *Zobrest* therefore expressly rejected the notion—relied on in *Ball* and *Aguilar*—that, solely because of her presence on private school property, a public employee will be presumed to inculcate religion in the students. *Zobrest* also implicitly repudiated another assumption on which *Ball* and *Aguilar* turned: that the presence of a public employee on private school property creates an impermissible "symbolic link" between government and religion.

Second, we have departed from the rule relied on in *Ball* that all government aid that directly aids the educational function of religious schools is invalid. In *Witters v. Washington Dept. of Servs. for Blind* (1986), we held that the Establishment Clause did not bar a State from issuing a vocational tuition grant to a blind person who wished to use the grant to attend a Christian college and become a pastor, missionary, or youth director. Even though the grant recipient clearly would use the money to obtain religious education, we observed that the tuition grants were " 'made available generally without regard to the sectarian-nonsectarian, or public-nonpublic nature of the institution benefited.' " The grants were disbursed directly to students, who then used the money to pay for tuition at the educational institution of their choice. In our view, this transaction was no different from a State's issuing a paycheck to one of its employees, knowing that the employee would donate part or all of the check to a religious institution. In both situations, any money that ultimately went to religious institutions did so "only as a result of the genuinely independent and private choices of" individuals. The same logic applied in *Zobrest*, where we allowed the State to provide an interpreter, even though she would be a mouthpiece for religious instruction, because the IDEA's neutral eligibility criteria ensured that the interpreter's presence in a sectarian school was a "result of the private decision of individual parents" and "[could] not be attributed to state decisionmaking." (emphasis added). Because the private school would not have provided an interpreter on its own, we also concluded that the aid in *Zobrest* did not indirectly finance religious education by "reliev[ing] the sectarian schoo[l] of costs [it] otherwise would have borne in educating [its] students."

Zobrest and *Witters* make clear that, under current law, the Shared Time program in *Ball* and New York City's Title I program in *Aguilar* will not, as a matter of law, be deemed to have the effect of advancing religion through indoctrination. Indeed, each of the premises upon which we relied in *Ball* to reach a contrary conclusion is no longer valid. First, there is no reason to presume that, simply because she enters a parochial school classroom, a full-time public employee such as a Title I teacher will depart from her assigned duties and instructions and embark on religious indoctrination. . . .

As discussed above, *Zobrest* also repudiates *Ball*'s assumption that the presence of Title I teachers in parochial school classrooms will, without more, create the impression of a "symbolic union" between church and state. . . . We do not see any perceptible (let alone dispositive) difference in the degree of symbolic union between a student receiving remedial instruction in a classroom on his sectarian school's campus and one receiving instruction in a van parked just at the school's curbside. To draw this line based solely on the location of the public employee is neither "sensible" nor "sound," and the Court in *Zobrest* rejected it.

Nor under current law can we conclude that a program placing full-time public employees on parochial campuses to provide Title I instruction would impermissibly finance religious indoctrination. In all relevant respects, the provision of instructional services under Title I is indistinguishable from the provision of sign-language interpreters under the IDEA. Both programs make aid available only to eligible recipients. That aid is provided to students at whatever school they choose to attend. Although Title I instruction is provided to several students at once, whereas an interpreter provides translation to a single student, this distinction is not constitutionally significant. Moreover, as in *Zobrest*, Title I services are by law supplemental to the regular curricula. These services do not, therefore, "reliev[e] sectarian schools of costs they otherwise would have borne in educating their students." [Quoting *Zobrest*.] . . .

We are also not persuaded that Title I services supplant the remedial instruction and guidance counseling already provided in New York City's sectarian schools. . . . We are unwilling to speculate that all sectarian schools provide remedial instruction and guidance counseling to their students, and are unwilling to presume that the Board would violate Title I regulations by continuing to provide Title I services to students who attend a sectarian school that has curtailed its remedial instruction program in response to Title I. Nor are we willing to conclude that the constitutionality of an aid program depends on the number of sectarian school students who happen to receive the otherwise neutral aid. *Zobrest* did not turn on the fact that James Zobrest had, at the time of litigation, been the only child using a publicly funded sign-language interpreter to attend a parochial school. . . .

What is most fatal to the argument that New York City's Title I program directly subsidizes religion is that it applies with equal force when those services are provided off-campus, and *Aguilar* implied that providing the services off-campus is entirely consistent with the Establishment Clause. . . . [W]e find no logical basis upon which to conclude that Title I services are an impermissible subsidy of religion when offered on-campus, but not when offered off-campus. Accordingly, contrary to our conclusion in *Aguilar*, placing full-time employees on parochial school campuses does not as a matter of law have the impermissible effect of advancing religion through indoctrination.

2

Although we examined in *Witters* and *Zobrest* the criteria by which an aid program identifies its beneficiaries, we did so solely to assess whether any use of that aid to indoctrinate religion could be attributed to the State. A number of our Establishment Clause cases have found that the criteria used for identifying beneficiaries are relevant in a second respect, apart from enabling a court to evaluate whether the program subsidizes religion. Specifically, the criteria might themselves have the effect of advancing religion by creating a financial incentive to undertake religious indoctrination. . . . This incentive is not present, however, where the aid is allocated on the basis of neutral, secular criteria that neither favor nor disfavor religion, and is made available to both religious and secular beneficiaries on a nondiscriminatory basis. Under such circumstances, the aid is less likely to have the effect of advancing religion. . . .

In *Ball* and *Aguilar*, the Court gave this consideration no weight. Before and since those decisions, we have sustained programs that provided aid to all eligible children regardless of where they attended school. . . .

Applying this reasoning to New York City's Title I program, it is clear that Title I services are allocated on the basis of criteria that neither favor nor disfavor religion. The services are available to all children who meet the Act's eligibility requirements, no matter what their religious beliefs or where they go to school. The Board's program does not, therefore, give aid recipients any incentive to modify their religious beliefs or practices in order to obtain those services.

3

We turn now to *Aguilar*'s conclusion that New York City's Title I program resulted in an excessive entanglement between church and state. Whether a government aid program results in such an entanglement has consistently been an aspect of our Establishment Clause analysis. We have considered entanglement both in the course of assessing whether an aid program has an impermissible effect of advancing religion, *Walz v. Tax Comm'n of City of New York* (1970), and as a factor separate and apart from "effect," *Lemon v. Kurtzman* [1971]. Regardless of how we have characterized the issue, however, the factors we use to assess whether an entanglement is "excessive" are similar to the factors we use to examine "effect." That is, to assess entanglement, we have looked to "the character and purposes of the institutions that are benefited, the nature of the aid that the State provides, and the resulting relationship between the government and religious authority." [Quoting *Lemon.*] Similarly, we have assessed a law's "effect" by examining the character of the institutions benefited (e.g., whether the religious institutions were "predominantly religious"); and the nature of the aid that the State provided (e.g., whether it was neutral and nonideological). Indeed, in *Lemon* itself, the entanglement that the Court found "independently" to necessitate the program's invalidation also was found to have the effect of inhibiting religion. . . . Thus, it is simplest to recognize why entanglement is significant and treat it—as we did in *Walz*—as an aspect of the inquiry into a statute's effect.

Not all entanglements, of course, have the effect of advancing or inhibiting religion. Interaction between church and state is inevitable, and we have always tolerated some level of involvement between the two. Entanglement must be "excessive" before it runs afoul of the Establishment Clause. . . .

The pre-*Aguilar* Title I program does not result in an "excessive" entanglement that advances or inhibits religion. As discussed previously, the Court's finding of "excessive" entanglement in *Aguilar* rested on three grounds: (i) the program would require "pervasive monitoring by public authorities" to ensure that Title I employees did not inculcate religion; (ii) the program required "administrative cooperation" between the Board and parochial schools; and (iii) the program might increase the dangers of "political divisiveness." Under our current understanding of the Establishment Clause, the last two considerations are insufficient by themselves to create an "excessive" entanglement. They are present no matter where Title I services are offered, and no court has held that Title I services cannot be offered off-campus. [Citing lower court cases.] Further, the assumption underlying the first consideration has been undermined. In *Aguilar*, the Court presumed that full-time public employees on parochial school grounds would be tempted to inculcate religion, despite the ethical standards they were required to uphold. Because of this risk pervasive monitoring would be required. But after *Zobrest* we no longer presume that public employees will inculcate religion simply because they happen to be in a sectarian environment. Since we have abandoned the assumption that properly instructed public employees will fail to discharge their duties faithfully, we must also discard the assumption that pervasive monitoring of Title I teachers is required. There is no suggestion in the record before us that unannounced monthly visits of public supervisors are insufficient to prevent or to detect inculcation of religion by public employees. Moreover, we have not found excessive entanglement in cases in which States imposed far more onerous burdens on religious institutions than the monitoring system at issue here.

To summarize, New York City's Title I program does not run afoul of any of three primary criteria we currently use to evaluate whether government aid has the effect of advancing religion: it does not result in governmental indoctrination; define its recipients by reference to religion; or create an excessive entanglement. We therefore hold that a federally funded program providing supplemental, remedial instruction to disadvantaged children on a neutral basis is not invalid under the Establishment Clause when such instruction is given on the premises of sectarian schools by government employees pursuant to a program containing safeguards such as those present here. The same considerations that justify this holding require us to conclude that this carefully constrained program also cannot reasonably be viewed as an endorsement of religion. . . . Accordingly, we must acknowledge that *Aguilar*, as well as the portion of *Ball* addressing Grand Rapids' Shared Time program, are no longer good law.

C

The doctrine of *stare decisis* does not preclude us from recognizing the change in our law and overruling *Aguilar* and those portions of *Ball* inconsistent with our more recent decisions. As we have often noted, "*[s]tare decisis* is not an inexorable command," but instead reflects a policy judgment that "in most matters it is more important that the applicable rule of law be settled than that it be settled right." That policy is at its weakest when we interpret the Constitution because our interpretation can be altered only by constitutional amendment or by overruling our prior decisions. . . . Thus, we have held in several cases that *stare decisis* does not prevent us from overruling a previous decision where there has been a significant change in or subsequent development of our constitutional law. . . . As discussed above, our Establishment Clause jurisprudence has changed significantly since we decided *Ball* and *Aguilar*, so our decision to overturn those cases rests on far more than "a present doctrinal disposition to come out differently from the Court of [1985]." [Quoting *Planned Parenthood of Southeastern Pa. v. Casey* (1992).] We therefore overrule *Ball* and *Aguilar* to the extent those decisions are inconsistent with our current understanding of the Establishment Clause.

Nor does the "law of the case" doctrine place any additional constraints on our ability to overturn *Aguilar*. Under this doctrine, a court should not reopen issues decided in earlier stages of the same litigation. The doctrine does not apply if the court is "convinced that [its prior decision] is clearly erroneous and would work a manifest injustice." In light of our conclusion that *Aguilar* would be decided differently under our current Establishment Clause law, we think adherence to that decision would undoubtedly work a "manifest injustice," such that the law of the case doctrine does not apply. . . .

IV

We therefore conclude that our Establishment Clause law has "significant[ly] change[d]" since we decided *Aguilar*. We are only left to decide whether this change in law entitles petitioners to relief under Rule 60(b)(5). We conclude that it does. Our general practice is to apply the rule of law we announce in a case to the parties before us. *Rodriguez de Quijas v. Shearson/American Express, Inc.* (1989). . . . We adhere to this practice even when we overrule a case. . . .

We do not acknowledge, and we do not hold, that other courts should conclude our more recent cases have, by implication, overruled an earlier precedent. We reaffirm that "if a precedent of this Court has direct application in a case, yet appears to rest on reasons rejected in some other line of decisions, the Court of Appeals should follow the case which directly controls, leaving to this Court the prerogative of overruling its own decisions." [Quoting *Rodriguez de Quijas.*] Adherence to this teaching by the District Court and Court of Appeals in this case does not insulate a legal principle on which they relied from our review to determine its continued vitality. The trial court acted within its discretion in entertaining the motion with supporting allegations, but it was also correct to recognize that the motion had to be denied unless and until this Court reinterpreted the binding precedent.

Respondents and JUSTICE GINSBURG urge us to adopt a different analysis because we are reviewing the District Court's denial of petitioners' Rule 60(b)(5) motion for an abuse of discretion. It is true that the trial court has discretion, but the exercise of discretion cannot be permitted to stand if we find it rests upon a legal principle that can no longer be sustained. The standard of review we employ in this litigation does not therefore require us to depart from our general practice.

Respondents nevertheless contend that we should not grant Rule 60(b)(5) relief here, in spite of its propriety in other contexts. They contend that petitioners have used Rule 60(b)(5) in an unprecedented way—not as a means of recognizing changes in the law, but as a vehicle for effecting them. If we were to sanction this use of Rule 60(b)(5), respondents argue, we would encourage litigants to burden the federal courts with a deluge of Rule 60(b)(5) motions premised on nothing more than the claim that various judges or Justices have stated that the law has changed. . . . We think their fears are overstated. As we noted above, a judge's stated belief that a case should be overruled does not make it so.

Most importantly, our decision today is intimately tied to the context in which it arose. This litigation involves a party's request under Rule 60(b)(5) to vacate a continuing injunction entered some years ago in light of a bona fide, significant change in subsequent law. The clause of Rule 60(b)(5) that petitioners invoke applies by its terms only to "judgment[s] hav[ing] prospective application." Intervening developments in the law by themselves rarely constitute the extraordinary circumstances required for relief under Rule 60(b)(6), the only remaining avenue for relief on this basis from judgments lacking any prospective component. Our decision will have no effect outside the context of ordinary civil litigation where the propriety of continuing prospective relief is at issue. . . . Given that Rule 60(b)(5) specifically contemplates the grant of relief in the circumstances presented here, it can hardly be said that we have somehow warped the Rule into a means of "allowing an 'anytime' rehearing." [Quoting GINSBURG, J., dissenting.]

Respondents further contend that "[p]etitioners' [p]roposed [u]se of Rule 60(b) [w]ill [e]rode the [i]nstitutional [i]ntegrity of the Court." Respondents do not explain how a proper application of Rule 60(b)(5) undermines our legitimacy. Instead, respondents focus on the harm occasioned if we were to overrule *Aguilar*. But as discussed above, we do no violence to the doctrine of *stare decisis* when we recognize bona fide changes in our decisional law. And in those circumstances, we do no violence to the legitimacy we derive from reliance on that doctrine.

As a final matter, we see no reason to wait for a "better vehicle" in which to evaluate the impact of subsequent cases on *Aguilar*'s continued vitality. To evaluate the Rule 60(b)(5) motion properly before us today in no way undermines "integrity in the interpretation of procedural rules" or signals any departure from "the responsive, non-agenda-setting character of this Court." (GINSBURG, J., dissenting). Indeed, under these circumstances, it would be particularly inequitable for us to bide our time waiting for another case to arise while the city of New York labors under a continuing injunction forcing it to spend millions of dollars on mobile instructional units and leased sites when it could instead be spending that money to give economically disadvantaged children a better chance at success in life by means of a program that is perfectly consistent with the Establishment Clause.

For these reasons, we reverse the judgment of the Court of Appeals and remand to the District Court with instructions to vacate its September 26, 1985, order.

It is so ordered.

JUSTICE SOUTER, with whom JUSTICE STEVENS and JUSTICE GINSBURG join, and with whom JUSTICE BREYER joins as to Part II, dissenting.

In this novel proceeding, petitioners seek relief from an injunction the District Court entered 12 years ago to implement our decision in *Aguilar v. Felton* (1985). For the reasons given by JUSTICE GINSBURG, the Court's holding that petitioners are entitled to relief under Rule 60(b) is seriously mistaken. The Court's misapplication of the rule is tied to its equally erroneous reading of our more recent Establishment Clause cases, which the Court describes as having rejected the underpinnings of *Aguilar* and portions of *Aguilar*'s companion case, *School Dist. of Grand Rapids v. Ball* (1985). The result is to repudiate the very reasonable line drawn in *Aguilar* and *Ball*, and to authorize direct state aid to religious institutions on an unparalleled scale, in violation of the Establishment Clause's central prohibition against religious subsidies by the government.

I respectfully dissent.

I

In both *Aguilar* and *Ball*, we held that supplemental instruction by public school teachers on the premises of religious schools during regular school hours violated the Establishment Clause. . . .

. . . I believe *Aguilar* was a correct and sensible decision, and my only reservation about its opinion is that the emphasis on the excessive entanglement produced by monitoring religious instructional content obscured those facts that independently called for the application of two central tenets of Establishment Clause jurisprudence. The State is forbidden to subsidize religion directly and is just as surely forbidden to act in any way that could reasonably be viewed as religious endorsement. . . .

. . . [T]he flat ban on subsidization antedates the Bill of Rights and has been an unwavering rule in Establishment Clause cases, qualified only by the conclusion two Terms ago that state exactions from college students are not the sort of public revenues subject to the ban. *Rosenberger v. Rector and Visitors of Univ. of Va.* (1995). The rule expresses the hard lesson learned over and over again in the American past and in the experiences of the countries from which we have come, that religions supported by governments are compromised just as surely as the religious freedom of dissenters is burdened when the government supports religion. . . . The ban against state endorsement of religion addresses the same historical lessons. Governmental approval of religion tends to reinforce the religious message (at least in the short run) and, by the same token, to carry a message of exclusion to those of less favored views. . . .

These principles were violated by the programs at issue in *Aguilar* and *Ball*, as a consequence of several significant features common to both Title I, as implemented in New York City before *Aguilar*, and the Grand Rapids Shared Time program: each provided classes on the premises of the religious schools, covering a wide range of subjects including some at the core of primary and secondary education, like reading and mathematics; while their services were termed "supplemental," the programs and their instructors necessarily assumed responsibility for teaching subjects that the religious schools would otherwise have been obligated to provide. . . ; the public employees carrying out the programs had broad responsibilities involving the exercise of considerable discretion . . . ; while the programs offered aid to nonpublic school students generally (and Title I went to public school students as well), participation by religious school students in each program was extensive. . . ; and, finally, aid under Title I and Shared Time flowed directly to the schools in the form of classes and programs, as distinct from indirect aid that reaches schools only as a result of independent private choice. . . .

What, therefore, was significant in *Aguilar* and *Ball* about the placement of state-paid teachers into the physical and social settings of the religious schools was not only the consequent temptation of some of those teachers to reflect the schools' religious missions in the rhetoric of their instruction, with a resulting need for monitoring and the certainty of entanglement. What was so remarkable was that the schemes in issue assumed a teaching responsibility indistinguishable from the responsibility of the schools themselves. The obligation of primary and secondary schools to teach reading necessarily extends to teaching those who are having a hard time at it, and the same is true of math. Calling some classes remedial does not distinguish their subjects from the schools' basic subjects, however inadequately the schools may have been addressing them.

What was true of the Title I scheme as struck down in *Aguilar* will be just as true when New York reverts to the old practices with the Court's approval after today. There is simply no line that can be drawn between the instruction paid for at taxpayers' expense and the instruction in any subject that is not identified as formally religious. While it would be an obvious sham, say, to channel cash to religious schools to be credited only against the expense of "secular" instruction, the line between "supplemental" and general education is likewise impossible to draw. If a State may constitutionally enter the schools to teach in the manner in question, it must in constitutional principle be free to assume, or assume payment for, the entire cost of instruction provided in any ostensibly secular subject in any religious school. . . .

In sum, if a line is to be drawn short of barring all state aid to religious schools for teaching standard subjects, the *Aguilar-Ball* line was a sensible one capable of principled adherence. It is no less sound, and no less necessary, today.

II

The Court today ignores this doctrine and claims that recent cases rejected the elemental assumptions underlying *Aguilar* and much of *Ball*. But the Court errs. Its holding that *Aguilar* and the portion of *Ball* addressing the Shared Time program are "no longer good law" rests on mistaken reading.

A

Zobrest v. Catalina Foothills School Dist. [1993] held that the Establishment Clause does not prevent a school district from providing a sign-language interpreter to a deaf student enrolled in a sectarian school. The Court today relies solely on *Zobrest* to support its contention that we have "abandoned the presumption erected in *Meek* [*v. Pittenger* (1975)] and *Ball* that the placement of public employees on parochial school grounds inevitably results in the impermissible effect of state-sponsored indoctrination or constitutes a symbolic union between government and religion." *Zobrest*, however, is no such sanction for overruling *Aguilar* or any portion of *Ball*.

In *Zobrest* the Court did indeed recognize that the Establishment Clause lays down no absolute bar to placing public employees in a sectarian school, but the rejection of such a per se rule was hinged expressly on the nature of the employee's job, sign-language interpretation (or signing) and the circumscribed role of the signer. . . .

. . . The Court may disagree with *Ball*'s assertion that a publicly employed teacher working in a sectarian school is apt to reinforce the pervasive inculcation of religious beliefs, but its disagreement is fresh law.

The Court tries to press *Zobrest* into performing another service beyond its reach. The Court says that *Ball* and *Aguilar* assumed "that the presence of a public employee on private school property creates an impermissible 'symbolic link' between government and religion," and that *Zobrest* repudiated this assumption. First, *Ball* and *Aguilar* said nothing about the "mere presence" of public employees at religious schools. It was *Ball* that specifically addressed the point and held only that when teachers employed by public schools are placed in religious schools to provide instruction to students during the schoolday a symbolic union of church and state is created and will reasonably be seen by the students as endorsement; *Aguilar* adopted the same conclusion by reference. *Zobrest* did not, implicitly or otherwise, repudiate the view that the involvement of public teachers in the instruction provided within sectarian schools looks like a partnership or union and implies approval of the sectarian aim. On the subject of symbolic unions and the strength of their implications, the lesson of *Zobrest* is merely that less is less.

B

The Court next claims that *Ball* rested on the assumption that "any and all public aid that directly aids the educational function of religious schools impermissibly finances religious indoctrination, even if the aid reaches such schools as a consequence of private decisionmaking." . . .

Ball did not establish that "any and all" such aid to religious schools necessarily violates the Establishment Clause. It held that the Shared Time program subsidized the religious functions of the parochial schools by taking over a significant portion of their responsibility for teaching secular subjects. The Court . . . enquired whether the effect of the proffered aid was "direct and substantial" (and, so, unconstitutional) or merely "indirect and incidental," (and, so, permissible), emphasizing that the question "is one of degree." *Witters* [*v. Washington Dept. of Servs. for Blind* (1986)] and *Zobrest* did nothing to repudiate the principle, emphasizing rather the limited nature of the aid at issue in each case as well as the fact that religious institutions did not receive it directly from the State. . . .

It is accordingly puzzling to find the Court insisting that the aid scheme administered under Title I and considered in *Aguilar* was comparable to the programs in *Witters* and *Zobrest*. Instead of aiding isolated individuals within a school system, New York City's Title I program before *Aguilar* served about 22,000 private school students, all but 52 of whom attended religious schools. Instead of serving individual blind or deaf students, as such, Title I as administered in New York City before *Aguilar* (and as now to be revived) funded instruction in core subjects (remedial reading, reading skills, remedial mathematics, English as a second language) and provided guidance services. Instead of providing a service the school would not otherwise furnish, the Title I services necessarily relieved a religious school of "an expense that it otherwise would have assumed" and freed its funds for other, and sectarian uses.

Finally, instead of aid that comes to the religious school indirectly . . . , a public educational agency distributes Title I aid in the form of programs and services directly to the religious schools. In *Zobrest* and *Witters*, it was fair to say that individual students were themselves applicants for individual benefits on a scale that could not amount to a systemic supplement. But under Title I, a local educational agency . . . may receive federal funding by proposing programs approved to serve individual students who meet the criteria of need, which it then uses to provide such programs at the religious schools; students eligible for such programs may not apply directly for Title I funds. The aid, accordingly, is not even formally aid to the individual students (and even formally individual aid must be seen as aid to a school system when so many individuals receive it that it becomes a significant feature of the system).

In sum, nothing since *Ball* and *Aguilar* and before this case has eroded the distinction between "direct and substantial" and "indirect and incidental." That principled line is being breached only here and now.

C

The Court notes that aid programs providing benefits solely to religious groups may be constitutionally suspect, while aid allocated under neutral, secular criteria is less likely to have the effect of advancing religion. . . . [E]venhandedness is a necessary but not a sufficient condition for an aid program to satisfy constitutional scrutiny. . . . If a scheme of government aid results in support for religion in some substantial degree, or in endorsement of its value, the formal neutrality of the scheme does not render the Establishment Clause helpless or the holdings in *Aguilar* and *Ball* inapposite.

III

Finally, there is the issue of precedent. *Stare decisis* is no barrier in the Court's eyes because it reads *Aguilar* and *Ball* for exaggerated propositions that *Witters* and *Zobrest* are supposed to have limited to the point of abandoned doctrine. The Court's dispensation from *stare decisis* is, accordingly, no more convincing than its reading of those cases. . . .

The continuity of the law, indeed, is matched by the persistence of the facts. When *Aguilar* was decided everyone knew that providing Title I services off the premises of the religious schools would come at substantial cost in efficiency, convenience, and money. Title I had begun off the premises in New York, after all, and dissatisfaction with the arrangement was what led the City to put the public school teachers into the religious schools in the first place. When *Aguilar* required the end of that arrangement, conditions reverted to those of the past and they have remained unchanged: teaching conditions are often poor, it is difficult to move children around, and it costs a lot of money. That is, the facts became once again what they were once before, as everyone including the Members of this Court knew they would be. . . .

That is not to deny that the facts just recited are regrettable; the object of Title I is worthy without doubt, and the cost of compliance is high. In the short run there is much that is genuinely unfortunate about the administration of the scheme under *Aguilar*'s rule. But constitutional lines have to be drawn, and on one side of every one of them is an otherwise sympathetic case that provokes impatience with the Constitution and with the line. But constitutional lines are the price of constitutional government.

JUSTICE GINSBURG, with whom JUSTICE STEVENS, JUSTICE SOUTER, and JUSTICE BREYER join, dissenting.

The Court today finds a way to rehear a legal question decided in respondents' favor in this very case some 12 years ago. Subsequent decisions, the majority says, have undermined *Aguilar* and justify our immediate reconsideration. This Court's Rules do not countenance the rehearing here granted. For good reason, a proper application of those rules and the Federal Rules of Civil Procedure would lead us to defer reconsideration of *Aguilar* until we are presented with the issue in another case.

We have a rule on rehearing, Rule 44, but it provides only for petitions filed within 25 days of the entry of the judgment in question. Although the Court or a Justice may "shorte[n] or exten[d]" this period, I am aware of no case in which we have extended the time for rehearing years beyond publication of our adjudication on the merits. . . . Moreover, nothing in our procedures allows us to grant rehearing, timely or not, "except . . . at the instance of a Justice who concurred in the judgment or decision." Petitioners have not been so bold (or so candid) as to style their plea as one for rehearing in this Court, and the Court has not taken up the petition at the instance of JUSTICE STEVENS, the only still-sitting member of the *Aguilar* majority.

Lacking any rule or practice allowing us to reconsider the *Aguilar* judgment directly, the majority accepts as a substitute a rule governing relief from judgments or orders of the federal trial courts. The service to which Rule 60(b) has been impressed is unprecedented, and neither the Court nor those urging reconsideration of *Aguilar* contend otherwise. . . . The Court makes clear, fortunately, that any future efforts to expand today's ruling will not be favored. I therefore anticipate that the extraordinary action taken in this case will remain aberrational.

Rule 60(b) provides, in relevant part:

> "On motion and upon such terms as are just, the [district] court may relieve a party or a party's legal representative from a final judgment, order, or proceeding for the following reasons: . . . (5) . . . it is no longer equitable that the judgment should have prospective application."

Under that rule, a district court may, in its discretion, grant relief from a final judgment with prospective effect if the party seeking modification can show "a significant change either in factual conditions or in law" that renders continued operation of the judgment inequitable. . . .

Appellate courts review denials of Rule 60(b) motions for abuse of discretion. . . . As we recognized in our unanimous opinion in *Browder* [*v. Director, Dept. of Corrections of Ill.* (1978)], "an appeal from denial of Rule 60(b) relief does not bring up the underlying judgment for review." . . .

In short, relitigation of the legal or factual claims underlying the original judgment is not permitted in a Rule 60(b) motion or an appeal therefrom. . . . Thus, under settled practice, the sole question legitimately presented on appeal of the District Court's decision denying petitioners' Rule 60(b)(5) motion to modify the *Aguilar* injunction would be: Did the District Court abuse its discretion when it concluded that neither the facts nor the law had so changed as to warrant alteration of the injunction?

The majority acknowledges that there has been no significant change in factual conditions. The majority also recognizes that *Aguilar* had not been overruled, but remained the governing Establishment Clause law, until this very day. Because *Aguilar* had not been overruled at the time the District Court acted, the law the District Court was bound to respect had not changed. The District Court therefore did not abuse its discretion in denying petitioners' Rule 60(b) motion. . . .

In an effort to make today's use of Rule 60(b) appear palatable, the Court describes its decision not as a determination of whether *Aguilar* should be overruled, but as an exploration whether *Aguilar* already has been "so undermined . . . that it is no longer good law." But nothing can disguise the reality that, until today, *Aguilar* had not been overruled. Good or bad, it was in fact the law.

Despite the problematic use of Rule 60(b), the Court "see[s] no reason to wait for a 'better vehicle.'" There are such vehicles in motion, and the Court does not say otherwise. [Citing pending cases.] . . .

Unlike the majority, I find just cause to await the arrival of [some other case] in which our review appropriately may be sought, before deciding whether *Aguilar* should remain the law of the land. That cause lies in the maintenance of integrity in the interpretation of procedural rules, preservation of the responsive, non-agenda-setting character of this Court, and avoidance of invitations to reconsider old cases based on "speculat[ions] on chances from changes in [the Court's membership]."

No. 95-2074

City of Boerne, Petitioner v. P. F. Flores, Archbishop of San Antonio and United States

On writ of certiorari to the United States Court
of Appeals for the Fifth Circuit

[June 25, 1997]

JUSTICE KENNEDY delivered the opinion of the Court. [JUSTICE SCALIA joins all but Part III-A-1 of this opinion.]

A decision by local zoning authorities to deny a church a building permit was challenged under the Religious Freedom Restoration Act of 1993 (RFRA). The case calls into question the authority of Congress to enact RFRA. We conclude the statute exceeds Congress' power.

I

Situated on a hill in the city of Boerne, Texas, some 28 miles northwest of San Antonio, is St. Peter Catholic Church. Built in 1923, the church's structure replicates the mission style of the region's earlier history. The church seats about 230 worshippers, a number too small for its growing parish. Some 40 to 60 parishioners cannot be accommodated at some Sunday masses. In order to meet the needs of the congregation the Archbishop of San Antonio gave permission to the parish to plan alterations to enlarge the building.

A few months later, the Boerne City Council passed an ordinance authorizing the city's Historic Landmark Commission to prepare a preservation plan with proposed historic landmarks and districts. Under the ordinance, the Commission must preapprove construction affecting historic landmarks or buildings in a historic district.

Soon afterwards, the Archbishop applied for a building permit so construction to enlarge the church could proceed. City authorities, relying on the ordinance and the designation of a historic district (which, they argued, included the church), denied the application. The Archbishop brought this suit challenging the permit denial in the United States District Court for the Western District of Texas.

The complaint contained various claims, but to this point the litigation has centered on RFRA and the question of its constitutionality. The Archbishop relied upon RFRA as one basis for relief from the refusal to issue the permit. The District Court concluded that by enacting RFRA Congress exceeded the scope of its enforcement power under §5 of the Fourteenth Amendment. (1995). The court certified its order for interlocutory appeal and the Fifth Circuit reversed, finding RFRA to be constitutional. (1996). We granted certiorari (1996) and now reverse.

II

Congress enacted RFRA in direct response to the Court's decision in *Employment Div., Dept. of Human Resources of Ore. v. Smith* (1990). There we considered a Free Exercise Clause claim brought by members of the Native American Church who were denied unemployment benefits when they lost their jobs because they had used peyote. Their practice was to ingest peyote for sacramental purposes, and they challenged an Oregon statute of general applicability which made use of the drug criminal. In evaluating the claim, we declined to apply the balancing test set forth in *Sherbert v. Verner* (1963), under which we would have asked whether Oregon's prohibition substantially burdened a religious practice and, if it did, whether the burden was justified by a compelling government interest. . . . The application of the *Sherbert* test, the *Smith* decision explained, would have produced an anomaly in the law, a constitutional right to ignore neutral laws of general applicability. The anomaly would have been accentuated, the Court reasoned, by the difficulty of determining whether a particular practice was central to an individual's religion. . . .

Four Members of the Court disagreed. They argued the law placed a substantial burden on the Native American Church members so that it could be upheld only if the law served a compelling state interest and was narrowly tailored to achieve that end. JUSTICE O'CONNOR concluded Oregon had satisfied the test, while Justice Blackmun, joined by Justice Brennan and Justice Marshall, could see no compelling interest justifying the law's application to the members.

These points of constitutional interpretation were debated by Members of Congress in hearings and floor debates. Many criticized the Court's reasoning, and this disagreement resulted in the passage of RFRA. Congress announced:

> "(1) [T]he framers of the Constitution, recognizing free exercise of religion as an unalienable right, secured its protection in the First Amendment to the Constitution;
> "(2) laws 'neutral' toward religion may burden religious exercise as surely as laws intended to interfere with religious exercise;
> "(3) governments should not substantially burden religious exercise without compelling justification;
> "(4) in *Employment Division v. Smith* (1990), the Supreme Court virtually eliminated the requirement that the government justify burdens on religious exercise imposed by laws neutral toward religion; and
> "(5) the compelling interest test as set forth in prior Federal court rulings is a workable test for striking sensible balances between religious liberty and competing prior governmental interests."

The Act's stated purposes are:

> "(1) to restore the compelling interest test as set forth in *Sherbert v. Verne* (1963) and *Wisconsin v. Yoder* (1972) and to guarantee its application in all cases where free exercise of religion is substantially burdened; and
> "(2) to provide a claim or defense to persons whose religious exercise is substantially burdened by government."

RFRA prohibits "[g]overnment" from "substantially burden[ing]" a person's exercise of religion even if the burden results from a rule of general applicability unless the government can demonstrate the burden "(1) is in furtherance of a compelling governmental interest; and (2) is the least restrictive means of furthering that compelling governmental interest." The Act's mandate applies to any "branch, department, agency, instrumentality, and official (or other person acting under color of law) of the United States," as well as to any "State, or . . . subdivision of a State." The Act's universal coverage is confirmed in [one section], under which RFRA "applies to all Federal and State law, and the implementation of that law, whether statutory or otherwise, and whether adopted before or after [RFRA's enactment]." In accordance with RFRA's usage of the term, we shall use "state law" to include local and municipal ordinances.

III

A

Under our Constitution, the Federal Government is one of enumerated powers. The judicial authority to determine the constitutionality of laws, in cases and controversies, is based on the premise that the "powers of the legislature are defined and limited; and that those limits may not be mistaken, or forgotten, the constitution is written."

Congress relied on its Fourteenth Amendment enforcement power in enacting the most far reaching and substantial of RFRA's provisions, those which impose its requirements on the States. The Fourteenth Amendment provides, in relevant part:

"Section 1. . . . No State shall make or enforce any law which shall abridge the privileges or immunities of citizens of the United States; nor shall any State deprive any person of life, liberty, or property, without due process of law; nor deny to any person within its jurisdiction the equal protection of the laws.

. . . .

"Section 5. The Congress shall have power to enforce, by appropriate legislation, the provisions of this article."

The parties disagree over whether RFRA is a proper exercise of Congress' §5 power "to enforce" by "appropriate legislation" the constitutional guarantee that no State shall deprive any person of "life, liberty, or property, without due process of law" nor deny any person "equal protection of the laws."

In defense of the Act respondent contends, with support from the United States as *amicus*, that RFRA is permissible enforcement legislation. Congress, it is said, is only protecting by legislation one of the liberties guaranteed by the Fourteenth Amendment's Due Process Clause, the free exercise of religion, beyond what is necessary under *Smith*. It is said the congressional decision to dispense with proof of deliberate or overt discrimination and instead concentrate on a law's effects accords with the settled understanding that §5 includes the power to enact legislation designed to prevent as well as remedy constitutional violations. It is further contended that Congress' §5 power is not limited to remedial or preventive legislation.

All must acknowledge that §5 is "a positive grant of legislative power" to Congress. . . . Legislation which deters or remedies constitutional violations can fall within the sweep of Congress' enforcement power even if in the process it prohibits conduct which is not itself unconstitutional and intrudes into "legislative spheres of autonomy previously reserved to the States." For example, the Court upheld a suspension of literacy tests and similar voting requirements under Congress' parallel power to enforce the provisions of the Fifteenth Amendment, see U. S. Const., Amdt. 15, §2, as a measure to combat racial discrimination in voting, *South Carolina v. Katzenbach* (1966), despite the facial constitutionality of the tests. . . . We have also concluded that other measures protecting voting rights are within Congress' power to enforce the Fourteenth and Fifteenth Amendments, despite the burdens those measures placed on the States. [Citations omitted.] . . .

Congress' power under §5, however, extends only to "enforc[ing]" the provisions of the Fourteenth Amendment. The Court has described this power as "remedial." The design of the Amendment and the text of §5 are inconsistent with the suggestion that Congress has the power to decree the substance of the Fourteenth Amendment's restrictions on the States. Legislation which alters the meaning of the Free Exercise Clause cannot be said to be enforcing the Clause. Congress does not enforce a constitutional right by changing what the right is. . . .

While the line between measures that remedy or prevent unconstitutional actions and measures that make a substantive change in the governing law is not easy to discern, and Congress must have wide latitude in determining where it lies, the distinction exists and must be observed. There must be a congruence and proportionality between the injury to be prevented or remedied and the means adopted to that end. Lacking such a connection, legislation may become substantive in operation and effect. History and our case law support drawing the distinction, one apparent from the text of the Amendment.

1

The Fourteenth Amendment's history confirms the remedial, rather than substantive, nature of the Enforcement Clause. . . . [In a lengthy historical section, Kennedy noted that the first draft of what was to become the Fourteenth Amendment would have given Congress sweeping powers "to make all laws which shall be necessary and proper to secure to the citizens of each State all privileges and immunities of citizens in the several States, and to all persons in the several States equal protection in the rights of life, liberty, and property." The final version, giving Congress "power, to enforce by appropriate legislation, the provisions of this article," was adopted following criticism that the original proposal would have given Congress too much power.]

. . . The design of the Fourteenth Amendment has proved significant also in maintaining the traditional separation of powers between Congress and the Judiciary. The first eight Amendments to the Constitution set forth self-executing prohibitions on governmental action, and this Court has had primary authority to interpret those prohibitions. . . .

As enacted, the Fourteenth Amendment confers substantive rights against the States which, like the provisions of the Bill of Rights, are self-executing. The power to interpret the Constitution in a case or controversy remains in the Judiciary.

2

The remedial and preventive nature of Congress' enforcement power, and the limitation inherent in the power, were confirmed in our earliest cases on the Fourteenth Amendment. [Discussion of cases omitted.]

Recent cases have continued to revolve around the question of whether §5 legislation can be considered remedial. In *South Carolina v. Katzenbach*, we emphasized that "[t]he constitutional propriety of [legislation adopted under the Enforcement Clause] must be judged with reference to the historical experience . . . it reflects." There we upheld various provisions of the Voting Rights Act of 1965, finding them to be "remedies aimed at areas where voting discrimination has been most flagrant," and necessary to "banish the blight of racial discrimination in voting, which has infected the electoral process in parts of our country for nearly a century." . . .

After *South Carolina v. Katzenbach*, the Court continued to acknowledge the necessity of using strong remedial and preventive measures to respond to the widespread and persisting deprivation of constitutional rights resulting from this country's history of racial discrimination. . . .

3

Any suggestion that Congress has a substantive, nonremedial power under the Fourteenth Amendment is not supported by our case law. In *Oregon v. Mitchell* [1970], a majority of the Court concluded Congress had exceeded its enforcement powers by enacting legislation lowering the minimum age of voters from 21 to 18 in state and local elections. The five Members of the Court who reached this conclusion explained that the legislation intruded into an area reserved by the Constitution to the States. . . . Four of these five were explicit in rejecting the position that §5 endowed Congress with the power to establish the meaning of constitutional provisions. Justice Black's rejection of this position might be inferred from his disagreement with Congress' interpretation of the Equal Protection Clause. . . .

If Congress could define its own powers by altering the Fourteenth Amendment's meaning, no longer would the Constitution be "superior paramount law, unchangeable by ordinary means." . . . Under this approach, it is difficult to conceive of a principle that would limit congressional power. Shifting legislative majorities could change the Constitution and effectively circumvent the difficult and detailed amendment process contained in Article V.

We now turn to consider whether RFRA can be considered enforcement legislation under §5 of the Fourteenth Amendment.

B

Respondent contends that RFRA is a proper exercise of Congress' remedial or preventive power. The Act, it is said, is a reasonable means of protecting the free exercise of religion as defined by *Smith*. It prevents and remedies laws which are enacted with the unconstitutional object of targeting religious beliefs and practices. . . . To avoid the difficulty of proving such violations, it is said, Congress can simply invalidate any law which imposes a substantial burden on a religious practice unless it is justified by a compelling interest and is the least restrictive means of accomplishing that interest. If Congress can prohibit laws with discriminatory effects in order to prevent racial discrimination in violation of the Equal Protection Clause, then it can do the same, respondent argues, to promote religious liberty.

While preventive rules are sometimes appropriate remedial measures, there must be a congruence between the means used and the ends to be achieved. The appropriateness of remedial measures must be considered in light of the evil presented. Strong measures appropriate to address one harm may be an unwarranted response to another, lesser one.

A comparison between RFRA and the Voting Rights Act is instructive. In contrast to the record which confronted Congress and the judiciary in the voting rights cases, RFRA's legislative record lacks examples of modern instances of generally applicable laws passed because of religious bigotry. The history of persecution in this country detailed in the hearings mentions no episodes occurring in the past 40 years. [Citing testimony.] . . . Rather, the emphasis of the hearings was on laws of general applicability which place incidental burdens on religion. Much of the discussion centered upon anecdotal evidence of autopsies performed on Jewish individuals and Hmong immigrants in violation of their religious beliefs . . . , and on zoning regulations and historic preservation laws (like the one at issue here), which as an incident of their normal operation, have adverse effects on churches and synagogues. It is difficult to maintain that they are examples of legislation enacted or enforced due to animus or hostility to the burdened religious practices or that they indicate some widespread pattern of religious discrimination in this country. Congress' concern was with the incidental burdens imposed, not the object or purpose of the legislation. This lack of support in the legislative record, however, is not RFRA's most serious shortcoming. Judicial deference, in most cases, is based not on the state of the legislative record Congress compiles but "on due regard for the decision of the body constitutionally appointed to decide." As a general matter, it is for Congress to determine the method by which it will reach a decision.

Regardless of the state of the legislative record, RFRA cannot be considered remedial, preventive legislation, if those terms are to have any meaning. RFRA is so out of proportion to a supposed remedial or preventive object that it cannot be understood as responsive to, or designed to prevent, unconstitutional behavior. It appears, instead, to attempt a substantive change in constitutional protections. Preventive measures prohibiting certain types of laws may be appropriate when there is reason to believe that many of the laws affected by the congressional enactment have a significant likelihood of being unconstitutional. . . . Remedial legislation under §5 "should be adapted to the mischief and wrong which the [Fourteenth] [A]mendment was intended to provide against."

RFRA is not so confined. Sweeping coverage ensures its intrusion at every level of government, displacing laws and prohibiting official actions of almost every description and regardless of subject matter. RFRA's restrictions apply to every agency and official of the Federal, State, and local Governments. RFRA applies to all federal and state law, statutory or otherwise, whether adopted before or after its enactment. RFRA has no termination date or termination mechanism. Any law is subject to challenge at any time by any individual who alleges a substantial burden on his or her free exercise of religion.

The reach and scope of RFRA distinguish it from other measures passed under Congress' enforcement power, even in the area of voting rights. In *South Carolina v. Katzenbach*, the challenged provisions were confined to those regions of the country where voting discrimination had been most flagrant and affected a discrete class of state laws, i.e., state voting laws. Furthermore, to ensure that the reach of the Voting Rights Act was limited to those cases in which constitutional violations were most likely (in order to reduce the possibility of overbreadth), the coverage under the Act would terminate "at the behest of States and political subdivisions in which the danger of substantial voting discrimination has not materialized during the preceding five years." The provisions restricting and banning literacy tests, upheld in *Katzenbach v. Morgan* (1966) and *Oregon v. Mitchell* (1970) attacked a particular type of voting qualification, one with a long history as a "notorious means to deny and abridge voting rights on racial grounds." . . .

The stringent test RFRA demands of state laws reflects a lack of proportionality or congruence between the means adopted and the legitimate end to be achieved. If an objector can show a substantial burden on his free exercise, the State must demonstrate a compelling governmental interest and show that the law is the least restrictive means of furthering its interest. Claims that a law substantially burdens someone's exercise of religion will often be difficult to contest. . . . Requiring a State to demonstrate a compelling interest and show that it has adopted the least restrictive means of achieving that interest is the most demanding test known to constitutional law. . . . Laws valid under *Smith* would fall under RFRA without regard to whether they had the object of stifling or punishing free exercise. We make these observations not to reargue the position of the majority in *Smith* but to illustrate the substantive alteration of its holding attempted by RFRA. Even assuming RFRA would be interpreted in effect to mandate some lesser test, say one equivalent to intermediate scrutiny, the statute nevertheless would require searching judicial scrutiny of state law with the attendant likelihood of invalidation. This is a considerable congressional intrusion into the States' traditional prerogatives and general authority to regulate for the health and welfare of their citizens.

The substantial costs RFRA exacts, both in practical terms of imposing a heavy litigation burden on the States and in terms of curtailing their traditional general regulatory power, far exceed any pattern or practice of unconstitutional conduct under the Free Exercise Clause as interpreted in *Smith*. Simply put, RFRA is not designed to identify and counteract state laws likely to be unconstitutional because of their treatment of religion. In most cases, the state laws to which RFRA applies are not ones which will have been motivated by religious bigotry. If a state law disproportionately burdened a particular class of religious observers, this circumstance might be evidence of an impermissible legislative motive. RFRA's substantial burden test, however, is not even a discriminatory effects or disparate impact test. It is a reality of the modern regulatory state that numerous state laws, such as the zoning regulations at issue here, impose a substantial burden on a large class of individuals. When the exercise of religion has been burdened in an incidental way by a law of general application, it does not follow that the persons affected have been burdened any more than other citizens, let alone burdened because of their religious beliefs. In addition, the Act imposes in every case a least restrictive means requirement—a requirement that was not used in the pre-*Smith* jurisprudence RFRA purported to codify—which also indicates that the legislation is broader than is appropriate if the goal is to prevent and remedy constitutional violations.

When Congress acts within its sphere of power and responsibilities, it has not just the right but the duty to make its own informed judgment on the meaning and force of the Constitution. This has been clear from the early days of the Republic. In 1789, when a Member of the House of Representatives objected to a debate on the constitutionality of legislation based on the theory that "it would be officious" to consider the constitutionality of a measure that did not affect the House, James Madison explained that "it is incontrovertibly of as much importance to this branch of the Government as to any other, that the constitution should be preserved entire. It is our duty." Were it otherwise, we would not afford Congress the presumption of validity its enactments now enjoy.

Our national experience teaches that the Constitution is preserved best when each part of the government respects both the Constitution and the proper actions and determinations of the other branches. When the Court has interpreted the Constitution, it has acted within the province of the Judicial Branch, which embraces the duty to say what the law is. When the political branches of the Government act against the background of a judicial interpretation of the Constitution already issued, it must be understood that in later cases and controversies the Court will treat its precedents with the respect due them under settled principles, including *stare decisis*, and contrary expectations must be disappointed. RFRA was designed to control cases and controversies, such as the one before us; but as the provisions of the federal statute here invoked are beyond congressional authority, it is this Court's precedent, not RFRA, which must control.

* * *

It is for Congress in the first instance to "determin[e] whether and what legislation is needed to secure the guarantees of the Fourteenth Amendment," and its conclusions are entitled to much deference. Congress' discretion is not unlimited, however, and the courts retain the power, as they have since *Marbury v. Madison* [1803], to determine if Congress has exceeded its authority under the Constitution. Broad as the power of Congress is under the Enforcement Clause of the Fourteenth Amendment, RFRA contradicts vital principles necessary to maintain separation of powers and the federal balance. The judgment of the Court of Appeals sustaining the Act's constitutionality is reversed.

It is so ordered.

JUSTICE STEVENS, concurring.

In my opinion, the Religious Freedom Restoration Act of 1993 (RFRA) is a "law respecting an establishment of religion" that violates the First Amendment to the Constitution.

If the historic landmark on the hill in Boerne happened to be a museum or an art gallery owned by an atheist, it would not be eligible for an exemption from the city ordinances that forbid an enlargement of the structure. Because the landmark is owned by the Catholic Church, it is claimed that RFRA gives its owner a federal statutory entitlement to an exemption from a generally applicable, neutral civil law. Whether the Church would actually prevail under the statute or not, the statute has provided the Church with a legal weapon that no atheist or agnostic can obtain. This governmental preference for religion, as opposed to irreligion, is forbidden by the First Amendment.

JUSTICE SCALIA, with whom JUSTICE STEVENS joins, concurring in part.

I write to respond briefly to the claim of JUSTICE O'CONNOR's dissent (hereinafter "the dissent") that historical materials support a result contrary to the one reached in *Employment Div., Dept. of Human Resources of Ore. v. Smith* (1990). . . . The material that the dissent claims is at odds with *Smith* either has little to say about the issue or is in fact more consistent with *Smith* than with the dissent's interpretation of the Free Exercise Clause. . . .

It seems to me that the most telling point made by the dissent is to be found, not in what it says, but in what it fails to say. Had the understanding in the period surrounding the ratification of the Bill of Rights been that the various forms of accommodation discussed by the dissent were constitutionally required (either by State Constitutions or by the Federal Constitution), it would be surprising not to find a single state or federal case refusing to enforce a generally applicable statute because of its failure to make accommodation. Yet the dissent cites none—and to my knowledge, and to the knowledge of the academic defenders of the dissent's position, none exists. . . .

. . . The dissent's approach has, of course, great popular attraction. Who can possibly be against the abstract proposition that government should not, even in its general, nondiscriminatory laws, place unreasonable burdens upon religious practice? Unfortunately, however, that abstract proposition must ultimately be reduced to concrete cases. The issue presented by *Smith* is, quite simply, whether the people, through their elected representatives, or rather this Court, shall control the outcome of those concrete cases. For example, shall it be the determination of this Court, or rather of the people, whether (as the dissent apparently believes) church construction will be exempt from zoning laws? The historical evidence put forward by the dissent does nothing to undermine the conclusion we reached in *Smith*: It shall be the people.

JUSTICE O'CONNOR, with whom JUSTICE BREYER joins except as to a portion of Part I, dissenting.

I dissent from the Court's disposition of this case. I agree with the Court that the issue before us is whether the Religious Freedom Restoration Act (RFRA) is a proper exercise of Congress' power to enforce §5 of the Fourteenth Amendment. But as a yardstick for measuring the constitutionality of RFRA, the Court uses its holding in *Employment Div., Dept. of Human Resources of Ore. v. Smith* (1990), the decision that prompted Congress to enact RFRA as a means of more rigorously enforcing the Free Exercise Clause. I remain of the view that *Smith* was wrongly decided, and I would use this case to reexamine the Court's holding there. Therefore, I would direct the parties to brief the question whether *Smith* represents the correct understanding of the Free Exercise Clause and set the case for reargument. If the Court were to correct the misinterpretation of the Free Exercise Clause set forth in *Smith*, it would simultaneously put our First Amendment jurisprudence back on course and allay the legitimate concerns of a majority in Congress who believed that *Smith* improperly restricted religious liberty. We would then be in a position to review RFRA in light of a proper interpretation of the Free Exercise Clause.

I

I agree with much of the reasoning set forth in Part III-A of the Court's opinion. Indeed, if I agreed with the Court's standard in *Smith*, I would join the opinion. As the Court's careful and thorough historical analysis shows, Congress lacks the "power to decree the substance of the Fourteenth Amendment's restrictions on the States." Rather, its power under §5 of the Fourteenth Amendment extends only to enforcing the Amendment's provisions. In short, Congress lacks the ability independently to define or expand the scope of constitutional rights by statute. Accordingly, whether Congress has exceeded its §5 powers turns on whether there is a "congruence and proportionality between the injury to be prevented or remedied and the means adopted to that end." This recognition does not, of course, in any way diminish Congress' obligation to draw its own conclusions regarding the Constitution's meaning. Congress, no less than this Court, is called upon to consider the requirements of the Constitution and to act in accordance with its dictates. But when it enacts legislation in furtherance of its delegated powers, Congress must make its judgments consistent with this Court's exposition of the Constitution and with the limits placed on its legislative authority by provisions such as the Fourteenth Amendment.

The Court's analysis of whether RFRA is a constitutional exercise of Congress' §5 power, set forth in Part III-B of its opinion, is premised on the assumption that *Smith* correctly interprets the Free Exercise Clause. This is an assumption that I do not accept. I continue to believe that *Smith* adopted an improper standard for deciding free exercise claims. In *Smith*, five Members of this Court—without briefing or argument on the issue—interpreted the Free Exercise Clause to permit the government to prohibit, without justification, conduct mandated by an individual's religious beliefs, so long as the prohibition is generally applicable. Contrary to the Court's holding in that case, however, the Free Exercise Clause is not simply an antidiscrimination principle that protects only against those laws that single out religious practice for unfavorable treatment. Rather, the Clause is best understood as an affirmative guarantee of the right to participate in religious practices and conduct without impermissible governmental interference, even when such conduct conflicts with a neutral, generally applicable law. Before *Smith*, our free exercise cases were generally in keeping with this idea: where a law substantially burdened religiously motivated conduct—regardless whether it was specifically targeted at religion or applied generally—we required government to justify that law with a compelling state interest and to use means narrowly tailored to achieve that interest. [Citation of cases omitted.]

The Court's rejection of this principle in *Smith* is supported neither by precedent nor, as discussed below, by history. The decision has harmed religious liberty. For example, a Federal District Court, in reliance on *Smith*, ruled that the Free Exercise Clause was not implicated where Hmong natives objected on religious grounds to their son's autopsy, conducted pursuant to a generally applicable state law. The Court of Appeals for the Eighth Circuit held that application of a city's zoning laws to prevent a church from conducting services in an area zoned for commercial uses raised no free exercise concerns, even though the city permitted secular not-for-profit organizations in that area. [Citation of other cases omitted.] These cases demonstrate that lower courts applying *Smith* no longer find necessary a searching judicial inquiry into the possibility of reasonably accommodating religious practice.

Stare decisis concerns should not prevent us from revisiting our holding in *Smith*. . . . I believe that, in light of both our precedent and our Nation's tradition of religious liberty, *Smith* is demonstrably wrong. Moreover, it is a recent decision. As such, it has not engendered the kind of reliance on its continued application that would militate against overruling it.

Accordingly, I believe that we should reexamine our holding in *Smith*, and do so in this very case. In its place, I would return to a rule that requires government to justify any substantial burden on religiously motivated conduct by a compelling state interest and to impose that burden only by means narrowly tailored to achieve that interest.

II

I shall not restate what has been said in other opinions, which have demonstrated that *Smith* is gravely at odds with our earlier free exercise precedents. . . . Rather, I examine here the early American tradition of religious free exercise to gain insight into the original understanding of the Free Exercise Clause—an inquiry the Court in *Smith* did not undertake. We have previously recognized the importance of interpreting the Religion Clauses in light of their history. . . .

The historical evidence casts doubt on the Court's current interpretation of the Free Exercise Clause. The record instead reveals that its drafters and ratifiers more likely viewed the Free Exercise Clause as a guarantee that government may not unnecessarily hinder believers from freely practicing their religion, a position consistent with our pre-*Smith* jurisprudence.

[O'Connor marshaled evidence from the history of the adoption of the First Amendment, colonial charters and state constitutions, and the practices of the colonies and early states to contend that the principle of religious "free exercise" was understood to mean that "government should, when possible, accommodate religious practice." She concluded by quoting writings from some of the early leaders, including George Washington, Thomas Jefferson, and James Madison:]

. . . Obviously, since these thinkers approached the issue of religious freedom somewhat differently, it is not possible to distill their thoughts into one tidy formula. Nevertheless, a few general principles may be discerned. Foremost, these early leaders accorded religious exercise a special constitutional status. The right to free exercise was a substantive guarantee of individual liberty, no less important than the right to free speech or the right to just compensation for the taking of property. . . .

Second, all agreed that government interference in religious practice was not to be lightly countenanced. Finally, all shared the conviction that "'true religion and good morals are the only solid foundation of public liberty and happiness.'". . . To give meaning to these ideas—particularly in a society characterized by religious pluralism and pervasive regulation—there will be times when the Constitution requires government to accommodate the needs of those citizens whose religious practices conflict with generally applicable law.

III

The Religion Clauses of the Constitution represent a profound commitment to religious liberty. Our Nation's Founders conceived of a Republic receptive to voluntary religious expression, not of a secular society in which religious expression is tolerated only when it does not conflict with a generally applicable law. As the historical sources discussed above show, the Free Exercise Clause is properly understood as an affirmative guarantee of the right to participate in religious activities without impermissible governmental interference, even where a believer's conduct is in tension with a law of general application. Certainly, it is in no way anomalous to accord heightened protection to a right identified in the text of the First Amendment. For example, it has long been the Court's position that freedom of speech—a right enumerated only a few words after the right to free exercise—has special constitutional status. Given the centrality of freedom of speech and religion to the American concept of personal liberty, it is altogether reasonable to conclude that both should be treated with the highest degree of respect.

Although it may provide a bright line, the rule the Court declared in *Smith* does not faithfully serve the purpose of the Constitution. Accordingly, I believe that it is essential for the Court to reconsider its holding in *Smith*—and to do so in this very case. I would therefore direct the parties to brief this issue and set the case for reargument.

I respectfully dissent from the Court's disposition of this case.

JUSTICE SOUTER, dissenting.

To decide whether the Fourteenth Amendment gives Congress sufficient power to enact the Religious Freedom Restoration Act, the Court measures the legislation against the free-exercise standard of *Employment Div., Dept. of Human Resources of Ore. v. Smith* (1990). For the reasons stated in my opinion in *Church of Lukumi Babalu Aye, Inc. v. Hialeah* (1993) (opinion concurring in part and concurring in judgment), I have serious doubts about the precedential value of the *Smith* rule and its entitlement to adherence. These doubts are intensified today by the historical arguments going to the original understanding of the Free Exercise Clause presented in JUSTICE O'CONNOR's opinion. . . . But without briefing and argument on the merits of that rule (which this Court has never had in any case, including *Smith* itself), I am not now prepared to join JUSTICE O'CONNOR in rejecting it or the majority in assuming it to be correct. In order to provide full adversarial consideration, this case should be set down for reargument permitting plenary reexamination of the issue. Since the Court declines to follow that course, our free-exercise law remains marked by an "intolerable tension," and the constitutionality of the Act of Congress to enforce the free-exercise right cannot now be soundly decided. I would therefore dismiss the writ of certiorari as improvidently granted, and I accordingly dissent from the Court's disposition of this case.

JUSTICE BREYER, dissenting.

I agree with JUSTICE O'CONNOR that the Court should direct the parties to brief the question whether *Employment Div., Dept. of Human Resources of Ore. v. Smith* (1990) was correctly decided, and set this case for reargument. I do not, however, find it necessary to consider the question whether, assuming *Smith* is correct, §5 of the Fourteenth Amendment would authorize Congress to enact the legislation before us. Thus, while I agree with some of the views expressed in the first paragraph of Part I of JUSTICE O'CONNOR's dissent, I do not necessarily agree with all of them. I therefore join JUSTICE O'CONNOR's dissent, with the exception of the first paragraph of Part I.

□□□

No. 96-511

Janet Reno, Attorney General of the United States, et al., Appellants v. American Civil Liberties Union et al.

On appeal from the United States District Court
for the Eastern District of Pennsylvania

[June 26, 1997]

JUSTICE STEVENS delivered the opinion of the Court.

At issue is the constitutionality of two statutory provisions enacted to protect minors from "indecent" and "patently offensive" communications on the Internet. Notwithstanding the legitimacy and importance of the congressional goal of protecting children from harmful materials, we agree with the three-judge District Court that the statute abridges "the freedom of speech" protected by the First Amendment.

I

The District Court made extensive findings of fact, most of which were based on a detailed stipulation prepared by the parties. (1996). The findings describe the character and the dimensions of the Internet, the availability of sexually explicit material in that medium, and the problems confronting age verification for recipients of Internet communications. Because those findings provide the underpinnings for the legal issues, we begin with a summary of the undisputed facts.

The Internet

The Internet is an international network of interconnected computers. It is the outgrowth of what began in 1969 as a military program called "ARPANET" [acronym for network developed by Advanced Research Project Agency], which was designed to enable computers operated by the military, defense contractors, and universities conducting defense-related research to communicate with one another by redundant channels even if some portions of the network were damaged in a war. While the ARPANET no longer exists, it provided an example for the development of a number of civilian networks that, eventually linking with each other, now enable tens of millions of people to communicate with one another and to access vast amounts of information from around the world. The Internet is "a unique and wholly new medium of worldwide human communication."

The Internet has experienced "extraordinary growth." The number of "host" computers—those that store information and relay communications—increased from about 300 in 1981 to approximately 9,400,000 by the time of the trial in 1996. Roughly 60% of these hosts are located in the United States. About 40 million people used the Internet at the time of trial, a number that is expected to mushroom to 200 million by 1999.

Individuals can obtain access to the Internet from many different sources, generally hosts themselves or entities with a host affiliation. Most colleges and universities provide access for their students and faculty; many corporations provide their employees with access through an office network; many communities and local libraries provide free access; and an increasing number of storefront "computer coffee shops" provide access for a small hourly fee. Several major national "online services" such as America Online, CompuServe, the Microsoft Network, and Prodigy offer access to their own extensive proprietary networks as well as a link to the much larger resources of the Internet. These commercial online services had almost 12 million individual subscribers at the time of trial.

Anyone with access to the Internet may take advantage of a wide variety of communication and information retrieval methods. These methods are constantly evolving and difficult to categorize precisely. But, as presently constituted, those most relevant to this case are electronic mail ("e-mail"), automatic mailing list services ("mail exploders," sometimes referred to as "listservs"), "newsgroups," "chat rooms," and the "World Wide Web." All of these methods can be used to transmit text; most can transmit sound, pictures, and moving video images. Taken together, these tools constitute a unique medium—known to its users as "cyberspace"—located in no particular geographical location but available to anyone, anywhere in the world, with access to the Internet.

E-mail enables an individual to send an electronic message—generally akin to a note or letter—to another individual or to a group of addressees. The message is generally stored electronically, sometimes waiting for the recipient to check her "mailbox" and sometimes making its receipt known through some type of prompt. A mail exploder is a sort of e-mail group. Subscribers can send messages to a common e-mail address, which then forwards the message to the group's other subscribers. Newsgroups also serve groups of regular participants, but these postings may be read by others as well. There are thousands of such groups, each serving to foster an exchange of information or opinion on a particular topic running the gamut from, say, the music of Wagner to Balkan politics to AIDS prevention to the Chicago Bulls. About 100,000 new messages are posted every day. In most newsgroups, postings are automatically purged at regular intervals. In addition to posting a message that can be read later, two or more individuals wishing to communicate more immediately can enter a chat room to engage in real-time dialogue—in other words, by typing messages to one another that appear almost immediately on the others' computer screens. The District Court found that at any given time "tens of thousands of users are engaging in conversations on a huge range of subjects." It is "no exaggeration to conclude that the content on the Internet is as diverse as human thought."

The best known category of communication over the Internet is the World Wide Web, which allows users to search for and retrieve information stored in remote computers, as well as, in some cases, to communicate back to designated sites. In concrete terms, the Web consists of a vast number of documents stored in different computers all over the world. Some of these documents are simply files containing information. However, more elaborate documents, commonly known as Web "pages," are also prevalent. Each has its own address—"rather like a telephone number." Web pages frequently contain information and sometimes allow the viewer to communicate with the page's (or "site's") author. They generally also contain "links" to other documents created by that site's author or to other (generally) related sites. Typically, the links are either blue or underlined text—sometimes images.

Navigating the Web is relatively straightforward. A user may either type the address of a known page or enter one or more keywords into a commercial "search engine" in an effort to locate sites on a subject of interest. A particular Web page may contain the information sought by the "surfer," or, through its links, it may be an avenue to other documents located anywhere on the Internet. Users generally explore a given Web page, or move to another, by clicking a computer "mouse" on one of the page's icons or links. Access to most Web pages is freely available, but some allow access only to those who have purchased the right from a commercial provider. The Web is thus comparable, from the readers' viewpoint, to both a vast library including millions of readily available and indexed publications and a sprawling mall offering goods and services.

From the publishers' point of view, it constitutes a vast platform from which to address and hear from a world-wide audience of millions of readers, viewers, researchers, and buyers. Any person or organization with a computer connected to the Internet can "publish" information. Publishers include government agencies, educational institutions, commercial entities, advocacy groups, and individuals. Publishers may either make their material available to the entire pool of Internet users, or confine access to a selected group, such as those willing to pay for the privilege. "No single organization controls any membership in the Web, nor is there any centralized point from which individual Web sites or services can be blocked from the Web."

Sexually Explicit Material

Sexually explicit material on the Internet includes text, pictures, and chat and "extends from the modestly titillating to the hardest-core." These files are created, named, and posted in the same manner as material that is not sexually explicit, and may be accessed either deliberately or unintentionally during the course of an imprecise search. "Once a provider posts its content on the Internet, it cannot prevent that content from entering any community." Thus, for example,

> "when the UCR/California Museum of Photography posts to its Web site nudes by Edward Weston and Robert Mapplethorpe to announce that its new exhibit will travel to Baltimore and New York City, those images are available not only in Los Angeles, Baltimore, and New York City, but also in Cincinnati, Mobile, or Beijing—wherever Internet users live. Similarly, the safer sex instructions that Critical Path posts to its Web site, written in street language so that the teenage receiver can understand them, are available not just in Philadelphia, but also in Provo and Prague." [Quoting from Findings of Fact.]

Some of the communications over the Internet that originate in foreign countries are also sexually explicit.

Though such material is widely available, users seldom encounter such content accidentally. ". . . Almost all sexually explicit images are preceded by warnings as to the content." For that reason, the "odds are slim" that a user would enter a sexually explicit site by accident. Unlike communications received by radio or television, "the receipt of information on the Internet requires a series of affirmative steps more deliberate and directed than merely turning a dial. A child requires some sophistication and some ability to read to retrieve material and thereby to use the Internet unattended."

Systems have been developed to help parents control the material that may be available on a home computer with Internet access. A system may either limit a computer's access to an approved list of sources that have been identified as containing no adult material, it may block designated inappropriate sites, or it may attempt to block messages containing identifiable objectionable features. "Although parental control software currently can screen for certain suggestive words or for known sexually explicit sites, it cannot now screen for sexually explicit images." Nevertheless, the evidence indicates that "a reasonably effective method by which parents can prevent their children from accessing sexually explicit and other material which parents may believe is inappropriate for their children will soon be available."

Age Verification

The problem of age verification differs for different uses of the Internet. The District Court categorically determined that there "is no effective way to determine the identity or the age of a user who is accessing material through e-mail, mail exploders, newsgroups or chat rooms." The Government offered no evidence that there was a reliable way to screen recipients and participants in such fora for age. Moreover, even if it were technologically feasible to block minors' access to newsgroups and chat rooms containing discussions of art, politics or other subjects that potentially elicit "indecent" or "patently offensive" contributions, it would not be possible to block their access to that material and "still allow them access to the remaining content, even if the overwhelming majority of that content was not indecent."

Technology exists by which an operator of a Web site may condition access on the verification of requested information such as a credit card number or an adult password. Credit card verification is only feasible, however, either in connection with a commercial transaction in which the card is used, or by payment to a verification agency. Using credit card possession as a surrogate for proof of age would impose costs on noncommercial Web sites that would require many of them to shut down. For that reason, at the time of the trial, credit card verification was "effectively unavailable to a substantial number of Internet content providers." Moreover, the imposition of such a requirement "would completely bar adults who do not have a credit card and lack the resources to obtain one from accessing any blocked material."

Commercial pornographic sites that charge their users for access have assigned them passwords as a method of age verification. The record does not contain any evidence concerning the reliability of these technologies. Even if passwords are effective for commercial purveyors of indecent material, the District Court found that an adult password requirement would impose significant burdens on noncommercial sites, both because they would discourage users from accessing their sites and because the cost of creating and maintaining such screening systems would be "beyond their reach."

. . . .

In sum, the District Court found:

"Even if credit card verification or adult password verification were implemented, the Government presented no testimony as to how such systems could ensure that the user of the password or credit card is in fact over 18. The burdens imposed by credit card verification and adult password verification systems make them effectively unavailable to a substantial number of Internet content providers."

II

The Telecommunications Act of 1996 was an unusually important legislative enactment. . . . [I]ts primary purpose was to reduce regulation and encourage "the rapid deployment of new telecommunications technologies." The major components of the statute have nothing to do with the Internet; they were designed to promote competition in the local telephone service market, the multichannel video market, and the market for over-the-air broadcasting. The Act includes seven Titles, six of which are the product of extensive committee hearings and the subject of discussion in Reports prepared by Committees of the Senate and the House of Representatives. By contrast, Title V—known as the "Communications Decency Act of 1996" (CDA)—contains provisions that were either added in executive committee after the hearings were concluded or as amendments offered during floor debate on the legislation. An amendment offered in the Senate was the source of the two statutory provisions challenged in this case. They are informally described as the "indecent transmission" provision and the "patently offensive display" provision.

The first, 47 U. S. C. A. §223(a), prohibits the knowing transmission of obscene or indecent messages to any recipient under 18 years of age. It provides in pertinent part:

> "(a) Whoever—
> "(1) in interstate or foreign communications—
>
> . . . .
>
> "(B) by means of a telecommunications device knowingly—
> "(i) makes, creates, or solicits, and
> "(ii) initiates the transmission of,
> "any comment, request, suggestion, proposal, image, or other communication which is obscene or indecent, knowing that the recipient of the communication is under 18 years of age, regardless of whether the maker of such communication placed the call or initiated the communication;
>
> . . . .
>
> "(2) knowingly permits any telecommunications facility under his control to be used for any activity prohibited by paragraph (1) with the intent that it be used for such activity, "shall be fined under Title 18, or imprisoned not more than two years, or both."

The second provision, §223(d), prohibits the knowing sending or displaying of patently offensive messages in a manner that is available to a person under 18 years of age. It provides:

> "(d) Whoever—
> "(1) in interstate or foreign communications knowingly—
> "(A) uses an interactive computer service to send to a specific person or persons under 18 years of age, or
> "(B) uses any interactive computer service to display in a manner available to a person under 18 years of age,
> "any comment, request, suggestion, proposal, image, or other communication that, in context, depicts or describes, in terms patently offensive as measured by contemporary community standards, sexual

or excretory activities or organs, regardless of whether the user of
such service placed the call or initiated the communication; or

"(2) knowingly permits any telecommunications facility under such
person's control to be used for an activity prohibited by paragraph (1)
with the intent that it be used for such activity, "shall be fined under Title
18, or imprisoned not more than two years, or both."

The breadth of these prohibitions is qualified by two affirmative defenses. One
covers those who take "good faith, reasonable, effective, and appropriate actions" to
restrict access by minors to the prohibited communications. §223(e)(5)(A). The
other covers those who restrict access to covered material by requiring certain designated forms of age proof, such as a verified credit card or an adult identification
number or code. §223(e)(5)(B).

III

On February 8, 1996, immediately after the President signed the statute, 20
plaintiffs filed suit against the Attorney General of the United States and the Department of Justice challenging the constitutionality of §§223(a)(1) and 223(d). A
week later, based on his conclusion that the term "indecent" was too vague to provide the basis for a criminal prosecution, District Judge Buckwalter entered a temporary restraining order against enforcement of §223(a)(1)(B)(ii) insofar as it applies
to indecent communications. A second suit was then filed by 27 additional plaintiffs, the two cases were consolidated, and a three-judge District Court was convened
pursuant to §561 of the Act. After an evidentiary hearing, that Court entered a
preliminary injunction against enforcement of both of the challenged provisions.
Each of the three judges wrote a separate opinion, but their judgment was unanimous. [Summary of opinions omitted.]

The judgment of the District Court enjoins the Government from enforcing
the prohibitions in §223(a)(1)(B) insofar as they relate to "indecent" communications, but expressly preserves the Government's right to investigate and prosecute
the obscenity or child pornography activities prohibited therein. The injunction
against enforcement of §§223(d)(1) and (2) is unqualified because those provisions contain no separate reference to obscenity or child pornography.

The Government appealed under the Act's special review provisions, §561,
and we noted probable jurisdiction (1996). In its appeal, the Government argues
that the District Court erred in holding that the CDA violated both the First Amendment because it is overbroad and the Fifth Amendment because it is vague. While
we discuss the vagueness of the CDA because of its relevance to the First Amendment overbreadth inquiry, we conclude that the judgment should be affirmed without reaching the Fifth Amendment issue. We begin our analysis by reviewing the
principal authorities on which the Government relies. Then, after describing the
overbreadth of the CDA, we consider the Government's specific contentions, including its submission that we save portions of the statute either by severance or by
fashioning judicial limitations on the scope of its coverage.

IV

In arguing for reversal, the Government contends that the CDA is plainly constitutional under three of our prior decisions: (1) *Ginsberg v. New York* (1968); (2)

FCC v. Pacifica Foundation (1978); and (3) *Renton v. Playtime Theatres, Inc.* (1986). A close look at these cases, however, raises—rather than relieves—doubts concerning the constitutionality of the CDA.

[Stevens summarized and analyzed the three decisions. In *Ginsberg*, he said, the Court upheld the constitutionality of a New York statute that prohibited selling to minors under 17 years of age material that was considered obscene as to them even if not obscene as to adults. Stevens said the New York law was narrower than the CDA in four respects: it did not bar parents from purchasing the materials for their children if they wished; it applied only to commercial transactions; it applied only to material that was "utterly without redeeming social importance for minors"; and it applied only to persons under the age of seventeen, not eighteen, as the CDA provides.

[In *Pacifica*, Stevens continued, the Court upheld a declaratory order of the Federal Communications Commission, holding that the broadcast of a recording of a 12-minute monologue entitled "Filthy Words" that had previously been delivered to a live audience "could have been the subject of administrative sanctions." He noted several distinctions between that order and the CDA—including the facts that the CDA is "punitive," permitting a criminal prosecution; and that broadcasting had traditionally received "the most limited First Amendment protection."

[Finally, Stevens said that in *Renton* the Court upheld a zoning ordinance that kept adult movie theatres out of residential neighborhoods because of the "secondary effects," such as crime and deteriorating property values. By contrast, he said, the CDA "applies broadly to the entire universe of cyberspace." And the purpose of the CDA, he added, was to "protect children from the primary effects of 'indecent' and 'patently offensive' speech, rather than any 'secondary' effect of such speech."]

These precedents, then, surely do not require us to uphold the CDA and are fully consistent with the application of the most stringent review of its provisions.

V

. . . [S]ome of our cases have recognized special justifications for regulation of the broadcast media that are not applicable to other speakers. In these cases, the Court relied on the history of extensive government regulation of the broadcast medium; the scarcity of available frequencies at its inception; and its "invasive" nature.

Those factors are not present in cyberspace. Neither before nor after the enactment of the CDA have the vast democratic fora of the Internet been subject to the type of government supervision and regulation that has attended the broadcast industry. Moreover, the Internet is not as "invasive" as radio or television. The District Court specifically found that "[c]ommunications over the Internet do not 'invade' an individual's home or appear on one's computer screen unbidden. Users seldom encounter content 'by accident.'" It also found that "[a]lmost all sexually explicit images are preceded by warnings as to the content," and cited testimony that " 'odds are slim' that a user would come across a sexually explicit sight by accident." . . .

Finally, unlike the conditions that prevailed when Congress first authorized regulation of the broadcast spectrum, the Internet can hardly be considered a "scarce" expressive commodity. It provides relatively unlimited, low-cost capacity for communication of all kinds. The Government estimates that "[a]s many as 40 million people use the Internet today, and that figure is expected to grow to 200 million by

1999." This dynamic, multifaceted category of communication includes not only traditional print and news services, but also audio, video, and still images, as well as interactive, real-time dialogue. Through the use of chat rooms, any person with a phone line can become a town crier with a voice that resonates farther than it could from any soapbox. Through the use of Web pages, mail exploders, and newsgroups, the same individual can become a pamphleteer. As the District Court found, "the content on the Internet is as diverse as human thought." We agree with its conclusion that our cases provide no basis for qualifying the level of First Amendment scrutiny that should be applied to this medium.

VI

Regardless of whether the CDA is so vague that it violates the Fifth Amendment, the many ambiguities concerning the scope of its coverage render it problematic for purposes of the First Amendment. For instance, each of the two parts of the CDA uses a different linguistic form. The first uses the word "indecent," 47 U. S. C. A. §223(a), while the second speaks of material that "in context, depicts or describes, in terms patently offensive as measured by contemporary community standards, sexual or excretory activities or organs," §223(d). Given the absence of a definition of either term, this difference in language will provoke uncertainty among speakers about how the two standards relate to each other and just what they mean. Could a speaker confidently assume that a serious discussion about birth control practices, homosexuality, the First Amendment issues raised by the Appendix to our *Pacifica* opinion, or the consequences of prison rape would not violate the CDA? This uncertainty undermines the likelihood that the CDA has been carefully tailored to the congressional goal of protecting minors from potentially harmful materials.

The vagueness of the CDA is a matter of special concern for two reasons. First, the CDA is a content-based regulation of speech. The vagueness of such a regulation raises special First Amendment concerns because of its obvious chilling effect on free speech. Second, the CDA is a criminal statute. In addition to the opprobrium and stigma of a criminal conviction, the CDA threatens violators with penalties including up to two years in prison for each act of violation. The severity of criminal sanctions may well cause speakers to remain silent rather than communicate even arguably unlawful words, ideas, and images. . . .

The Government argues that the statute is no more vague than the obscenity standard this Court established in *Miller v. California* (1973). But that is not so. [Stevens stated and analyzed the three-part definition of obscenity established in *Miller*: a work, taken as a whole, appeals to the prurient interest; depicts sexual conduct in a patently offensive way; and lacks "serious literary, artistic, political, or scientific value." Stevens said the CDA provision was broader, in particular because it did not include the "societal value" requirement.]

In contrast to *Miller* and our other previous cases, the CDA . . . presents a greater threat of censoring speech that, in fact, falls outside the statute's scope. Given the vague contours of the coverage of the statute, it unquestionably silences some speakers whose messages would be entitled to constitutional protection. That danger provides further reason for insisting that the statute not be overly broad. The CDA's burden on protected speech cannot be justified if it could be avoided by a more carefully drafted statute.

VII

We are persuaded that the CDA lacks the precision that the First Amendment requires when a statute regulates the content of speech. In order to deny minors access to potentially harmful speech, the CDA effectively suppresses a large amount of speech that adults have a constitutional right to receive and to address to one another. That burden on adult speech is unacceptable if less restrictive alternatives would be at least as effective in achieving the legitimate purpose that the statute was enacted to serve.

In evaluating the free speech rights of adults, we have made it perfectly clear that "[s]exual expression which is indecent but not obscene is protected by the First Amendment." *Sable* [*Communications of Cal., Inc. v. FCC* (1989)]. . . .

It is true that we have repeatedly recognized the governmental interest in protecting children from harmful materials. But that interest does not justify an unnecessarily broad suppression of speech addressed to adults. . . .

The District Court was correct to conclude that the CDA effectively resembles the ban on "dial-a-porn" invalidated in *Sable*. In *Sable*, this Court rejected the argument that we should defer to the congressional judgment that nothing less than a total ban would be effective in preventing enterprising youngsters from gaining access to indecent communications. *Sable* thus made clear that the mere fact that a statutory regulation of speech was enacted for the important purpose of protecting children from exposure to sexually explicit material does not foreclose inquiry into its validity. . . .

In arguing that the CDA does not so diminish adult communication, the Government relies on the incorrect factual premise that prohibiting a transmission whenever it is known that one of its recipients is a minor would not interfere with adult-to-adult communication. The findings of the District Court make clear that this premise is untenable. Given the size of the potential audience for most messages, in the absence of a viable age verification process, the sender must be charged with knowing that one or more minors will likely view it. Knowledge that, for instance, one or more members of a 100-person chat group will be minor—and therefore that it would be a crime to send the group an indecent message—would surely burden communication among adults.

The District Court found that at the time of trial existing technology did not include any effective method for a sender to prevent minors from obtaining access to its communications on the Internet without also denying access to adults. The Court found no effective way to determine the age of a user who is accessing material through e-mail, mail exploders, newsgroups, or chat rooms. As a practical matter, the Court also found that it would be prohibitively expensive for noncommercial—as well as some commercial—speakers who have Web sites to verify that their users are adults. These limitations must inevitably curtail a significant amount of adult communication on the Internet. By contrast, the District Court found that "[d]espite its limitations, currently available *user-based* software suggests that a reasonably effective method by which *parents* can prevent their children from accessing sexually explicit and other material which *parents* may believe is inappropriate for their children will soon be widely available" (emphases added).

The breadth of the CDA's coverage is wholly unprecedented. Unlike the regulations upheld in *Ginsberg* and *Pacifica*, the scope of the CDA is not limited to commercial speech or commercial entities. Its open-ended prohibitions embrace all nonprofit entities and individuals posting indecent messages or displaying them on their own computers in the presence of minors. The general, undefined terms "indecent" and "patently offensive" cover large amounts of nonpornographic material with serious educational or other value. Moreover, the "community standards" criterion as applied to the Internet means that any communication available to a nationwide audience will be judged by the standards of the community most likely to be offended by the message. The regulated subject matter includes any of the seven "dirty words" used in the Pacifica monologue, the use of which the Government's expert acknowledged could constitute a felony. It may also extend to discussions about prison rape or safe sexual practices, artistic images that include nude subjects, and arguably the card catalogue of the Carnegie Library.

For the purposes of our decision, we need neither accept nor reject the Government's submission that the First Amendment does not forbid a blanket prohibition on all "indecent" and "patently offensive" messages communicated to a 17-year-old—no matter how much value the message may contain and regardless of parental approval. It is at least clear that the strength of the Government's interest in protecting minors is not equally strong throughout the coverage of this broad statute. Under the CDA, a parent allowing her 17-year-old to use the family computer to obtain information on the Internet that she, in her parental judgment, deems appropriate could face a lengthy prison term. Similarly, a parent who sent his 17-year-old college freshman information on birth control via e-mail could be incarcerated even though neither he, his child, nor anyone in their home community, found the material "indecent" or "patently offensive," if the college town's community thought otherwise.

The breadth of this content-based restriction of speech imposes an especially heavy burden on the Government to explain why a less restrictive provision would not be as effective as the CDA. It has not done so. The arguments in this Court have referred to possible alternatives such as requiring that indecent material be "tagged" in a way that facilitates parental control of material coming into their homes, making exceptions for messages with artistic or educational value, providing some tolerance for parental choice, and regulating some portions of the Internet—such as commercial web sites—differently than others, such as chat rooms. Particularly in the light of the absence of any detailed findings by the Congress, or even hearings addressing the special problems of the CDA, we are persuaded that the CDA is not narrowly tailored if that requirement has any meaning at all.

VIII

In an attempt to curtail the CDA's facial overbreadth, the Government advances three additional arguments for sustaining the Act's affirmative prohibitions: (1) that the CDA is constitutional because it leaves open ample "alternative channels" of communication; (2) that the plain meaning of the Act's "knowledge" and "specific person" requirement significantly restricts its permissible applications; and (3) that the Act's prohibitions are "almost always" limited to material lacking redeeming social value.

[Stevens rejected all three arguments. He said the government's argument about alternative channels of communication was "immaterial," saying it was "equivalent to arguing that a statute could ban leaflets on certain subjects as long as individuals are free to publish books." The government's argument that the "knowledge" requirement and "specific child" element would limit the scope of the act was "untenable," Stevens continued. "This argument ignores the fact that most Internet fora—including chat rooms, newsgroups, mail exploders, and the Web—are open to all comers," he wrote. Finally, Stevens said there was "no textual support" for the government's argument that the law would not apply to works with redeeming social value.]

IX

The Government's three remaining arguments focus on the defenses provided in §223(e)(5). First, relying on the "good faith, reasonable, effective, and appropriate actions" provision, the Government suggests that "tagging" provides a defense that saves the constitutionality of the Act. The suggestion assumes that transmitters may encode their indecent communications in a way that would indicate their contents, thus permitting recipients to block their reception with appropriate software. It is the requirement that the good faith action must be "effective" that makes this defense illusory. The Government recognizes that its proposed screening software does not currently exist. Even if it did, there is no way to know whether a potential recipient will actually block the encoded material. Without the impossible knowledge that every guardian in America is screening for the "tag," the transmitter could not reasonably rely on its action to be "effective."

For its second and third arguments concerning defenses—which we can consider together—the Government relies on the latter half of §223(e)(5), which applies when the transmitter has restricted access by requiring use of a verified credit card or adult identification. Such verification is not only technologically available but actually is used by commercial providers of sexually explicit material. These providers, therefore, would be protected by the defense. Under the findings of the District Court, however, it is not economically feasible for most noncommercial speakers to employ such verification. Accordingly, this defense would not significantly narrow the statute's burden on noncommercial speech. Even with respect to the commercial pornographers that would be protected by the defense, the Government failed to adduce any evidence that these verification techniques actually preclude minors from posing as adults. . . . The Government thus failed to prove that the proffered defense would significantly reduce the heavy burden on adult speech produced by the prohibition on offensive displays.

We agree with the District Court's conclusion that the CDA places an unacceptably heavy burden on protected speech, and that the defenses do not constitute the sort of "narrow tailoring" that will save an otherwise patently invalid unconstitutional provision. In *Sable*, we remarked that the speech restriction at issue there amounted to " 'burn[ing] the house to roast the pig.' " The CDA, casting a far darker shadow over free speech, threatens to torch a large segment of the Internet community.

X

At oral argument, the Government relied heavily on its ultimate fall-back position: If this Court should conclude that the CDA is insufficiently tailored, it urged, we should save the statute's constitutionality by honoring the severability clause and construing nonseverable terms narrowly. In only one respect is this argument acceptable.

. . . The "indecency" provision applies to "any comment, request, suggestion, proposal, image, or other communication which is *obscene or indecent*" (emphasis added). Appellees do not challenge the application of the statute to obscene speech, which, they acknowledge, can be banned totally because it enjoys no First Amendment protection. . . . Therefore, we will sever the term "or indecent" from the statute, leaving the rest of §223(a) standing. In no other respect, however, can §223(a) or §223(d) be saved by such a textual surgery. . . .

XI

In this Court, though not in the District Court, the Government asserts that—in addition to its interest in protecting children—its "[e]qually significant" interest in fostering the growth of the Internet provides an independent basis for upholding the constitutionality of the CDA. The Government apparently assumes that the unregulated availability of "indecent" and "patently offensive" material on the Internet is driving countless citizens away from the medium because of the risk of exposing themselves or their children to harmful material.

We find this argument singularly unpersuasive. The dramatic expansion of this new marketplace of ideas contradicts the factual basis of this contention. The record demonstrates that the growth of the Internet has been and continues to be phenomenal. As a matter of constitutional tradition, in the absence of evidence to the contrary, we presume that governmental regulation of the content of speech is more likely to interfere with the free exchange of ideas than to encourage it. The interest in encouraging freedom of expression in a democratic society outweighs any theoretical but unproven benefit of censorship.

For the foregoing reasons, the judgment of the district court is affirmed.

It is so ordered.

JUSTICE O'CONNOR, with whom THE CHIEF JUSTICE joins, concurring in the judgment in part and dissenting in part.

I write separately to explain why I view the Communications Decency Act of 1996 (CDA) as little more than an attempt by Congress to create "adult zones" on the Internet. Our precedent indicates that the creation of such zones can be constitutionally sound. Despite the soundness of its purpose, however, portions of the CDA are unconstitutional because they stray from the blueprint our prior cases have developed for constructing a "zoning law" that passes constitutional muster. . . .

I

Our cases make clear that a "zoning" law is valid only if adults are still able to obtain the regulated speech. If they cannot, the law does more than simply keep children away from speech they have no right to obtain—it interferes with the rights of adults to obtain constitutionally protected speech and effectively "reduce[s] the adult population . . . to reading only what is fit for children." *Butler v. Michigan* (1957). The First Amendment does not tolerate such interference. . . .

The Court in *Ginsberg* [*v. New York* (1968)] concluded that the New York law created a constitutionally adequate adult zone simply because, on its face, it denied access only to minors. The Court did not question—and therefore necessarily assumed—that an adult zone, once created, would succeed in preserving adults' access while denying minors' access to the regulated speech. Before today, there was no reason to question this assumption, for the Court has previously only considered laws that operated in the physical world, a world with two characteristics that make it possible to create "adult zones": geography and identity. A minor can see an adult dance show only if he enters an establishment that provides such entertainment. And should he attempt to do so, the minor will not be able to conceal completely his identity (or, consequently, his age). Thus, the twin characteristics of geography and identity enable the establishment's proprietor to prevent children from entering the establishment, but to let adults inside.

The electronic world is fundamentally different. Because it is no more than the interconnection of electronic pathways, cyberspace allows speakers and listeners to mask their identities. Cyberspace undeniably reflects some form of geography; chat rooms and Web sites, for example, exist at fixed "locations" on the Internet. Since users can transmit and receive messages on the Internet without revealing anything about their identities or ages, however, it is not currently possible to exclude persons from accessing certain messages on the basis of their identity.

Cyberspace differs from the physical world in another basic way: Cyberspace is malleable. Thus, it is possible to construct barriers in cyberspace and use them to screen for identity, making cyberspace more like the physical world and, consequently, more amenable to zoning laws. This transformation of cyberspace is already underway. . . . Internet speakers (users who post material on the Internet) have begun to zone cyberspace itself through the use of "gateway" technology. Such technology requires Internet users to enter information about themselves—perhaps an adult identification number or a credit card number—before they can access certain areas of cyberspace, much like a bouncer checks a person's driver's license before admitting him to a nightclub. Internet users who access information have not attempted to zone cyberspace itself, but have tried to limit their own power to access information in cyberspace, much as a parent controls what her children watch on television by installing a lock box. This user-based zoning is accomplished through the use of screening software (such as Cyber Patrol or SurfWatch) or browsers with screening capabilities, both of which search addresses and text for keywords that are associated with "adult" sites and, if the user wishes, blocks access to such sites. The Platform for Internet Content Selection (PICS) project is designed to facilitate user-based zoning by encouraging Internet speakers to rate the content of their speech using codes recognized by all screening programs.

Despite this progress, the transformation of cyberspace is not complete. Although gateway technology has been available on the World Wide Web for some time now, it is not available to all Web speakers and is just now becoming technologically feasible for chat rooms and USENET newsgroups. Gateway technology is not ubiquitous in cyberspace, and because without it "there is no means of age verification," cyberspace still remains largely unzoned—and unzoneable. User-based zoning is also in its infancy. For it to be effective, (i) an agreed-upon code (or "tag") would have to exist; (ii) screening software or browsers with screening capabilities would have to be able to recognize the "tag"; and (iii) those programs would have to be widely available–and widely used—by Internet users. At present, none of these conditions is true. Screening software "is not in wide use today" and "only a handful of browsers have screening capabilities." There is, moreover, no agreed-upon "tag" for those programs to recognize.

Although the prospects for the eventual zoning of the Internet appear promising, I agree with the Court that we must evaluate the constitutionality of the CDA as it applies to the Internet as it exists today. Given the present state of cyberspace, I agree with the Court that the "display" provision cannot pass muster. Until gateway technology is available throughout cyberspace, and it is not in 1997, a speaker cannot be reasonably assured that the speech he displays will reach only adults because it is impossible to confine speech to an "adult zone." Thus, the only way for a speaker to avoid liability under the CDA is to refrain completely from using indecent speech. But this forced silence impinges on the First Amendment right of adults to make and obtain this speech. . . .

The "indecency transmission" and "specific person" provisions present a closer issue, for they are not unconstitutional in all of their applications. . . . [T]he "indecency transmission" provision makes it a crime to transmit knowingly an indecent message to a person the sender knows is under 18 years of age. The "specific person" provision proscribes the same conduct, although it does not as explicitly require the sender to know that the intended recipient of his indecent message is a minor. Appellant urges the Court to construe the provision to impose such a knowledge requirement, and I would do so. . . .

So construed, both provisions are constitutional as applied to a conversation involving only an adult and one or more minors—*e.g.*, when an adult speaker sends an e-mail knowing the addressee is a minor, or when an adult and minor converse by themselves or with other minors in a chat room. In this context, these provisions are no different from the law we sustained in *Ginsberg*. Restricting what the adult may say to the minors in no way restricts the adult's ability to communicate with other adults. He is not prevented from speaking indecently to other adults in a chat room (because there are no other adults participating in the conversation) and he remains free to send indecent e-mails to other adults. The relevant universe contains only one adult, and the adult in that universe has the power to refrain from using indecent speech and consequently to keep all such speech within the room in an "adult" zone.

The analogy to *Ginsberg* breaks down, however, when more than one adult is a party to the conversation. If a minor enters a chat room otherwise occupied by adults, the CDA effectively requires the adults in the room to stop using indecent speech. If they did not, they could be prosecuted under the "indecency transmission" and "specific person" provisions for any indecent statements they make to the group, since they would be transmitting an indecent message to specific persons, one of whom is a minor. The CDA is therefore akin to a law that makes it a crime for a bookstore owner to sell pornographic magazines to anyone once a minor enters his store. Even assuming such a law might be constitutional in the physical world as a reasonable alternative to excluding minors completely from the store, the absence of any means of excluding minors from chat rooms in cyberspace restricts the rights of adults to engage in indecent speech in those rooms. The "indecency transmission" and "specific person" provisions share this defect.

But these two provisions do not infringe on adults' speech in all situations. And as discussed below, I do not find that the provisions are overbroad in the sense that they restrict minors' access to a substantial amount of speech that minors have the right to read and view. Accordingly, the CDA can be applied constitutionally in some situations. Normally, this fact would require the Court to reject a direct facial challenge. . . . Appellees' claim arises under the First Amendment, however, and they argue that the CDA is facially invalid because it is "substantially overbroad." . . . I agree with the Court that the provisions are overbroad in that they cover any and all communications between adults and minors, regardless of how many adults might be part of the audience to the communication.

This conclusion does not end the matter, however. . . . There is no question that Congress intended to prohibit certain communications between one adult and one or more minors. . . . There is also no question that Congress would have enacted a narrower version of these provisions had it known a broader version would be declared unconstitutional. . . . I would therefore sustain the "indecency transmission" and "specific person" provisions to the extent they apply to the transmission of Internet communications where the party initiating the communication knows that all of the recipients are minors.

II

Whether the CDA substantially interferes with the First Amendment rights of minors, and thereby runs afoul of the second characteristic of valid zoning laws, presents a closer question. In *Ginsberg*, the New York law we sustained prohibited the sale to minors of magazines that were "harmful to minors." Under that law, a magazine was "harmful to minors" only if it was obscene as to minors. . . .

The Court neither "accept[s] nor reject[s]" the argument that the CDA is facially overbroad because it substantially interferes with the First Amendment rights of minors. I would reject it. *Ginsberg* established that minors may constitutionally be denied access to material that is obscene as to minors. As *Ginsberg* explained, material is obscene as to minors if it (i) is "patently offensive to prevailing standards in the adult community as a whole with respect to what is suitable . . . for minors"; (ii) appeals to the prurient interest of minors; and (iii) is "utterly without redeeming social importance for minors." Because the CDA denies minors the right to obtain material that is "patently offensive"—even if it has some redeeming value for minors and even if it does not appeal to their prurient interests—Congress' rejection of the *Ginsberg* "harmful to minors" standard means that the CDA could ban some speech that is "indecent" (*i.e.*, "patently offensive") but that is not obscene as to minors.

I do not deny this possibility, but to prevail in a facial challenge, it is not enough for a plaintiff to show "some" overbreadth. Our cases require a proof of "real" and "substantial" overbreadth, and appellees have not carried their burden in this case. In my view, the universe of speech constitutionally protected as to minors but banned by the CDA—*i.e.*, the universe of material that is "patently offensive," but which nonetheless has some redeeming value for minors or does not appeal to their prurient interest—is a very small one. Appellees cite no examples of speech falling within this universe and do not attempt to explain why that universe is substantial "in relation to the statute's plainly legitimate sweep." That the CDA might deny minors the right to obtain material that has some "value" is largely beside the point. While discussions about prison rape or nude art may have some redeeming education value for *adults*, they do not necessarily have any such value *for minors*. . . . There is also no evidence in the record to support the contention that "many [e]-mail transmissions from an adult to a minor are conversations between family members," and no support for the legal proposition that such speech is absolutely immune from regulation. Accordingly, in my view, the CDA does not burden a substantial amount of minors' constitutionally protected speech.

Thus, the constitutionality of the CDA as a zoning law hinges on the extent to which it substantially interferes with the First Amendment rights of adults. Because the rights of adults are infringed only by the "display" provision and by the "indecency transmission" and "specific person" provisions as applied to communications involving more than one adult, I would invalidate the CDA only to that extent. Insofar as the "indecency transmission" and "specific person" provisions prohibit the use of indecent speech in communications between an adult and one or more minors, however, they can and should be sustained. The Court reaches a contrary conclusion, and from that holding I respectfully dissent.

□□□

No. 96-110

Washington, et al., Petitioners v. Harold Glucksberg et al.

On writ of certiorari to the United States Court
of Appeals for the Ninth Circuit

[June 26, 1997]

CHIEF JUSTICE REHNQUIST delivered the opinion of the Court.

The question presented in this case is whether Washington's prohibition against "caus[ing]" or "aid[ing]" a suicide offends the Fourteenth Amendment to the United States Constitution. We hold that it does not.

It has always been a crime to assist a suicide in the State of Washington. . . . Today, Washington law provides: "A person is guilty of promoting a suicide attempt when he knowingly causes or aids another person to attempt suicide." "Promoting a suicide attempt" is a felony, punishable by up to five years' imprisonment and up to a $10,000 fine. At the same time, Washington's Natural Death Act, enacted in 1979, states that the "withholding or withdrawal of life-sustaining treatment" at a patient's direction "shall not, for any purpose, constitute a suicide."

Petitioners in this case are the State of Washington and its Attorney General. Respondents Harold Glucksberg, M. D., Abigail Halperin, M. D., Thomas A. Preston, M. D., and Peter Shalit, M. D., are physicians who practice in Washington. These doctors occasionally treat terminally ill, suffering patients, and declare that they would assist these patients in ending their lives if not for Washington's assisted-suicide ban. In January 1994, respondents, along with three gravely ill, pseudonymous plaintiffs who have since died and Compassion in Dying, a nonprofit organization that counsels people considering physician-assisted suicide, sued in the United States District Court, seeking a declaration that [the state law banning assisted suicide] is, on its face, unconstitutional.

The plaintiffs asserted "the existence of a liberty interest protected by the Four-

---

Note: Concurring opinions in *Washington v. Glucksberg* and *Vacco v. Quill* follow the opinion for the Court in *Vacco*.

teenth Amendment which extends to a personal choice by a mentally competent, terminally ill adult to commit physician-assisted suicide." Relying primarily on *Planned Parenthood v. Casey* (1992) and *Cruzan v. Director, Missouri Dept. of Health* (1990), the District Court agreed and concluded that Washington's assisted-suicide ban is unconstitutional because it "places an undue burden on the exercise of [that] constitutionally protected liberty interest." The District Court also decided that the Washington statute violated the Equal Protection Clause's requirement that " 'all persons similarly situated . . . be treated alike.' " (1994).

A panel of the Court of Appeals for the Ninth Circuit reversed, emphasizing that "[i]n the two hundred and five years of our existence no constitutional right to aid in killing oneself has ever been asserted and upheld by a court of final jurisdiction." (1995). The Ninth Circuit reheard the case *en banc*, reversed the panel's decision, and affirmed the District Court. (1996). Like the District Court, the *en banc* Court of Appeals emphasized our *Casey* and *Cruzan* decisions. The court also discussed what it described as "historical" and "current societal attitudes" toward suicide and assisted suicide, and concluded that "the Constitution encompasses a due process liberty interest in controlling the time and manner of one's death—that there is, in short, a constitutionally-recognized 'right to die.' " After "[w]eighing and then balancing" this interest against Washington's various interests, the court held that the State's assisted-suicide ban was unconstitutional "as applied to terminally ill competent adults who wish to hasten their deaths with medication prescribed by their physicians." The court did not reach the District Court's equal-protection holding. We granted certiorari (1996) and now reverse.

I

We begin, as we do in all due-process cases, by examining our Nation's history, legal traditions, and practices. . . .

. . . [F]or over 700 years, the Anglo-American common-law tradition has punished or otherwise disapproved of both suicide and assisting suicide. . . .

For the most part, the early American colonies adopted the common-law approach. . . .

Over time, however, the American colonies abolished . . . harsh common-law penalties. . . . [T]he movement away from the common law's harsh sanctions did not represent an acceptance of suicide; rather, . . . this change reflected the growing consensus that it was unfair to punish the suicide's family for his wrongdoing. . . .

That suicide remained a grievous, though nonfelonious, wrong is confirmed by the fact that colonial and early state legislatures and courts did not retreat from prohibiting assisting suicide. . . .

Though deeply rooted, the States' assisted-suicide bans have in recent years been reexamined and, generally, reaffirmed. Because of advances in medicine and technology, Americans today are increasingly likely to die in institutions, from chronic illnesses. Public concern and democratic action are therefore sharply focused on how best to protect dignity and independence at the end of life, with the result that there have been many significant changes in state laws and in the attitudes these laws reflect. Many States, for example, now permit "living wills," surrogate health-care decisionmaking, and the withdrawal or refusal of life-sustaining medical treatment. At the same time, however, voters and legislators continue for the most part to reaffirm their States' prohibitions on assisting suicide.

The Washington statute at issue in this case, Wash. Rev. Code §9A.36.060 (1994), was enacted in 1975 as part of a revision of that State's criminal code. Four years later, Washington passed its Natural Death Act, which specifically stated that the "withholding or withdrawal of life-sustaining treatment . . . shall not, for any purpose, constitute a suicide" and that "[n]othing in this chapter shall be construed to condone, authorize, or approve mercy killing. . . ." In 1991, Washington voters rejected a ballot initiative which, had it passed, would have permitted a form of physician-assisted suicide. Washington then added a provision to the Natural Death Act expressly excluding physician-assisted suicide.

California voters rejected an assisted-suicide initiative similar to Washington's in 1992. On the other hand, in 1994, voters in Oregon enacted, also through ballot initiative, that State's "Death With Dignity Act," which legalized physician-assisted suicide for competent, terminally ill adults. Since the Oregon vote, many proposals to legalize assisted-suicide have been and continue to be introduced in the States' legislatures, but none has been enacted. And just last year, Iowa and Rhode Island joined the overwhelming majority of States explicitly prohibiting assisted suicide.

Thus, the States are currently engaged in serious, thoughtful examinations of physician-assisted suicide and other similar issues. For example, New York State's Task Force on Life and the Law—an ongoing, blue-ribbon commission composed of doctors, ethicists, lawyers, religious leaders, and interested laymen—was convened in 1984 and commissioned with "a broad mandate to recommend public policy on issues raised by medical advances. . . . After studying physician-assisted suicide . . . , the Task Force unanimously concluded that "[l]egalizing assisted suicide and euthanasia would pose profound risks to many individuals who are ill and vulnerable. . . . [T]he potential dangers of this dramatic change in public policy would outweigh any benefit that might be achieved."

Attitudes toward suicide itself have changed . . . , but our laws have consistently condemned, and continue to prohibit, assisting suicide. Despite changes in medical technology and notwithstanding an increased emphasis on the importance of end-of-life decision-making, we have not retreated from this prohibition. Against this backdrop of history, tradition, and practice, we now turn to respondents' constitutional claim.

II

The Due Process Clause guarantees more than fair process, and the "liberty" it protects includes more than the absence of physical restraint. . . . The Clause also provides heightened protection against government interference with certain fundamental rights and liberty interests. [Listing of cases omitted.] We have also assumed, and strongly suggested, that the Due Process Clause protects the traditional right to refuse unwanted lifesaving medical treatment. *Cruzan.*

But we "ha[ve] always been reluctant to expand the concept of substantive due process because guideposts for responsible decisionmaking in this unchartered area are scarce and open-ended." By extending constitutional protection to an asserted right or liberty interest, we, to a great extent, place the matter outside the arena of public debate and legislative action. We must therefore "exercise the utmost care whenever we are asked to break new ground in this field," lest the liberty protected by the Due Process Clause be subtly transformed into the policy preferences of the members of this Court. . . .

Turning to the claim at issue here, the Court of Appeals stated that "[p]roperly analyzed, the first issue to be resolved is whether there is a liberty interest in determining the time and manner of one's death," or, in other words, "[i]s there a right to die?" Similarly, respondents assert a "liberty to choose how to die" and a right to "control of one's final days," and describe the asserted liberty as "the right to choose a humane, dignified death" and "the liberty to shape death." . . . The Washington statute at issue in this case prohibits "aid[ing] another person to attempt suicide," and, thus, the question before us is whether the "liberty" specially protected by the Due Process Clause includes a right to commit suicide which itself includes a right to assistance in doing so.

We now inquire whether this asserted right has any place in our Nation's traditions. Here, . . . we are confronted with a consistent and almost universal tradition that has long rejected the asserted right, and continues explicitly to reject it today, even for terminally ill, mentally competent adults. To hold for respondents, we would have to reverse centuries of legal doctrine and practice, and strike down the considered policy choice of almost every State. . . .

Respondents contend, however, that the liberty interest they assert is consistent with this Court's substantive due-process line of cases, if not with this Nation's history and practice. Pointing to *Casey* and *Cruzan*, respondents read our jurisprudence in this area as reflecting a general tradition of "self-sovereignty," and as teaching that the "liberty" protected by the Due Process Clause includes "basic and intimate exercises of personal autonomy." . . . According to respondents, our liberty jurisprudence, and the broad, individualistic principles it reflects, protects the "liberty of competent, terminally ill adults to make end-of-life decisions free of undue government interference." The question presented in this case, however, is whether the protections of the Due Process Clause include a right to commit suicide with another's assistance. With this "careful description" of respondents' claim in mind, we turn to *Casey* and *Cruzan*.

[In summarizing the two decisions, Rehnquist said that *Cruzan*'s recognition of a right to refuse life-sustaining medical treatment stemmed from "a long line of relevant state cases" holding that patients may reject unwanted medical treatment. As for the right to abortion recognized in *Casey*, Rehnquist said the ruling followed the Court's "tradition" of interpreting the Due Process Clause to protect "personal decisions relating to marriage, procreation, contraception, family relationships, child rearing, and education. . . ." Neither of those decisions, he said, "warrant the sweeping conclusion that any and all important, intimate, and personal decisions are so protected."]

The history of the law's treatment of assisted suicide in this country has been and continues to be one of the rejection of nearly all efforts to permit it. That being the case, our decisions lead us to conclude that the asserted "right" to assistance in committing suicide is not a fundamental liberty interest protected by the Due Process Clause. The Constitution also requires, however, that Washington's assisted-suicide ban be rationally related to legitimate government interests. This requirement is unquestionably met here. As the court below recognized, Washington's assisted-suicide ban implicates a number of state interests.

First, Washington has an "unqualified interest in the preservation of human life." The State's prohibition on assisted suicide, like all homicide laws, both reflects and advances its commitment to this interest. . . .

Respondents admit that "[t]he State has a real interest in preserving the lives of those who can still contribute to society and enjoy life." The Court of Appeals also recognized Washington's interest in protecting life, but held that the "weight" of this interest depends on the "medical condition and the wishes of the person whose life is at stake." Washington, however, has rejected this sliding-scale approach and, through its assisted-suicide ban, insists that all persons' lives, from beginning to end, regardless of physical or mental condition, are under the full protection of the law. . . .

Relatedly, all admit that suicide is a serious public-health problem, especially among persons in otherwise vulnerable groups. . . . The State has an interest in preventing suicide, and in studying, identifying, and treating its causes. . . .

Those who attempt suicide—terminally ill or not—often suffer from depression or other mental disorders. . . . Research indicates, however, that many people who request physician-assisted suicide withdraw that request if their depression and pain are treated. . . . The New York Task Force, however, expressed its concern that, because depression is difficult to diagnose, physicians and medical professionals often fail to respond adequately to seriously ill patients' needs. Thus, legal physician-assisted suicide could make it more difficult for the State to protect depressed or mentally ill persons, or those who are suffering from untreated pain, from suicidal impulses.

The State also has an interest in protecting the integrity and ethics of the medical profession. In contrast to the Court of Appeals' conclusion that "the integrity of the medical profession would [not] be threatened in any way by [physician-assisted suicide]," the American Medical Association, like many other medical and physicians' groups, has concluded that "[p]hysician-assisted suicide is fundamentally incompatible with the physician's role as healer." American Medical Association, Code of Ethics §2.211 (1994). . . . And physician-assisted suicide could, it is argued, undermine the trust that is essential to the doctor-patient relationship by blurring the time-honored line between healing and harming. . . .

Next, the State has an interest in protecting vulnerable groups—including the poor, the elderly, and disabled persons—from abuse, neglect, and mistakes. The Court of Appeals dismissed the State's concern that disadvantaged persons might be pressured into physician-assisted suicide as "ludicrous on its face." We have recognized, however, the real risk of subtle coercion and undue influence in end-of-life situations. [Citing *Cruzan.*] Similarly, the New York Task Force warned that "[l]egalizing physician-assisted suicide would pose profound risks to many individuals who are ill and vulnerable. . . . The risk of harm is greatest for the many individuals in our society whose autonomy and well-being are already compromised by poverty, lack of access to good medical care, advanced age, or membership in a stigmatized social group." . . . If physician-assisted suicide were permitted, many might resort to it to spare their families the substantial financial burden of end-of-life health-care costs.

The State's interest here goes beyond protecting the vulnerable from coercion; it extends to protecting disabled and terminally ill people from prejudice, negative and inaccurate stereotypes, and "societal indifference." The State's assisted-suicide ban reflects and reinforces its policy that the lives of terminally ill, disabled, and elderly people must be no less valued than the lives of the young and healthy, and that a seriously disabled person's suicidal impulses should be interpreted and treated the same way as anyone else's. . . .

Finally, the State may fear that permitting assisted suicide will start it down the path to voluntary and perhaps even involuntary euthanasia. The Court of Appeals struck down Washington's assisted-suicide ban only "as applied to competent, terminally ill adults who wish to hasten their deaths by obtaining medication prescribed by their doctors." Washington insists, however, that the impact of the court's decision will not and cannot be so limited. If suicide is protected as a matter of constitutional right, it is argued, "every man and woman in the United States must enjoy it." The Court of Appeals' decision, and its expansive reasoning, provide ample support for the State's concerns. . . . Thus, it turns out that what is couched as a limited right to "physician-assisted suicide" is likely, in effect, a much broader license, which could prove extremely difficult to police and contain. Washington's ban on assisting suicide prevents such erosion.

This concern is further supported by evidence about the practice of euthanasia in the Netherlands. The Dutch government's own study revealed that in 1990, there were 2,300 cases of voluntary euthanasia (defined as "the deliberate termination of another's life at his request"), 400 cases of assisted suicide, and more than 1,000 cases of euthanasia without an explicit request. In addition to these latter 1,000 cases, the study found an additional 4,941 cases where physicians administered lethal morphine overdoses without the patients' explicit consent. This study suggests that, despite the existence of various reporting procedures, euthanasia in the Netherlands has not been limited to competent, terminally ill adults who are enduring physical suffering, and that regulation of the practice may not have prevented abuses in cases involving vulnerable persons, including severely disabled neonates and elderly persons suffering from dementia. . . . The New York Task Force, citing the Dutch experience, observed that "assisted suicide and euthanasia are closely linked," and concluded that the "risk of . . . abuse is neither speculative nor distant." Washington, like most other States, reasonably ensures against this risk by banning, rather than regulating, assisting suicide. . . .

We need not weigh exactingly the relative strengths of these various interests. They are unquestionably important and legitimate, and Washington's ban on assisted suicide is at least reasonably related to their promotion and protection. We therefore hold that Wash. Rev. Code §9A.36.060(1) does not violate the Fourteenth Amendment, either on its face or "as applied to competent, terminally ill adults who wish to hasten their deaths by obtaining medication prescribed by their doctors."

[Rehnquist added this significant footnote: ". . . We emphasize that we today reject the Court of Appeals' specific holding that the statute is unconstitutional 'as applied' to a particular class. JUSTICE STEVENS agrees with this holding, but would not 'foreclose the possibility that an individual plaintiff seeking to hasten her death, or a doctor whose assistance was sought, could prevail in a more particularized challenge.' Our opinion does not absolutely foreclose such a claim. However, given our holding that the Due Process Clause of the Fourteenth Amendment does not provide heightened protection to the asserted liberty interest in ending one's life with a physician's assistance, such a claim would have to be quite different from the ones advanced by respondents here."]

* * *

Throughout the Nation, Americans are engaged in an earnest and profound debate about the morality, legality, and practicality of physician-assisted suicide. Our holding permits this debate to continue, as it should in a democratic society. The decision of the en banc Court of Appeals is reversed, and the case is remanded for further proceedings consistent with this opinion.

It is so ordered.

No. 95-1858

Dennis C. Vacco, Attorney General of New York, et al., Petitioners v. Timothy E. Quill et al.

On writ of certiorari to the United States Court
of Appeals for the Second Circuit

[June 26, 1997]

CHIEF JUSTICE REHNQUIST delivered the opinion of the Court.

In New York, as in most States, it is a crime to aid another to commit or attempt suicide, but patients may refuse even lifesaving medical treatment. The question presented by this case is whether New York's prohibition on assisting suicide therefore violates the Equal Protection Clause of the Fourteenth Amendment. We hold that it does not.

Petitioners are various New York public officials. Respondents Timothy E. Quill, Samuel C. Klagsbrun, and Howard A. Grossman are physicians who practice in New York. They assert that although it would be "consistent with the standards of [their] medical practice[s]" to prescribe lethal medication for "mentally competent, terminally ill patients" who are suffering great pain and desire a doctor's help in taking their own lives, they are deterred from doing so by New York's ban on assisting suicide. Respondents, and three gravely ill patients who have since died, sued the State's Attorney General in the United States District Court. They urged that because New York permits a competent person to refuse life-sustaining medical treatment, and because the refusal of such treatment is "essentially the same thing" as physician-assisted suicide, New York's assisted-suicide ban violates the Equal Protection Clause. (1994).

The District Court disagreed: "[I]t is hardly unreasonable or irrational for the State to recognize a difference between allowing nature to take its course, even in the most severe situations, and intentionally using an artificial death-producing device." . . .

The Court of Appeals for the Second Circuit reversed. (1996). The court determined that, despite the assisted-suicide ban's apparent general applicability, "New York law does not treat equally all competent persons who are in the final stages of fatal illness and wish to hasten their deaths," because "those in the final stages of terminal illness who are on life-support systems are allowed to hasten their deaths by directing the removal of such systems; but those who are similarly situated, except for the previous attachment of life-sustaining equipment, are not allowed to hasten death by self-administering prescribed drugs." In the court's view, "[t]he ending of life by [the withdrawal of life-support systems] is *nothing more nor less than assisted suicide.*" (emphasis added) The Court of Appeals then examined whether this supposed unequal treatment was rationally related to any legitimate state interests, and concluded that "to the extent that [New York's statutes] prohibit a physician from prescribing medications to be self-administered by a mentally competent, terminally-ill person in the final stages of his terminal illness, they are not rationally related to any legitimate state interest." We granted certiorari (1996) and now reverse.

The Equal Protection Clause commands that no State shall "deny to any person within its jurisdiction the equal protection of the laws." This provision creates no substantive rights. Instead, it embodies a general rule that States must treat like cases alike but may treat unlike cases accordingly. . . .

New York's statutes outlawing assisting suicide affect and address matters of profound significance to all New Yorkers alike. They neither infringe fundamental rights nor involve suspect classifications. . . . These laws are therefore entitled to a "strong presumption of validity."

On their faces, neither New York's ban on assisting suicide nor its statutes permitting patients to refuse medical treatment treat anyone differently than anyone else or draw any distinctions between persons. Everyone, regardless of physical condition, is entitled, if competent, to refuse unwanted lifesaving medical treatment; no one is permitted to assist a suicide. Generally speaking, laws that apply evenhandedly to all "unquestionably comply" with the Equal Protection Clause. . . .

The Court of Appeals, however, concluded that some terminally ill people— those who are on life-support systems—are treated differently than those who are not, in that the former may "hasten death" by ending treatment, but the latter may not "hasten death" through physician-assisted suicide. This conclusion depends on the submission that ending or refusing lifesaving medical treatment "is nothing more nor less than assisted suicide." Unlike the Court of Appeals, we think the distinction between assisting suicide and withdrawing life-sustaining treatment, a distinction widely recognized and endorsed in the medical profession and in our legal traditions, is both important and logical; it is certainly rational.

The distinction comports with fundamental legal principles of causation and intent. First, when a patient refuses life-sustaining medical treatment, he dies from an underlying fatal disease or pathology; but if a patient ingests lethal medication prescribed by a physician, he is killed by that medication. . . .

Furthermore, a physician who withdraws, or honors a patient's refusal to begin, life-sustaining medical treatment purposefully intends, or may so intend, only to respect his patient's wishes and "to cease doing useless and futile or degrading things to the patient when [the patient] no longer stands to benefit from them." [Quoting testimony of Dr. Leon R. Kass, before House Judiciary Subcommittee on the Constitution, 1996.] The same is true when a doctor provides aggressive palliative care; in some cases, painkilling drugs may hasten a patient's death, but the physician's purpose and intent is, or may be, only to ease his patient's pain. A doctor who assists a suicide, however, "must, necessarily and indubitably, intend primarily that the patient be made dead." Similarly, a patient who commits suicide with a doctor's aid necessarily has the specific intent to end his or her own life, while a patient who refuses or discontinues treatment might not. . . .

The law has long used actors' intent or purpose to distinguish between two acts that may have the same result. . . . Put differently, the law distinguishes actions taken "because of" a given end from actions taken "in spite of" their unintended but fore-seen consequences. . . .

Given these general principles, it is not surprising that many courts, including New York courts, have carefully distinguished refusing life-sustaining treatment from suicide. [Citations omitted.] In fact, the first state-court decision explicitly to autho-rize withdrawing lifesaving treatment noted the "real distinction between the self-infliction of deadly harm and a self-determination against artificial life support." *In re Quinlan* [New Jersey Supreme Court, 1976]. And recently, the Michigan Supreme Court also rejected the argument that the distinction "between acts that artificially sustain life and acts that artificially curtail life" is merely a "distinction without con-stitutional significance—a meaningless exercise in semantic gymnastics," insisting that "the *Cruzan* [*v. Director, Mo. Dept. of Health* (1990)] majority disagreed and so do we." [*People v.*] *Kevorkian* [1994].

Similarly, the overwhelming majority of state legislatures have drawn a clear line between assisting suicide and withdrawing or permitting the refusal of unwanted lifesaving medical treatment by prohibiting the former and permitting the latter. And "nearly all states expressly disapprove of suicide and assisted suicide either in statutes dealing with durable powers of attorney in health-care situations, or in 'liv-ing will' statutes." [Quoting from *Kevorkian.*] Thus, even as the States move to pro-tect and promote patients' dignity at the end of life, they remain opposed to physician-assisted suicide.

New York is a case in point. The State enacted its current assisted-suicide stat-utes in 1965. Since then, New York has acted several times to protect patients' com-mon-law right to refuse treatment. [Citing laws passed in 1987, 1990, and 1994, permitting "Do Not Resuscitate Orders" and authorizing appointment of "Health Care Agents and Proxies."] In so doing, however, the State has neither endorsed a general right to "hasten death" nor approved physician-assisted suicide. Quite the opposite: The State has reaffirmed the line between "killing" and "letting die." . . . More recently, the New York State Task Force on Life and the Law studied assisted suicide and euthanasia and, in 1994, unanimously recommended against legaliza-tion. . . .

This Court has also recognized, at least implicitly, the distinction between let-ting a patient die and making that patient die. In *Cruzan v. Director, Mo. Dept. of Health* (1990), we concluded that "[t]he principle that a competent person has a constitutionally protected liberty interest in refusing unwanted medical treatment may be inferred from our prior decisions," and we assumed the existence of such a right for purposes of that case. But our assumption of a right to refuse treatment was grounded not, as the Court of Appeals supposed, on the proposition that patients have a general and abstract "right to hasten death," but on well established, tradi-tional rights to bodily integrity and freedom from unwanted touching. . . . *Cruzan* therefore provides no support for the notion that refusing life-sustaining medical treatment is "nothing more nor less than suicide."

For all these reasons, we disagree with respondents' claim that the distinction between refusing lifesaving medical treatment and assisted suicide is "arbitrary" and "irrational." Granted, in some cases, the line between the two may not be clear, but certainty is not required, even were it possible. Logic and contemporary practice support New York's judgment that the two acts are different, and New York may therefore, consistent with the Constitution, treat them differently. By permitting everyone to refuse unwanted medical treatment while prohibiting anyone from assisting a suicide, New York law follows a longstanding and rational distinction.

New York's reasons for recognizing and acting on this distinction—including prohibiting intentional killing and preserving life; preventing suicide; maintaining physicians' role as their patients' healers; protecting vulnerable people from indifference, prejudice, and psychological and financial pressure to end their lives; and avoiding a possible slide towards euthanasia—are discussed in greater detail in our opinion in [*Washington v.*] *Glucksberg* [1997]. These valid and important public interests easily satisfy the constitutional requirement that a legislative classification bear a rational relation to some legitimate end.

The judgment of the Court of Appeals is reversed.

It is so ordered.

JUSTICE O'CONNOR, concurring.

[JUSTICE GINSBURG concurs in the Court's judgments substantially for the reasons stated in this opinion. JUSTICE BREYER joins this opinion except insofar as it joins the opinions of the Court.]

Death will be different for each of us. For many, the last days will be spent in physical pain and perhaps the despair that accompanies physical deterioration and a loss of control of basic bodily and mental functions. Some will seek medication to alleviate that pain and other symptoms.

The Court frames the issue in this case as whether the Due Process Clause of the Constitution protects a "right to commit suicide which itself includes a right to assistance in doing so," and concludes that our Nation's history, legal traditions, and practices do not support the existence of such a right. I join the Court's opinions because I agree that there is no generalized right to "commit suicide." But respondents urge us to address the narrower question whether a mentally competent person who is experiencing great suffering has a constitutionally cognizable interest in controlling the circumstances of his or her imminent death. I see no need to reach that question in the context of the facial challenges to the New York and Washington laws at issue here. . . . The parties and *amici* agree that in these States a patient who is suffering from a terminal illness and who is experiencing great pain has no legal barriers to obtaining medication, from qualified physicians, to alleviate that suffering, even to the point of causing unconsciousness and hastening death. In this light, even assuming that we would recognize such an interest, I agree that the State's interests in protecting those who are not truly competent or facing imminent death, or those whose decisions to hasten death would not truly be voluntary, are sufficiently weighty to justify a prohibition against physician-assisted suicide.

Every one of us at some point may be affected by our own or a family member's terminal illness. There is no reason to think the democratic process will not strike the proper balance between the interests of terminally ill, mentally competent individuals who would seek to end their suffering and the State's interests in protecting those who might seek to end life mistakenly or under pressure. As the Court recognizes, States are presently undertaking extensive and serious evaluation of physician-assisted suicide and other related issues. In such circumstances, "the . . . challenging task of crafting appropriate procedures for safeguarding . . . liberty interests is entrusted to the 'laboratory' of the States . . . in the first instance." *Cruzan v. Director, Mo. Dept. of Health* (1990) (O'CONNOR, J., concurring).

In sum, there is no need to address the question whether suffering patients have a constitutionally cognizable interest in obtaining relief from the suffering that they may experience in the last days of their lives. There is no dispute that dying patients in Washington and New York can obtain palliative care, even when doing so would hasten their deaths. The difficulty in defining terminal illness and the risk that a dying patient's request for assistance in ending his or her life might not be truly voluntary justifies the prohibitions on assisted suicide we uphold here.

JUSTICE STEVENS, concurring in the judgments.

The Court ends its opinion with the important observation that our holding today is fully consistent with a continuation of the vigorous debate about the "morality, legality, and practicality of physician-assisted suicide" in a democratic society. I write separately to make it clear that there is also room for further debate about the limits that the Constitution places on the power of the States to punish the practice.

I, II [OMITTED]

III

The state interests supporting a general rule banning the practice of physician-assisted suicide do not have the same force in all cases. First and foremost of these interests is the "'unqualified interest in the preservation of human life,'" which is equated with "'the sanctity of life.'" That interest not only justifies—it commands— maximum protection of every individual's interest in remaining alive, which in turn commands the same protection for decisions about whether to commence or to terminate life-support systems or to administer pain medication that may hasten death. Properly viewed, however, this interest is not a collective interest that should always outweigh the interests of a person who because of pain, incapacity, or sedation finds her life intolerable, but rather, an aspect of individual freedom.

Many terminally ill people find their lives meaningful even if filled with pain or dependence on others. Some find value in living through suffering; some have an abiding desire to witness particular events in their families' lives; many believe it a sin to hasten death. Individuals of different religious faiths make different judgments and choices about whether to live on under such circumstances. There are those who will want to continue aggressive treatment; those who would prefer terminal sedation; and those who will seek withdrawal from life-support systems and death by gradual starvation and dehydration. Although as a general matter the State's interest in the contributions each person may make to society outweighs the person's interest in ending her life, this interest does not have the same force for a terminally ill patient faced not with the choice of whether to live, only of how to die. Allowing the individual, rather than the State, to make judgments "'about the "quality" of life that a particular individual may enjoy'" does not mean that the lives of terminally-ill, disabled people have less value than the lives of those who are healthy. Rather, it gives proper recognition to the individual's interest in choosing a final chapter that accords with her life story, rather than one that demeans her values and poisons memories of her. . . .

Similarly, the State's legitimate interests in preventing suicide, protecting the vulnerable from coercion and abuse, and preventing euthanasia are less significant in this context. I agree that the State has a compelling interest in preventing persons from committing suicide because of depression, or coercion by third parties. But the State's legitimate interest in preventing abuse does not apply to an individual who is not victimized by abuse, who is not suffering from depression, and who makes a rational and voluntary decision to seek assistance in dying. . . .

Relatedly, the State and *amici* express the concern that patients whose physical pain is inadequately treated will be more likely to request assisted suicide. Encouraging the development and ensuring the availability of adequate pain treatment is of utmost importance; palliative care, however, cannot alleviate all pain and suffering. . . . An individual adequately informed of the care alternatives thus might make a rational choice for assisted suicide. For such an individual, the State's interest in preventing potential abuse and mistake is only minimally implicated.

The final major interest asserted by the State is its interest in preserving the traditional integrity of the medical profession. The fear is that a rule permitting physicians to assist in suicide is inconsistent with the perception that they serve their patients solely as healers. But for some patients, it would be a physician's refusal to dispense medication to ease their suffering and make their death tolerable and dignified that would be inconsistent with the healing role. . . . For doctors who have long-standing relationships with their patients, who have given their patients advice on alternative treatments, who are attentive to their patient's individualized needs, and who are knowledgeable about pain symptom management and palliative care options, heeding a patient's desire to assist in her suicide would not serve to harm the physician-patient relationship. Furthermore, because physicians are already involved in making decisions that hasten the death of terminally ill patients—through termination of life support, withholding of medical treatment, and terminal sedation—there is in fact significant tension between the traditional view of the physician's role and the actual practice in a growing number of cases.

As the New York State Task Force on Life and the Law recognized, a State's prohibition of assisted suicide is justified by the fact that the "'ideal'" case in which "patients would be screened for depression and offered treatment, effective pain medication would be available, and all patients would have a supportive committed family and doctor" is not the usual case. Although, as the Court concludes today, these potential harms are sufficient to support the State's general public policy against assisted suicide, they will not always outweigh the individual liberty interest of a particular patient. Unlike the Court of Appeals, I would not say as a categorical matter that these state interests are invalid as to the entire class of terminally ill, mentally competent patients. I do not, however, foreclose the possibility that an individual plaintiff seeking to hasten her death, or a doctor whose assistance was sought, could prevail in a more particularized challenge. Future cases will determine whether such a challenge may succeed.

IV

In New York, a doctor must respect a competent person's decision to refuse or to discontinue medical treatment even though death will thereby ensue, but the same doctor would be guilty of a felony if she provided her patient assistance in committing suicide. Today we hold that the Equal Protection Clause is not violated by the resulting disparate treatment of two classes of terminally ill people who may have the same interest in hastening death. I agree that the distinction between permitting death to ensue from an underlying fatal disease and causing it to occur by the administration of medication or other means provides a constitutionally sufficient basis for the State's classification. Unlike the Court, however, I am not persuaded that in all cases there will in fact be a significant difference between the intent of the physicians, the patients or the families in the two situations.

There may be little distinction between the intent of a terminally-ill patient who decides to remove her life-support and one who seeks the assistance of a doctor in ending her life; in both situations, the patient is seeking to hasten a certain, impending death. The doctor's intent might also be the same in prescribing lethal medication as it is in terminating life support. A doctor who fails to administer medical treatment to one who is dying from a disease could be doing so with an intent to harm or kill that patient. Conversely, a doctor who prescribes lethal medication does not necessarily intend the patient's death—rather that doctor may seek simply to ease the patient's suffering and to comply with her wishes. The illusory character of any differences in intent or causation is confirmed by the fact that the American Medical Association unequivocally endorses the practice of terminal sedation—the administration of sufficient dosages of pain-killing medication to terminally ill patients to protect them from excruciating pain even when it is clear that the time of death will be advanced. The purpose of terminal sedation is to ease the suffering of the patient and comply with her wishes, and the actual cause of death is the administration of heavy doses of lethal sedatives. This same intent and causation may exist when a doctor complies with a patient's request for lethal medication to hasten her death.

Thus, although the differences the majority notes in causation and intent between terminating life-support and assisting in suicide support the Court's rejection of the respondents' facial challenge, these distinctions may be inapplicable to particular terminally ill patients and their doctors. Our holding today in *Vacco v. Quill* that the Equal Protection Clause is not violated by New York's classification, just like our holding in *Washington v. Glucksberg* that the Washington statute is not invalid on its face, does not foreclose the possibility that some applications of the New York statute may impose an intolerable intrusion on the patient's freedom.

There remains room for vigorous debate about the outcome of particular cases that are not necessarily resolved by the opinions announced today. How such cases may be decided will depend on their specific facts. In my judgment, however, it is clear that the so-called "unqualified interest in the preservation of human life" is not itself sufficient to outweigh the interest in liberty that may justify the only possible means of preserving a dying patient's dignity and alleviating her intolerable suffering.

JUSTICE SOUTER, concurring in the judgment [in *Washington v. Glucksberg*].
Three terminally ill individuals and four physicians who sometimes treat terminally ill patients brought this challenge to the Washington statute making it a crime "knowingly . . . [to] ai[d] another person to attempt suicide," claiming on behalf of both patients and physicians that it would violate substantive due process to enforce the statute against a doctor who acceded to a dying patient's request for a drug to be taken by the patient to commit suicide. The question is whether the statute sets up one of those "arbitrary impositions" or "purposeless restraints" at odds with the Due

Process Clause of the Fourteenth Amendment. [Quoting from dissenting opinion by Justice Harlan from ruling in *Poe v. Ullman* (1961), declining to rule on challenge to state law banning married couples from using contraceptives.] I conclude that the statute's application to the doctors has not been shown to be unconstitutional, but I write separately to give my reasons for analyzing the substantive due process claims as I do, and for rejecting this one.

I, II, III [OMITTED]

IV

. . . I take it that the basic concept of judicial review with its possible displacement of legislative judgment bars any finding that a legislature has acted arbitrarily when the following conditions are met: there is a serious factual controversy over the feasibility of recognizing the claimed right without at the same time making it impossible for the State to engage in an undoubtedly legitimate exercise of power; facts necessary to resolve the controversy are not readily ascertainable through the judicial process; but they are more readily subject to discovery through legislative factfinding and experimentation. It is assumed in this case, and must be, that a State's interest in protecting those unable to make responsible decisions and those who make no decisions at all entitles the State to bar aid to any but a knowing and responsible person intending suicide, and to prohibit euthanasia. How, and how far, a State should act in that interest are judgments for the State, but the legitimacy of its action to deny a physician the option to aid any but the knowing and responsible is beyond question.

The capacity of the State to protect the others if respondents were to prevail is, however, subject to some genuine question, underscored by the responsible disagreement over the basic facts of the Dutch experience. . . . Since there is little experience directly bearing on the issue, the most that can be said is that whichever way the Court might rule today, events could overtake its assumptions, as experimentation in some jurisdictions confirmed or discredited the concerns about progression from assisted suicide to euthanasia.

Legislatures, on the other hand, have superior opportunities to obtain the facts necessary for a judgment about the present controversy. Not only do they have more flexible mechanisms for factfinding than the Judiciary, but their mechanisms include the power to experiment, moving forward and pulling back as facts emerge within their own jurisdictions. There is, indeed, good reason to suppose that in the absence of a judgment for respondents here, just such experimentation will be attempted in some of the States.

I do not decide here what the significance might be of legislative foot-dragging in ascertaining the facts going to the State's argument that the right in question could not be confined as claimed. Sometimes a court may be bound to act regardless of the institutional preferability of the political branches as forums for addressing constitutional claims. Now, it is enough to say that our examination of legislative reasonableness should consider the fact that the Legislature of the State of Washington is no more obviously at fault than this Court is in being uncertain about what would happen if respondents prevailed today. We therefore have a clear question about which institution, a legislature or a court, is relatively more competent to deal with an emerging issue as to which facts currently unknown could be dispositive. The answer has to be, for the reasons already stated, that the legislative process is to be preferred. There is a closely related further reason as well.

One must bear in mind that the nature of the right claimed, if recognized as one constitutionally required, would differ in no essential way from other constitutional rights guaranteed by enumeration or derived from some more definite textual source than "due process." An unenumerated right should not therefore be recognized, with the effect of displacing the legislative ordering of things, without the assurance that its recognition would prove as durable as the recognition of those other rights differently derived. To recognize a right of lesser promise would simply create a constitutional regime too uncertain to bring with it the expectation of finality that is one of this Court's central obligations in making constitutional decisions.

Legislatures, however, are not so constrained. The experimentation that should be out of the question in constitutional adjudication displacing legislative judgments is entirely proper, as well as highly desirable, when the legislative power addresses an emerging issue like assisted suicide. The Court should accordingly stay its hand to allow reasonable legislative consideration. While I do not decide for all time that respondents' claim should not be recognized, I acknowledge the legislative institutional competence as the better one to deal with that claim at this time.

[Souter wrote a brief, separate opinion in *Vacco v. Quill*, also concurring in the judgment: ". . . The reasons that lead me to conclude in *Glucksberg* that the prohibition on assisted suicide is not arbitrary under the due process standard also support the distinction between assistance to suicide, which is banned, and practices such as termination of artificial life support and death-hastening pain medication, which are permitted. I accordingly concur in the judgment of the Court."]

JUSTICE GINSBURG, concurring in the judgments.

I concur in the Court's judgments in these cases substantially for the reasons stated by JUSTICE O'CONNOR in her concurring opinion.

JUSTICE BREYER, concurring in the judgments.

I believe that JUSTICE O'CONNOR's views, which I share, have greater legal significance than the Court's opinion suggests. I join her separate opinion, except insofar as it joins the majority. And I concur in the judgments. I shall briefly explain how I differ from the Court.

I agree with the Court in *Vacco v. Quill* that the articulated state interests justify the distinction drawn between physician-assisted suicide and withdrawal of life-support. I also agree with the Court that the critical question in both of the cases before us is whether "the 'liberty' specially protected by the Due Process Clause includes a right" of the sort that the respondents assert. I do not agree, however, with the Court's formulation of that claimed "liberty" interest. The Court describes it as a "right to commit suicide with another's assistance." But I would not reject the respondents' claim without considering a different formulation, for which our legal tradition may provide greater support. That formulation would use words roughly like a "right to die with dignity." But irrespective of the exact words used, at its core would lie personal control over the manner of death, professional medical assistance, and the avoidance of unnecessary and severe physical suffering—combined.

. . . The respondents here . . . argue that one can find a "right to die with dignity" by examining the protection the law has provided for . . . interests relating to personal dignity, medical treatment, and freedom from state-inflicted pain. . . .

I do not believe, however, that this Court need or now should decide whether or a not such a right is "fundamental." That is because, in my view, the avoidance of severe physical pain (connected with death) would have to comprise an essential part of any successful claim and because, as JUSTICE O'CONNOR points out, the laws before us do not force a dying person to undergo that kind of pain. Rather, the laws of New York and of Washington do not prohibit doctors from providing patients with drugs sufficient to control pain despite the risk that those drugs themselves will kill. And under these circumstances the laws of New York and Washington would overcome any remaining significant interests and would be justified, regardless.

Medical technology, we are repeatedly told, makes the administration of pain-relieving drugs sufficient, except for a very few individuals for whom the ineffectiveness of pain control medicines can mean, not pain, but the need for sedation which can end in a coma. We are also told that there are many instances in which patients do not receive the palliative care that, in principle, is available, but that is so for institutional reasons or inadequacies or obstacles, which would seem possible to overcome, and which do *not* include *a prohibitive set of laws.* . . .

This legal circumstance means that the state laws before us do not infringe directly upon the (assumed) central interest (what I have called the core of the interest in dying with dignity). . . .

Were the legal circumstances different—for example, were state law to prevent the provision of palliative care, including the administration of drugs as needed to avoid pain at the end of life—then the law's impact upon serious and otherwise unavoidable physical pain (accompanying death) would be more directly at issue. And as JUSTICE O'CONNOR suggests, the Court might have to revisit its conclusions in these cases.

□□□

Nos. 95-1478 and 95-1503

Jay Printz, Sheriff/Coroner, Ravalli County, Montana, Petitioner v. United States

Richard Mack, Petitioner v. United States

On writs of certiorari to the United States Court
of Appeals for the Ninth Circuit

[June 27, 1997]

JUSTICE SCALIA delivered the opinion of the Court.

The question presented in these cases is whether certain interim provisions of the Brady Handgun Violence Prevention Act, commanding state and local law enforcement officers to conduct background checks on prospective handgun purchasers and to perform certain related tasks, violate the Constitution.

I

The Gun Control Act of 1968 (GCA), 18 U. S. C. §921 *et seq.*, establishes a detailed federal scheme governing the distribution of firearms. It prohibits firearms dealers from transferring handguns to any person under 21, not resident in the dealer's State, or prohibited by state or local law from purchasing or possessing firearms. It also forbids possession of a firearm by, and transfer of a firearm to, convicted felons, fugitives from justice, unlawful users of controlled substances, persons adjudicated as mentally defective or committed to mental institutions, aliens unlawfully present in the United States, persons dishonorably discharged from the Armed Forces, persons who have renounced their citizenship, and persons who have been subjected to certain restraining orders or been convicted of a misdemeanor offense involving domestic violence.

In 1993, Congress amended the GCA by enacting the Brady Act. The Act requires the Attorney General to establish a national instant background check system by November 30, 1998, and immediately puts in place certain interim provisions until that system becomes operative. Under the interim provisions, a firearms dealer who proposes to transfer a handgun must first: (1) receive from the transferee a statement (the Brady Form), §922(s)(1)(A) (i)(I), containing the name, address and date of birth of the proposed transferee along with a sworn statement that the transferee is not among any of the classes of prohibited purchasers, §922(s)(3); (2) verify the identity of the transferee by examining an identification document, §922(s)(1)(A)(i)(II); and (3) provide the "chief law enforcement officer" (CLEO) of the transferee's residence with notice of the contents (and a copy) of the Brady Form, §§922(s)(1)(A)(i)(III) and (IV). With some exceptions, the dealer must then wait five business days before consummating the sale, unless the CLEO earlier notifies the dealer that he has no reason to believe the transfer would be illegal. §922(s)(1)(A)(ii).

The Brady Act creates two significant alternatives to the foregoing scheme. A dealer may sell a handgun immediately if the purchaser possesses a state handgun permit issued after a background check, §922(s)(1)(C), or if state law provides for an instant background check, §922(s)(1)(D). In States that have not rendered one of these alternatives applicable to all gun purchasers, CLEOs are required to perform certain duties. When a CLEO receives the required notice of a proposed transfer from the firearms dealer, the CLEO must "make a reasonable effort to ascertain within 5 business days whether receipt or possession would be in violation of the law, including research in whatever State and local recordkeeping systems are available and in a national system designated by the Attorney General." §922(s)(2). The Act does not require the CLEO to take any particular action if he determines that a pending transaction would be unlawful; he may notify the firearms dealer to that effect, but is not required to do so. If, however, the CLEO notifies a gun dealer that a prospective purchaser is ineligible to receive a handgun, he must, upon request, provide the would-be purchaser with a written statement of the reasons for that determination. §922(s)(6)(C). Moreover, if the CLEO does not discover any basis for objecting to the sale, he must destroy any records in his possession relating to the transfer, including his copy of the Brady Form. §922(s)(6)(B)(i). Under a separate provision of the GCA, any person who "knowingly violates [the section of the GCA amended by the Brady Act] shall be fined under this title, imprisoned for no more than 1 year, or both." §924(a)(5).

Petitioners Jay Printz and Richard Mack, the CLEOs for Ravalli County, Montana, and Graham County, Arizona, respectively, filed separate actions challenging the constitutionality of the Brady Act's interim provisions. In each case, the District Court held that the provision requiring CLEOs to perform background checks was unconstitutional, but concluded that that provision was severable from the remainder of the Act, effectively leaving a voluntary background-check system in place. (1994). A divided panel of the Court of Appeals for the Ninth Circuit reversed, finding none of the Brady Act's interim provisions to be unconstitutional. (1995). We granted certiorari. (1996).

II

. . . [T]he Brady Act purports to direct state law enforcement officers to participate, albeit only temporarily, in the administration of a federally enacted regulatory scheme. Regulated firearms dealers are required to forward Brady Forms not to a federal officer or employee, but to the CLEOs, whose obligation to accept those forms is implicit in the duty imposed upon them to make "reasonable efforts" within five days to determine whether the sales reflected in the forms are lawful. While the CLEOs are subjected to no federal requirement that they prevent the sales determined to be unlawful . . . , they are empowered to grant, in effect, waivers of the federally prescribed 5-day waiting period for handgun purchases by notifying the gun dealers that they have no reason to believe the transactions would be illegal.

The petitioners here object to being pressed into federal service, and contend that congressional action compelling state officers to execute federal laws is unconstitutional. Because there is no constitutional text speaking to this precise question, the answer to the CLEOs' challenge must be sought in historical understanding and practice, in the structure of the Constitution, and in the jurisprudence of this Court. We treat those three sources, in that order, in this and the next two sections of this opinion.

Petitioners contend that compelled enlistment of state executive officers for the administration of federal programs is, until very recent years at least, unprecedented. The Government contends, to the contrary, that "the earliest Congresses enacted statutes that required the participation of state officials in the implementation of federal laws." . . .

The Government observes that statutes enacted by the first Congresses required state courts to record applications for citizenship, to transmit abstracts of citizenship applications and other naturalization records to the Secretary of State, and to register aliens seeking naturalization and issue certificates of registry. It may well be, however, that these requirements applied only in States that authorized their courts to conduct naturalization proceedings. . . . Other statutes of that era apparently or at least arguably required state courts to perform functions unrelated to naturalization, such as resolving controversies between a captain and the crew of his ship concerning the seaworthiness of the vessel, hearing the claims of slave owners who had apprehended fugitive slaves and issuing certificates authorizing the slave's forced removal to the State from which he had fled, taking proof of the claims of Canadian refugees who had assisted the United States during the Revolutionary War, and ordering the deportation of alien enemies in times of war.

These early laws establish, at most, that the Constitution was originally understood to permit imposition of an obligation on state *judges* to enforce federal prescriptions, insofar as those prescriptions related to matters appropriate for the judicial power. [Scalia said that assumption was "explicit" in the Supremacy Clause, Art. VI, cl. 2, which stated that "the Laws of the United States . . . shall be the supreme Law of the Land; and the Judges in every State shall be bound thereby." In addition, he said, the assumption was "perhaps implicit" in the Framers' decision to make the creation of lower federal courts optional with Congress, since it was "obvious that the Supreme Court alone could not hear all federal cases throughout the United States."]

For these reasons, we do not think the early statutes imposing obligations on state courts imply a power of Congress to impress the state executive into its service. Indeed, it can be argued that the numerousness of these statutes, contrasted with the utter lack of statutes imposing obligations on the States' executive . . . , suggests an assumed *absence* of such power. The only early federal law the Government has brought to our attention that imposed duties on state executive officers is the Extradition Act of 1793, which required the "executive authority" of a State to cause the arrest and delivery of a fugitive from justice upon the request of the executive authority of the State from which the fugitive had fled. That was in direct implementation, however, of the Extradition Clause of the Constitution itself, see Art. IV, §2.

Not only do the enactments of the early Congresses . . . contain no evidence of an assumption that the Federal Government may command the States' executive power in the absence of a particularized constitutional authorization, they contain some indication of precisely the opposite assumption. On September 23, 1789[,] . . . the First Congress enacted a law aimed at obtaining state assistance of the most rudimentary and necessary sort for the enforcement of the new Government's laws: the holding of federal prisoners in state jails at federal expense. Significantly, the law issued not a command to the States' executive, but a recommendation to their legislatures. . . . Moreover, when Georgia refused to comply with the request, Congress's only reaction was a law authorizing the marshal in any State that failed to comply . . . to rent a temporary jail until provision for a permanent one could be made.

[Scalia commented at length on passages from The Federalist cited by the government and by Justice Souter in his dissenting opinion to try to show that the Framers anticipated that the national government could use state officers to carry out federal functions, such as collecting federal taxes. In particular, the government and Justice Souter both emphasized passages written by Alexander Hamilton in Federalist No. 27. The government pointed to a passage in which Hamilton said that the Constitution would "enable the [national] government to employ the ordinary magistracy of each [State] in the execution of its laws." Scalia contended that this and other passages cited by the government "appear to rest on the natural assumption that the States would consent to allowing their officials to assist the Federal Government. . . ."

[Souter emphasized an additional passage by Hamilton: "Thus, the legislatures, courts, and magistrates, of the respective members will be incorporated into the operations of the national government as far as its just and constitutional authority extends; and will be rendered auxiliary to the enforcement of its laws." Scalia responded that Souter's interpretation would lead to untenable conclusions that state officials as well as state legislatures were automatically bound to carry out federal law. "But no one has ever thought, and no one asserts in the present litigation, that that is the law," Scalia concluded.]

To complete the historical record, we must note that there is not only an absence of executive-commandeering statutes in the early Congresses, but there is an absence of them in our later history as well, at least until very recent years. The Government points to the Act of August 3, 1882, which enlisted state officials "to take charge of the local affairs of immigration in the ports within such State, and to provide for the support and relief of such immigrants therein landing as may fall into distress or need of public aid"; to inspect arriving immigrants and exclude any person found to be a "convict, lunatic, idiot," or indigent; and to send convicts back to their country of origin "without compensation." The statute did not, however, *mandate* those duties, but merely empowered the Secretary of the Treasury "to *enter into contracts* with such State . . . officers as *may be designated* for that purpose by *the governor* of any State." (Emphasis added.)

The Government cites the World War I selective draft law that authorized the President "to utilize the service of any or all departments and any or all officers or agents of the United States *and of the several States*, Territories, and the District of Columbia, and subdivisions thereof, in the execution of this Act," and made any person who refused to comply with the President's directions guilty of a misdemeanor. Act of May 18, 1917 (emphasis added). However, it is far from clear that the authorization "to utilize the service" of state officers was an authorization to compel the service of state officers; and the misdemeanor provision surely applied only to refusal to comply with the President's *authorized* directions, which might not have included directions to officers of States whose governors had not volunteered their services. . . .

The Government points to a number of federal statutes enacted within the past few decades that require the participation of state or local officials in implementing federal regulatory schemes. Some of these are connected to federal funding measures, and can perhaps be more accurately described as conditions upon the grant of federal funding than as mandates to the States; others, which require only the provision of information to the Federal Government, do not involve the precise issue before us here, which is the forced participation of the States' executive in the actual administration of a federal program. We of course do not address these or other currently operative enactments that are not before us; it will be time enough to do so if and when their validity is challenged in a proper case. . . .

III

The constitutional practice we have examined above tends to negate the existence of the congressional power asserted here, but is not conclusive. We turn next to consideration of the structure of the Constitution, to see if we can discern among its "essential postulate[s]" a principle that controls the present cases.

A

It is incontestible that the Constitution established a system of "dual sovereignty." Although the States surrendered many of their powers to the new Federal Government, they retained "a residuary and inviolable sovereignty," The Federalist No. 39 (J. Madison). This is reflected throughout the Constitution's text, including (to mention only a few examples) the prohibition on any involuntary reduction or combination of a State's territory, Art. IV, §3; the Judicial Power Clause, Art. III, §2, and the Privileges and Immunities Clause, Art. IV, §2, which speak of the "Citizens" of the States; the amendment provision, Article V, which requires the votes of three-fourths of the States to amend the Constitution; and the Guarantee Clause, Art. IV, §4, which "presupposes the continued existence of the states and . . . those means and instrumentalities which are the creation of their sovereign and reserved rights." Residual state sovereignty was also implicit, of course, in the Constitution's conferral upon Congress of not all governmental powers, but only discrete, enumerated ones, Art. I, §8, which implication was rendered express by the Tenth Amendment's assertion that "[t]he powers not delegated to the United States by the Constitution, nor prohibited by it to the States, are reserved to the States respectively, or to the people."

The Framers' experience under the Articles of Confederation had persuaded them that using the States as the instruments of federal governance was both ineffectual and provocative of federal-state conflict. . . . [T]he Framers rejected the concept of a central government that would act upon and through the States, and instead designed a system in which the state and federal governments would exercise concurrent authority over the people. . . . We have set forth the historical record in more detail elsewhere [*New York v. United States* (1992)]. . . . It suffices to repeat the conclusion: "The Framers explicitly chose a Constitution that confers upon Congress the power to regulate individuals, not States." . . . The Constitution thus contemplates that a State's government will represent and remain accountable to its own citizens. . . .

This separation of the two spheres is one of the Constitution's structural protections of liberty. . . . The power of the Federal Government would be augmented immeasurably if it were able to impress into its service—and at no cost to itself—the police officers of the 50 States.

B

. . . [F]ederal control of state officers . . . would also have an effect upon . . . the separation and equilibration of powers between the three branches of the Federal Government itself. The Constitution does not leave to speculation who is to administer the laws enacted by Congress; the President, it says, "shall take Care that the Laws be faithfully executed," Art. II, §3, personally and through officers whom he appoints. . . . The Brady Act effectively transfers this responsibility to thousands of CLEOs in the 50 States, who are left to implement the program without meaningful Presidential control. . . . The insistence of the Framers upon unity in the Federal Executive—to insure both vigor and accountability—is well known. That unity would be shattered, and the power of the President would be subject to reduction, if Congress could act as effectively without the President as with him, by simply requiring state officers to execute its laws.

C

The dissent of course resorts to the last, best hope of those who defend *ultra vires* congressional action, the Necessary and Proper Clause. It reasons, that the power to regulate the sale of handguns under the Commerce Clause, coupled with the power to "make all Laws which shall be necessary and proper for carrying into Execution the foregoing Powers," Art. I, §8, conclusively establishes the Brady Act's constitutional validity, because the Tenth Amendment imposes no limitations on the exercise of *delegated* powers but merely prohibits the exercise of powers "not delegated to the United States." What destroys the dissent's Necessary and Proper Clause argument, however, is not the Tenth Amendment but the Necessary and Proper Clause itself. When a "La[w] . . . for carrying into Execution" the Commerce Clause violates the principle of state sovereignty reflected in the various constitutional provisions we mentioned earlier, it is not a "La[w] . . . *proper* for carrying into Execution the Commerce Clause." . . .

IV

Finally, and most conclusively in the present litigation, we turn to the prior jurisprudence of this Court. Federal commandeering of state governments is such a novel phenomenon that this Court's first experience with it did not occur until the 1970's, when the Environmental Protection Agency promulgated regulations requiring States to prescribe auto emissions testing, monitoring and retrofit programs, and to designate preferential bus and carpool lanes. The Courts of Appeals for the Fourth and Ninth Circuits invalidated the regulations on statutory grounds in order to avoid what they perceived to be grave constitutional issues; and the District of Columbia Circuit invalidated the regulations on both constitutional and statutory grounds. After we granted certiorari to review the statutory and constitutional validity of the regulations, the Government declined even to defend them, and instead rescinded some and conceded the invalidity of those that remained, leading us to vacate the opinions below and remand for consideration of mootness. [*EPA v. Brown* (1977).]

Although we had no occasion to pass upon the subject in *Brown*, later opinions of ours have made clear that the Federal Government may not compel the States to implement, by legislation or executive action, federal regulatory programs. In *Hodel v. Virginia Surface Mining & Reclamation Assn., Inc.* (1981) and *FERC v. Mississippi* (1982), we sustained statutes against constitutional challenge only after assuring ourselves that they did not require the States to enforce federal law. In *Hodel* we cited the lower court cases in *EPA v. Brown, supra,* but concluded that the Surface Mining Control and Reclamation Act did not present the problem they raised because it merely made compliance with federal standards a precondition to continued state regulation in an otherwise pre-empted field. In *FERC*, we construed the most troubling provisions of the Public Utility Regulatory Policies Act of 1978, to contain only the "command" that state agencies "consider" federal standards, and again only as a precondition to continued state regulation of an otherwise pre-empted field. . . .

When we were at last confronted squarely with a federal statute that unambiguously required the States to enact or administer a federal regulatory program, our decision should have come as no surprise. At issue in *New York v. United States* were the so-called "take title" provisions of the Low-Level Radioactive Waste Policy Amendments Act of 1985, which required States either to enact legislation providing for the disposal of radioactive waste generated within their borders, or to take title to, and possession of the waste—effectively requiring the States either to legislate pursuant to Congress's directions, or to implement an administrative solution. We concluded that Congress could constitutionally require the States to do neither. "The Federal Government," we held, "may not compel the States to enact or administer a federal regulatory program."

The Government contends that *New York* is distinguishable on the following ground: unlike the "take title" provisions invalidated there, the background-check provision of the Brady Act does not require state legislative or executive officials to make policy, but instead issues a final directive to state CLEOs. It is permissible, the Government asserts, for Congress to command state or local officials to assist in the implementation of federal law so long as "Congress itself devises a clear legislative solution that regulates private conduct" and requires state or local officers to provide only "limited, non-policymaking help in enforcing that law." . . .

The Government's distinction between "making" law and merely "enforcing" it, between "policymaking" and mere "implementation," is an interesting one. . . . Executive action that has utterly no policy-making component is rare, particularly at an executive level as high as a jurisdiction's chief law-enforcement officer. Is it really true that there is no policymaking involved in deciding, for example, what "reasonable efforts" shall be expended to conduct a background check? . . . It is quite impossible . . . to draw the Government's proposed line at "no policymaking," and we would have to fall back upon a line of "not too much policymaking." How much is too much is not likely to be answered precisely; and an imprecise barrier against federal intrusion upon state authority is not likely to be an effective one.

Even assuming, moreover, that the Brady Act leaves no "policymaking" discretion with the States, we fail to see how that improves rather than worsens the intrusion upon state sovereignty. . . . It is an essential attribute of the States' retained sovereignty that they remain independent and autonomous within their proper sphere of authority. It is no more compatible with this independence and autonomy that their officers be "dragooned" (as Judge Fernandez put it in his dissent below) into administering federal law, than it would be compatible with the independence and autonomy of the United States that its officers be impressed into service for the execution of state laws.

The Government purports to find support for its proffered distinction of *New York* in our decisions in *Testa v. Katt* (1947) and *FERC v. Mississippi*. We find neither case relevant. *Testa* stands for the proposition that state courts cannot refuse to apply federal law—a conclusion mandated by the terms of the Supremacy Clause ("the Judges in every State shall be bound [by federal law]"). As we have suggested earlier, that says nothing about whether state executive officers must administer federal law. As for *FERC*, it . . . upheld the statutory provisions at issue precisely because they did not commandeer state government, but merely imposed preconditions to continued state regulation of an otherwise pre-empted field, in accord with *Hodel*, and required state administrative agencies to apply federal law while acting in a judicial capacity, in accord with *Testa*.

The Government also maintains that requiring state officers to perform discrete, ministerial tasks specified by Congress does not violate the principle of *New York* because it does not diminish the accountability of state or federal officials. This argument fails even on its own terms. By forcing state governments to absorb the financial burden of implementing a federal regulatory program, Members of Congress can take credit for "solving" problems without having to ask their constituents to pay for the solutions with higher federal taxes. And even when the States are not forced to absorb the costs of implementing a federal program, they are still put in the position of taking the blame for its burdensomeness and for its defects. Under the present law, for example, it will be the CLEO and not some federal official who stands between the gun purchaser and immediate possession of his gun. And it will likely be the CLEO, not some federal official, who will be blamed for any error (even one in the designated federal database) that causes a purchaser to be mistakenly rejected.

The dissent makes no attempt to defend the Government's basis for distinguishing *New York*, but instead advances what seems to us an even more implausible theory. The Brady Act, the dissent asserts, is different from the "take title" provisions invalidated in *New York* because the former is addressed to individuals—namely CLEOs—while the latter were directed to the State itself. That is certainly a difference, but it cannot be a constitutionally significant one. While the Brady Act is directed to "individuals," it is directed to them in their official capacities as state officers; it controls their actions, not as private citizens, but as the agents of the State. . . . To say that the Federal Government cannot control the State, but can control all of its officers, is to say nothing of significance. . . . By resorting to this, the dissent not so much distinguishes *New York* as disembowels it.

Finally, the Government puts forward a cluster of arguments that can be grouped under the heading: "The Brady Act serves very important purposes, is most efficiently administered by CLEOs during the interim period, and places a minimal and only temporary burden upon state officers." There is considerable disagreement over the extent of the burden, but we need not pause over that detail. Assuming all the mentioned factors were true, they might be relevant if we were evaluating whether the incidental application to the States of a federal law of general applicability excessively interfered with the functioning of state governments. [Citation of cases omitted.] But where, as here, it is the whole object of the law to direct the functioning of the state executive, and hence to compromise the structural framework of dual sovereignty, such a "balancing" analysis is inappropriate. It is the very principle of separate state sovereignty that such a law offends, and no comparative assessment of the various interests can overcome that fundamental defect. . . . We expressly rejected such an approach in *New York*. . . . We adhere to that principle today, and conclude categorically, as we concluded categorically in *New York*: "The Federal Government may not compel the States to enact or administer a federal regulatory program." The mandatory obligation imposed on CLEOs to perform background checks on prospective handgun purchasers plainly runs afoul of that rule.

V

What we have said makes it clear enough that the central obligation imposed upon CLEOs by the interim provisions of the Brady Act—the obligation to "make a reasonable effort to ascertain within 5 business days whether receipt or possession [of a handgun] would be in violation of the law, including research in whatever State and local recordkeeping systems are available and in a national system designated by the Attorney General"—is unconstitutional. Extinguished with it, of course, is the duty implicit in the background-check requirement that the CLEO accept notice of the contents of, and a copy of, the completed Brady Form, which the firearms dealer is required to provide to him.

[Scalia said the ruling also eliminated the effect of two other challenged provisions, which required a chief law enforcement officer to destroy Brady forms and to notify a would-be purchaser of the reasons for any determination that the individual is ineligible to receive a handgun.]

There is involved in this Brady Act conundrum a severability question . . . :

whether firearms dealers in the jurisdictions at issue here, and in other jurisdictions, remain obliged to forward to the CLEO (even if he will not accept it) the requisite notice of the contents (and a copy) of the Brady Form; and to wait five business days before consummating the sale. These are important questions, but we have no business answering them in these cases. These provisions burden only firearms dealers and purchasers, and no plaintiff in either of those categories is before us here. We decline to speculate regarding the rights and obligations of parties not before the Court. . . .

* * *

We held in *New York* that Congress cannot compel the States to enact or enforce a federal regulatory program. Today we hold that Congress cannot circumvent that prohibition by conscripting the State's officers directly. The Federal Government may neither issue directives requiring the States to address particular problems, nor command the States' officers, or those of their political subdivisions, to administer or enforce a federal regulatory program. It matters not whether policymaking is involved, and no case-by-case weighing of the burdens or benefits is necessary; such commands are fundamentally incompatible with our constitutional system of dual sovereignty. Accordingly, the judgment of the Court of Appeals for the Ninth Circuit is reversed.

It is so ordered.

JUSTICE O'CONNOR, concurring.

Our precedent and our Nation's historical practices support the Court's holding today. The Brady Act violates the Tenth Amendment to the extent it forces States and local law enforcement officers to perform background checks on prospective handgun owners and to accept Brady Forms from firearms dealers. Our holding, of course, does not spell the end of the objectives of the Brady Act. States and chief law enforcement officers may voluntarily continue to participate in the federal program. Moreover, the directives to the States are merely interim provisions scheduled to terminate November 30, 1998. Congress is also free to amend the interim program to provide for its continuance on a contractual basis with the States if it wishes, as it does with a number of other federal programs. See, *e.g.*, 23 U. S. C. §402 (conditioning States' receipt of federal funds for highway safety program on compliance with federal requirements).

In addition, the Court appropriately refrains from deciding whether other purely ministerial reporting requirements imposed by Congress on state and local authorities pursuant to its Commerce Clause powers are similarly invalid. See, *e.g.*, 42 U. S. C. §5779(a) (requiring state and local law enforcement agencies to report cases of missing children to the Department of Justice). The provisions invalidated here, however, which directly compel state officials to administer a federal regulatory program, utterly fail to adhere to the design and structure of our constitutional scheme.

JUSTICE THOMAS, concurring.

The Court today properly holds that the Brady Act violates the Tenth Amendment in that it compels state law enforcement officers to "administer or enforce a federal regulatory program." Although I join the Court's opinion in full, I write separately to emphasize that the Tenth Amendment affirms the undeniable notion that under our Constitution, the Federal Government is one of enumerated, hence limited, powers. . . .

In my "revisionist" view [quoting dissent by STEVENS, J.], the Federal Government's authority under the Commerce Clause, which merely allocates to Congress the power "to regulate Commerce . . . among the several states," does not extend to the regulation of wholly intrastate, point-of-sale transactions. See *United States v. Lopez* (1995) (concurring opinion). Absent the underlying authority to regulate the intrastate transfer of firearms, Congress surely lacks the corollary power to impress state law enforcement officers into administering and enforcing such regulations. . . .

Even if we construe Congress' authority to regulate interstate commerce to encompass those intrastate transactions that "substantially affect" interstate commerce, I question whether Congress can regulate the particular transactions at issue here. The Constitution . . . places whole areas outside the reach of Congress' regulatory authority. The First Amendment, for example, is fittingly celebrated for preventing Congress from "prohibiting the free exercise" of religion or "abridging the freedom of speech." The Second Amendment similarly appears to contain an express limitation on the government's authority. That Amendment provides: "[a] well regulated Militia, being necessary to the security of a free State, the right of the people to keep and bear arms, shall not be infringed." This Court has not had recent occasion to consider the nature of the substantive right safeguarded by the Second Amendment. If, however, the Second Amendment is read to confer a *personal* right to "keep and bear arms," a colorable argument exists that the Federal Government's regulatory scheme, at least as it pertains to the purely intrastate sale or possession of firearms, runs afoul of that Amendment's protections. As the parties did not raise this argument, however, we need not consider it here. . . . In the meantime, I join the Court's opinion striking down the challenged provisions of the Brady Act as inconsistent with the Tenth Amendment.

JUSTICE STEVENS, with whom JUSTICE SOUTER, JUSTICE GINSBURG, and JUSTICE BREYER join, dissenting.

When Congress exercises the powers delegated to it by the Constitution, it may impose affirmative obligations on executive and judicial officers of state and local governments as well as ordinary citizens. This conclusion is firmly supported by the text of the Constitution, the early history of the Nation, decisions of this Court, and a correct understanding of the basic structure of the Federal Government.

These cases do not implicate the more difficult questions associated with congressional coercion of state legislatures addressed in *New York v. United States* (1992). Nor need we consider the wisdom of relying on local officials rather than federal agents to carry out aspects of a federal program, or even the question whether such officials may be required to perform a federal function on a permanent basis. The question is whether Congress, acting on behalf of the people of the entire Nation, may require local law enforcement officers to perform certain duties during the interim needed for the development of a federal gun control program. . . .

Indeed, since the ultimate issue is one of power, we must consider its implications in times of national emergency. Matters such as the enlistment of air raid wardens, the administration of a military draft, the mass inoculation of children to forestall an epidemic, or perhaps the threat of an international terrorist, may require a national response before federal personnel can be made available to respond. If the Constitution empowers Congress and the President to make an appropriate response, is there anything in the Tenth Amendment, "in historical understanding and practice, in the structure of the Constitution, [or] in the jurisprudence of this Court," that forbids the enlistment of state officers to make that response effective? More narrowly, what basis is there in any of those sources for concluding that it is the Members of this Court, rather than the elected representatives of the people, who should determine whether the Constitution contains the unwritten rule that the Court announces today?

Perhaps today's majority would suggest that no such emergency is presented by the facts of these cases. But such a suggestion is itself an expression of a policy judgment. And Congress' view of the matter is quite different from that implied by the Court today.

The Brady Act was passed in response to what Congress described as an "epidemic of gun violence." The Act's legislative history notes that 15,377 Americans were murdered with firearms in 1992, and that 12,489 of these deaths were caused by handguns. Congress expressed special concern that "[t]he level of firearm violence in this country is, by far, the highest among developed nations." The partial solution contained in the Brady Act, a mandatory background check before a handgun may be purchased, has met with remarkable success. Between 1994 and 1996, approximately 6,600 firearm sales each month to potentially dangerous persons were prevented by Brady Act checks; over 70% of the rejected purchasers were convicted or indicted felons. Whether or not the evaluation reflected in the enactment of the Brady Act is correct as to the extent of the danger and the efficacy of the legislation, the congressional decision surely warrants more respect than it is accorded in today's unprecedented decision.

I

The text of the Constitution provides a sufficient basis for a correct disposition of this case.

Article I, §8, grants the Congress the power to regulate commerce among the States. Putting to one side the revisionist views expressed by JUSTICE THOMAS in his concurring opinion in *United States v. Lopez* (1995), there can be no question that that provision adequately supports the regulation of commerce in handguns effected by the Brady Act. Moreover, the additional grant of authority in that section of the Constitution "[t]o make all Laws which shall be necessary and proper for carrying into Execution the foregoing Powers" is surely adequate to support the temporary enlistment of local police officers in the process of identifying persons who should not be entrusted with the possession of handguns. In short, the affirmative delegation of power in Article I provides ample authority or the congressional enactment.

. . . [T]he Tenth Amendment imposes no restriction on the exercise of delegated powers. Using language that plainly refers only to powers that are "not" delegated to Congress, it provides:

> "The powers not delegated to the United States by the Constitution, nor prohibited by it to the States, are reserved to the States respectively, or to the people." U. S. Const., Amdt. 10.

The Amendment confirms the principle that the powers of the Federal Government are limited to those affirmatively granted by the Constitution, but it does not purport to limit the scope or the effectiveness of the exercise of powers that are delegated to Congress. . . . Thus, the Amendment provides no support for a rule that immunizes local officials from obligations that might be imposed on ordinary citizens. Indeed, it would be more reasonable to infer that federal law may impose greater duties on state officials than on private citizens because another provision of the Constitution requires that "all executive and judicial Officers, both of the United States and of the several States, shall be bound by Oath or Affirmation, to support this Constitution." U. S. Const., Art. VI, cl. 3. . . .

There is not a clause, sentence, or paragraph in the entire text of the Constitution of the United States that supports the proposition that a local police officer can ignore a command contained in a statute enacted by Congress pursuant to an express delegation of power enumerated in Article I.

II

Under the Articles of Confederation the National Government had the power to issue commands to the several sovereign states, but it had no authority to govern individuals directly. Thus, it raised an army and financed its operations by issuing requisitions to the constituent members of the Confederacy, rather than by creating federal agencies to draft soldiers or to impose taxes.

That method of governing proved to be unacceptable, not because it demeaned the sovereign character of the several States, but rather because it was cumbersome and inefficient. . . . The basic change in the character of the government that the Framers conceived was designed to enhance the power of the national government, not to provide some new, unmentioned immunity for state officers. . . .

Indeed, the historical materials strongly suggest that the Founders intended to enhance the capacity of the federal government by empowering it—as a part of the new authority to make demands directly on individual citizens—to act through local officials. [Stevens cited passages by Alexander Hamilton in The Federalist No. 27, among other contemporaneous sources, to contend that the Framers believed that "state judicial and executive branch officials may be required to implement federal law where the National Government acts within the scope of its affirmative powers."]

Bereft of support in the history of the founding, the Court rests its conclusion on the claim that there is little evidence the National Government actually exercised such a power in the early years of the Republic. This reasoning is misguided in principle and in fact. . . . [W]e have never suggested that the failure of the early Congresses to address the scope of federal power in a particular area or to exercise a particular authority was an argument against its existence. . . .

More importantly, the fact that Congress did elect to rely on state judges and the clerks of state courts to perform a variety of executive functions is surely evidence of a contemporary understanding that their status as state officials did not immunize them from federal service. The majority's description of these early statutes is both incomplete and at times misleading.

For example, statutes of the early Congresses required in mandatory terms that state judges and their clerks perform various executive duties with respect to applications for citizenship. [Description of acts of 1790, 1798, and 1802 omitted.]

Similarly, the First Congress enacted legislation requiring state courts to serve, functionally, like contemporary regulatory agencies in certifying the seaworthiness of vessels. The majority casts this as an adjudicative duty, but that characterization is misleading. . . . The statute sets forth, in essence, procedures for an expert inquisitorial proceeding, supervised by a judge but otherwise more characteristic of executive activity. . . .

The Court's evaluation of the historical evidence, furthermore, fails to acknowledge the important difference between policy decisions that may have been influenced by respect for state sovereignty concerns, and decisions that are compelled by the Constitution. Thus, for example, the decision by Congress to give President Wilson the authority to utilize the services of state officers in implementing the World War I draft surely indicates that the national legislature saw no constitutional impediment to the enlistment of state assistance during a federal emergency. The fact that the President was able to implement the program by respectfully "request[ing]" state action, rather than bluntly commanding it, is evidence that he was an effective statesman, but surely does not indicate that he doubted either his or Congress' power to use mandatory language if necessary. . . .

. . . [T]he majority's opinion consists almost entirely of arguments against the substantial evidence weighing in opposition to its view; the Court's ruling is strikingly lacking in affirmative support. Absent even a modicum of textual foundation for its judicially crafted constitutional rule, there should be a presumption that if the Framers had actually intended such a rule, at least one of them would have mentioned it.

III

The Court's "structural" arguments are not sufficient to rebut that presumption. The fact that the Framers intended to preserve the sovereignty of the several States simply does not speak to the question whether individual state employees may be required to perform federal obligations, such as registering young adults for the draft, creating state emergency response commissions designed to manage the release of hazardous substances, collecting and reporting data on underground storage tanks that may pose an environmental hazard, and reporting traffic fatalities and missing children to a federal agency.

As we explained in *Garcia v. San Antonio Metropolitan Transit Authority* (1985): "[T]he principal means chosen by the Framers to ensure the role of the States in the federal system lies in the structure of the Federal Government itself. . . ." Given the fact that the Members of Congress are elected by the people of the several States, with each State receiving an equivalent number of Senators in order to ensure that even the smallest States have a powerful voice in the legislature, it is quite unrealistic to assume that they will ignore the sovereignty concerns of their constituents. It is far more reasonable to presume that their decisions to impose modest burdens on state officials from time to time reflect a considered judgment that the people in each of the States will benefit therefrom. . . .

Recent developments demonstrate that the political safeguards protecting our Federalism are effective. The majority expresses special concern that were its rule not adopted the Federal Government would be able to avail itself of the services of state government officials "at no cost to itself." . . . But this specific problem of federal actions that have the effect of imposing so-called "unfunded mandates" on the States has been identified and meaningfully addressed by Congress in recent legislation. See Unfunded Mandates Reform Act of 1995 [requring explicit decision by Congress to impose on states any unfunded mandate of over $50 million]. . . . Whatever the ultimate impact of the new legislation, its passage demonstrates that unelected judges are better off leaving the protection of federalism to the political process in all but the most extraordinary circumstances.

Perversely, the majority's rule seems more likely to damage than to preserve the safeguards against tyranny provided by the existence of vital state governments. By limiting the ability of the Federal Government to enlist state officials in the implementation of its programs, the Court creates incentives for the National Govern ment to aggrandize itself. In the name of State's rights, the majority would have the Federal Government create vast national bureaucracies to implement its policies. This is exactly the sort of thing that the early Federalists promised would not occur, in part as a result of the National Government's ability to rely on the magistracy of the states.

With colorful hyperbole, the Court suggests that the unity in the Executive Branch of the Federal Government "would be shattered, and the power of the President would be subject to reduction, if Congress could . . . require . . . state officers to execute its laws." Putting to one side the obvious tension between the majority's claim that impressing state police officers will unduly tip the balance of power in favor of the federal sovereign and this suggestion that it will emasculate the Presidency, the Court's reasoning contradicts *New York v. United States*.

That decision squarely approved of cooperative federalism programs, designed at the national level but implemented principally by state governments. *New York* disapproved of a particular method of putting such programs into place, not the existence of federal programs implemented locally. . . . Indeed, nothing in the majority's holding calls into question the three mechanisms for constructing such programs that *New York* expressly approved. Congress may require the States to implement its programs as a condition of federal spending, in order to avoid the threat of unilateral federal action in the area, or as a part of a program that affects States and private parties alike. The majority's suggestion in response to this dissent that Congress' ability to create such programs is limited is belied by the importance and sweep of the federal statutes that meet this description, some of which we described in *New York*. [Noting references to the Clean Water Act, the Occupational Safety and Health Act of 1970, and the Resource Conservation and Recovery Act of 1976.]

Nor is there force to the assumption undergirding the Court's entire opinion that if this trivial burden on state sovereignty is permissible, the entire structure of federalism will soon collapse. These cases do not involve any mandate to state legislatures to enact new rules. . . . [T]his case . . . merely involves the imposition of modest duties on individual officers. . . .

Far more important than the concerns that the Court musters in support of its new rule is the fact that the Framers entrusted Congress with the task of creating a working structure of intergovernmental relationships around the framework that the Constitution authorized. Neither explicitly nor implicitly did the Framers issue any command that forbids Congress from imposing federal duties on private citizens or on local officials. As a general matter, Congress has followed the sound policy of authorizing federal agencies and federal agents to administer federal programs. That general practice, however, does not negate the existence of power to rely on state officials in occasional situations in which such reliance is in the national interest. Rather, the occasional exceptions confirm the wisdom of Justice Holmes' reminder that "the machinery of government would not work if it were not allowed a little play in its joints."

IV

Finally, the Court advises us that the "prior jurisprudence of this Court" is the most conclusive support for its position. That "prior jurisprudence" is *New York v. United States.* . . .

[Stevens summarized the decision as striking down a provision of a federal statute that "gave the States the option either of adopting regulations dictated by Congress or of taking title to and possession of low level radioactive waste" generated within their borders. "The Court concluded," Stevens continued, "that, because Congress had no power to compel the state governments to take title to the waste, the 'option' really amounted to a simple command to the States to enact and enforce a federal regulatory program." On that basis, he said, the Court held the provision was "inconsistent with the federal structure of our Government established by the Constitution."]

Our statements . . . clearly did not decide the question presented here, whether state executive officials—as opposed to state legislators—may in appropriate circumstances be enlisted to implement federal policy. . . .

The majority relies upon dictum in *New York* to the effect that "[t]he Federal Government may not compel the States to enact *or administer* a federal regulatory program." (Emphasis added). But that language was wholly unnecessary to the decision of the case. It is, of course, beyond dispute that we are not bound by the dicta of our prior opinions. . . . To the extent that it has any substance at all, *New York*'s administration language may have referred to the possibility that the State might have been able to take title to and devise an elaborate scheme for the management of the radioactive waste through purely executive policymaking. But despite the majority's effort to suggest that similar activities are required by the Brady Act, it is hard to characterize the minimal requirement that CLEOs perform background checks as one involving the exercise of substantial policymaking discretion on that essentially legislative scale. . . .

Importantly, the majority either misconstrues or ignores three cases that are more directly on point. In *FERC* [*v. Mississippi* (1982)], we upheld a federal statute requiring state utilities commissions, *inter alia*, to take the affirmative step of considering federal energy standards in a manner complying with federally specified notice and comment procedures, and to report back to Congress periodically. . . . The burden on state officials that we approved in *FERC* was far more extensive than the minimal, temporary imposition posed by the Brady Act. Similarly, in *Puerto Rico v. Branstad* (1987), we . . . held that the Extradition Act of 1793 permitted the Commonwealth of Puerto Rico to seek extradition of a fugitive from its laws without constitutional barrier. . . .

Finally, the majority provides an incomplete explanation of our decision in *Testa v. Katt* (1947) and demeans its importance. In that case the Court unanimously held that state courts of appropriate jurisdiction must occupy themselves adjudicating claims brought by private litigants under the federal Emergency Price Control Act of 1942, regardless of how otherwise crowded their dockets might be with state law matters. That is a much greater imposition on state sovereignty than the Court's characterization of the case as merely holding that "state courts cannot refuse to apply federal law." . . .

Even if the Court were correct in its suggestion that it was the reference to judges in the Supremacy Clause, rather than the central message of the entire Clause, that dictated the result in *Testa*, the Court's implied . . . argument that the Framers therefore did not intend to permit the enlistment of other state officials is implausible. . . . The notion that the Framers would have had no reluctance to "press state judges into federal service" against their will but would have regarded the imposition of a similar—indeed, far lesser—burden on town constables as an intolerable affront to principles of state sovereignty, can only be considered perverse. If such a distinction had been contemplated by the learned and articulate men who fashioned the basic structure of our government, surely some of them would have said so.

* * *

The provision of the Brady Act that crosses the Court's newly defined constitutional threshold is more comparable to a statute requiring local police officers to report the identity of missing children to the Crime Control Center of the Department of Justice than to an offensive federal command to a sovereign state. If Congress believes that such a statute will benefit the people of the Nation, and serve the interests of cooperative federalism better than an enlarged federal bureaucracy, we should respect both its policy judgment and its appraisal of its constitutional power.

Accordingly, I respectfully dissent.

JUSTICE SOUTER, dissenting.

I join JUSTICE STEVENS's dissenting opinion, but subject to the following qualifications. While I do not find anything dispositive in the paucity of early examples of federal employment of state officers for executive purposes, . . . neither would I find myself in dissent with no more to go on than those few early instances in the administration of naturalization laws, for example, or such later instances as state support for federal emergency action. . . .

In deciding these cases, which I have found closer than I had anticipated, it is The Federalist that finally determines my position. I believe that the most straightforward reading of No. 27 is authority for the Government's position here. . . .

Hamilton in No. 27 first notes that because the new Constitution would authorize the National Government to bind individuals directly through national law, it could "employ the ordinary magistracy of each [State] in the execution of its laws." The Federalist No. 27. Were he to stop here, he would not necessarily be speaking of anything beyond the possibility of cooperative arrangements by agreement. But he then addresses the combined effect of the proposed Supremacy Clause, U. S. Const., Art. VI, cl. 2, and state officers's oath requirement, U. S. Const., Art. VI, cl. 3, and he states that "the Legislatures, Courts and Magistrates of the respective members will be incorporated into the operations of the national government, *as far as its just and constitutional authority extends;* and will be rendered auxiliary to the enforcement of its laws." (Emphasis in original). The natural reading of this language is not merely that the officers of the various branches of state governments may be employed in the performance of national functions; Hamilton says that the state governmental machinery "will be incorporated" into the Nation's operation, and because the "auxiliary" status of the state officials will occur because they are "bound by the sanctity of an oath," I take him to mean that their auxiliary functions will be the products of their obligations thus undertaken to support federal law, not of their own, or the States', unfettered choices.

. . . To be sure, it does not follow that any conceivable requirement may be imposed on any state official. I continue to agree, for example, that Congress may not require a state legislature to enact a regulatory scheme and that *New York v. United States* (1992) was rightly decided (even though I now believe its dicta went too far toward immunizing state administration as well as state enactment of such a scheme from congressional mandate); after all, the essence of legislative power, within the limits of legislative jurisdiction, is a discretion not subject to command. But insofar as national law would require nothing from a state officer inconsistent with the power proper to his branch of tripartite state government . . . , I suppose that the reach of federal law as Hamilton described it would not be exceeded. . . .

. . . I do not read any of The Federalist material as requiring the conclusion that Congress could require administrative support without an obligation to pay fair value for it. . . . If, therefore, my views were prevailing in these cases, I would remand for development and consideration of petitioners' points, that they have no budget provision for work required under the Act and are liable for unauthorized expenditures.

JUSTICE BREYER, with whom JUSTICE STEVENS joins, dissenting.

I would add to the reasons JUSTICE STEVENS sets forth the fact that the United States is not the only nation that seeks to reconcile the practical need for a central authority with the democratic virtues of more local control. . . . The federal systems of Switzerland, Germany, and the European Union, for example, all provide that constituent states, not federal bureaucracies, will themselves implement many of the laws, rules, regulations, or decrees enacted by the central "federal" body. They do so in part because they believe that such a system interferes less, not more, with the independent authority of the "state," member nation, or other subsidiary government, and helps to safeguard individual liberty as well.

Of course, we are interpreting our own Constitution, not those of other nations. . . . But their experience . . . offers empirical confirmation of the implied answer to a question JUSTICE STEVENS asks: Why, or how, would what the majority sees as a constitutional alternative—the creation of a new federal gun-law bureaucracy, or the expansion of an existing federal bureaucracy—better promote either state sovereignty or individual liberty? . . .

Regardless, as JUSTICE STEVENS points out, the Constitution itself is silent on the matter. Precedent supports the Government's position here. And the fact that there is not more precedent—that direct federal assignment of duties to state officers is not common—likely reflects, not a widely shared belief that any such assignment is incompatible with basic principles of federalism, but rather a widely shared practice of assigning such duties in other ways. Thus, there is neither need nor reason to find in the Constitution an absolute principle, the inflexibility of which poses a surprising and technical obstacle to the enactment of a law that Congress believed necessary to solve an important national problem.

For these reasons and those set forth in JUSTICE STEVENS' opinion, I join his dissent.

How the Court Works

The Constitution makes the Supreme Court the final arbiter in "cases" and "controversies" arising under the Constitution or the laws of the United States. As the interpreter of the law, the Court often is viewed as the least mutable and most tradition-bound of the three branches of the federal government. But the Court has undergone innumerable changes in its history, some of which have been mandated by law. Some of these changes are embodied in Court rules; others are informal adaptations to needs and circumstances.

The Schedule of the Term

Annual Terms

By law the Supreme Court begins its regular annual term on the first Monday in October, and the term lasts approximately nine months. This session is known as the October term. The summer recess, which is not determined by statute or Court rules, generally begins in late June or early July of the following year. This system—staying in continuous session throughout the year, with periodic recesses—makes it unnecessary to convene a special term to deal with matters arising in the summer.

The justices actually begin work before the official opening of the term. They hold their initial conference during the last week in September. When the justices formally convene on the first Monday in October, oral arguments begin.

Arguments and Conferences

At least four justices must request that a case be argued before it can be accepted. Arguments are heard on Monday, Tuesday, and Wednesday for seven two-week sessions, beginning in the first week in October and ending in mid-April. Recesses of two weeks or longer occur between the sessions of oral arguments so that justices can consider the cases and deal with other Court business.

The schedule for oral arguments is 10:00 a.m. to noon and 1 p.m. to 3 p.m. Because most cases receive one hour apiece for argument, the Court can hear up to twelve cases a week.

The Court holds conferences on the Friday just before the two-week oral argument periods and on Wednesday and Friday during the weeks when oral arguments are scheduled. The conferences are designed for consideration of cases already heard in oral argument.

Before each of the Friday conferences, the chief justice circulates a "discuss" list—a list of cases deemed important enough for discussion and a vote. Appeals are placed on the discuss list almost automatically, but as many as three-quarters of the petitions for certiorari are denied. No case is denied review during conference, however, without an initial examination by the justices and their law clerks. Any justice can have a case placed on the Court's conference agenda for review. Most of the cases scheduled for the discuss list also are denied review in the end but only after discussion by the justices during the conference.

Although the last oral arguments have been heard by mid-April each year, the conferences of the justices continue until the end of the term to consider cases remaining on the Court's agenda. All conferences are held in secret, with no legal assistants or other staff present. The attendance of six justices constitutes a quorum. Conferences begin with handshakes all around. In discussing a case, the chief justice speaks first, followed by each justice in order of seniority.

Decision Days

Opinions are released on Tuesdays and Wednesdays during the weeks that the Court is hearing oral arguments; during other weeks, they are released on Mondays. In addition to opinions, the Court also releases an "orders" list—the summary of the Court's action granting or denying review. The orders list is posted at the beginning of the Monday session. It is not announced orally but can be obtained from the clerk and the public information officer. When urgent or important matters arise, the Court's summary orders may be made available on a day other than Monday.

Unlike its orders, decisions of the Court are announced orally in open Court. The justice who wrote the opinion announces the Court's decision, and justices writing concurring or dissenting opinions may state their views as well. When more than one decision is to be rendered, the justices who wrote the opinion make their announcements in reverse order of seniority. Occasionally, all or a large portion of the opinion is read aloud. More often the author summarizes the opinion or simply announces the result and states that a written opinion has been filed.

Reviewing Cases

In determining whether to accept a case for review, the Court has considerable discretion, subject only to the restraints imposed by the Constitution

---

Visiting the Supreme Court

The Supreme Court building has six levels, two of which—the ground and main floors—are accessible to the public. The basement contains a parking garage, a printing press, and offices for security guards and maintenance personnel. On the ground floor are the John Marshall statue, the exhibition area, the public information office, and a cafeteria. The main corridor, known as the Great Hall, the courtroom, and justices' offices are on the main floor. The second floor contains dining rooms, the justices' reading room, and other offices; the third floor, the Court library; and the fourth floor, the gym and storage areas.

From October to mid-April, the Court hears oral arguments Monday through Wednesday for about two weeks a month. These sessions begin at 10 a.m. and continue until 3 p.m., with a one-hour recess starting at noon. They are open to the public on a first-come, first-served basis.

Visitors may inspect the Supreme Court chamber any time the Court is not in session. Historical exhibits and a free motion picture on how the Court works also are available throughout the year. The Supreme Court building is open from 9 a.m. to 4:30 p.m. Monday through Friday, except for legal holidays. When the Court is not in session, lectures are given in the courtroom every hour on the half hour between 9:30 a.m. and 3:30 p.m.

---

and Congress. Article III, section 2, of the Constitution provides that "In all Cases affecting Ambassadors, other public Ministers and Consuls, and those in which a State shall be Party, the supreme Court shall have original Jurisdiction. In all the other Cases . . . the supreme Court shall have appellate Jurisdiction, both as to Law and Fact, with such Exceptions, and under such Regulations as the Congress shall make."

Original jurisdiction refers to the right of the Supreme Court to hear a case before any other court does. Appellate jurisdiction is the right to review the decision of a lower court. The vast majority of cases reaching the Supreme Court are appeals from rulings of the lower courts; generally only a handful of original jurisdiction cases are filed each term.

After enactment of the Judiciary Act of 1925, the Supreme Court gained broad discretion to decide for itself what cases it would hear. In 1988 Congress virtually eliminated the Court's mandatory jurisdiction, which obliged it to hear most appeals. Since then that discretion has been nearly unlimited.

Methods of Appeal

Cases come to the Supreme Court in several ways: through petitions for writs of certiorari, appeals, and requests for certification.

In petitioning for a writ of certiorari, a litigant who has lost a case in a lower court sets out the reasons why the Supreme Court should review the case. If a writ is granted, the Court requests a certified record of the case from the lower court.

The main difference between the certiorari and appeal routes is that the Court has complete discretion to grant a request for a writ of certiorari but is under more obligation to accept and decide a case that comes to it on appeal.

Most cases reach the Supreme Court by means of the writ of certiorari. In the relatively few cases to reach the Court by means of appeal, the appellant must file a jurisdictional statement explaining why the case qualifies for review and why the Court should grant it a hearing. Often the justices dispose of these cases by deciding them summarily, without oral argument or formal opinion.

Those whose petitions for certiorari have been granted must pay the Court's standard $300 fee for docketing the case. The U.S. government does not have to pay these fees, nor do persons too poor to afford them. The latter may file in forma pauperis (in the character or manner of a pauper) petitions. Another, seldom used, method of appeal is certification, the request by a lower court—usually a court of appeals—for a final answer to questions of law in a particular case. The Court, after examining the certificate, may order the case argued before it.

Process of Review

In recent terms the Court has been asked to review around 7,000 cases. All petitions are examined by the staff of the clerk of the Court; those found to be in reasonably proper form are placed on the docket and given a number. All cases, except those falling within the Court's original jurisdiction, are placed on a single docket, known simply as "the docket." Only in the numbering of the cases is a distinction made between prepaid and in forma pauperis cases on the docket. The first case filed in the 1996–1997 term, for example, would be designated 96–1. In forma pauperis cases contain the year and begin with the number 5001. The second in forma pauperis case filed in the 1996–1997 term would thus be number 96–5002.

Each justice, aided by law clerks, is responsible for reviewing all cases on the docket. In recent years a number of justices have used a "cert pool" system in this review. Their clerks work together to examine cases, writing a pool memo on several petitions. The memo then is given to the justices who determine if more research is needed. Other justices may prefer to review each petition themselves or have their clerks do it.

Petitions on the docket vary from elegantly printed and bound documents, of which multiple copies are submitted to the Court, to single sheets of prison stationery scribbled in pencil. The decisions to grant or deny review of cases are made in conferences, which are held in the conference room adjacent to the chief justice's chambers. Justices are summoned to the conference room by a buzzer, usually between 9:30 and 10:00 a.m. They shake hands with each other and take their appointed seats, and the chief justice then begins the discussion.

Discuss and Orders Lists

A few days before the conference convenes, the chief justice compiles the discuss list of cases deemed important enough for discussion and a vote. As many as three-quarters of the petitions for certiorari are denied a place on the list and thus rejected without further consideration. Any justice can have a case placed on the discuss list simply by requesting that it be placed there.

Only the justices attend conferences; no legal assistants or staff are present. The junior associate justice acts as doorkeeper and messenger, sending for reference material and receiving messages and data. Unlike with other parts of the federal government, few leaks have occurred about what transpires during the conferences.

At the start of the conference, the chief justice makes a brief statement outlining the facts of each case. Then each justice, beginning with the senior associate justice, comments on the case, usually indicating in the course of the comments how he or she intends to vote. A traditional but unwritten rule is that four affirmative votes puts a case on the schedule for oral argument.

Petitions for certiorari, appeals, and in forma pauperis motions that are approved for review or denied review during conference are placed on a certified orders list to be released the next Monday in open court.

Arguments

Once the Court announces it will hear a case, the clerk of the Court arranges the schedule for oral argument. Cases are argued roughly in the order in which they were granted review, subject to modification if more time is needed to acquire all the necessary documents. Cases generally are heard not sooner than three months after the Court has agreed to review

The Supreme Court's law library contains about 300,000 volumes and houses the most complete available set of the printed briefs, appendices, and records of Court cases.

them. Under special circumstances the date scheduled for oral argument can be advanced or postponed.

Well before oral argument takes place, the justices receive the briefs and records from counsel in the case. The measure of attention the brief receives—from a thorough and exhaustive study to a cursory glance—depends both on the nature of the case and the work habits of the justice.

As one of the two public functions of the Court, oral arguments are viewed by some as very important. Others dispute the significance of oral arguments, contending that by the time a case is heard most of the justices already have made up their minds.

Time Limits

The time allowed each side for oral argument is thirty minutes. Because the time allotted must accommodate any questions the justices may wish to ask, the actual time for presentation may be considerably shorter than thirty minutes. Under the current rules of the Court, one counsel only will be heard for each side, except by special permission.

An exception is made for an amicus curiae, a "friend of the court," a person who volunteers or is invited to take part in matters before a court but is not a party in the case. Counsel for an amicus curiae may participate in oral argument if the party supported by the amicus allows use of part of its argument time or the Court grants a motion permitting argument by this counsel. The motion must show, the rules state, that the amicus's argument "is thought to provide assistance to the Court not otherwise available." The Court is generally unreceptive to such motions.

Court rules provide advice to counsel presenting oral arguments before the Court: "Oral argument should emphasize and clarify the written arguments appearing in the briefs on the merits." That same rule warns—with italicized emphasis—that the Court "looks with disfavor on oral argument read from a prepared text." Most attorneys appearing before the Court use an outline or notes to make sure they cover the important points.

Circulating the Argument

The Supreme Court has tape-recorded oral arguments since 1955. In 1968 the Court, in addition to its own recording, began contracting with private firms to tape and transcribe all oral arguments. The contract stipulates that the transcript "shall include everything spoken in argument, by Court, counsel, or others, and nothing shall be omitted from the transcript unless the Chief Justice or Presiding Justice so directs." But "the names of Justices asking questions shall not be recorded or transcribed; questions shall be indicated by the letter 'Q.'"

The marshal of the Court keeps the tapes during the term, and their use usually is limited to the justices and their law clerks. At the end of the term, the tapes are sent to the National Archives. Persons wishing to listen to the tapes or buy a copy of a transcript can apply to the Archives for permission to do so.

Transcripts made by a private firm can be acquired more quickly. These transcripts usually are available a week after arguments are heard. Transcripts can be read in the Court's library or public information office. Those who purchase the transcripts must agree that they will not be photographically reproduced. In addition, transcripts of oral arguments are available on the Westlaw electronic data retrieval system.

Proposals have been made to tape arguments for television and radio use or to permit live broadcast coverage of arguments. The Court has rejected these proposals.

Use of Briefs

The brief of the petitioner or appellant must be filed within forty-five days of the Court's announced decision to hear the case. Except for in forma pauperis cases, forty copies of the brief must be filed with the Court. For in forma pauperis proceedings, the Court requires only that documents be legible. The opposing brief from the respondent or appellee is to be filed within thirty days of receipt of the brief of the petitioner or appellant. Either party may appeal to the clerk for an extension of time in filing the brief.

Court Rule 24 sets forth the elements that a brief should contain. These are: the questions presented for review; a list of all parties to the proceeding; a table of contents and table of authorities; citations of the opinions and judgments delivered in the lower courts; "a concise statement of the grounds on which the jurisdiction of this Court is invoked"; constitutional provisions, treaties, statutes, ordinances, and regulations involved; "a concise statement of the case containing all that is material to the consideration of the questions presented"; a summary of argument; the argument, which exhibits "clearly the points of fact and of law being presented and citing the authorities and statutes relied upon"; and a conclusion "specifying with particularity the relief which the party seeks."

The form and organization of the brief are covered by rules 33 and 34. The rules limit the number of pages in various types of briefs. The rules also set out a color code for the covers of different kinds of briefs. Petitions are white; motions opposing them are orange. Petitioner's briefs on the merits are light blue, while those of respondents are red. Reply briefs are yellow; amicus curiae, green; and documents filed by the United States, gray.

Questioning

During oral argument the justices may interrupt with questions or remarks as often as they wish. Unless counsel has been granted special permission extending the thirty-minute limit, he or she can continue talking after the time has expired only to complete a sentence.

The frequency of questioning, as well as the manner in which questions are asked, depends on the style of the justices and their interest in a particular case. Of the current justices, all but Clarence Thomas participate, more or less actively, in questioning during oral arguments; Thomas asks questions very, very rarely.

Questions from the justices may upset and unnerve counsel by interrupting a well-rehearsed argument and introducing an unexpected element. Nevertheless, questioning has several advantages. It serves to alert counsel about what aspects of the case need further elaboration or more information. For the Court, questions can bring out weak points in an argument— and sometimes strengthen it.

Conferences

Cases for which oral arguments have been heard are then dealt with in conference. During the Wednesday afternoon conference, the cases that

The Supreme Court's bench, angled at the ends, allows justices to see each other during oral arguments.

were argued the previous Monday are discussed and decided. At the all-day Friday conference, the cases argued on the preceding Tuesday and Wednesday are discussed and decided. Justices also consider new motions, appeals, and petitions while in conference.

Conferences are conducted in complete secrecy. No secretaries, clerks, stenographers, or messengers are allowed into the room. This practice began many years ago when the justices became convinced that decisions were being disclosed prematurely.

The justices meet in an oak-paneled, book-lined conference room adjacent to the chief justice's suite. Nine chairs surround a large rectangular table, each chair bearing the nameplate of the justice who sits there. The chief justice sits at the east end of the table, and the senior associate justice at the west end. The other justices take their places in order of seniority. The junior justice is charged with sending for and receiving documents or other information the Court needs.

On entering the conference room the justices shake hands with each other, a symbol of harmony that began in the 1880s. The chief justice begins the conference by calling the first case to be decided and discussing it. When the chief justice is finished, the senior associate justice speaks, followed by the other justices in order of seniority.

The justices can speak for as long as they wish, but they practice restraint because of the amount of business to be completed. By custom each justice speaks without interruption. Other than these procedural arrangements, little is known about what transpires in conference. Although discussions generally are said to be polite and orderly, occasionally they can be acrimonious. Likewise, consideration of the issues in a particular case may be full and probing, or perfunctory, leaving the real debate on the question until later when the written drafts of opinions are circulated up and down the Court's corridors between chambers.

Generally the discussion of the case clearly indicates how a justice plans to vote on it. A majority vote is needed to decide a case—five votes if all nine justices are participating.

Opinions

After the justices have voted on a case, the writing of the opinion or opinions begins. An opinion is a reasoned argument explaining the legal issues in the case and the precedents on which the opinion is based. Soon after a case is decided in conference, the task of writing the majority opinion is assigned. When in the majority, the chief justice designates the writer. When the chief justice is in the minority, the senior associate justice voting with the majority assigns the job of writing the majority opinion.

Any justice may write a separate opinion. If in agreement with the Court's decision but not with some of the reasoning in the majority opinion, the justice writes a concurring opinion giving his or her reasoning. If in disagreement with the majority, the justice writes a dissenting opinion or simply goes on record as a dissenter without an opinion. More than one justice can sign a concurring opinion or a dissenting opinion.

The amount of time between the vote on a case and the announcement of the decision varies from case to case. In simple cases where few points of law are at issue, the opinion sometimes can be written and cleared by the other justices in a week or less. In more complex cases, especially those with several dissenting or concurring opinions, the process can take six months or more. Some cases may have to be reargued or the initial decision reversed after the drafts of opinions have been circulated.

The assigning justice may consider the points made by majority justices during the conference discussion, the workload of the other justices, the need to avoid the more extreme opinions within the majority, and expertise in the particular area of law involved in a case.

The style of writing a Court opinion—majority, concurring, or dissenting—depends primarily on the individual justice. In some cases, the justice may prefer to write a restricted and limited opinion; in others, he or she may take a broader approach to the subject. The decision likely is to be influenced by the need to satisfy the other justices in the majority.

When a justice is satisfied that the written opinion is conclusive or "unanswerable," it goes into print. Draft opinions are circulated, revised, and printed on a computerized typesetting system. The circulation of the drafts—whether computer-to-computer or on paper—provokes further discussion in many cases. Often the suggestions and criticisms require the writer to juggle opposing views. To retain a majority, the author of the draft opinion frequently feels obliged to make major emendations to satisfy justices who are unhappy with the initial draft. Some opinions have to be rewritten several times.

One reason for the secrecy surrounding the circulation of drafts is that some of the justices who voted with the majority may find the majority draft opinion so unpersuasive—or one or more of the dissenting drafts so convincing—that they change their vote. If enough justices alter their votes, the majority may shift, so that a former dissent becomes the majority opinion. When a new majority emerges from this process, the task of writing, printing, and circulating a new majority draft begins all over again.

When the drafts of an opinion—including dissents and concurring views—have been written, circulated, discussed, and revised, if necessary, the final versions then are printed. Before the opinion is produced the reporter of decisions adds a "headnote" or syllabus summarizing the decision and a "lineup" showing how the justices voted.

Two hundred copies of the "bench opinion" are made. As the decision is announced in Court, the bench opinion is distributed to journalists and others in the public information office. Another copy, with any necessary corrections noted on it, is sent to the U.S. Government Printing Office, which prints 3,397 "slip" opinions, which are distributed to federal and state courts and agencies. The Court receives 400 of these, and they are available to the public free through the Public Information Office as long as supplies last. The Government Printing Office also prints the opinion for inclusion in *United States Reports,* the official record of Supreme Court opinions.

The Court also makes opinions available electronically, through its so-called Hermes system, to a number of large legal publishers, the Government Printing Office, and other information services. These organizations allow redistribution of the opinions to their own subscribers and users. Opinions are available on the Internet through Case Western Reserve University. The Hermes system was established as a pilot project in 1991 and expanded and made permanent in 1993.

In 1996 the Court also established its own electronic bulletin board system (BBS) that provides anyone with a personal computer online access to the Court's opinions, docket, argument calendar, and other information and publications. The telephone number for the Court's BBS is (202) 554-2570.

The public announcement of opinions in Court probably is the Court's most dramatic function. It may also be the most expendable. Depending on who delivers the opinion and how, announcements can take a considerable amount of the Court's time. Opinions are given simultaneously to the public information officer for distribution. Nevertheless, those who are in the courtroom to hear the announcement of a ruling are participating in a very old tradition. The actual delivery may be tedious or exciting, depending on the nature of the case, the eloquence of the opinion, and the style of its oral delivery.

Brief Biographies

William Hubbs Rehnquist

Born: October 1, 1924, Milwaukee, Wisconsin.

Education: Stanford University, B.A., Phi Beta Kappa, and M.A., 1948; Harvard University, M.A., 1949; Stanford University Law School, LL.B., 1952.

Family: Married Natalie Cornell, 1953; died, 1991; two daughters, one son.

Career: Law clerk to Justice Robert H. Jackson, U.S. Supreme Court, 1952–1953; practiced law, 1953–1969; assistant U.S. attorney general, Office of Legal Counsel, 1969–1971.

Supreme Court Service: Nominated as associate justice of the U.S. Supreme Court by President Richard Nixon, October 21, 1971; confirmed, 68–26, December 10, 1971; nominated as chief justice of the United States by President Ronald Reagan, June 17, 1986; confirmed, 65–33, September 17, 1986.

President Reagan's appointment of William H. Rehnquist as chief justice in 1986 was a deliberate effort to shift the Court to the right. Since his

early years as an associate justice in the 1970s, Rehnquist had been the Court's strongest conservative voice. And as chief justice, Rehnquist has helped move the Court to the right in a number of areas, including criminal law, states' rights, civil rights, and church-state issues.

Rehnquist, the fourth associate justice to become chief, argues that the original intent of the Framers of the Constitution and the Bill of Rights is the proper standard for interpreting those documents today. He also takes a literal approach to individual rights. These beliefs have led him to dissent from the Court's rulings protecting a woman's privacy-based right to abortion, to argue that no constitutional barrier exists to school prayer, and to side with police and prosecutors on questions of criminal law. In 1991 he wrote the Court's decision upholding an administration ban on abortion counseling at publicly financed clinics. The next year he vigorously dissented from the Court's affirmation of *Roe v. Wade*, the 1973 opinion that made abortion legal nationwide.

A native of Milwaukee, Rehnquist attended Stanford University, where he earned both a B.A. and an M.A. He received a second M.A. from Harvard before returning to Stanford for law school. His classmates there recalled him as an intelligent student with already well-entrenched conservative views.

After graduating from law school in 1952, Rehnquist came to Washington, D.C., to serve as a law clerk to Supreme Court justice Robert H. Jackson. There he wrote a memorandum that later came back to haunt him during his Senate confirmation hearings. In the memo Rehnquist favored separate but equal schools for blacks and whites. Asked about those views by the Senate Judiciary Committee in 1971, Rehnquist repudiated them, declaring that they were Justice Jackson's, not his own.

Following his clerkship, Rehnquist decided to practice law in the Southwest. He moved to Phoenix and immediately became immersed in Arizona Republican politics. From his earliest days in the state, he was associated with the party's conservative wing. A 1957 speech denouncing the liberalism of the Warren Court typified his views at the time.

During the 1964 presidential race, Rehnquist campaigned ardently for Barry Goldwater. It was then that Rehnquist met and worked with Richard G. Kleindienst, who later, as President Richard Nixon's deputy attorney general, appointed Rehnquist to head the Justice Department's Office of Legal Counsel as an assistant attorney general. In 1971 Nixon nominated him to the Supreme Court.

Rehnquist drew opposition from liberals and civil rights organizations before winning confirmation and again before being approved as chief justice in 1986. The Senate voted to approve his nomination in December 1971 by a vote of 68–26 at the same time that another Nixon nominee, Lewis F. Powell Jr., was winning nearly unanimous confirmation.

In 1986 Rehnquist faced new accusations of having harassed voters as a Republican poll watcher in Phoenix in the 1950s and 1960s. He was also found to have accepted anti-Semitic restrictions in a property deed to a Vermont home. Despite the charges, the Senate approved his appointment as chief justice 65–33. Liberal Democratic senators cast most of the no votes in both confirmations.

Despite his strong views, Rehnquist is popular among his colleagues and staff. When he was nominated for chief justice, Justice William J. Brennan Jr., the leader of the Court's liberal bloc, said Rehnquist would be "a splendid chief justice." After becoming chief justice, Rehnquist was credited with speeding up the Court's conferences, in which the justices decide what cases to hear, vote on cases, and assign opinions.

Rehnquist was married to Natalie Cornell, who died in 1991. They had two daughters and a son. Recent news reports said that Rehnquist was dating Cynthia Holcomb Hall, a judge on the Ninth U.S. Circuit Court of Appeals.

John Paul Stevens

Born: April 20, 1920, Chicago, Illinois.

Education: University of Chicago, B.A., Phi Beta Kappa, 1941; Northwestern University School of Law, J.D., 1947.

Family: Married Elizabeth Jane Sheeren, 1942; three daughters, one son; divorced 1979; married Maryan Mulholland Simon, 1980.

Career: Law clerk to Justice Wiley B. Rutledge, U.S. Supreme Court, 1947–1948; practiced law, Chicago, 1949–1970; judge, U.S. Court of Appeals for the Seventh Circuit, 1970–1975.

Supreme Court Service: Nominated as associate justice of the U.S. Supreme Court by President Gerald R. Ford, November 28, 1975; confirmed, 98–0, December 17, 1975.

When President Gerald R. Ford nominated federal appeals court judge John Paul Stevens to the Supreme Court seat vacated by veteran liberal William O. Douglas in 1975, Court observers struggled to pin an ideological label on the new nominee. The consensus that finally emerged was that Stevens was neither a doctrinaire liberal nor conservative, but a judicial centrist. His subsequent opinions bear out this description, although in recent years he has moved steadily toward the liberal side.

Stevens is a soft-spoken, mild-mannered man who often sports a bow tie under his judicial robes. A member of a prominent Chicago family, he had a long record of excellence in scholarship, graduating Phi Beta Kappa from the University of Chicago in 1941. He earned the Bronze Star during a wartime stint in the navy and then returned to Chicago to enter Northwestern University Law School, from which he was graduated magna cum laude in 1947. From there Stevens left for Washington, where he served as a law clerk to Supreme Court justice Wiley B. Rutledge. He returned to Chicago to join the prominent law firm of Poppenhusen, Johnston, Thompson & Raymond, which specialized in antitrust law. Stevens developed a reputation as a pre-eminent antitrust lawyer and three years later in 1952 formed his own firm, Rothschild, Stevens, Barry & Myers. He remained there, engaging in private practice and teaching part-time at Northwestern and the University of Chicago law schools, until his appointment by President Richard Nixon in 1970 to the U.S. Court of Appeals for the Seventh Circuit.

Stevens developed a reputation as a political moderate during his undergraduate days at the University of Chicago, then an overwhelmingly liberal campus. Although he is a registered Republican, he has never been active in partisan politics. Nevertheless, Stevens served as Republican counsel in 1951 to the House Judiciary Subcommittee on the Study of Monopoly Power. He also served from 1953 to 1955, during the Eisenhower administration, as a member of the attorney general's committee to study antitrust laws.

In his five years on the federal appeals court, Stevens earned a reputation as an independent-minded judicial craftsman. President Ford, who took office after Nixon's forced resignation, wanted to nominate a moderate of impeccable legal reputation to help restore confidence in government after the Watergate scandals. Stevens was confirmed without dissent, 98–0, on December 17, 1975, and took office two days later.

Stevens has frequently dissented from the most conservative rulings of the Burger and Rehnquist Courts. For example, he dissented from the Burger Court's 1986 decision upholding state antisodomy laws and the Rehnquist Court's 1989 decision permitting states to execute someone for committing a murder at the age of sixteen or seventeen. He has taken liberal positions on abortion rights, civil rights, and church-state issues.

In his second full term on the Court, Stevens wrote the main opinion in a case upholding the right of the Federal Communications Commission to penalize broadcasters for airing indecent material at times when children are in the audience. But in 1997, he led the Court in a major victory for First Amendment interests by striking down a newly enacted law aimed at blocking sexually explicit materials from children on the Internet. In the same year, he wrote the opinion holding that presidents have no immunity while in office from civil suits for private conduct unrelated to their office.

In 1942 Stevens married Elizabeth Jane Sheeren. They have four children. They were divorced in 1979. Stevens subsequently married Maryan Mulholland Simon, a longtime neighbor in Chicago.

Sandra Day O'Connor

Born: March 26, 1930, El Paso, Texas.

Education: Stanford University, B.A., 1950; Stanford University Law School, LL.B., 1952.

Family: Married John J. O'Connor III, 1952; three sons.

Career: Deputy county attorney, San Mateo, California, 1952–1953; assistant attorney general, Arizona, 1965–1969; Arizona state senator, 1969–1975; Arizona Senate majority leader, 1972–1975; judge, Maricopa County Superior Court, 1974–1979; judge, Arizona Court of Appeals, 1979–1981.

Supreme Court Service: Nominated as associate justice of the U.S. Supreme Court by President Ronald Reagan August 19, 1981; confirmed, 99–0, September 21, 1981.

Sandra Day O'Connor, the first woman to serve on the Court, has been a pivotal figure in forming a conservative majority on a range of issues but has also moderated the Rehnquist Court's stance on some questions, including abortion rights and affirmative action.

Pioneering came naturally to O'Connor. Her grandfather left Kansas in 1880 to take up ranching in the desert land that eventually became the state of Arizona. O'Connor, born in El Paso, Texas, where her mother's parents lived, was raised on the Lazy B Ranch, the 198,000-acre spread that her grandfather founded in southeastern Arizona near Duncan. She spent her school years in El Paso, living with her grandmother. She graduated from high school at age sixteen and then entered Stanford University.

Six years later, in 1952, Sandra Day had won degrees with great distinction, both from the university, in economics, and from Stanford Law School. At Stanford she met John J. O'Connor III, her future husband, and William H. Rehnquist, a future colleague on the Supreme Court. While in law school, Sandra Day was an editor of the *Stanford Law Review* and a member of Order of the Coif, the academic honor society.

Despite her record, O'Connor had difficulty finding a job as an attorney in 1952 when relatively few women were practicing law. She applied, among other places, to the firm in which William French Smith—first attorney general in the Reagan administration—was a partner, only to be offered a job as a secretary.

After she completed a short stint as deputy county attorney for San Mateo County (California) while her new husband completed law school at Stanford, the O'Connors moved with the U.S. Army to Frankfurt, Germany. There Sandra O'Connor worked as a civilian attorney for the army, while John O'Connor served his tour of duty. In 1957 they returned to Phoenix, where, during the next eight years, their three sons were born. O'Connor's life was a mix of parenthood, homemaking, volunteer work, and some "miscellaneous legal tasks" on the side.

In 1965 she resumed her legal career on a full-time basis, taking a job as an assistant attorney general for Arizona. After four years in that post she was appointed to fill a vacancy in the state Senate, where she served on the judiciary committee. In 1970 she was elected to the same body and two years later was chosen its majority leader, the first woman in the nation to hold such a post. O'Connor was active in Republican Party politics, serving as co-chair of the Arizona Committee for the Re-election of the President in 1972.

In 1974 she was elected to the Superior Court for Maricopa County, where she served for five years. Then in 1979 Democratic governor Bruce

Babbitt appointed O'Connor to the Arizona Court of Appeals. It was from that post that President Reagan chose her as his first nominee to the Supreme Court, succeeding Potter Stewart, who retired. Reagan described her as "a person for all seasons." The Senate confirmed her on September 21, 1981, by a vote of 99–0.

O'Connor brings to the Court a conservative viewpoint and a cautious, case-by-case decisionmaking style. On criminal law issues, she has generally voted to give broader discretion to police, uphold death penalty cases, and restrict the use of federal habeas corpus to challenge state court convictions. She was a strong supporter of limiting punitive damage awards in state courts and relaxing restrictions on government support for religion.

In two important areas, however, O'Connor's cautious approach has disappointed conservatives. While she voted in many decisions in the 1980s to limit abortion rights, she joined in 1992 with two other Republican-appointed justices, Anthony M. Kennedy and David H. Souter, to form a majority for preserving a modified form of the Court's original abortion rights ruling, *Roe v. Wade*. In a jointly authored opinion the three justices said that *Roe*'s "essential holding"—guaranteeing a woman's right to an abortion during most of her pregnancy—should be reaffirmed. But the joint opinion also said that states could regulate abortion procedures as long as they did not impose "an undue burden" on a woman's choice—a test that O'Connor had advocated in previous opinions.

O'Connor has also voted to limit racial preferences in employment and government contracting and wrote the Court's first opinion restricting the use of race in drawing legislative and congressional districts. But she also joined the majority in a critical 1987 case upholding voluntary affirmative action by government employers to remedy past discrimination against women. And she has refused to limit all consideration of race in redistricting cases.

Antonin Scalia

Born: March 11, 1936, Trenton, New Jersey.

Education: Georgetown University, A.B., 1957; Harvard University Law School, LL.B., 1960.

Family: Married Maureen McCarthy, 1960; five sons, four daughters.

Career: Practiced law, Cleveland, 1960–1967; taught at the University of Virginia, 1967–1971; general counsel, White House Office of Telecommunications Policy, 1971–1972; chairman, Administrative Conference of the United States, 1972–1974; head, Justice Department Office of Legal Counsel, 1974–1977; taught at the University of Chicago Law School, 1977–1982; judge, U.S. Court of Appeals for the District of Columbia Circuit, 1982–1986.

Supreme Court Service: Nominated as associate justice of the U.S. Supreme Court by President Ronald Reagan June 17, 1986; confirmed, 98–0, September 17, 1986.

After Warren E. Burger retired from the Court and Ronald Reagan named William H. Rehnquist to succeed him as chief justice, the president's next move—appointing Antonin Scalia as associate justice—was not surprising. On issues dear to Reagan, Scalia clearly met the president's tests for conservatism. Scalia, whom Reagan had named to the U.S. Court of Appeals for the District of Columbia Circuit in 1982, became the first Supreme Court justice of Italian ancestry. A Roman Catholic, he opposes abortion. He has also strongly opposed "affirmative action" preferences for minorities.

In contrast to the heated debate over Rehnquist's nomination as chief justice, only a few, brief speeches were given before the Senate confirmed the equally conservative Scalia, 98–0. He has since become the scourge of some members of Congress because of his suspicion of committee reports, floor speeches, and other elements of legislative history that courts traditionally use to interpret statutes.

Born in Trenton, New Jersey, March 11, 1936, Scalia grew up in Queens, New York. His father was a professor of Romance languages at Brooklyn College, and his mother was a schoolteacher. He was first in his graduating class at an all-male military academy in Manhattan, St. Francis Xavier, and class valedictorian at Georgetown University, where he graduated in 1957. He received his law degree in 1960 from Harvard Law School, where he served as note editor of the *Harvard Law Review*. He worked for six years for the firm of Jones, Day, Cockley & Reavis in Cleveland and then taught contract, commercial, and comparative law at the University of Virginia Law School.

Scalia was a specialist in administrative law and a strong advocate of deregulation. He served as general counsel of the White House Office of Telecommunications Policy from 1971 to 1972. He then headed the Administrative Conference of the United States, a group that advises the government on questions of administrative law and procedure. From 1974 through the Ford administration he headed the Justice Department's Office of Legal Counsel, a post Rehnquist had held three years earlier. Scalia then returned to academia to teach at the University of Chicago Law School. From 1977 to 1982 he was editor of the magazine *Regulation,* published by the American Enterprise Institute for Public Policy Research.

President Ronald Reagan appointed Scalia to the U.S. Court of Appeals for the District of Columbia Circuit in 1982. There, Scalia showed himself to be a hard worker, an aggressive interrogator, and an articulate advocate. He had a marked impatience with what he saw as regulatory or judicial over-reaching. In 1983 he dissented from a ruling requiring the Food and Drug Administration (FDA) to consider whether drugs used for lethal injections met FDA standards as safe and effective. The Supreme Court agreed, reversing the appeals court in 1985.

Scalia was thought to be the principal author of an unsigned decision in 1986 that declared major portions of the Gramm-Rudman-Hollings budget-balancing act unconstitutional. The Supreme Court upheld the decision later in the year.

On the Supreme Court Scalia quickly became a forceful voice for conservative positions. He joined in conservative decisions limiting procedural rights in criminal cases and in a series of rulings in 1989 limiting remedies in employment discrimination cases. He also strongly dissented from rulings upholding affirmative action and reaffirming abortion rights. In 1997, he wrote an important decision that struck down on states' rights grounds a federal law requiring state and local law enforcement agencies to conduct background checks on prospective gun purchasers.

In many of his constitutional law opinions, Scalia argued for an "original intent" approach that limited rights to those intended when the Constitution was adopted. He also sharply challenged the use of legislative history in interpreting statutes. He argued that judges should look only to the words of the statute itself.

Scalia expressed his conservative views in aggressive questioning from the bench and in frequently acerbic opinions, especially in dissent.

Anthony McLeod Kennedy

Born: July 23, 1936, Sacramento, California.

Education: Stanford University, A.B., Phi Beta Kappa, 1958; Harvard University Law School, LL.B., 1961.

Family: Married Mary Davis, 1963; two sons, one daughter.

Career: Practiced law, San Francisco, 1961–1963, Sacramento, 1963–1975; professor of constitutional law, McGeorge School of Law, University of the Pacific, 1965–1988; judge, U.S. Court of Appeals for the Ninth Circuit, 1975–1988.

Supreme Court Service: Nominated as associate justice of the U.S. Supreme Court by President Ronald Reagan November 11, 1987; confirmed, 97–0, February 3, 1988.

Quiet, scholarly Anthony M. Kennedy, President Reagan's third choice for his third appointment to the Supreme Court, helped form a conservative majority on many issues in his initial years after joining the Court in

1988. While he adheres to generally conservative views, Kennedy has taken moderate stands on some issues that often make him a pivotal vote between the Court's conservative and liberal blocs.

Before Kennedy's nomination in November 1987, the Senate and the country had agonized through Reagan's two unsuccessful attempts to replace retiring Justice Lewis F. Powell Jr., first with Robert H. Bork and then with Douglas H. Ginsburg. The Senate rejected Bork's nomination after contentious hearings, where opponents depicted the federal appeals court judge as a conservative ideologue. Reagan then turned to Ginsburg, a colleague of Bork's on the federal appeals court in Washington, but he withdrew his name amid controversy about his admitted past use of marijuana.

A quiet sense of relief prevailed when Reagan finally selected a nominee who could be confirmed without another wrenching confrontation. Kennedy spent twelve years as a judge on the U.S. Court of Appeals for the Ninth Circuit. But unlike Bork, who wrote and spoke extensively for twenty years, Kennedy's record was confined mostly to his approximately five hundred judicial opinions, where he generally decided issues narrowly instead of using his opinions as a testing ground for constitutional theories. The Senate voted to confirm him without dissent, 97–0, on February 3, 1988.

A native Californian, Kennedy attended Stanford University from 1954 to 1957 and the London School of Economics from 1957 to 1958. He received an A.B. from Stanford in 1958 and an LL.B. from Harvard Law School in 1961. Admitted to the California bar in 1962, he was in private law practice until 1975, when President Gerald R. Ford appointed him to the appeals court. From 1965 to 1988 he taught constitutional law at McGeorge School of Law, University of the Pacific.

In his first full term on the Court, Kennedy provided a crucial fifth vote for the Court's conservative wing in a number of civil rights cases. He generally favored law enforcement in criminal cases. And in a closely watched abortion-rights case, he voted along with Chief Justice William H. Rehnquist and Justices Byron R. White and Antonin Scalia to overturn the 1973 ruling, *Roe v. Wade*, that first established a constitutional right to abortion.

Many observers viewed Kennedy's arrival as ushering in a new conservative era. But in 1992 he sorely disappointed conservatives in two major cases. In one he provided the critical fifth vote and wrote the majority opinion in a decision barring officially sponsored prayers at public high school graduation ceremonies. In the other he reversed himself on the abortion issue, joining with Justices Sandra Day O'Connor and David H. Souter in an opinion that upheld a modified version of *Roe v. Wade*.

Kennedy has proved to be a strong free speech advocate in First Amendment cases. In 1989 he helped form the 5–4 majority that overturned state laws against burning or desecrating the U.S. flag. The former constitutional law professor has also displayed a special interest in equal protection and federalism issues. He has voted with other conservatives in rulings that limited racially motivated congressional districting and backed states in disputes over federal power. But he was the swing vote in a 1995 decision to bar the states from imposing term limits on members of Congress. And in 1996 he wrote the opinion striking down Colorado's anti–gay rights amendment prohibiting enactment of any laws to bar discrimination against homosexuals.

David Hackett Souter

Born: September 17, 1939, Melrose, Massachusetts.

Education: Harvard College, B.A., 1961; Rhodes scholar, Oxford University, 1961–1963; Harvard University Law School, LL.B., 1966.

Family: Unmarried.

Career: Private law practice, Concord, New Hampshire, 1966–1968; assistant attorney general, New Hampshire, 1968–1971; deputy attorney general, New Hampshire, 1971–1976; attorney general, New Hampshire, 1976–1978; associate justice, New Hampshire Superior Court, 1978–1983; associate justice, New Hampshire Supreme Court, 1983–1990; judge, U.S. Court of Appeals for the First Circuit, 1990.

Supreme Court Service: Nominated as associate justice of the U.S. Supreme Court by President George Bush July 23, 1990; confirmed, 90–9, October 2, 1990.

At first the Senate did not know what to make of David H. Souter, a cerebral, button-down nominee who was President Bush's first appointment to the Court. Souter was little known outside his home state of New Hampshire, where he had been attorney general, a trial judge, and a state supreme court justice. He had virtually no scholarly writings to dissect and little federal court experience to scrutinize. Only three months earlier Bush had appointed him to the U.S. Court of Appeals for the First Circuit. Souter had yet to write a legal opinion on the appeals court.

During his confirmation hearings, the Harvard graduate and former Rhodes scholar demonstrated intellectual rigor and a masterly approach to constitutional law. His earlier work as state attorney general and New Hampshire Supreme Court justice had a conservative bent, but he came across as more moderate during the hearings.

Under persistent questioning from Democratic senators, Souter refused to say how he would vote on the issue of abortion rights. Abortion rights supporters feared he would provide a fifth vote for overturning the 1973 *Roe v. Wade* decision. Senators in both parties, however, said they were impressed with his legal knowledge. He was confirmed by the Senate 90–9; dissenting senators cited his refusal to take a stand on abortion.

On the bench Souter proved to be a tenacious questioner but reserved in his opinions. He generally voted with the Court's conservative majority in his first term. But in the 1991–1992 term he staked out a middle ground with Justices Sandra Day O'Connor and Anthony M. Kennedy in two crucial cases. In a closely watched abortion case Souter joined with the other two Republican-appointed justices in writing the main opinion reaffirming the "essential holding" of *Roe v. Wade.* The three also joined in forming a 5–4 majority to prohibit school-sponsored prayers at public high school graduation ceremonies.

In the Court's next several terms Souter moved markedly to the left. He joined with liberals in dissenting from cases that restricted racial redistricting. He also voted with the Court's liberal bloc on church-state and some criminal law issues.

Despite his experience in state government, Souter has proved to be a strong supporter of federal power in cases affecting states' rights. He joined the dissenters in a 1995 decision striking down on states' rights grounds a federal law banning the possession of guns near schools. And in 1996 he wrote a massive and scholarly dissent from the Court's decision limiting Congress's power to authorize private citizens to sue states in federal courts to enforce federal law.

Souter is known for his intensely private, ascetic life. He was born September 17, 1939, in Melrose, Massachusetts. An only child, he moved with his parents to Weare, New Hampshire, at age eleven. Except for college, he lived in Weare until 1990.

Graduating from Harvard College in 1961, Souter attended Oxford University on a Rhodes Scholarship from 1961 to 1963, then returned to Cambridge for Harvard Law School. Graduating in 1966, he worked for two years in a Concord law firm. In 1968 he became an assistant attorney general, rose to deputy attorney general in 1971, and in 1976 was appointed attorney general. Souter served as attorney general until 1978, when he was named to the state's trial court. Five years later Gov. John H. Sununu appointed Souter to the state supreme court. Sununu was Bush's chief of staff when Souter was named to the U.S. Supreme Court.

Souter, a bachelor, is a nature enthusiast and avid hiker.

Clarence Thomas

Born: June 23, 1948, Savannah, Georgia.

Education: Immaculate Conception Seminary, 1967–1968; Holy Cross College, B.A., 1971; Yale University Law School, J.D., 1974.

Family: Married Kathy Grace Ambush, 1971; one son; divorced 1984; married Virginia Lamp, 1987.

Career: Assistant attorney general, Missouri, 1974–1977; attorney, Monsanto Co., 1977–1979; legislative assistant to Sen. John C. Danforth, R-Mo., 1979–1981; assistant secretary of education for civil rights, 1981–1982; chairman, Equal Employment Opportunity Commission, 1982–1990; judge, U.S. Court of Appeals for the District of Columbia Circuit, 1990–1991.

Supreme Court Service: Nominated as associate justice of the U.S. Supreme Court by President George Bush July 1, 1991; confirmed, 52–48, October 15, 1991.

Clarence Thomas won a narrow confirmation to the Supreme Court in 1991 after surviving dramatic accusations of sexual harassment. He generated continuing controversy with outspoken conservative views as a justice.

The Senate's 52–48 vote on Thomas was the closest Supreme Court confirmation vote in more than a century. It followed a tumultuous nomination process that included close scrutiny of Thomas's judicial philosophy and sensational charges of sexual harassment brought by a former aide. Thomas denied the charges and accused the Senate Judiciary Committee of conducting a "high-tech lynching."

President George Bush nominated Thomas to succeed Thurgood Marshall, the Court's first black justice and a pioneer of the civil rights movement. Thomas came to prominence as a black conservative while serving as chairman of the Equal Employment Opportunity Commission during the Reagan and Bush administrations. Bush appointed him to the U.S. Court of Appeals for the District of Columbia Circuit in 1990.

Thomas was only forty-three at the time of his nomination to the Court, and senators noted that he likely would be affecting the outcome of major constitutional rulings well into the twenty-first century. Democratic senators closely questioned him on a range of constitutional issues—in particular, abortion. Thomas declined to give his views on abortion, saying he had never discussed the issue.

The committee decided to end its hearings even though it had received an allegation from a University of Oklahoma law professor, Anita Hill, that

Thomas had sexually harassed her while she worked for him at the U.S. Department of Education and the EEOC. When the accusation leaked out, the Judiciary Committee reopened the hearing to take testimony from Hill, Thomas, and other witnesses.

In the end most senators said they could not resolve the conflict between Hill's detailed allegations and Thomas's categorical denials. Instead, senators fell back on their previous positions. Supporters praised his determined character and rise from poverty in rural Georgia. Opponents questioned whether Thomas had been candid with the committee in discussing his judicial philosophy.

After joining the Court, Thomas became one of the Court's most conservative members. He closely aligned himself with fellow conservative Antonin Scalia, voting with Scalia about 90 percent of the time. In 1992 he voted as his opponents had warned to overturn the 1973 abortion rights ruling, *Roe v. Wade*, but the Court reaffirmed the decision by a 5–4 vote.

In later cases Thomas wrote lengthy opinions sharply challenging existing legal doctrines. In 1994 he called for scrapping precedents that allowed courts to order the creation of majority-black districts for legislative or congressional seats. In 1995 he authored opinions that called for restricting the basis for Congress to regulate interstate commerce and for re-examining federal courts' role in desegregating public schools. In a campaign finance case in 1996, he urged the Court to overturn all laws limiting political contributions as an infringement on the First Amendment.

Thomas graduated from Yale Law School in 1974 and became an assistant attorney general of Missouri and, three years later, a staff attorney for Monsanto Company. He worked for Sen. John C. Danforth, R-Mo., as a legislative assistant and served in the Department of Education as assistant secretary for civil rights for one year before being named chairman of the EEOC.

Thomas's wife, the former Virginia Lamp, is a lawyer who served as a legislative official with the U.S. Department of Labor during the Bush administration and since 1993 as a senior policy analyst with the House Republican Conference. They were married in 1987. He has a son from his first marriage, which ended in divorce in 1984.

Ruth Bader Ginsburg

Born: March 15, 1933, Brooklyn, New York.

Education: Cornell University, B.A., 1954; attended Harvard University Law School, 1956–1958; graduated Columbia Law School, J.D., 1959.

Family: Married Martin D. Ginsburg, 1954; one daughter, one son.

Career: Law clerk to U.S. District Court Judge Edmund L. Palmieri, 1959–1961; Columbia Law School Project on International Procedure, 1961–1963; professor, Rutgers University School of Law, 1963–1972; director,

Women's Rights Project, American Civil Liberties Union, 1972–1980; professor, Columbia Law School, 1972–1980; judge, U.S. Court of Appeals for the District of Columbia Circuit, 1980–1993.

Supreme Court Service: Nominated as associate justice of the U.S. Supreme Court by President Bill Clinton, June 22, 1993; confirmed, 96–3, August 3, 1993.

Ruth Bader Ginsburg's path to the U.S. Supreme Court is a classic American story of overcoming obstacles and setbacks through intelligence, persis-

tence, and quiet hard work. Her achievements as a student, law teacher, advocate, and judge came against a background of personal adversity and institutional discrimination against women. Ginsburg not only surmounted those hurdles for herself but also charted the legal strategy in the 1970s that helped broaden opportunities for women by establishing constitutional principles limiting sex discrimination in the law.

Born into a Jewish family of modest means in Brooklyn, Ruth Bader was greatly influenced by her mother, Celia, who imparted a love of learning and a determination to be independent. Celia Bader died of cancer on the eve of her daughter's high school graduation in 1948.

Ruth Bader attended Cornell University, where she graduated first in her class and met her future husband, Martin Ginsburg, who became a tax lawyer and later a professor at Georgetown University Law Center in Washington.

At Harvard Law School Ruth Bader Ginsburg made law review, cared for an infant daughter, and then helped her husband complete his studies after he was diagnosed with cancer. He recovered, graduated, and got a job in New York, and she transferred to Columbia for her final year of law school.

Although she was tied for first place in her class when she graduated, Ginsburg was unable to land a Supreme Court clerkship or job with a top New York law firm. Instead, she won a two-year clerkship with a federal district court judge. She then accepted a research position at Columbia that took her to Sweden, where she studied civil procedure and began to be stirred by feminist thought.

Ginsburg taught at Rutgers law school in New Jersey from 1963 to 1972. She also worked with the New Jersey affiliate of the American Civil Liberties Union (ACLU), where her caseload included several early sex discrimination complaints. In 1972 Ginsburg became the first woman to be named to a tenured position on the Columbia Law School faculty. As director of the national ACLU's newly established Women's Rights Project, she also handled the cases that over the course of several years led the Supreme Court to require heightened scrutiny of legal classifications based on sex. Ginsburg won five of the six cases she argued before the Court.

President Jimmy Carter named Ginsburg to the U.S. Court of Appeals for the District of Columbia Circuit in 1980. There she earned a reputation as a judicial moderate on a sharply divided court. When Justice Byron R. White announced plans for his retirement in March 1993, Ginsburg was among the large field of candidates President Bill Clinton considered for the vacancy. Clinton considered and passed over two other leading candidates for the position before deciding to interview Ginsburg. White House aides told reporters later that Clinton had been especially impressed with Ginsburg's life story. Reaction to the nomination was overwhelmingly positive.

In three days of confirmation hearings before the Senate Judiciary Committee, Ginsburg depicted herself as an advocate of judicial restraint, but she also said courts sometimes had a role to play in bringing about social change. On specific issues she strongly endorsed abortion rights, equal rights for women, and the constitutional right to privacy. But she declined to give her views on many other issues, including capital punishment. Some senators said that she had been less than forthcoming, but the committee voted unanimously to recommend her for confirmation. The full Senate confirmed her four days later by a vote of 96–3.

Ginsburg was sworn in August 10, 1993, as the Court's second female justice—joining Justice Sandra Day O'Connor—and the first Jewish justice since 1969.

In her first weeks on the bench, Ginsburg startled observers and drew some criticism with her unusually active questioning, but she eased up later. In her voting, she took liberal positions on women's rights, civil rights, church-state, states' rights, and First Amendment issues, but she had a more mixed record in other areas, including criminal law. In 1996 she wrote the Court's opinion in an important sex discrimination case, requiring the all-male Virginia Military Institute to admit women or give up its public funding.

Stephen Gerald Breyer

Born: August 15, 1938, San Francisco, California.

Education: Stanford University, A.B., Phi Beta Kappa, 1959; Oxford University, B.A. (Marshall scholar), 1961; Harvard Law School, LL.B., 1964.

Family: Married Joanna Hare, 1967; two daughters, one son.

Career: Law clerk to Justice Arthur J. Goldberg, U.S. Supreme Court, 1964–1965; assistant to assistant attorney general, antitrust, U.S. Justice Department, 1965–1967; professor, Harvard Law School, 1967–1981; assistant special prosecutor, Watergate Special Prosecution Force, 1973; special counsel, Senate Judiciary Committee, 1974–1975; chief counsel, Senate Judiciary

Committee, 1979–1980; judge, U.S. Court of Appeals for the First Circuit, 1980–1994.

Supreme Court Service: Nominated as associate justice of the U.S. Supreme Court by President Bill Clinton May 17, 1994; confirmed, 87–9, July 29, 1994.

When President Bill Clinton introduced Stephen G. Breyer, his second Supreme Court nominee, at a White House ceremony on May 16, 1994, he

described the federal appeals court judge as a "consensus-builder." The reaction to the nomination proved his point. Senators from both parties quickly endorsed Breyer. The only vocal dissents came from a few liberals and consumer advocates, who said Breyer was too probusiness.

Breyer, chosen to replace the retiring liberal justice Harry A. Blackmun, won a reputation as a centrist in fourteen years on the federal appeals court in Boston and two earlier stints as a staff member for the Senate Judiciary Committee. Breyer's work crossed ideological lines. He played a critical role in enacting airline deregulation in the 1970s and writing federal sentencing guidelines in the 1980s.

Born in 1938 to a politically active family in San Francisco, Breyer earned degrees from Stanford University and Harvard Law School. He clerked for Supreme Court Justice Arthur J. Goldberg and helped draft Goldberg's influential opinion in the 1965 case establishing the right of married couples to use contraceptives. Afterward he served two years in the Justice Department's antitrust division and then took a teaching position at Harvard Law School in 1967.

Breyer took leave from Harvard to serve as an assistant prosecutor in the Watergate investigation in 1973, special counsel to the Judiciary Committee's Administrative Practices Subcommittee from 1974 to 1975, and the full committee's chief counsel from 1979 to 1980. He worked for Sen. Edward Kennedy, D-Mass., but also had good relationships with Republican committee members. His ties to senators paid off when President Jimmy Carter nominated him for the federal appeals court in November 1980. Even though Ronald Reagan had been elected president, GOP senators allowed a vote on Breyer's nomination.

As a judge, Breyer was regarded as scholarly, judicious, and open-minded, with generally conservative views on economic issues and more liberal views on social questions. He wrote two books on regulatory reform that criticized economic regulations as anticompetitive and questioned priorities in some environmental and health rulemaking. He also served as a member of the newly created United States Sentencing Commission from 1985 to 1989. Later he defended the commission's guidelines against criticism from judges and others who viewed them as overly restrictive.

President Clinton interviewed Breyer before his first Supreme Court appointment in 1993 but chose Ruth Bader Ginsburg instead. He picked Breyer in 1994 after Senate Majority Leader George Mitchell took himself out of consideration and problems developed with two other leading candidates.

In his confirmation hearings before the Senate Judiciary Committee, Breyer defused two potential controversies by saying that he accepted Supreme Court precedents upholding abortion rights and capital punishment. The only contentious issue in the confirmation process concerned Breyer's investment in the British insurance syndicate Lloyd's of London. Some senators said Breyer should have recused himself from several environmental pollution cases because of the investment. Breyer told the committee that the cases could not have affected his holdings but also promised to get out of Lloyd's as soon as possible. The panel went on to recommend the nomination unanimously.

One Republican senator, Indiana's Richard Lugar, raised the Lloyd's issue during debate, but Breyer was strongly supported by senators from both parties. The Senate voted to confirm Breyer 87–9. Breyer disposed of his investment in Lloyd's shortly after taking office.

In his first two terms, Breyer has compiled a moderately liberal record on the Court. He dissented from several conservative rulings on race and religion and wrote the dissenting opinion for the four liberal justices in a decision that struck down a federal law prohibiting the possession of firearms near schools. But he had a more conservative record on criminal law issues and joined the Court's 1995 opinion permitting random drug testing of high school athletes.

Breyer joined Ginsburg as the Court's second Jewish justice. The Court had two Jewish members only once before, in the 1930s when Louis Brandeis and Benjamin Cardozo served together for six years.

Glossary of Legal Terms

Accessory. In criminal law, a person not present at the commission of an offense who commands, advises, instigates, or conceals the offense.

Acquittal. A person is acquitted when a jury returns a verdict of not guilty. A person also may be acquitted when a judge determines that insufficient evidence exists to convict him or that a violation of due process precludes a fair trial.

Adjudicate. To determine finally by the exercise of judicial authority, to decide a case.

Affidavit. A voluntary written statement of facts or charges affirmed under oath.

A fortiori. With stronger force, with more reason.

Amicus curiae. Friend of the court; a person, not a party to litigation, who volunteers or is invited by the court to give his or her views on a case.

Appeal. A legal proceeding to ask a higher court to review or modify a lower court decision. In a civil case, either the plaintiff or the defendant can appeal an adverse ruling. In criminal cases a defendant can appeal a conviction, but the Double Jeopardy Clause prevents the government from appealing an acquittal. In Supreme Court practice an appeal is a case that falls within the Court's mandatory jurisdiction as opposed to a case that the Court agrees to review under the discretionary writ of certiorari. With the virtual elimination of the Court's mandatory jurisdiction in 1988, the Court now hears very few true appeals, but petitions for certiorari are often referred to imprecisely as appeals.

Appellant. The party who appeals a lower court decision to a higher court.

Appellee. One who has an interest in upholding the decision of a lower court and is compelled to respond when the case is appealed to a higher court by an appellant.

Arraignment. The formal process of charging a person with a crime, reading that person the charge, asking whether he or she pleads guilty or not guilty, and entering the plea.

Attainder, Bill of. A legislative act pronouncing a particular individual guilty of a crime without trial or conviction and imposing a sentence.

Bail. The security, usually money, given as assurance of a prisoner's due appearance at a designated time and place (as in court) to procure in the interim the prisoner's release from jail.

Bailiff. A minor officer of a court, usually serving as an usher or a messenger.

Brief. A document prepared by counsel to serve as the basis for an argument in court, setting out the facts of and the legal arguments in support of the case.

Burden of proof. The need or duty of affirmatively providing a fact or facts that are disputed.

Case law. The law as defined by previously decided cases, distinct from statutes and other sources of law.

Cause. A case, suit, litigation, or action, civil or criminal.

Certiorari, Writ of. A writ issued from the Supreme Court, at its discretion, to order a lower court to prepare the record of a case and send it to the Supreme Court for review.

Civil law. Body of law dealing with the private rights of individuals, as distinguished from criminal law.

Class action. A lawsuit brought by one person or group on behalf of all persons similarly situated.

Code. A collection of laws, arranged systematically.

Comity. Courtesy, respect; usually used in the legal sense to refer to the proper relationship between state and federal courts.

Common law. Collection of principles and rules of action, particularly from unwritten English law, that derive their authority from longstanding usage and custom or from courts recognizing and enforcing these customs. Sometimes used synonymously with case law.

Consent decree. A court-sanctioned agreement settling a legal dispute and entered into by the consent of the parties.

Contempt (civil and criminal). Civil contempt arises from a failure to follow a court order for the benefit of another party. Criminal contempt occurs when a person willfully exhibits disrespect for the court or obstructs the administration of justice.

Conviction. Final judgment or sentence that the defendant is guilty as charged.

Criminal law. The branch of law that deals with the enforcement of laws and the punishment of persons who, by breaking laws, commit crimes.

Declaratory judgment. A court pronouncement declaring a legal right or interpretation but not ordering a specific action.

De facto. In fact, in reality.

Defendant. In a civil action, the party denying or defending itself against charges brought by a plaintiff. In a criminal action, the person indicted for commission of an offense.

De jure. As a result of law or official action.

De novo. Anew; afresh; a second time.

Deposition. Oral testimony from a witness taken out of court in response to written or oral questions, committed to writing, and intended to be used in the preparation of a case.

Dicta. *See* Obiter dictum.

Dismissal. Order disposing of a case without a trial.

Docket. A calendar prepared by the clerks of the court listing the cases set to be tried.

Due process. Fair and regular procedure. The Fifth and Fourteenth amendments guarantee persons that they will not be deprived of life, liberty, or property by the government until fair and usual procedures have been followed.

Error, Writ of. A writ issued from an appeals court to a lower court requiring it to send to the appeals court the record of a case in which it has entered a final judgment and which the appeals court will review for error.

Ex parte. Only from, or on, one side. Application to a court for some ruling or action on behalf of only one party.

Ex post facto. After the fact; an ex post facto law makes an action a crime after it already has been committed, or otherwise changes the legal consequences of some past action.

Ex rel. Upon information from; the term is usually used to describe legal proceedings begun by an official in the name of the state but at the instigation of, and with information from, a private individual interested in the matter.

Grand jury. Group of twelve to twenty-three persons impanelled to hear, in private, evidence presented by the state against an individual or persons accused of a criminal act and to issue indictments when a majority of the jurors find probable cause to believe that the accused has committed a crime. Called a "grand" jury because it comprises a greater number of persons than a "petit" jury.

Grand jury report. A public report, often called "presentments," released by a grand jury after an investigation into activities of public officials that fall short of criminal actions.

Guilty. A word used by a defendant in entering a plea or by a jury in returning a verdict, indicating that the defendant is legally responsible as charged for a crime or other wrongdoing.

Habeas corpus. Literally, "you have the body"; a writ issued to inquire whether a person is lawfully imprisoned or detained. The writ demands that the persons holding the prisoner justify the detention or release the prisoner.

Immunity. A grant of exemption from prosecution in return for evidence or testimony.

In camera. In chambers. Refers to court hearings in private without spectators.

In forma pauperis. In the manner of a pauper, without liability for court costs.

In personam. Done or directed against a particular person.

In re. In the affair of, concerning. Frequent title of judicial proceedings in which there are no adversaries but instead where the matter itself—such as a bankrupt's estate—requires judicial action.

In rem. Done or directed against the thing, not the person.

Indictment. A formal written statement, based on evidence presented by the prosecutor, from a grand jury. Decided by a majority vote, an indictment charges one or more persons with specified offenses.

Information. A written set of accusations, similar to an indictment, but filed directly by a prosecutor.

Injunction. A court order prohibiting the person to whom it is directed from performing a particular act.

Interlocutory decree. A provisional decision of the court before completion of a legal action that temporarily settles an intervening matter.

Judgment. Official decision of a court based on the rights and claims of the parties to a case that was submitted for determination.

Juries. *See* Grand jury; Petit jury.

Jurisdiction. The power of a court to hear a case in question, which exists when the proper parties are present and when the point to be decided is within the issues authorized to be handled by the particular court.

Magistrate. A judicial officer having jurisdiction to try minor criminal cases and conduct preliminary examinations of persons charged with serious crimes.

Majority opinion. An opinion joined by a majority of the justices explaining the legal basis for the Court's decision and regarded as binding precedent for future cases.

Mandamus. "We command." An order issued from a superior court directing a lower court or other authority to perform a particular act.

Moot. Unsettled, undecided. A moot question also is one that no longer is material; a moot case is one that has become hypothetical.

Motion. Written or oral application to a court or a judge to obtain a rule or an order.

Nolo contendere. "I will not contest it." A plea entered by a defendant at the discretion of the judge with the same legal effect as a plea of guilty, but it may not be cited in other proceedings as an admission of guilt.

Obiter dictum. Statements by a judge or justice expressing an opinion and included with, but not essential to, an opinion resolving a case before the court. Dicta are not necessarily binding in future cases.

Parole. A conditional release from imprisonment under conditions that, if the prisoner abides by the law and other restrictions that may be imposed, the prisoner will not have to serve the remainder of the sentence.

Per curiam. "By the court." An unsigned opinion of the court, or an opinion written by the whole court.

Petit jury. A trial jury, originally a panel of twelve persons who tried to reach a unanimous verdict on questions of fact in criminal and civil proceedings. Since 1970 the Supreme Court has upheld the legality of state juries with fewer than twelve persons. Fewer persons serve on a "petit" jury than on a "grand" jury.

Petitioner. One who files a petition with a court seeking action or relief, including a plaintiff or an appellant. But a petitioner also is a person who files for other court action where charges are not necessarily made; for example, a party may petition the court for an order requiring another person or party to produce documents. The opposite party is called the respondent.

   When a writ of certiorari is granted by the Supreme Court, the parties to the case are called petitioner and respondent in contrast to the appellant and appellee terms used in an appeal.

Plaintiff. A party who brings a civil action or sues to obtain a remedy for injury to his or her rights. The party against whom action is brought is termed the defendant.

Plea bargaining. Negotiations between a prosecutor and the defendant aimed at exchanging a plea of guilty from the defendant for concessions by the prosecutor, such as reduction of the charges or a request for leniency.

Pleas. *See* Guilty; Nolo contendere.

Plurality opinion. An opinion supported by the largest number of justices but less than a majority. A plurality opinion typically is not regarded as establishing a binding precedent for future cases.

Precedent. A judicial decision that may be used as a basis for ruling on subsequent similar cases.

Presentment. *See* Grand jury report.

Prima facie. At first sight; referring to a fact or other evidence presumably sufficient to establish a defense or a claim unless otherwise contradicted.

Probation. Process under which a person convicted of an offense, usually a first offense, receives a suspended sentence and is given freedom, usually under the guardianship of a probation officer.

Quash. To overthrow, annul, or vacate; as to quash a subpoena.

Recognizance. An obligation entered into before a court or magistrate requiring the performance of a specified act—usually to appear in court at a later date. It is an alternative to bail for pretrial release.

Remand. To send back. When a decision is remanded, it is sent back by a higher court to the court from which it came for further action.

Respondent. One who is compelled to answer the claims or questions posed in court by a petitioner. A defendant and an appellee may be called respondents, but the term also includes those parties who answer in court during actions where charges are not necessarily brought or where the Supreme Court has granted a writ of certiorari.

Seriatim. Separately, individually, one by one.

Stare decisis. "Let the decision stand." The principle of adherence to settled cases, the doctrine that principles of law established in earlier judicial decisions should be accepted as authoritative in similar subsequent cases.

Statute. A written law enacted by a legislature. A collection of statutes for a particular governmental division is called a code.

Stay. To halt or suspend further judicial proceedings.

Subpoena. An order to present oneself before a grand jury, court, or legislative hearing.

Subpoena duces tecum. An order to produce specified documents or papers.

Tort. An injury or wrong to the person or property of another.

Transactional immunity. Protects a witness from prosecution for any offense mentioned in or related to his or her testimony, regardless of independent evidence against the witness.

Use immunity. Protects a witness from the use of his or her testimony against the witness in prosecution.

Vacate. To make void, annul, or rescind.

Writ. A written court order commanding the designated recipient to perform or not perform specified acts.

United States Constitution

We the People of the United States, in Order to form a more perfect Union, establish Justice, insure domestic Tranquility, provide for the common defence, promote the general Welfare, and secure the Blessings of Liberty to ourselves and our Posterity, do ordain and establish this Constitution for the United States of America.

Article I

Section 1. All legislative Powers herein granted shall be vested in a Congress of the United States, which shall consist of a Senate and House of Representatives.

Section 2. The House of Representatives shall be composed of Members chosen every second Year by the People of the several States, and the Electors in each State shall have the Qualifications requisite for Electors of the most numerous Branch of the State Legislature.

No Person shall be a Representative who shall not have attained to the age of twenty five Years, and been seven Years a Citizen of the United States, and who shall not, when elected, be an Inhabitant of that State in which he shall be chosen.

[Representatives and direct Taxes shall be apportioned among the several States which may be included within this Union, according to their respective Numbers, which shall be determined by adding to the whole Number of free Persons, including those bound to Service for a Term of Years, and excluding Indians not taxed, three fifths of all other Persons.][1] The actual Enumeration shall be made within three Years after the first Meeting of the Congress of the United States, and within every subsequent Term of ten Years, in such Manner as they shall by Law direct. The Number of Representatives shall not exceed one for every thirty Thousand, but each State shall have at Least one Representative; and until such enumeration shall be made, the State of New Hampshire shall be entitled to chuse three, Massachusetts eight, Rhode-Island and Providence Plantations one, Connecticut five, New-York six, New Jersey four, Pennsylvania eight, Delaware one, Maryland six, Virginia ten, North Carolina five, South Carolina five, and Georgia three.

When vacancies happen in the Representation from any State, the Executive Authority thereof shall issue Writs of Election to fill such Vacancies.

The House of Representatives shall chuse their Speaker and other Officers; and shall have the sole Power of Impeachment.

Section 3. The Senate of the United States shall be composed of two Senators from each State, [chosen by the Legislature thereof,][2] for six Years; and each Senator shall have one Vote.

Immediately after they shall be assembled in Consequence of the first Election, they shall be divided as equally as may be into three Classes. The Seats of the Senators of the first Class shall be vacated at the Expiration of the second Year, of the second Class at the Expiration of the fourth Year, and of the third Class at the Expiration of the sixth Year, so that one third may be chosen every second Year; [and if Vacancies happen by Resignation, or otherwise, during the Recess of the Legislature of any State, the Executive thereof may make temporary Appointments until the next Meeting of the Legislature, which shall then fill such Vacancies.]³

No Person shall be a Senator who shall not have attained to the Age of thirty Years, and been nine Years a Citizen of the United States, and who shall not, when elected, be an Inhabitant of that State for which he shall be chosen.

The Vice President of the United States shall be President of the Senate, but shall have no Vote, unless they be equally divided.

The Senate shall chuse their other Officers, and also a President pro tempore, in the Absence of the Vice President, or when he shall exercise the Office of President of the United States.

The Senate shall have the sole Power to try all Impeachments. When sitting for that Purpose, they shall be on Oath or Affirmation. When the President of the United States is tried, the Chief Justice shall preside: And no Person shall be convicted without the Concurrence of two thirds of the Members present.

Judgment in Cases of Impeachment shall not extend further than to removal from Office, and disqualification to hold and enjoy any Office of honor, Trust or Profit under the United States: but the Party convicted shall nevertheless be liable and subject to Indictment, Trial, Judgment and Punishment, according to Law.

Section 4. The Times, Places and Manner of holding Elections for Senators and Representatives, shall be prescribed in each State by the Legislature thereof; but the Congress may at any time by Law make or alter such Regulations, except as to the Places of chusing Senators.

The Congress shall assemble at least once in every Year, and such Meeting shall [be on the first Monday in December],⁴ unless they shall by Law appoint a different Day.

Section 5. Each House shall be the Judge of the Elections, Returns and Qualifications of its own Members, and a Majority of each shall constitute a Quorum to do Business; but a smaller Number may adjourn from day to day, and may be authorized to compel the Attendance of absent Members, in such Manner, and under such Penalties as each House may provide.

Each House may determine the Rules of its Proceedings, punish its Members for disorderly Behaviour, and, with the Concurrence of two thirds, expel a Member.

Each House shall keep a Journal of its Proceedings, and from time to time publish the same, excepting such Parts as may in their Judgment require Secrecy; and the Yeas and Nays of the Members of either House on any question shall, at the Desire of one fifth of those Present, be entered on the Journal.

Neither House, during the Session of Congress, shall, without the Consent of the other, adjourn for more than three days, nor to any other Place than that in which the two Houses shall be sitting.

Section 6. The Senators and Representatives shall receive a Compensation for their Services, to be ascertained by Law, and paid out of the Treasury of the United States. They shall in all Cases, except Treason, Felony and Breach of the Peace, be privileged from Arrest during their Attendance at the Session of their respective

Houses, and in going to and returning from the same; and for any Speech or Debate in either House, they shall not be questioned in any other Place.

No Senator or Representative shall, during the Time for which he was elected, be appointed to any civil Office under the Authority of the United States, which shall have been created, or the Emoluments whereof shall have been encreased during such time; and no Person holding any Office under the United States, shall be a Member of either House during his Continuance in Office.

Section 7. All Bills for raising Revenue shall originate in the House of Representatives; but the Senate may propose or concur with Amendments as on other Bills.

Every Bill which shall have passed the House of Representatives and the Senate, shall, before it become a Law, be presented to the President of the United States; If he approve he shall sign it, but if not he shall return it, with his Objections to that House in which it shall have originated, who shall enter the Objections at large on their Journal, and proceed to reconsider it. If after such Reconsideration two thirds of that House shall agree to pass the Bill, it shall be sent, together with the Objections, to the other House, by which it shall likewise be reconsidered, and if approved by two thirds of that House, it shall become a Law. But in all such Cases the Votes of both Houses shall be determined by yeas and Nays, and the Names of the Persons voting for and against the Bill shall be entered on the Journal of each House respectively. If any Bill shall not be returned by the President within ten Days (Sundays excepted) after it shall have been presented to him, the Same shall be a Law, in like Manner as if he had signed it, unless the Congress by their Adjournment prevent its Return, in which Case it shall not be a Law.

Every Order, Resolution, or Vote to which the Concurrence of the Senate and House of Representatives may be necessary (except on a question of Adjournment) shall be presented to the President of the United States; and before the Same shall take Effect, shall be approved by him, or being disapproved by him, shall be repassed by two thirds of the Senate and House of Representatives, according to the Rules and Limitations prescribed in the Case of a Bill.

Section 8. The Congress shall have Power To lay and collect Taxes, Duties, Imposts and Excises, to pay the Debts and provide for the common Defence and general Welfare of the United States; but all Duties, Imposts and Excises shall be uniform throughout the United States;

To borrow Money on the credit of the United States;

To regulate Commerce with foreign Nations, and among the several States, and with the Indian Tribes;

To establish an uniform Rule of Naturalization, and uniform Laws on the subject of Bankruptcies throughout the United States;

To coin Money, regulate the Value thereof, and of foreign Coin, and fix the Standard of Weights and Measures;

To provide for the Punishment of counterfeiting the Securities and current Coin of the United States;

To establish Post Offices and post Roads;

To promote the Progress of Science and useful Arts, by securing for limited Times to Authors and Inventors the exclusive Right to their respective Writings and Discoveries;

To constitute Tribunals inferior to the supreme Court;

To define and punish Piracies and Felonies committed on the high Seas, and Offences against the Law of Nations;

To declare War, grant Letters of Marque and Reprisal, and make Rules concerning Captures on Land and Water;

To raise and support Armies, but no Appropriation of Money to that Use shall be for a longer Term than two Years;

To provide and maintain a Navy;

To make Rules for the Government and Regulation of the land and naval Forces;

To provide for calling forth the Militia to execute the Laws of the Union, suppress Insurrections and repel Invasions;

To provide for organizing, arming, and disciplining, the Militia, and for governing such Part of them as may be employed in the Service of the United States, reserving to the States respectively, the Appointment of the Officers, and the Authority of training the Militia according to the discipline prescribed by Congress;

To exercise exclusive Legislation in all Cases whatsoever, over such District (not exceeding ten Miles square) as may, by Cession of particular States, and the Acceptance of Congress, become the Seat of the Government of the United States, and to exercise like Authority over all Places purchased by the Consent of the Legislature of the State in which the Same shall be, for the Erection of Forts, Magazines, Arsenals, dock-Yards, and other needful Buildings; — And

To make all Laws which shall be necessary and proper for carrying into Execution the foregoing Powers, and all other Powers vested by this Constitution in the Government of the United States, or in any Department or Officer thereof.

Section 9. The Migration or Importation of such Persons as any of the States now existing shall think proper to admit, shall not be prohibited by the Congress prior to the Year one thousand eight hundred and eight, but a Tax or duty may be imposed on such Importation, not exceeding ten dollars for each Person.

The Privilege of the Writ of Habeas Corpus shall not be suspended, unless when in Cases of Rebellion or Invasion the public Safety may require it.

No Bill of Attainder or ex post facto Law shall be passed.

No Capitation, or other direct, Tax shall be laid, unless in Proportion to the Census or Enumeration herein before directed to be taken.[5]

No Tax or Duty shall be laid on Articles exported from any State.

No Preference shall be given by any Regulation of Commerce or Revenue to the Ports of one State over those of another; nor shall Vessels bound to, or from, one State, be obliged to enter, clear, or pay Duties in another.

No Money shall be drawn from the Treasury, but in Consequence of Appropriations made by Law; and a regular Statement and Account of the Receipts and Expenditures of all public Money shall be published from time to time.

No Title of Nobility shall be granted by the United States: And no Person holding any Office of Profit or Trust under them, shall, without the Consent of the Congress, accept of any present, Emolument, Office, or Title, of any kind whatever, from any King, Prince, or foreign State.

Section 10. No State shall enter into any Treaty, Alliance, or Confederation; grant Letters of Marque and Reprisal; coin Money; emit Bills of Credit; make any

Thing but gold and silver Coin a Tender in Payment of Debts; pass any Bill of Attainder, ex post facto Law, or Law impairing the Obligation of Contracts, or grant any Title of Nobility.

No State shall, without the Consent of the Congress, lay any Imposts or Duties on Imports or Exports, except what may be absolutely necessary for executing it's inspection Laws: and the net Produce of all Duties and Imposts, laid by any State on Imports or Exports, shall be for the Use of the Treasury of the United States; and all such Laws shall be subject to the Revision and Controul of the Congress.

No State shall, without the Consent of Congress, lay any Duty of Tonnage, keep Troops, or Ships of War in time of Peace, enter into any Agreement or Compact with another State, or with a foreign Power, or engage in War, unless actually invaded, or in such imminent Danger as will not admit of delay.

Article II

Section 1. The executive Power shall be vested in a President of the United States of America. He shall hold his Office during the Term of four Years, and, together with the Vice President, chosen for the same Term, be elected, as follows

Each State shall appoint, in such Manner as the Legislature thereof may direct, a Number of Electors, equal to the whole Number of Senators and Representatives to which the State may be entitled in the Congress: but no Senator or Representative, or Person holding an Office of Trust or Profit under the United States, shall be appointed an Elector.

[The Electors shall meet in their respective States, and vote by Ballot for two Persons, of whom one at least shall not be an Inhabitant of the same State with themselves. And they shall make a List of all the Persons voted for, and of the Number of Votes for each; which List they shall sign and certify, and transmit sealed to the Seat of the Government of the United States, directed to the President of the Senate. The President of the Senate shall, in the Presence of the Senate and House of Representatives, open all the Certificates, and the Votes shall then be counted. The Person having the greatest Number of Votes shall be the President, if such Number be a Majority of the whole Number of Electors appointed; and if there be more than one who have such Majority, and have an equal Number of Votes, then the House of Representatives shall immediately chuse by Ballot one of them for President; and if no Person have a Majority, then from the five highest on the list the said House shall in like Manner chuse the President. But in chusing the President, the Votes shall be taken by States, the Representation from each State having one Vote; A quorum for this Purpose shall consist of a Member or Members from two thirds of the States, and a Majority of all the States shall be necessary to a Choice. In every Case, after the Choice of the President, the Person having the greatest Number of Votes of the Electors shall be the Vice President. But if there should remain two or more who have equal Votes, the Senate shall chuse from them by Ballot the Vice President.][6]

The Congress may determine the Time of chusing the Electors, and the Day on which they shall give their Votes; which Day shall be the same throughout the United States.

No Person except a natural born Citizen, or a Citizen of the United States, at the time of the Adoption of this Constitution, shall be eligible to the Office of President; neither shall any Person be eligible to that Office who shall not have attained to the Age of thirty five Years, and been fourteen Years a Resident within the United States.

In Case of the Removal of the President from Office, or of his Death, Resignation, or Inability to discharge the Powers and Duties of the said Office,[7] the Same shall devolve on the Vice President, and the Congress may by Law provide for the Case of Removal, Death, Resignation or Inability, both of the President and Vice President, declaring what Officer shall then act as President, and such Officer shall act accordingly, until the Disability be removed, or a President shall be elected.

The President shall, at stated Times, receive for his Services, a Compensation, which shall neither be encreased nor diminished during the Period for which he shall have been elected, and he shall not receive within that Period any other Emolument from the United States, or any of them.

Before he enter on the Execution of his Office, he shall take the following Oath or Affirmation:—"I do solemnly swear (or affirm) that I will faithfully execute the Office of President of the United States, and will to the best of my Ability, preserve, protect and defend the Constitution of the United States."

Section 2. The President shall be Commander in Chief of the Army and Navy of the United States, and of the Militia of the several States, when called into the actual Service of the United States; he may require the Opinion, in writing, of the principal Officer in each of the executive Departments, upon any Subject relating to the Duties of their respective Offices, and he shall have Power to grant Reprieves and Pardons for Offences against the United States, except in Cases of Impeachment.

He shall have Power, by and with the Advice and Consent of the Senate, to make Treaties, provided two thirds of the Senators present concur; and he shall nominate, and by and with the Advice and Consent of the Senate, shall appoint Ambassadors, other public Ministers and Consuls, Judges of the supreme Court, and all other Officers of the United States, whose Appointments are not herein otherwise provided for, and which shall be established by Law: but the Congress may by Law vest the Appointment of such inferior Officers, as they think proper, in the President alone, in the Courts of Law, or in the Heads of Departments.

The President shall have Power to fill up all Vacancies that may happen during the Recess of the Senate, by granting Commissions which shall expire at the End of their next Session.

Section 3. He shall from time to time give to the Congress Information of the State of the Union, and recommend to their Consideration such Measures as he shall judge necessary and expedient; he may, on extraordinary Occasions, convene both Houses, or either of them, and in Case of Disagreement between them, with Respect to the Time of Adjournment, he may adjourn them to such Time as he shall think proper; he shall receive Ambassadors and other public Ministers; he shall take Care that the Laws be faithfully executed, and shall Commission all the Officers of the United States.

Section 4. The President, Vice President and all civil Officers of the United States, shall be removed from Office on Impeachment for, and Conviction of, Treason, Bribery, or other high Crimes and Misdemeanors.

Article III

Section 1. The judicial Power of the United States, shall be vested in one supreme Court, and in such inferior Courts as the Congress may from time to time ordain and establish. The Judges, both of the supreme and inferior Courts, shall hold their Offices during good Behaviour, and shall, at stated Times, receive for their Services, a Compensation, which shall not be diminished during their Continuance in Office.

Section 2. The judicial Power shall extend to all Cases, in Law and Equity, arising under this Constitution, the Laws of the United States, and Treaties made, or which shall be made, under their Authority; — to all Cases affecting Ambassadors, other public Ministers and Consuls; — to all Cases of admiralty and maritime Jurisdiction; — to Controversies to which the United States shall be a Party; — to Controversies between two or more States; — between a State and Citizens of another State;[8] — between Citizens of different States; — between Citizens of the same State claiming Lands under Grants of different States, and between a State, or the Citizens thereof, and foreign States, Citizens or Subjects.[8]

In all Cases affecting Ambassadors, other public Ministers and Consuls, and those in which a State shall be Party, the supreme Court shall have original Jurisdiction. In all the other Cases before mentioned, the supreme Court shall have appellate Jurisdiction, both as to Law and Fact, with such Exceptions, and under such Regulations as the Congress shall make.

The Trial of all Crimes, except in Cases of Impeachment, shall be by Jury; and such Trial shall be held in the State where the said Crimes shall have been committed; but when not committed within any State, the Trial shall be at such Place or Places as the Congress may by Law have directed.

Section 3. Treason against the United States, shall consist only in levying War against them, or in adhering to their Enemies, giving them Aid and Comfort. No Person shall be convicted of Treason unless on the Testimony of two Witnesses to the same overt Act, or on Confession in open Court.

The Congress shall have Power to declare the Punishment of Treason, but no Attainder of Treason shall work Corruption of Blood, or Forfeiture except during the Life of the Person attainted.

Article IV

Section 1. Full Faith and Credit shall be given in each State to the public Acts, Records, and judicial Proceedings of every other State. And the Congress may by general Laws prescribe the Manner in which such Acts, Records and Proceedings shall be proved, and the Effect thereof.

Section 2. The Citizens of each State shall be entitled to all Privileges and Immunities of Citizens in the several States.

A Person charged in any State with Treason, Felony, or other Crime, who shall flee from Justice, and be found in another State, shall on Demand of the executive Authority of the State from which he fled, be delivered up, to be removed to the State having Jurisdiction of the Crime.

[No Person held to Service or Labour in one State, under the Laws thereof, escaping into another, shall, in Consequence of any Law or Regulation therein, be discharged from such Service or Labour, but shall be delivered up on Claim of the Party to whom such Service or Labour may be due.][9]

Section 3. New States may be admitted by the Congress into this Union; but no new State shall be formed or erected within the Jurisdiction of any other State; nor any State be formed by the Junction of two or more States, or Parts of States, without the Consent of the Legislatures of the States concerned as well as of the Congress.

The Congress shall have Power to dispose of and make all needful Rules and Regulations respecting the Territory or other Property belonging to the United States; and nothing in this Constitution shall be so construed as to Prejudice any Claims of the United States, or of any particular State.

Section 4. The United States shall guarantee to every State in this Union a Republican Form of Government, and shall protect each of them against Invasion; and on Application of the Legislature, or of the Executive (when the Legislature cannot be convened) against domestic Violence.

Article V

The Congress, whenever two thirds of both Houses shall deem it necessary, shall propose Amendments to this Constitution, or, on the Application of the Legislatures of two thirds of the several States, shall call a Convention for proposing Amendments, which, in either Case, shall be valid to all Intents and Purposes, as Part of this Constitution, when ratified by the Legislatures of three fourths of the several States, or by Conventions in three fourths thereof, as the one or the other Mode of Ratification may be proposed by the Congress; Provided [that no Amendment which may be made prior to the Year One thousand eight hundred and eight shall in any Manner affect the first and fourth Clauses in the Ninth Section of the first Article; and][10] that no State, without its Consent, shall be deprived of its equal Suffrage in the Senate.

Article VI

All Debts contracted and Engagements entered into, before the Adoption of this Constitution, shall be as valid against the United States under this Constitution, as under the Confederation.

This Constitution, and the Laws of the United States which shall be made in Pursuance thereof; and all Treaties made, or which shall be made, under the Authority of the United States, shall be the supreme Law of the Land; and the Judges in every State shall be bound thereby, any Thing in the Constitution or Laws of any State to the Contrary notwithstanding.

The Senators and Representatives before mentioned, and the Members of the several State Legislatures, and all executive and judicial Officers, both of the United States and of the several States, shall be bound by Oath or Affirmation, to support this Constitution; but no religious Test shall ever be required as a Qualification to any Office or public Trust under the United States.

Article VII

The Ratification of the Conventions of nine States, shall be sufficient for the Establishment of this Constitution between the States so ratifying the Same.

Done in Convention by the Unanimous Consent of the States present the Seventeenth Day of September in the Year of our Lord one thousand seven hundred and Eighty seven and of the Independence of the United States of America the Twelfth. IN WITNESS whereof We have hereunto subscribed our Names,

George Washington,
President and
deputy from Virginia.

New Hampshire: John Langdon,
                                   Nicholas Gilman.

Massachusetts: Nathaniel Gorham,
                                   Rufus King.

Connecticut: William Samuel Johnson,
                                   Roger Sherman.

New York: Alexander Hamilton.

New Jersey: William Livingston,
                                   David Brearley,
                                   William Paterson,
                                   Jonathan Dayton.

Pennsylvania: Benjamin Franklin,
                                   Thomas Mifflin,
                                   Robert Morris,
                                   George Clymer,
                                   Thomas FitzSimons,
                                   Jared Ingersoll,
                                   James Wilson,
                                   Gouverneur Morris.

Delaware: George Read,
                                   Gunning Bedford Jr.,
                                   John Dickinson,
                                   Richard Bassett,
                                   Jacob Broom.

Maryland: James McHenry,
                                   Daniel of St. Thomas Jenifer,
                                   Daniel Carroll.

| Virginia: | John Blair, |
| | James Madison Jr. |

Virginia: John Blair,
James Madison Jr.

North Carolina: William Blount,
Richard Dobbs Spaight,
Hugh Williamson.

South Carolina: John Rutledge,
Charles Cotesworth Pinckney,
Charles Pinckney,
Pierce Butler.

Georgia: William Few,
Abraham Baldwin.

[The language of the original Constitution, not including the Amendments, was adopted by a convention of the states on September 17, 1787, and was subsequently ratified by the states on the following dates: Delaware, December 7, 1787; Pennsylvania, December 12, 1787; New Jersey, December 18, 1787; Georgia, January 2, 1788; Connecticut, January 9, 1788; Massachusetts, February 6, 1788; Maryland, April 28, 1788; South Carolina, May 23, 1788; New Hampshire, June 21, 1788.

Ratification was completed on June 21, 1788.

The Constitution subsequently was ratified by Virginia, June 25, 1788; New York, July 26, 1788; North Carolina, November 21, 1789; Rhode Island, May 29, 1790; and Vermont, January 10, 1791.]

Amendments

Amendment I

(First ten amendments ratified December 15, 1791.)

Congress shall make no law respecting an establishment of religion, or prohibiting the free exercise thereof; or abridging the freedom of speech, or of the press; or the right of the people peaceably to assemble, and to petition the Government for a redress of grievances.

Amendment II

A well regulated Militia, being necessary to the security of a free State, the right of the people to keep and bear Arms, shall not be infringed.

Amendment III

No Soldier shall, in time of peace be quartered in any house, without the consent of the Owner, nor in time of war, but in a manner to be prescribed by law.

Amendment IV

The right of the people to be secure in their persons, houses, papers, and effects, against unreasonable searches and seizures, shall not be violated, and no Warrants shall issue, but upon probable cause, supported by Oath or affirmation, and particularly describing the place to be searched, and the persons or things to be seized.

Amendment V

No person shall be held to answer for a capital, or otherwise infamous crime, unless on a presentment or indictment of a Grand Jury, except in cases arising in the land or naval forces, or in the Militia, when in actual service in time of War or public danger; nor shall any person be subject for the same offence to be twice put in jeopardy of life or limb; nor shall be compelled in any criminal case to be a witness against himself, nor be deprived of life, liberty, or property, without due process of law; nor shall private property be taken for public use, without just compensation.

Amendment VI

In all criminal prosecutions, the accused shall enjoy the right to a speedy and public trial, by an impartial jury of the State and district wherein the crime shall have been committed, which district shall have been previously ascertained by law, and to be informed of the nature and cause of the accusation; to be confronted with the witnesses against him; to have compulsory process for obtaining witnesses in his favor, and to have the Assistance of Counsel for his defence.

Amendment VII

In Suits at common law, where the value in controversy shall exceed twenty dollars, the right of trial by jury shall be preserved, and no fact tried by a jury, shall be otherwise re-examined in any Court of the United States, than according to the rules of the common law.

Amendment VIII

Excessive bail shall not be required, nor excessive fines imposed, nor cruel and unusual punishments inflicted.

Amendment IX

The enumeration in the Constitution, of certain rights, shall not be construed to deny or disparage others retained by the people.

Amendment X

The powers not delegated to the United States by the Constitution, nor prohibited by it to the States, are reserved to the States respectively, or to the people.

Amendment XI

(Ratified February 7, 1795)

The Judicial power of the United States shall not be construed to extend to any suit in law or equity, commenced or prosecuted against one of the United States by Citizens of another State, or by Citizens or Subjects of any Foreign State.

Amendment XII

(Ratified June 15, 1804)

The Electors shall meet in their respective states and vote by ballot for President and Vice-President, one of whom, at least, shall not be an inhabitant of the same state with themselves; they shall name in their ballots the person voted for as President, and in distinct ballots the person voted for as Vice-President, and they shall make distinct lists of all persons voted for as President, and of all persons voted for as Vice-President, and of the number of votes for each, which lists they shall sign and certify, and transmit sealed to the seat of the government of the United States, directed to the President of the Senate; — The President of the Senate shall, in the presence of the Senate and House of Representatives, open all the certificates and the votes shall then be counted; — The person having the greatest number of votes for President, shall be the President, if such number be a majority of the whole number of Electors appointed; and if no person have such majority, then from the persons having the highest numbers not exceeding three on the list of those voted for as President, the House of Representatives shall choose immediately, by ballot, the President. But in choosing the President, the votes shall be taken by states, the representation from each state having one vote; a quorum for this purpose shall consist of a member or members from two-thirds of the states, and a majority of all the states shall be necessary to a choice. [And if the House of Representatives shall not choose a President whenever the right of choice shall devolve upon them, before the fourth day of March next following, then the Vice-President shall act as President, as in the case of the death or other constitutional disability of the President. —][11] The person having the greatest number of votes as Vice-President, shall be the Vice-President, if such number be a majority of the whole number of Electors appointed, and if no person have a majority, then from the two highest numbers on the list, the Senate shall choose the Vice-President; a quorum for the purpose shall consist of two-thirds of the whole number of Senators, and a majority of the whole number shall be necessary to a choice. But no person constitutionally ineligible to the office of President shall be eligible to that of Vice-President of the United States.

Amendment XIII

(Ratified December 6, 1865)

Section 1. Neither slavery nor involuntary servitude, except as a punishment for crime whereof the party shall have been duly convicted, shall exist within the United States, or any place subject to their jurisdiction.

Section 2. Congress shall have power to enforce this article by appropriate legislation.

Amendment XIV

(Ratified July 9, 1868)

Section 1. All persons born or naturalized in the United States, and subject to the jurisdiction thereof, are citizens of the United States and of the State wherein they reside. No State shall make or enforce any law which shall abridge the privileges or immunities of citizens of the United States; nor shall any State deprive any person of life, liberty, or property, without due process of law; nor deny to any person within its jurisdiction the equal protection of the laws.

Section 2. Representatives shall be apportioned among the several States according to their respective numbers, counting the whole number of persons in each State, excluding Indians not taxed. But when the right to vote at any election for the choice of electors for President and Vice President of the United States, Representatives in Congress, the Executive and Judicial officers of a State, or the members of the Legislature thereof, is denied to any of the male inhabitants of such State, being twenty-one years of age,[12] and citizens of the United States, or in any way abridged, except for participation in rebellion, or other crime, the basis of representation therein shall be reduced in the proportion which the number of such male citizens shall bear to the whole number of male citizens twenty-one years of age in such State.

Section 3. No person shall be a Senator or Representative in Congress, or elector of President and Vice President, or hold any office, civil or military, under the United States, or under any State, who, having previously taken an oath, as a member of Congress, or as an officer of the United States, or as a member of any State legislature, or as an executive or judicial officer of any State, to support the Constitution of the United States, shall have engaged in insurrection or rebellion against the same, or given aid or comfort to the enemies thereof. But Congress may by a vote of two-thirds of each House, remove such disability.

Section 4. The validity of the public debt of the United States, authorized by law, including debts incurred for payment of pensions and bounties for services in suppressing insurrection or rebellion, shall not be questioned. But neither the United States nor any State shall assume or pay any debt or obligation incurred in aid of insurrection or rebellion against the United States, or any claim for the loss or emancipation of any slave; but all such debts, obligations and claims shall be held illegal and void.

Section 5. The Congress shall have power to enforce, by appropriate legislation, the provisions of this article.

Amendment XV

(Ratified February 3, 1870)

Section 1. The right of citizens of the United States to vote shall not be denied or abridged by the United States or by any State on account of race, color, or previous condition of servitude.

Section 2. The Congress shall have power to enforce this article by appropriate legislation.

Amendment XVI

(Ratified February 3, 1913)

The Congress shall have power to lay and collect taxes on incomes, from whatever source derived, without apportionment among the several States, and without regard to any census or enumeration.

Amendment XVII

(Ratified April 8, 1913)

The Senate of the United States shall be composed of two Senators from each State, elected by the people thereof, for six years; and each Senator shall have one vote. The electors in each State shall have the qualifications requisite for electors of the most numerous branch of the State legislatures.

When vacancies happen in the representation of any State in the Senate, the executive authority of such State shall issue writs of election to fill such vacancies: *Provided,* That the legislature of any State may empower the executive thereof to make temporary appointments until the people fill the vacancies by election as the legislature may direct.

This amendment shall not be so construed as to affect the election or term of any Senator chosen before it becomes valid as part of the Constitution.

Amendment XVIII

(Ratified January 16, 1919)[13]

Section 1. After one year from the ratification of this article the manufacture, sale, or transportation of intoxicating liquors within, the importation thereof into, or the exportation thereof from the United States and all territory subject to the jurisdiction thereof for beverage purposes is hereby prohibited.

Section 2. The Congress and the several States shall have concurrent power to enforce this article by appropriate legislation.

Section 3. This article shall be inoperative unless it shall have been ratified as an amendment to the Constitution by the legislatures of the several States, as provided in the Constitution, within seven years from the date of the submission hereof to the States by the Congress.

Amendment XIX

(Ratified August 18, 1920)

The right of citizens of the United States to vote shall not be denied or abridged by the United States or by any State on account of sex.

Congress shall have power to enforce this article by appropriate legislation.

Amendment XX

(Ratified January 23, 1933)

Section 1. The terms of the President and Vice President shall end at noon on the 20th day of January, and the terms of Senators and Representatives at noon on the 3d day of January, of the years in which such terms would have ended if this article had not been ratified; and the terms of their successors shall then begin.

Section 2. The Congress shall assemble at least once in every year, and such meeting shall begin at noon on the 3d day of January, unless they shall by law appoint a different day.

Section 3.[14] If, at the time fixed for the beginning of the term of the President, the President elect shall have died, the Vice President elect shall become President. If a President shall not have been chosen before the time fixed for the beginning of his term, or if the President elect shall have failed to qualify, then the Vice President elect shall act as President until a President shall have qualified; and the Congress may by law provide for the case wherein neither a President elect nor a Vice President elect shall have qualified, declaring who shall then act as President, or the manner in which one who is to act shall be selected, and such person shall act accordingly until a President or Vice President shall have qualified.

Section 4. The Congress may by law provide for the case of the death of any of the persons from whom the House of Representatives may choose a President whenever the right of choice shall have devolved upon them, and for the case of the death of any of the persons from whom the Senate may choose a Vice President whenever the right of choice shall have devolved upon them.

Section 5. Sections 1 and 2 shall take effect on the 15th day of October following the ratification of this article.

Section 6. This article shall be inoperative unless it shall have been ratified as an amendment to the Constitution by the legislatures of three-fourths of the several States within seven years from the date of its submission.

Amendment XXI

(Ratified December 5, 1933)

Section 1. The eighteenth article of amendment to the Constitution of the United States is hereby repealed.

Section 2. The transportation or importation into any State, Territory, or possession of the United States for delivery or use therein of intoxicating liquors, in violation of the laws thereof, is hereby prohibited.

Section 3. This article shall be inoperative unless it shall have been ratified as an amendment to the Constitution by conventions in the several States, as provided in the Constitution, within seven years from the date of the submission hereof to the States by the Congress.

Amendment XXII

(Ratified February 27, 1951)

Section 1. No person shall be elected to the office of the President more than twice, and no person who has held the office of President, or acted as President, for more than two years of a term to which some other person was elected President shall be elected to the office of the President more than once. But this Article shall not apply to any person holding the office of President when this Article was proposed by the Congress, and shall not prevent any person who may be holding the office of President, or acting as President, during the term within which this Article become operative from holding the office of President or acting as President during the remainder of such term.

Section 2. This article shall be inoperative unless it shall have been ratified as an amendment to the Constitution by the legislatures of three-fourths of the several States within seven years from the date of its submission to the States by the Congress.

Amendment XXIII

(Ratified March 29, 1961)

Section 1. The District constituting the seat of Government of the United States shall appoint in such manner as the Congress may direct:
A number of electors of President and Vice President equal to the whole number of Senators and Representatives in Congress to which the District would be entitled if it were a State, but in no event more than the least populous State; they shall be in addition to those appointed by the States, but they shall be considered, for the purposes of the election of President and Vice President, to be electors appointed by a State; and they shall meet in the District and perform such duties as provided by the twelfth article of amendment.

Section 2. The Congress shall have power to enforce this article by appropriate legislation.

Amendment XXIV

(Ratified January 23, 1964)

Section 1. The right of citizens of the United States to vote in any primary or other election for President or Vice President, for electors for President or Vice President, or for Senator or Representative in Congress, shall not be denied or abridged by the United States or any State by reason of failure to pay any poll tax or other tax.

Section 2. The Congress shall have power to enforce this article by appropriate legislation.

Amendment XXV

(Ratified February 10, 1967)

Section 1. In case of the removal of the President from office or of his death or resignation, the Vice President shall become President.

Section 2. Whenever there is a vacancy in the office of the Vice President, the President shall nominate a Vice President who shall take office upon confirmation by a majority vote of both Houses of Congress.

Section 3. Whenever the President transmits to the President pro tempore of the Senate and the Speaker of the House of Representatives his written declaration that he is unable to discharge the powers and duties of his office, and until he transmits to them a written declaration to the contrary, such powers and duties shall be discharged by the Vice President as Acting President.

Section 4. Whenever the Vice President and a majority of either the principal officers of the executive departments or of such other body as Congress may by law provide, transmit to the President pro tempore of the Senate and the Speaker of the House of Representatives their written declaration that the President is unable to discharge the powers and duties of his office, the Vice President shall immediately assume the powers and duties of the office as Acting President.

Thereafter, when the President transmits to the President pro tempore of the Senate and the Speaker of the House of Representatives his written declaration that no inability exists, he shall resume the powers and duties of his office unless the Vice President and a majority of either the principal officers of the executive department or of such other body as Congress may by law provide, transmit within four days to the President pro tempore of the Senate and the Speaker of the House of Representatives their written declaration that the President is unable to discharge the powers and duties of his office. Thereupon Congress shall decide the issue, assembling within forty-eight hours for that purpose if not in session. If the Congress, within twenty-one days after receipt of the latter written declaration, or, if Congress is not in session, within twenty-one days after Congress is required to assemble, determines by two-thirds vote of both Houses that the President is unable to discharge the powers and duties of his office, the Vice President shall continue to discharge the same as Acting President; otherwise, the President shall resume the powers and duties of his office.

Amendment XXVI

(Ratified July 1, 1971)

Section 1. The right of citizens of the United States, who are eighteen years of age or older, to vote shall not be denied or abridged by the United States or by any State on account of age.

Section 2. The Congress shall have power to enforce this article by appropriate legislation.

Amendment XXVII

(Ratified May 7, 1992)

No law varying the compensation for the services of the Senators and Representatives shall take effect, until an election of Representatives shall have intervened.

Notes

1. The part in brackets was by section 2 of the Fourteenth Amendment.
2. The part in brackets was changed by the first paragraph of the Seventeenth Amendment.
3. The part in brackets was changed by the second paragraph of the Seventeenth Amendment.
4. The part in brackets was changed by section 2 of the Twentieth Amendment.
5. The Sixteenth Amendment gave Congress the power to tax incomes.
6. The material in brackets has been superseded by the Twelfth Amendment.
7. This provision has been affected by the Twenty-fifth Amendment.
8. These clauses were affected by the Eleventh Amendment.
9. This paragraph has been superseded by the Thirteenth Amendment.
10. Obsolete.
11. The part in brackets has been superseded by section 3 of the Twentieth Amendment.
12. See the Nineteenth and Twenty-sixth Amendments.
13. This Amendment was repealed by section 1 of the Twenty-first Amendment.
14. See the Twenty-fifth Amendment.

Source: U.S. Congress, House, Committee on the Judiciary, *The Constitution of the United States of America, as Amended,* 100th Cong., 1st sess., 1987, H Doc 100-94.

Index

Abortion
    anti-abortion protesters, 7, 8, 26,
        77, 113–114
    parental notification, 112–113
    physician-only, 113
Abrams v. Johnson (1997), 98–99
ACLU. *See* American Civil Liberties
    Union
Addington v. Texas (1979), 59
Advertising, 12, 13, 25, 27, 104
Advocacy groups, 142
Affirmative action, 133, 134–137
Agostini v. Felton (1997), 21*t*, 54,
    108–109
Aguilar v. Felton (1985), 21*t*, 55–57, 109
*Alaska v. Native Village of Venetie Tribal
    Government*, 144–145
Albrecht v. Herald Tribune Co. (1968),
    138
*Allentown Mack Sales and Service, Inc. v.
    National Labor Relations Board*,
    147–148
Alstyne, William van, 22
Amchem Products, Inc. v. Windsor
    (1997), 62, 84–85
American Civil Liberties Union
    (ACLU)
    Internet anti-indecency law, 19,
        20*t*, 35–40, 110–111
    and physician-assisted suicide, 32
American Library Association,
    Internet anti-indecency law, 37
American Medical Association,
    physician-assisted suicide ban, 32
Americans for Death With Dignity, 32
Antiterrorism and Effective Death
    Penalty Act, 25, 91–92
Appeals, 83–84, 86
Arizona, official English law, 15, 21,
    120
Arizonans for Official English v. Arizona
    (1997), 120

*Arkansas Educational Television
    Commission v. Forbes*, 145
*Arkansas v. Farm Credit Services of
    Central Arkansas* (1997), 129
Asbestos-exposure claims, 16, 28,
    62–66, 84–85, 123–124, 125
Assisted suicide. *See* Physician-assisted
    suicide
Associates Commercial Corp. v. Rash
    (1997), 79–80
*AT&T Family Federal Credit Union v.
    First National Bank & Trust Co.*,
    137–138
*Atherton v. Federal Deposit Insurance
    Corporation* (1997), 79
Attorney-client privilege, 75
Attorney trust accounts, 139–140
Auer v. Robbins (1997), 120–121

Babbitt, Secretary of the Interior v. Youpee,
    20*t*, 106–107
Baker v. General Motors Corp., 139
Banking, *See also* Credit unions
    false statements for loans, 89
    savings and loans, 79
Bankruptcy, 79–80
Barry, Maryanne Trump, 135
Becker, Edward R., 64–65
Bennett, Robert S., 43, 44
Bennett v. Spear (1997), 102
Berman, Jerry, 40
*Bibles, Director, Oregon Bureau of Land
    Management v. Oregon Natural Desert
    Association* (1997), 105
Biskupic, Joan, 19, 40
Blackmun, Harry A., 18, 71
*Blessing, Director, Arizona Department of
    Economic Security v. Freestone* (1997),
    103
*Board of County Commissioners of Bryan
    County, Oklahoma v. Brown* (1997),
    115–116

Board of Education of Kiryas Joel School District v. Grumet (1994), 55–56
Bogan v. Scott-Harris, 147
Boggs v. Boggs (1997), 121–122
Bokat, Stephen, 27
Bolick, Clint, 137
Boundary disputes, 127–128, 134
Bracy v. Gramley, Warden (1997), 90
Bracy, William, 90
Brady Handgun Violence Prevention Act, 1, 4, 6–8, 13–14, 19, 20*t*, 22, 23, 45–49, 104–105
Brady, James S., 45, 46
Brady, Sarah, 45–46, 49
Brennan, William J., Jr., 55
Breyer, Stephen G.
    on abortion, 113, 114
    on Brady Act case, 45, 49
    on cable must-carry provisions, 71, 112
    on class action suits, 62, 65–66, 84–85
    on contempt of court, 87
    on damage suits, 115–116, 117, 118
    dissenting votes, 9*t*
    on federal regulation, 104–105
    on habeas corpus, 91, 92
    on insider trading, 69
    on Internet anti-indecency law, 38, 39
    on liability law, 16–17, 80
    on line-item veto, 108
    on maritime law, 80
    on parochial school aid, 54, 57, 108–109
    on pensions and benefits, 121–122
    on physician-assisted suicide, 35, 115
    on presidential immunity, 44, 108
    on racketeering, 131–132
    on redistricting, 98–99
    on religious freedom, 49, 52, 53, 109–110
    on remedies, 123–124
    on savings and loans, 79
    on sentencing, 95–96

Breyer, Stephen G. (*continued*)
    on sexual offenders, 17, 58, 61, 97–98
    on states' rights, 128–129
    on taxation, 81–83
    voting pattern, 5*t*, 12–13, 16–17
    on voting rights, 101–102
    on workers' compensation, 124–125
Brodsky, Edward, 70
Brooks, Melissa, 83–84
Buchanan v. Angelone, 141
Bullock, Scott, 20, 26
Bunton, Lucius Desha, III, 52
Burger, Warren E., 18
Business law, 16, 27–28, 79–80, 137–138

Cable television, must-carry provisions, 11, 13, 25, 27, 70–73, 111–112
California, physician-assisted suicide, 30
California Division of Labor Standards Enforcement v. Dillingham Construction, N.A., Inc. (1997), 122–123
California v. Roy (1997), 91
Cammarata, Joseph, 43, 44, 45
Camps Newfoundland/Owatonna, Inc. v. Town of Harrison, 20*t*, 129–130
Capital punishment, 86, 141
Carpenter v. United States (1987), 67
Caterpillar Inc. v. Lewis (1997), 84
Center for Claims Resolution (CCR), 63
Chandler v. Miller, Governor of Georgia (1997), 20*t*, 118–119
Chemerinsky, Erwin, 2, 4, 14, 17, 18, 24
Chiarella v. United States (1980), 67
Child-support enforcement, 21, 103
Church and state
    aid for parochial schools, 54–57, 108–109
    religious freedom law, 49–54, 109–110
City of Boerne v. Flores, Archbishop of San Antonio (1997), 20*t*, 49, 52, 54, 109–110

City of Chicago v. International College of Surgeons, 144
Civil Rights Act, 119–120
Class actions
    asbestos-exposure case, 16, 28, 62–66, 84–85
    requirements for suit, 63
Clinton administration
    affirmative action, 136
    gun control, 47
    Internet anti-indecency law, 36, 38, 40
    and physician-assisted suicide, 32
Clinton, Bill
    presidential immunity, 1, 13, 16, 27, 40–45, 107–108
    religious freedom, 51
    Whitewater affair, 40
Clinton, Hillary Rodham, 75
Clinton v. Jones (1997), 40–45, 107–108
Coats, Dan, 36
Colleges and universities, women's athletics, 74–75
Colorado, gay rights legislation, 6
Commerce Clause, 8, 23, 130
Commissioner of Internal Revenue v. Estate of Hubert (1997), 81–82
Commissioner of Internal Revenue v. Schleier (1995), 82
Communications Decency Act. *See* Internet anti-indecency law
Compassion in Dying, 31
Congress, Court limiting power of, 3, 12, 23
Conservative justices, 4–12
Contempt of court, 87
County of Sacramento v. Lewis, 146–147
Courts and procedure, 4, 22, 83–86, 138–140
Crawford-El v. Britton, 147
Credit unions, 137–138
Criminal law and procedure, 86–98, 140–142. *See also specific issues*
    defendants' rights, 4, 22, 23–24
    offenses, 87–88
    for sexual offenders, 4, 6, 21, 24, 58–61
Cruzan, Nancy Beth, 30

Cruzan v. Director, Missouri Department of Health (1990), 30, 31
Cummins, Anthony, 50

Damage suits, 115–118, 147
    for police chases, 146–147
Daubert v. Merrell Dow Pharmaceuticals, Inc. (1993), 138
Davis, Gilbert K., 43, 45
Death penalty, 13, 142
DeBuono, New York Commissioner of Health v. NYSA-ILA Medical and Clinical Services Fund (1997), 130–131
Dellinger, Walter, 43, 48, 56, 71
Department of Defense v. Federal Labor Relations Authority (1994), 105
Diller, Barry, 73
Discrimination
    affirmative action, 133
    job, 119–120
Dissenting opinions, 9t, 11. 12
Double Jeopardy Clause, 97, 140–141
Dreeben, Michael, 68
Drug testing, for state candidates, 7, 16, 20, 118–119
Due Process Clause, 6, 9, 13, 32, 35, 84
Dunn v. Commodity Futures Trading Commission (1997), 103–104

Edmond v. United States (1997), 106
Edwards v. Balisok (1997), 116
Election law, 142–143. *See also* Redistricting; Voting rights
    ballot access, 6, 16, 25–26, 98
Ellis Island, 134
Emergency Planning and Community Right-to-Know Act, 143
Employee Retirement Income Security Act (ERISA), 28, 121–122, 123, 130–131
Employer polling, 147–148
Employment Division v. Smith (1990), 50, 53, 110
Endangered Species Act, 7–8, 28, 102
English, as official language, 15, 21, 120
Ennis, Bruce J., 38

Environmental law, 102, 143–144
Equal Protection Clause, 32, 33, 84
ERISA. *See* Employee Retirement
Income Security Act
Espinosa v. Florida (1992), 91
Establishment Clause, 53, 56
Ex parte Young (1908), 128–129
Ex Post Facto Clause, 59, 61, 93, 97
Executive clemency, 142
Exon, James, 36
Expert testimony, 138–139

False claims, 85–86
Federal Communications Commission
(FCC), cable must-carry provisions,
70–73, 111–112
Federal Deposit Insurance Corpora-
tion (FDIC), 79
Federal Election Commission v. Akins, 142
Federal government
employees, 144
regulations, 103–105
Federalism rulings, 3, 22
Feldblum, Chai, 3, 13
Ferguson, Danny, 41
Firearms. *See also* Brady Handgun
Violence Prevention Act
near a school, 23
right to keep or bear, 8–9, 49
First Amendment. *See* Church and
state; Free Exercise Clause; Speech
and expression rights
Fitzpatrick, Larry, 66
Florida, early prison releases, 20*t*
Forbes, Ralph, 145
Foreman v. Dallas County, Texas (1997),
100
Foster v. Love, 143
Foucha v. Louisiana (1992), 59
Fourteenth Amendment. *See* Due
Process Clause; Equal Protection
Clause
Fourth Amendment. *See* Drug testing;
Search and seizure
Free Exercise Clause, 50, 54
Freedom of information, 105
Freedom of speech. *See* Speech and
expression rights
French, John, 68

Gay rights, 6
Gays, military policy, 77
General Electric Co. v. Joiner, 138–139
*General Motors Corp. v. Tracy, Tax
Commissioner of Ohio* (1997), 131
Georgia, drug testing for candidates, 7,
16, 20*t*
Gewirtz, Paul, 3
*Gilbert, President, East Stroudsburg
University v. Homar* (1997), 123
Ginsburg, Ruth Bader
on abortion, 113
on appeals process, 83–84
on bankruptcy, 79–80
on Brady Act case, 45, 49
on cable must-carry provisions, 70,
72, 111–112
on civil procedure, 15
on class action suits, 62, 65,
84–85
on damage suits, 115–116, 117
dissenting votes, 9*t*, 16
on drug testing, 118–119
on election law, 98
on English as official language,
120
on federal regulation, 104–105
on habeas corpus, 91, 92
on insider trading, 66, 69, 88–89
on Internet anti-indecency law,
39
on Native Americans, 106, 107
on parochial school aid, 15, 54,
56, 57, 108–109
on pensions and benefits,
121–122
on physician-assisted suicide, 32,
35, 115
on redistricting, 98–99
on remedies, 123–124
on sentencing, 95–96
on sexual offenders, 58, 61,
97–98
on states' rights, 128–129
on taxation, 82
voting pattern, 5*t*, 12–13, 15–16
on wage laws, 123
on workers' compensation,
124–125

Gleeson, John, 56
*Glickman, Secretary of Agriculture v.
  Wileman Brothers & Elliott, Inc.*
  (1997), 104
Glucksberg, Harold, 31
Grand Rapids School District v. Ball
  (1985), 55
Greene v. Georgia (1997), 86
Greenhouse, Linda, 4, 12
Griffin v. Illinois (1956), 84
Guilty pleas, 90
Gun control, *See also* Brady Handgun
  Violence Prevention Act
    background checks, 1, 45–49
    right to bear arms, 8
Gunther, Gerald, 23

Habeas corpus, 23, 24, 25, 90–92
Halbrook, Stephen, 47
Hamilton, Alexander, 2, 49
Hamilton, Marci, 52, 54
Hansen, Christopher, 136
Harbor Tug & Barge Co. v. Papai
  (1997), 124–125
Harlan, John Marshall, 35
Harper, Ernest, 93
Hatch, Orrin, 53
Hendricks, Leroy, 58–61, 97–98
Hinckley, John, Jr., 45–46
Hodel v. Irving (1987), 106
Homosexuals. *See* Gay rights
Hudson, John, 140
Hudson v. United States (1997), 140–141
*Hughes Aircraft Co. v. United States ex rel.
  Schumer* (1997), 85–86
Hunt, Donald, 61

Idaho v. Coeur d'Alene Tribe of Idaho
  (1997), 128–129
*Immigration and Naturalization Service v.
  Yang* (1997), 112
Immigration law, 112, 145–146
Immunity, states, 128–129. *See also*
  Presidential immunity
Indecency. *See* Internet anti-indecency
  law
Indian Land Consolidation Act, 20*t*, 106
Indian tribe, law suit against state
  official, 11

Individual rights, 112–120, 146–147
*Ingalls Shipbuilding, Inc. v. Director,
  Office of Workers' Compensation
  Programs, Department of Labor* (1997),
  125
Insider trading, 24, 66–70, 88–89
*Inter-Modal Rail Employees Association v.
  Atchison, Topeka & Santa Fe Railway
  Co.* (1997), 122
Interest on Lawyer Trust Accounts
  (IOLTA), 140
Internal Revenue Service (IRS), 81–83
Internet anti-indecency law, 1, 4, 13,
  19, 20*t*, 25, 27, 35–40, 110–111

Jails. *See* Prisons and jails
Job discrimination, 119–120
Johnson v. Frankell (1997), 117
Johnson v. United States (1997), 86
Jones, Paula Corbin, 1, 13, 27, 40–45,
  107–108
Jury selection, for capital punishment
  cases, 86

Kansas, "sexual predators" law, 21, 24,
  58–61, 97–98
Kansas v. Hendricks (1997), 58, 97–98
Kemler, Lisa, 23–24
Kennedy, Anthony M.
    on abortion protesters, 113–114
    on Brady Act case, 48
    on cable must-carry provisions,
      11, 71, 72
    on child-support enforcement,
      103
    on class action suits, 65
    on damage suits, 118
    dissenting votes, 9*t*, 11–12
    on drug testing, 7
    on habeas corpus, 91
    on insider trading, 69
    on Internet anti-indecency law, 39
    on judicial power, 22
    on parochial school aid, 55, 56, 57
    on pensions and benefits, 121–122
    on physician-assisted suicide, 32,
      34
    on police investigations at traffic
      stops, 24

Kennedy, Anthony M. (*continued*)
  on redistricting, 98–100
  on religious freedom, 10–11, 53,
    109–110
  on search and seizure, 93–94
  on sentencing, 95, 96
  on "sexual predators" law, 4, 6, 61
  on states' rights, 128–129
  on taxation, 81–82, 129
  voting pattern, 4, 5t, 6, 12
  on workers' compensation,
    124–125
Kennedy, John F., 42–43
Kevorkian, Jack, 29
King v. Erickson, 144
Klausner, Stephen, 135
Klehr v. A.O. Smith Corp. (1997),
  131–132
Kmiec, Douglas, 3, 7, 17, 18, 136

Labinger, Lynette, 74
Labor law, 120–126, 147–148
*Lambert, Gallatin County Attorney v.
  Wicklund* (1997), 112–113
*Lambrix v. Singletary, Secretary, Florida
  Department of Corrections* (1997), 91
Land use regulation, 126–127
Landmark preservation, 144
Lanier, David, 87
Lawyer v. Department of Justice (1997),
  99–100
Lawyer-client privilege. *See* Attorney-
  client privilege
Laycock, H. Douglas, 52–53
Lessig, Lawrence, 2
Levitt, Arthur, Jr., 69
Liability, 16
  product-defect suits, 80
Liberal justices, 12–17
Lie detector tests, 134, 140
Lindh v. Murphy, Warden (1997), 91–92
Line Item Veto Act, 7, 108
Louisiana, open primary, 143
Luftman, Michael, 73
*Lynce v. Mathis, Superintendent, Tomoka
  Correctional Institution* (1997), 20t,
  92–93
Lynn, Barry, 57

McConnell, Michael, 6, 14, 22
McFarland, Wendy, 61
McMillan v. Monroe County, Alabama
  (1997), 117
McMillan, Walter, 117
Mack, Richard, 47
Madison, James, 49
Madsen v. Women's Health Center, Inc.
  (1997), 114
Mahoney, Maureen, 28, 74
Maine, state tax dispute, 8, 20t,
  129–130
Maloney, Thomas J., 90
Marbury v. Madison (1803), 22
Maritime law, 80
Marshall, John, 22
Marshall, Thurgood, 55, 77
Maryland v. Wilson (1997), 93–94
Mauro, Tony, 77
*Mazurek, Attorney General of Montana v.
  Armstrong* (1997), 113
*Metro-North Commuter Railroad Co. v.
  Buckley* (1997), 123–124
Metropolitan Stevedore Co. v. Rambo
  (1997), 125–126
Military law, 106
Miller v. Albright, 145–146
Miller v. Johnson (1995), 98–99
Miner, Roger, 32
Misappropriation doctrine, 24, 67–69
M.L.B. v. S.L.J. (1997), 83–84
*Monell v. New York City Department of
  Social Services* (1978), 117
Morissey v. Brewer (1972), 93
Morrison, Alan, 19–20
Motor Voter Act. *See* National Voter
  Registration Act

*National Credit Union Administration v.
  First National Bank & Trust Co.,*
  137–138
National Labor Relations Board
  (NLRB), 147–148
National Voter Registration Act, 23, 102
Native Americans, 11, 20t, 106
  and civil suits, 107
  "Indian country" status, 144–145
  property rights, 106–107

New Jersey v. New York, 134
New York, physician-assisted suicide, 32–33
New York v. United States (1992), 47
Nixon, Richard M., 43
Nixon v. Fitzgerald (1982), 43

O'Brien, David M., 77
Occupational safety. *See* Asbestos-exposure claims
O'Connor, Sandra Day
    on affirmative action, 137
    on boundary disputes, 127
    on Brady Act case, 4, 47–48
    on cable must-carry provisions, 11, 70, 71, 72, 111–112
    on child-support enforcement, 103
    on damage suits, 115–116
    dissenting votes, 9*t*
    on evidence, 89
    on federal regulation, 105
    on habeas corpus, 91
    on insider trading, 68, 69
    on Internet anti-indecency law, 35, 38, 40, 110–111
    join-3 votes practice, 77
    on land use regulation, 126–127
    on maritime law, 80
    on parochial school aid, 10, 17, 54, 56–57, 108–109
    on pensions and benefits, 121–122
    on physician-assisted suicide, 6, 34, 35, 115
    on redistricting, 99–100
    on religious freedom, 10–11, 49, 51–52, 109–110
    on sentencing, 95
    on "sexual predators" law, 60, 61
    on taxation, 82
    voting pattern, 4, 5*t*, 6, 12
    voting rights, 100–101
    on workers' compensation, 125–126
O'Dell, Joseph, 92
O'Dell v. Netherland, Warden (1997), 92
Office of the President v. Office of the Independent Counsel (1997), 75

Official English law, 15, 21, 120
Ogilvie v. United States (1997), 82
O'Hagan, James, 66–70, 88–89
Ohio Adult Parole Authority v. Woodard, 142
Ohio v. Robinette (1997), 94
Old Chief v. United States (1997), 89
Olson, Theodore, 12
Oncale v. Sundowner Offshore Services, Inc., 146
Oregon, physician-assisted suicide, 30
Overtime pay, 120–121

Patents, equivalents doctrine, 10, 81
Pennsylvania v. Mimms (1977), 93–94
Pensions and benefits, 121–122
Phillips v. Washington Legal Foundation, 139–140
Physician-assisted suicide, 3, 4, 6, 14–15, 26, 28–35, 114–115
Piscataway Township Board of Education v. Taxman, 133–137
Planned Parenthood of Southeastern Pa. v. Casey (1992), 113
Police brutality, damage suits, 17, 27, 115–116
Police chases, 146–147
Police investigations
    no-knock searches, 22, 25, 94–95, 141
    at traffic stops, 7, 22, 24, 93–94
Pornography, on Internet. *See* Internet anti-indecency law
Pounders, Judge, Superior Court of California, Los Angeles County v. Watson (1997), 87
Pounders, William S., 87
Powell, Lewis F., Jr., 55
Presidential immunity, 1, 13, 16, 27, 40–45, 107–108
Price fixing, 138
Printz, Jay, 47, 49
Printz, Sheriff/Coroner, Ravalli County, Montana v. United States (1997), 20*t*, 45–49, 104–105
Prisons and jails, 92–93
    private prison guard immunity, 118

Property rights
    land use regulation, 126–127
    for Native Americans, 106–107
Public employees, 123
Public television, campaign debates,
    145
Putra, Cheryl, 96

Quill, Timothy, 29, 35
Quinlan, Karen Ann, 29

Racial redistricting. *See* Redistricting
Racketeer Influenced and Corrupt
    Organizations Act (RICO), 131–132
Racketeering, 131–132
Railroad industry, 122, 123
*Raines, Director, Office of Management
    and Budget v. Byrd* (1997), 108
Rambo, John, 125–126
Redistricting, 13, 26, 98–100
Reed, Lowell A., Jr., 64
*Regents of the University of California v.
    Doe* (1997), 129
Rehnquist, William H.
    on abortion protesters, 113–114
    on appeals, 83–84, 86
    on boundary disputes, 127–128
    on cable must-carry provisions, 72
    on class action suits, 65
    on damage suits, 117, 118
    dissenting votes, 7, 9*t*
    on drug testing, 7, 118–119
    on election law, 98
    on evidence, 89
    on federal regulation, 104
    on guilty pleas, 90
    on habeas corpus, 90, 91–92
    on insider trading, 66, 68, 88–89
    on Internet anti-indecency law,
        35, 40, 110–111
    join-3 votes practice, 77
    and judicial activism, 2, 6
    on line-item veto, 108
    on parochial school aid, 56, 57
    on pensions and benefits,
        121–122
    on physician-assisted suicide, 3, 6,
        28, 33–34, 114–115

Rehnquist, William H. (*continued*)
    on presidential immunity, 43
    on search and seizure, 93–94
    on "sexual predators" law, 61
    on taxation, 82, 129–130
    voting pattern, 4, 5*t*, 6–7
Reinhardt, Stephen, 32
Religious freedom, 1, 10–11
Religious Freedom Restoration Act
    (RFRA), 1, 20*t*, 22, 50
Remedies, 123–124
*Reno, Attorney General v. American Civil
    Liberties Union* (1997), 20*t*, 35,
    110–111
*Reno, Attorney General v. Bossier Parish
    School Board* (1997), 101
Richards v. Wisconsin (1997), 94–95
Richardson v. McKnight (1997), 118
Right-to-die movement. *See* Physician-
    assisted suicide
Robinson, Charles, 119
Robinson v. Shell Oil Co. (1997), 119
Roosevelt, Theodore, 42
Rubin, David B., 135

*Sable Communications of California, Inc.
    v. FCC* (1989), 37
Samp, Richard, 12, 23
*Saratoga Fishing Co. v. J.M. Martinac &
    Co.* (1997), 80
Savings and loans, gross negligence
    standard, 79
Scalia, Antonin
    on abortion protesters, 8,
        113–114
    on appeals process, 83–84
    on boundary disputes, 127–128
    on Brady Act case, 7, 45, 48
    on cable must-carry provisions,
        70, 71, 72, 111–112
    on child-support enforcement,
        103
    on class action suits, 65
    on damage suits, 116, 118
    dissenting opinions, 8, 9*t*
    on drug testing, 7
    on environmental law, 7–8, 102
    on evidence, 89

Scalia, Antonin (*continued*)
  on federal regulation, 104–105
  on habeas corpus, 91
  on immigration, 112
  on insider trading, 66, 69, 88–89
  on Internet anti-indecency law,
    38–39
  on job discrimination, 119–120
  on land use regulation, 126–127
  on maritime law, 80
  on military law, 106
  on overtime pay, 120–121
  on parochial school aid, 56, 57
  on physician-assisted suicide, 34
  on public employees, 123
  on redistricting, 99–100
  on religious freedom, 50–52
  on sentencing, 96
  on "sexual predators" law, 61
  on taxation, 81–82, 129–131
  voting pattern, 4, 5*t*, 6–8
  on workers' compensation,
    125–126
Scheidegger, Kent, 25
Schenck v. Pro-Choice of Western New York
  (1997), 113–114
School District of Grand Rapids v. Ball
  (1985), 21*t*
Schools, on parochial school aid, 6,
  10, 15, 17, 20–21, 54–57, 108–109
Schumer, Charles, 53
Screws v. United States (1945), 88
Search and seizure, 7, 22, 24, 93–95.
  See also Drug testing
Second Amendment. *See* Firearms,
  right to keep or bear, 8–9, 49
Securities and Exchange Commission
  (SEC), 24, 66–69
Sentencing, 9–10, 24–25, 95–97
Separation of powers, 107–108
Sexual assaults, by judge in chambers,
  24, 87–88
Sexual harassment, 1, 13, 16, 40–45.
  See also Presidential immunity
  same-sex, 134, 146
Sexual offenders, criminal procedures
  for, 6, 9, 21, 24, 58–61, 97–98
Shapiro, Steven R., 25

Shaw, Theodore, 26, 136
Sherbert v. Verner (1963), 50
Simmons v. South Carolina (1995), 92
Souter, David
  on banking, 89
  on Brady Act case, 14, 45, 49
  on cable must-carry provisions,
    71, 72
  on class action suits, 65
  on criminal offenses, 87–88
  on damage suits, 117
  dissenting votes, 9*t*, 14
  on election law, 98
  on evidence, 89
  on federal regulation, 104–105
  on habeas corpus, 91, 92
  on insider trading, 69
  on Internet anti-indecency law,
    39
  on land use regulation, 126–127
  on parochial school aid, 14, 54,
    56, 57, 108–109
  on physician-assisted suicide,
    14–15, 34–35
  on redistricting, 98–100
  on religious freedom, 49, 53,
    109–110
  on sexual offenders, 58, 97
  on states' rights, 128–129
  on taxation, 82, 131
  voting pattern, 5*t*, 12
  on voting rights, 101
Speech and expression rights. *See also*
  Advertising
  anti-abortion demonstrations, 8,
    26, 77, 113–114
  Internet anti-indecency law, 1, 4,
    13, 19, 25, 27, 35–45
Staniecki, Ted, 57
Stapleton, Walter K., 135–136
Starr, Kenneth, 75
State courts, 21–22
State Oil Co. v. Khan, 138
States' rights
  boundary disputes, 127–128, 134
  immunity, 128–129
Steel Co. v. Citizens for a Better Environ-
  ment, 143

Stevens, John Paul
    on abortion, 113
    on banking, 89
    on bankruptcy, 79–80
    on Brady Act case, 13–14, 45, 49
    on cable must-carry provisions,
        71, 72
    on class actions, 62, 84–85
    on contempt of court, 87
    on damage suits, 115–116, 117
    dissenting votes, 9*t*, 14
    on election law, 98
    on federal regulation, 103–105
    on habeas corpus, 91, 92
    on immunity, 128–129
    on insider trading, 69
    on Internet anti-indecency law,
        13, 39, 110–111
    on line-item veto, 108
    on Native American property
        rights, 106
    on parochial school aid, 54, 57,
        108–109
    on physician-assisted suicide, 14,
        34–35
    on police investigations at traffic
        stops, 24
    on presidential immunity, 13, 27,
        40, 43–44, 107–108
    on prisons and jails, 92–93
    on redistricting, 98–99
    on remedies, 123–124
    on search and seizure, 93–95
    on sentencing, 95–97
    on sexual offenders, 58, 61, 97–98
    on states' rights, 128–129
    on taxation, 82, 129–131
    voting pattern, 5*t*, 12, 14
    on voting rights, 101
    on workers' compensation,
        124–125
Story, Joseph, 9
Stovall, Carla J., 59, 61
*Strate, Associate Tribal Judge, Tribal Court
    of the Three Affiliated Tribes of the Fort
    Berthold Indian Reservation v. A-1
    Contractors* (1997), 107
Suicide. *See* Physician-assisted suicide

*Suitum v. Tahoe Regional Planning
    Agency* (1997), 126–127
Sunstein, Cass, 23
Supreme Court. *See also specific justices*
    appointments, 12, 17–18
    caseload, 19, 75, 76*f*
    case previews, 133–148
    future appointments, 17–18
    join-3 votes practice, 77
    judicial activism, 2–4, 6, 20
    per curiam opinions, 77, 78, 83,
        86, 87, 91, 96–97, 100, 105,
        112–113
    refusals to hear cases, 74–75,
        77
    reversals of earlier rulings, 21*t*
    unanimous decisions, 77–78
    vote divisions, 78, 78*f*
    vote patterns, 5*t*, 9*t*

Taxation, 129–131
    IRS summonses, 83
    and late filings, 82–83
    Maine tax exemption, 8, 20*t*
    on punitive damages, 82
Taxman, Sharon, 133, 135
Teague v. Lane (1989), 91
Telecommunications. *See* Cable
    television; Internet anti-indecency
    law; Public television
Thomas, Clarence
    abortion protesters, 113–114
    on appeals process, 83–84
    on boundary disputes, 127–128
    on Brady Act case, 48, 49
    on cable must-carry provisions,
        70, 72, 111–112
    on class action suits, 65
    on damage suits, 118
    dissenting votes, 9*t*
    on drug testing, 7
    on evidence, 89
    on false claims, 85–86
    on federal regulation, 104, 105
    on habeas corpus, 91, 92
    on insider trading, 66, 69, 88–89
    on Internet anti-indecency law, 39
    on job discrimination, 119

Thomas, Clarence (*continued*)
 on land use regulation, 126–127
 on maritime law, 80
 on parochial school aid, 55, 57
 on patents, 10, 81
 on physician-assisted suicide, 34
 on prisons and jails, 93
 on redistricting, 99–100
 on religious freedom, 53
 on right to bear arms, 8–9, 49
 on sentencing, 9–10
 on sexual offenders, 9, 58, 60–61,
  97–98
 on taxation, 8, 82, 129–131
 voting pattern, 4, 5*t*, 6–8
 on wage laws, 122–123
 on workers' compensation,
  125–126
Thomas, Oliver, 53
*Timmons, Acting Director, Ramsey County
 Department of Property Records v. Twin
 Cities Area New Party* (1997), 98
Torts, 15, 16, 131–132
Totenberg, Nina, 19
Toxic substances, right-to-know suits,
 143
Tribe, Laurence, 33, 35, 65
Truman, Harry S, 42
Tucker, Kathryn L., 32, 35
*Turner Broadcasting System, Inc. v.
 Federal Communications Commission*
 (1997), 70, 111–112

United States v. Alaska (1997), 127–128
United States v. Brockamp (1997), 82–83
United States v. Gaudin (1997), 86
United States v. Gonzales (1997), 95–96
United States v. Hyde (1997), 90
United States v. Jose (1997), 83
United States v. Lanier (1997), 87–88
United States v. Nixon (1974), 44
United States v. O'Hagan (1997), 66,
 88–89
United States v. Ramirez, 141
United States v. Scheffer, 140

United States v. Wells (1997), 89

*Vacco, Attorney General of New York v.
 Quill* (1997), 28, 35, 114–115
Volokh, Eugene, 3, 4, 12, 18
Voting rights, 100–102
Voting Rights Act, 26–27, 52, 99,
 100–102

Wage laws, 122–123
Wainwright v. Witt (1985), 86
*Walters v. Metropolitan Educational
 Enterprises, Inc.* (1997), 119–120
*Warner-Jenkinson Co., Inc. v. Hilton
 Davis Chemical Co.* (1997), 81
Washington, physician-assisted suicide,
 30–32
Washington v. Glucksberg (1997), 28, 35,
 115
Watson, Penelope, 87
Waxman, Seth, 38
Weilert, Thomas J., 60
Whistleblower testimony, 139–140
Whitewater affair, 40, 75
Williams, Debra, 133, 135
Williams, William L., 32–33
Wilson v. Arkansas (1995), 95
Winans, R. Foster, 67
Wisconsin v. Yoder (1972), 50
*Witters v. Washington Department of
 Services for the Blind* (1986), 55, 57,
 109
Women's athletics, 74–75
Woodard, Eugene, 142
Workers' compensation, 124–126
Wright, Susan Webber, 42, 44, 45
Wygant v. Jackson Board of Education
 (1986), 137

Young v. Fordice, Governor of Mississippi
 (1997), 101–102
Young v. Harper (1997), 93

Zobrest v. Catalina Foothills School District
 (1993), 55, 57, 109